Land, the State & the Unfinished Decolonisation Project in Africa:
Essays in Honour of Professor Sam Moyo

Edited by

Horman Chitonge & Yoichi Mine

Langaa Research & Publishing CIG
Mankon, Bamenda

Publisher:
Langaa RPCIG
Langaa Research & Publishing Common Initiative Group
P.O. Box 902 Mankon
Bamenda
North West Region
Cameroon
Langaagrp@gmail.com
www.langaa-rpcig.net

Distributed in and outside N. America by African Books Collective
orders@africanbookscollective.com
www.africanbookscollective.com

ISBN-10: 9956-550-58-2

ISBN-13: 978-9956-550-58-6

List of Contributors

Peter Lawrence is Professor Emeritus in the Keele School of Management (Economics) at Keele University, UK, and a founding editor of the *Review of African Political Economy*. His research interests include, African rural cooperation and industrialisation, privatisation in Eastern Europe and unemployment, corporate power and the world economy.

Elizabeth Tabot is a PhD candidate in African Studies, University of Cape Town. She holds a Masters degree in African Studies from the Centre of African Studies, Dalarna University, Sweden. Her major research interest includes Human Rights and African Socio-political and economic development, and land rights of minorities' in Africa. Her PHD study focuses on the land rights of the Mbororo in the Northwest Region of Cameroon.

Zhenke Zhang is professor of African Studies and Director of the Centre of African Studies at Nanjin University, Nanjing Province, China.

Moses Moyo is a PhD candidate in African Studies, University of Cape Town, South Africa. His research interests include agricultural institutions, poverty, livelihoods and rural development. His PhD looked at the effects of contract farming on rural institutions and livelihoods, focusing on Mazowe tobacco farmers.

Yoichi Mine is Professor at the Graduate School of Global Studies, Doshisha University, Japan, and Visiting Fellow at the JICA Research Institute. His research interests include human security, development economics and African area study.

Rangarirai Gavin Muchetu is a PhD candidate at the Graduate School of Global Studies, Doshisha University, Japan. He received a BSc (hons) and a Master's degree in Agricultural and Applied Economics from the University of Zimbabwe. He research interests include land use, food security, productivity, women's land rights, climate change, youth unemployment and illicit financial flows.

Shuichi Oyama is Associate Professor at Centre for African Area Studies, Kyoto University, Japan. His major research interests are geography and anthropology concerning land issues and people's livelihoods in Africa, specifically in northern Zambia and Niger. His main works include 'Land degradation and ecological knowledge-based land rehabilitation.

Malvern Kudakwashe Marewo is a PhD candidate in African Studies, University of Cape Town, South Africa. His research interests include land reform, agrarian labour dynamics, agrarian livelihoods and social relations. His PhD focuses on linkages between communal areas and A1 villagised settlements in Zvimba District, Zimbabwe.

Yumi Sakata is a research associate both at the Centre for Applied Social Sciences (CASS), University of Zimbabwe, and the Sam Moyo Institute of Agrarian Studies (SMIAS). She obtained a bachelor's degree in economics from Hosei University, Japan, and a master's degree in human sciences from Osaka University, Japan. Her research interests include contract farming and the economy of peasants. She is currently working as Second Secretary at the Embassy of Japan in Zimbabwe.

Senzeni Ncube is a Postdoctoral fellow at the Centre for African Studies, University of Cape Town, under the National Research Foundation (NRF) Chair of Land reform and Democracy in South Africa. Her research interests include land reform, social capital, livelihoods and the agrarian political economy of Africa. Her PhD thesis examined the role of social capital in the Fast Track Land Reform Programme (FTLRP) in Zimbabwe, focusing on Matabeleland North Province.

Chizuko Sato is a research fellow at the Institute of Developing Economies (IDE-JETRO), Chiba, Japan. Her current research interests include the challenge of land and agrarian reform, revival of Khoisan identities among "coloured" communities, and social integration of African migrants and refugees in South Africa.

Horman Chitonge is Associate Professor at the Centre for African Studies (CAS), University of Cape Town (UCT). His research interests include agrarian political economy, hydro-politics, and alternative strategies for inclusive economic growth and poverty reduction in Africa.

Table of Contents

The State and the Land Question in Africa: The Unfinished Business

Horman Chitonge & Yoichi Mine

Introduction

The way African states have dealt with land and agrarian issues has been a subject of scholarly debates for a long time now. As one would expect, the responses of African states to the land and agrarian issues in Africa has not been the same across countries and time; the responses have largely been shaped by the prevailing political, historical and socioeconomic context. What seems common, though, is that most African states, since independence, have been tinkering with the colonial legacy on land policy and governance structures. Although land and agrarian challenges in African countries have varied, the general sense one gets from the large body of literature accumulated over the years is that most countries have not succeeded in going beyond the colonial framework of land governance and administration in Africa. Indeed the colonial legacy on land in Africa is inscribed as a DNA code, still dictating, in a large measure, the way land is administered, accessed and used. In other words, most countries in Africa have not succeeded to decolonise land governance, administration and tenure arrangements. This is particularly true when it comes to land governance and land tenure issues, all of which are still influenced by the colonial social engineering. Most of the chapters in this volume discuss how these unresolved land issues in post-colonial Africa impact on agricultural production and rural development broadly. The idea that Africa's agrarian challenges today are shaped by the colonial social engineering was very central in Sam Moyo's scholarship, whose life and work we are remembering and celebrating in this book.

Chapters in this book were initially presented at a two-day colloquium in 2016, co-hosted by the Centre for African Studies

(CAS), University of Cape Town, and the Centre for African Area Studies at Kyoto University, Japan, to honour and celebrate the work and life of the late professor Sam Moyo, who passed on in November 2015.

As most of the chapters in this book highlight, Sam Moyo was one of the leading African scholars on the question of land and agrarian transformation in Africa, and how African States have addressed this question. He spent the larger part of his adult life reflecting on agrarian issues in Africa. This is borne out in Sam's extensive body of work (spanning almost four decades), which include work on land reform, class differentiation, state radicalization, rural social movements, and the colonial legacy on the agrarian structure in Africa. While his work mostly focused on his country of birth, Zimbabwe, Sam's scholarship covered different perspectives of land across the African continent and the Global South. Sam was not only a widely known, independent and critical scholar, he was also an influential activist who collaborated with rural various social movements in Africa, Latin America and Asia.

From the long experience of working on land issues in Africa, Sam came to the conclusion that the enduring land and agrarian questions in Africa can be attributed to what he calls "incomplete decolonisation" (see Moyo, 2008). In relation to land, Moyo (2004) argued that the failure of post-colonial African states to reconcile imported and indigenous tenure systems has left these states dancing to two tunes, leading to schizophrenic land and agrarian policies. This failure is manifested in various dimensions including the now rising land inequality and the neglect of the agricultural sector, particularly the small-scale and subsistence sectors. He observed that there are many factors which shape and define the land and agrarian question(s) in Africa today, including the "nature of state-civil society relations surrounding land, the nature of social movements... the nature of existing social formations... which underlie the African neo-colony, and the degree of rural marketization and economic incorporation into the global market system"(Moyo, 2003).

Africa's Land Question

While the hype around 'land grabbing' which surfaced in 2009 has almost died down, we have seen the change in the formal and informal rules that govern access to, control and use of land in many countries. But these changes in the rules governing access to land, which are often tailored to protect the interest of local and international elites, have not radically transformed the colonial land administrative structure and philosophy. This is particularly true when it comes to the relationship between customary and statutory tenure. The outcome of this uneasy co-existence of these two systems is contestation and conflict over the control of land in local communities. Sam Moyo (2004) attributed the growing contestation over land to the rising unequal distribution of land, which the new land policies and regulations have engendered. Moyo (2004) argues that the growing contestations "at varying scales and localities over escalating unequal access to and control of land represent Africa's real land question."

The broader context to this is the failure of African states to deal with the distortions introduced during colonial rule which resulted in indigenous tenure systems being regarded as inferior, in favour of the imported land tenure arrangements. For instance, despite the political decolonisation of the continent during the 1960 and 70s, customary land tenure in most African countries has tended to be devalued in favour of statutory tenure as exemplified in the practice of converting or 'formalising' customary land into statutory land. In a fundamental way, this failure to address the uneasy co-existence of customary and statutory land tenures in Africa has not only contributed to the growing unequal access to and ownership of land, but also to the challenges of transforming the agricultural sector and rural livelihoods more broadly. This is evident at two levels.

In the first instance, most African states have paid little attention to finding ways to render customary land more productive, particularly because there is a belief that this type of tenure is antithetical to progress and will eventually fade away. On the basis of this, it is widely believed that customary tenure is a transitory form of tenure which will die a natural death as Africa modernises, and as more people are looped into the capitalist relations of production. Secondly, and related to the first, is that little effort in most countries has been made to provide infrastructure on land under customary tenure; little has been done since independence.

It is not only the pattern of infrastructure development which shows the neglect of customary land, but even policies recently developed openly prefer statutory to customary tenure. The inclination to favour an imported over an indigenous land tenure system is evident in many land policies across the continent. Yet majority of the people in Africa still live under customary tenure, and there are no signs that this form of landholding is disappearing any time soon.

Land Tenure Dualism: A Reminder of Partial Decolonisation

While there have been prolonged debates around how African states should deal with the *dual* or *plural* system of land tenure, the underlying belief is that customary tenure should be adapted to statutory tenure, and there has been little effort made to explore the possibility of adapting statutory tenure to customary tenure. Can statutory tenure be adapted to customary tenure in a transforming Africa? This question has been largely ignored in the debates, which is a reflection of the stranglehold of colonial philosophy and practice on land administration in Africa. The existence of the two tenure systems in Africa, was for Sam Moyo a clear sign of an incomplete project of decolonising the African agrarian system. African states loom large in this failure, and as chapters in this book show, the state is central to resolving this fundamental agrarian challenge in Africa.

The need to complete the decolonisation project in Africa has been revitalised by students in South Africa through the "#RhodesMusFall" and "FeesMustFall" Movements. In addition to campaigning for free education, students have called for the decolonisation of the curriculum, not just in South Africa but across the African Continent. While the students have not yet clearly articulated what exactly decolonising the curriculum entails, they are clear that the current curriculum and the nature of the knowledge being circulated in Africa undermines African experiences and knowledges. They are calling for a curriculum which is envisioned to promote Africa-centred teaching, learning and production of knowledge. These calls by the students allude to the fact that the decolonisation process in Africa remains an incomplete project. Calls for decolonising the curriculum are a reminder that dislodging the colonial regimes on the continent was only the beginning of a process of decolonising Africa. A complete decolonisation of the continent has to go beyond political decolonisation to encompass all sectors of life in Africa including the African world view, the production of knowledge, cultural expressions, the learning process and structures, and issues around land and the economy. As most of the articles in this book allude to, the land question is one area where the failure to decolonise is most apparent, largely manifested in the failure to address the tension between imported and indigenous tenure systems.

The Task for African Scholars

The task for African scholars today is to understand the changing relations around land, and the role the state in Africa is and should be playing in this. Among the critical questions to ask are: How are African states responding to the changing relations around land? Are states in Africa promoting equitable access to land? Are African states complicit in the various forms of land grabbing occurring on the continent? How are states in Africa addressing tenure insecurity for vulnerable groups? Are policy measures put in place responsive to the various dimensions of the land question in Africa today, particularly the trends towards land concentration?

The fundamental issue when reflecting on the land question in Africa today is that while land itself is a fixed resource; the relations around it are always changing, shaped by many factors including the changing forms of land use as a result of growing population, urbanisation, economic growth, changing environmental conditions, and the changing social and economic objectives in society. For instance, in the context of rising demand for land in Africa, many African states are seeking to have more control over customary land resources which were previously left under the administration of traditional and local authorities. It is therefore not surprising that most land policies developed in the new millennium in Africa have sought to give the state more control over land resources in general, thereby altering the relations between the state and other key land stakeholders. While in the earlier periods we saw states in Africa focusing on addressing land tenure issues, there seems to be a gradual shift toward issues around land governance, leading to the sharpening of institutions responsible for land administration. This has increasingly led to many states in Africa seeking to directly (in some cases, indirectly) exert more control on how land, particularly customary land, is administered and governed.

This trend became much more visible in the after math of the 2008/2009 Global Financial crisis when demand for land in Africa and other developing regions of the world shot up as a result of over-accumulated global capital seeking more profitable investment outlets through large-scale land acquisitions. Leading international media houses widely reported on these large-scale land acquisitions from 2009, and have since flagged these deals (which are often referred to as 'land grabbing') as 'a major concern' in most developing countries, particularly in Africa[1]. Media stories on the acquisition of land by international investors, including foreign sovereign wealth funds in Africa, have highlighted the fact that African governments are, in fact, promoting these land deals by inviting investors, offering them the most generous terms and conditions for land acquisition. As it has been observed, it is actually the host African countries who are lobbying foreign companies and governments to acquire land in the name of attracting foreign investment. Suzan Payne, A chief executive of Emergent Asset Management, asserts that, "frankly we are seeing amenable terms because local groups, including governments, want us there". There are reports of investors actually targeting countries that are desperate for investment, but with weak institutions and regulatory environment.

Drawing mainly on Sam Moyo's scholarship, chapters in this volume are arranged in two related sections. The first set of chapters focus on the broader discussion of the implications of decolonisation on Africa's land and the economy, African states and the tendency to be co-opted by international interests. The potential for states in

Africa to resist the dictates of global forces by forming alliances which draw from African knowledges to solve African problems is also discussed under the broad theme of African Potentials. In this section of the book, the authors are reflecting on the broader question of finding alternative ways of thinking about the state and how it can resist capture from the narrow interests of capital and its various manifestations in the Global South. An example of how the Chinese government addressed the agrarian question and rural development forms part of the reflection on the challenges of rural development in Africa. The authors reflect on China's land and rural development policy, and poverty reduction strategies, focusing on what African countries can learn from the Chinese experience.

The second set of chapters are case studies on land relations and how these affect land, including agriculture production. Case studies from four African countries (Cameroon, Niger, South Africa and Zimbabwe) have discussed land related issues, particularly how land tenure reforms affect production and rural livelihoods. The authors in these case studies highlight the fact that at the centre of the land and agrarian questions in Africa is the way African states engage with other actors including people on customary land, beneficiaries of land reform and minority groups. The last chapter is a reflection on Steve Biko's Black Consciousness Movement and the Japanese Social Movements after 1968.

Half of the chapters in this book were published as journal articles in the *African Studies Monograph Journal (ASMJ)* No. 57 (2018). We are grateful to the ASMJ for the permission to republish these articles in this book.

Notes

(1) Although media houses such as *Reuters, BBC, Financial Times, The Economist, Economic Times, The Guardian (UK) Wall Street Journal* reported on large scale land acquisition, it was GRAIN, a Spanish Non-governmental organisation (NGO) that first drew public attention to land acquisition when it compiled a list of over 100 large-

scale land deals in an online briefing entitled, *Seized: The 2008 Land Grab for Food and Financial Security* (GRAIN, 2008).

Acknowledgement

The colloquium at which all the chapters in this volume were first presented would have not been possible without financial support from the African Potential Project (funded by the Japan Society for the Promotion of Science, Grant-in-Aid for Scientific Research) KAKENHI 16H06318 headed by Motoji Matsuda Kyoto University. The University of Cape Town Research Office, through the University Research Committee (URC) provided additional support through the HAC grant. We would like to express our deep gratitude to the scholars at the conference's host institution, the University of Cape Town, including Shamil Jeppie, Lungisile Ntsebeza, and Francis Nyamnjoh. Last but not least, we thank Walter Chambati, Deputy Director of the Sam Moyo African Institute for Agrarian Studies (SMAIAS), and Qondile Moyo (Sam's daughter), for delivering a powerful summary and interpretation of Sam's work and life.

Chapter 1

Perspectives on "African Potentials"

Sam Moyo & Yoichi Mine

Introduction

This chapter was originally presented by Professor Sam Moyo at the 5th African Forum of the "African Potentials" project organised at Addis Ababa from October 31 to November 1, 2015. The "African Potentials" project is an international research endeavour funded by the Japan Society for the Promotion of Science (JSPS), of which Sam was an active member and a respected mentor.[1] The chapter is an early version of the introductory chapter of *What Colonialism Ignored: "African Potentials" for Resolving Conflicts in Southern Africa* (edited by Sam Moyo & Yoichi Mine, Langaa RPCIG, 2016), a major posthumous work of Sam. At the time of the Addis Ababa Forum, we were still engaged in the rigorous co-writing of the introductory chapter by exchanging e-mails between Harare and Kyoto. Sam then took the lead in editing and reformatting the latest draft into this offshoot paper for the Forum.

I think this chapter is especially meaningful in two ways. First, this version reflects the elements of the proposition of "African Potentials" that Sam wanted to emphasise in person (though he respected the part of my modest contribution). Second, the last section of this chapter contains key initiatives that Sam crafted with care. To nurture and expand trans-regional research networks, he wanted to have these six-point initiatives widely discussed by the next generation African scholars and Japanese/Asian Africanists, and this is why I wanted to publish this version of our writing in *African Study Monographs* with only technical revisions.

Sadly, now, it is not possible to obtain Sam's explicit agreement any more, but I have no doubt that he would be very happy that this document is presented to the public in this form. In the "African Potentials" fora, Sam enjoyed conversation with African and Asian anthropologists and sociologists who then highly appreciated Sam's sharp political-economy interventions with his characteristic wide smile.

Narrow conceptual frameworks are often used to attribute violent conflicts to internal "dysfunction" and "barbarism" of African society. Yet, recently, the image of "rising Africa" has also become popular, given that the continent's export of primary goods to the global markets has increased on a much larger scale, leading to markedly high growth rates. However, this conceptual framework is limited to a shallow causality of trade expansion, prosperity and stability. This said, Afro-optimism can easily be shattered, when the present extroverted development pattern proves to be unsustainable. While powers in global capitalism regard Africa as the land of opportunity, their interventions produce and aggravate contradictions across African society, leading to renewed pessimism.

Although the call for African solutions to African problems has given rise to various new initiatives when it comes to addressing violence and poverty, these efforts have not been sufficient. New geo-political imperatives shape the "scramble for Africa," in which global capital acquires extraordinary shares of land and resources, as forms of trade, aid and foreign direct investment (FDI) shift. New Asian investments diversify Africa's international relations, gradually diminishing conventional Euro-American influence. This provides strategic opportunities to transform African societies, with their complex mix of diversity and commonality. The challenge for Africa is to release the potential of the people's agency to solve Africa's problems, transcending parochial identities and going beyond the dichotomy of "tradition/modernity."

The "Southern African Potentials" Forum organised in Harare in 2012 sought to challenge and shift the centre of gravity away from Euro-American scholarship to deepen intellectual collaboration in an alternative "East-South" frame. It brought together scholars in history, anthropology, sociology and political economy and, through intensive debate, elaborated the notion of "African Potentials" to explore mechanisms that are utilised to bring about "conflict resolution and co-existence" in the African settings from below. The Forum discussed the nature of violent conflicts in contemporary

Southern Africa, paying attention to the transformative dynamics of society and evaluating existing approaches for addressing conflicts, and sought an alternative vision called "African Potentials." An academic book jointly written by African scholars and Japanese Africanists will be published as a result.

The Southern African Conflict Regime: Violence and Disarticulation

Given that the Southern African conflict regime is complex, ambiguous and often paradoxical, it is proposed that its "Potentials" can only be realised when the structural violence embedded in global capitalism (shaped by the settler-colonial trajectory) is addressed in fundamental ways. Structural violence in the Southern African countryside entails a unique accumulation trajectory, as compared to the rest of the continent, although such trajectories seem to lead to a convergence. Elements of African Potentials are found in long historical processes: the historical mobility, flexibility and openness of African society. These elements contribute to the everyday practices that are a part of conflict resolution, which persist even today despite colonial and post-colonial distortions.

In 1994, South Africa's transition to the African non-racial majority rule promised a peace dividend to the entire region. However, the South African transition could barely contain conflicting aspirations and emotions, including "tribal identities." The social life of South African neoliberal cities is tormented by rampant crime, insecurities and growing inequalities, compared for instance to the relative calmness of everyday life in Harare, even though Zimbabwe is classified as a "failed state" by the Western powers. Yet, in the 2000s, relatively "stable" countries such as Zimbabwe, Lesotho and Madagascar continued to be affected by election-related violence.

Nevertheless, the GDP growth rates of Southern African countries surpassed 5 percent on average during the first decade and a half of the 21st century, largely due to the rising demand for natural resources in Asian economies. However, the present growth, induced by the export of primary products, has precipitated renewed insecurity and vulnerability in African society. As the wealth is increasingly possessed by a handful of land and mineral "grabbing" barons around economic enclaves, frustration is fermenting among the alienated masses. Furthermore, the recent burst of the commodity bubble has sharply shrunk external resource flows, making the life of peasants and workers, as well as the positions of ruling classes, much more precarious.

The "New Scramble for Africa" is changing the landscape of the countryside as land concentration leads toward a convergence of historical trajectories of capital accumulation based on large-scale farming and transnational agribusiness. The rise of Sinophobia and Sinophilia is found almost everywhere in African countries, as Chinese goods, labour and capital are entrenched at an unprecedented rate. The fact, however, is that global monopoly capital, both Western and Eastern, capitalise on "investment opportunities" created by neoliberal policies to assert control over land and resources in Africa, and the entry of China is used to impose a renewed, orderly "partition" of Africa that is deemed to be more "equitable" for all external and internal capitalist speculators. This process constitutes the most significant setting for violent conflict and renewed geopolitical militarisation in Africa (Moyo et al., 2012).

Compared to the magnitude of human suffering in global human history, according to Julius Nyerere (2000: xiv): "the surprising thing is not that there has been so much political instability in Africa but that there has been so much stability, although this fact is less publicized internationally." In the past quarter-century, however, parts of the relatively peaceful African countryside have been shaken successively by rebellious groups and armed rogues, alongside more disciplined attempts such as those in rural Zimbabwe to address the lingering colonial legacy.

These conflicts are connected to imperialist forces, which increasingly control the land and resources and take advantage of internal strife among Africans. The continent is entering an age of precarious transition and dynamic change, and the focus of these struggles is in the countryside. Continuous external interventions and evolving contradictions make the future of Africa much more complicated and unpredictable, although the resilience of African peoples and states is evident. Strong undercurrents of social processes that mediate conflicts and enable transformation throughout recent history of Africa suggest that legitimate "African Potentials" will be able to transform African society.

Three Predominant Perspectives on African Conflicts

The "African Potentials" Forum held at Harare discussed three predominant perspectives to understand the nature of violent confrontations. The first is the notion of Africa's "backwardness," which has been rife in the discourse of popular journalism as well as academic writings on Africa in the West. Within this framework, Africa is regarded as a continent of self-destruction, its society is intrinsically emotional, irrational and abusive since ancient times and will remain so forever. This perspective is buttressed by the theory of neopatrimonialism, a mainstream theoretical framework in African studies, based on the Weberian categorisation of human societies and the Eurocentric perception of the "otherness" of non-Western societies (see Bach & Gazibo, 2012; Mkandawire, 2013). With few exceptions, most academic writings pursue this culturalist line of thought, whereby the essence of African society is considered timeless, unchangeable and incapable of creating a new order. If there is anything worth engaging with in Africa, it is the land, minerals and natural resources, not the people.

This reductionist cultural discourse obscures reality, reflecting a Malthusian fear of population explosion at the periphery of the global capitalist system. However, such fears also reflect the real frustration of the majority of the world's population, who comprise a mass semi-proletariat living in the countryside and facing accelerated pauperisation and marginalisation. These are human persons enduring an ongoing process of enclosure and structural neglect. The current trajectory could lead to the genocide of half of humanity unless a democratic, labour-absorbing type of agricultural revolution firmly based on peasant production is pursued (Amin, 1990; 2011; Moyo & Yeros, 2005).

The second approach to addressing the African conflict discussed at the Forum involves the perspective of universal justice and human rights. Based on the flawed perception that local people are unable to realise post-conflict reconciliation by themselves, this approach seeks to implant universal principles from above. This is typically shown in the legal action taken by the International Criminal Court (ICC), which has largely prosecuted Africans. While the responsibility of some African political leaders for the gross violation of human rights is undeniable, the practitioners of international laws and human rights seldom pay attention to the attempts at social healing taking place at village and street levels, despite the fact that most atrocities were committed at these local levels. This approach also absolves external actors which generate the structural injustices underlying these conflicts.

Another variation of this top-down approach involves constitutional engineering to contain political confrontations and emotions, such as power-sharing arrangements to "normalise" the war-town states. Although the arrangements can be negotiated by local politicians through the mediation of a regional organization, theorists of social engineering still tend to regard their prescriptions as one-size-fits-all recipes (Mine et al., 2013). To this end, Paul Collier comes up with an extreme proposal suggesting that the Western players should force undemocratic leaders of African governments to accept election results by threatening military intervention while trusting the "rational" behaviours of dictators (Collier, 2009).

In the realm of economics, the proposition of individual property rights propounded by Hernando de Soto has been endorsed by the World Bank and has wielded influence over the policy making of national governments in Africa (Soto, 2000). Certain forms of justice, electoral democracy as well as the stabilization of land tenure system are all required for any government, but the problem is that most of these top-down attempts presuppose a convergence around an idealised Western liberal democracy, rather than developing hybrid systems accommodating local needs and participatory dynamics. South Africa's Truth and Reconciliation Commission (TRC) and its experiments of "inclusive governments," as well as other efforts at reconciliation, such as in Namibia (since 1990) and Zimbabwe from 1980 to 1990, fit into this latter mould to some extent.

Thirdly, a new "traditionalist" perspective was discussed, given that studies of history and anthropology have widely accepted that many of the seemingly "African" practices were "invented" under colonial power relations (Hobsbawm & Ranger, 1983; Mamdani, 2012). In post-colonial situations, there have been several attempts to realise conflict resolution and reconciliation at the societal level by resurrecting and reconstructing past practices of community justice through the "reinvention" of traditions. Attempts that have fully involved rural villagers include the Gacaca court in Rwanda, a community justice system established in 2001 to speed up the trial of the suspects of genocide crime (Clark, 2010). Aside from these formal experiments, traditional rituals were explicitly utilized as a method to heal the wounds of civil war at the village level in Mozambique (see also Hayner, 2001). Although these tradition-based practices of conflict resolution reflect bottom-up ingenuity, such institutions also have the risk of falling prey to post-colonial despots in the shadow of late colonial bifurcation of the "modern" world of urban citizens and the "traditional" world of rural peasants (Mamdani, 1996).

While the second universal approach and the third new traditionalist approach appear to be irreconcilable as opposites, in reality, they are embedded together within the single space of post-colonial Africa. The contradiction of modernity and tradition is especially palpable in Southern Africa, where indigenous communities have been exposed for more than a century to the political and cultural influence of settler communities. Furthermore, in this region, the duality of colonial rulers has sometimes resulted in unintended consequences of strengthening the practice of "divide and rule," as demonstrated in the case of the Herero and Ovambo division in Namibia. People claim that their own traditions are historically justifiable but they are often rendered inflexible and exploited by the overarching rulers.

African Potentials: An Alternative Approach?

African Potentials are tentatively defined as the capabilities of Africans to resolve contradictions among the people, utilising indigenous knowledge on human relations that has constantly

7

transformed and accumulated at the level of people's everyday life (Moyo & Mine, 2016). The development of the art of conflict resolution and transformation has persisted throughout pre-colonial, colonial and post-colonial times, and African Potentials can be reviewed in two dimensions related to space and time. However, a distinction ought to be made between *personal* (or *direct*) violence and *structural* (or *indirect*) violence (see Galtung, 1969).

When the military kills innocent civilians, that homicide is an act of personal violence. When rural children die of avoidable infectious diseases in the periphery of global capitalism, structural violence is committed; as the children's potential to have a long life is crushed by external influence and structural poverty. Similarly, the infringement of food sovereignty of nations in the South that imposes avoidable starvation on people is a clear manifestation of structural violence. While structural violence is often accompanied by personal violence and vice versa, these two notions of violence should not be confused. Absence of personal violence and absence of structural violence are both desirable goals of global transformation, and the former is called "negative peace" while the latter is called "positive peace."

The concept of structural violence illuminates the anti-human nature of poverty and exploitation, which are regarded here as a form of violence, even if they are caused by a system with no explicit intention of harming individuals; capitalists do not beat workers with their whips in person (Moyo & Mine, 2016). Polarisation of the world into the centre in which autocentric development is on track and the periphery in which disarticulation permeates economy and society, as well as unequal exchange embedded in the global trade system, does exist. However, it may not be visible unless we look at reality through the lens of a scientific theory of global capitalism (Amin, 1976). On the other hand, personal violence may function even without resorting to physical violence at all; a threat to use violence may suffice to fetter action on the part of the potential victims of violence. Exercise of personal violence may indeed trigger a chain of grave violence (e.g., the role of Western nations in the Rwandan Genocide and the toppling Gaddafi in Libya in the name of responsibility to protect). This kind of violence precipitated personal violence in

Maghreb, in the Sahel countries and in regions of Central Africa. The dichotomous world of centre-periphery is rife with both structural and personal violence, and Africa is in the line of fire.

While we define violence as the difference between the actual and the potential, the notion of African Potentials suggests further considerations. In an imaginary state in which both personal violence and structural violence are abolished, with the actual matching the potential, the actual shape of such an accomplished state remains vague. In terms of popular interpretation of human development, in such a state, all individuals would be able to enjoy longevity, a decent life, a good education with a fair distribution of resources. However, human potentials do not only cover the socio-economic well-being of individuals but are also closely tied to collective self-determination in the political and cultural spheres; the realization of national, communal and personal dignity is therefore essential. Given the diversity of value in use, a hypothetical society in which all potentials are realized will be substantially different from the average shape of homogeneous "global society." Such hypothetical spaces will be diverse, given the wide variety of local and regional histories and belief systems, as well as the diversity present in ecological systems. This is the reason why we speak about "African" potentials rather than abstract human potentials.

However, a blanket notion of Africa is problematic, as Africa is extremely diverse, not only in terms of ecosystems, cultures, religions and languages but also with relation to economic structures and political systems. The unique position of the Southern African region suggests that its conflict regime is based on the history of foreign control over land and other natural resources, testifying the glaring truth that primitive accumulation of capital is not just a one-off event but a sustained process. At the same time, the economic activities of monopoly capitalism have closely integrated the entire region, thereby making an agenda of the liberation of the whole region realistic.

Historically, Southern Africa has been a microcosm of global structural and personal violence, which has been consolidated by the legal and cultural superstructure of Euro-centric racism, as well as by sophisticated military machines targeting the whole region to protect the racial order of Apartheid. This historical path of agrarian accumulation in Southern Africa differs from the path travelled by the rest of the continent.

Structural Violence and Accumulation Trajectories in Africa

Patterns of conflict over land and resources in Africa continue to be defined by the agrarian structures that have taken shape through the history of colonial scramble for Africa in the past centuries. Three macro-scale trajectories of capital accumulation are discernible: first, the labour reserve political economies mainly in Southern Africa; second, the resource extraction concession enclaves mainly in Central Africa; third, the trade economies grounded on the extraction of surpluses from African peasantries across West and Eastern Africa (Amin, 1976). These diverse historical paths created intense but varied patterns of structural violence.

An "Africa of the labour reserves" emerged through land dispossession and displacement of the peasantry, which was conducive to monopolistic control over land and water resources as well as increased infrastructure investments for the benefit of white settlers. This plainly unequal structure is manifest in such places as South Africa, Zimbabwe, Namibia, Kenya and Algeria on a large scale, as well as in their neighbours such as Malawi, Zambia and Mozambique on a smaller scale (Denoon, 1972; Magubane, 1979). This process clearly shifted the main producers of food from African peasants toward large-scale European farmers with the support of state marketing boards and European merchants. In addition, from the 1950s, new enclaves of highly subsidised agro-industrial estates were expanded in this region.

Even though the continuous process of land dispossession seriously undermined the livelihoods of African peasantry (almost completely in South Africa) and caused "land hunger," this accumulation "from above" fell short of the total dispossession of peasant lands. Instead, based on a functional dualism that subjugated labour and repressed peasant farming, the process resulted in the creation and preservation of "labour reserves," the homes of migrant workers who were exposed to super-exploitation. This settler mode

10

of accumulation placed the burden of the social reproduction of cheap labour on the shoulders of peasantries in segregated "communal" areas, where "tribal" authority was preserved and recreated by the settler regime to regulate the systems (Moyo & Yeros, 2005). Today, domestic and foreign capitalist farmers seek to insert themselves into this arena through the mediation of chiefs and the state. This instrumentalisation of tradition and universal values (land and tenure) makes it imperative for us to discuss the ambiguity of the roles of traditional leaders in conceptualising African Potentials in Southern African contexts.

In an "Africa of the concessions," several significant agricultural and mining enclaves were formed around plantations with rudimentary agro-processing facilities, typically in Central Africa. This entailed the plunder of raw material and limited infrastructural investments by trading and mining conglomerates. This mode of accumulation entailed direct control of the resources by transnational capital, rather than the creation of a domestic bourgeoisie based on the indigenous population or European settlers. Such enclaves were sustained only by the merciless use of personal violence: military control and forcible recruitment of cheap labour. The pedigree of resistance to this enclave dispossession, for instance in Cameroon, is well documented (Crowder, 1968). The enclaves were not directly integrated into local economic development, though after independence the creation and incorporation of peasantries started to supplement the enclaves, except where large oil and mining enclaves overshadowed national policies.

In an "Africa of the *économie de traite*," seemingly autonomous peasants are forced to produce a quota of specific export products. This practice was developed and sustained for two centuries of European mercantilism, typically in West and Eastern Africa. Although this mode of accumulation was also premised on the rule of "traditional" chiefs buttressed by colonial administration along the line of "indirect rule" of Lord Lugard, the difference from the first path is that peasants were encouraged to produce more on the land. This type of colonisation led to the pervasive growth of "petty (agricultural) commodity production" among increasingly differentiated peasantries (Bernstein, 2002) or "small cultivators"

11

(Mafeje, 2003). Critically, this mode of colonization also gave rise to institutionalised labour migration based on various extra-economic measures other than forceful land alienation.

In West Africa, a vast number of farmers migrated from northern territories into the coastal and forest areas where agricultural commercialisation was focused on tropical crop exports. In the end, this trajectory has been conducive not only to the creation of diverse peasantries but also to intense land conflict in places like today's Côte d'Ivoire, where there have been attempts to deprive "alien northerners" of their entitlements. Even in the peasant societies of this third category, large-scale agricultural estates (e.g., palm oil) emerged from the 1940s and led to the creation of new enclaves as the drive to modernise agriculture grew.

The gradual transformation of the agro-based African political economy since the beginning of the 21st century and the prolonged crisis of the world capitalist system has produced a new wave of accumulation by land dispossession in Africa at large, partly through fraudulent land grabbing, as well as more generally through the erosion of both rural and urban incomes due to wage repression and price hikes, which brings social reproduction based in the African countryside into crisis (Moyo et al., 2013). The renewed interest in oil, gas and mineral extraction accompanies the most recent surge in land alienation, expanding the production of food, bio-fuels and natural resources for export at the expense of food sovereignty. The same process intensifies the exploitation of water resources and undermines the livelihoods of peasants and pastoralists.

Under present global neoliberal conditions, small and scattered forms of land concentration started to emerge in the 1990s even in non-settler Africa. This seems to have established a fragile merchant path of agrarian accumulation that involves non-rural capital gaining access to land. This accumulation path is now being overtaken by a wider process of large-scale land alienation led by both Western and Eastern foreign capital, often with African domestic allies. Although many "land deals" have not yet been confirmed, this uncertainty itself has fuelled political upheaval as occurred in Madagascar. This continental process of land and agrarian transformation is now installing a new "junker" path of accumulation across Africa, which is transforming parts of the African countryside to perform the function of impoverished labour reserves in parallel with the creation of more agricultural enclaves (Moyo et al., 2013).

This trend seems to suggest a gradual convergence of the three macro accumulation trajectories, with agrarian capital and expertise from Southern Africa playing an important role in the scramble for land. The varied and yet converging accumulation trajectories continue to be at the heart of uneven development, exclusion and poverty in Africa. This process constitutes a key factor of the major conflicts and provokes widespread resistances throughout the continent. The radicalisation of Zimbabwe since 1997 is a case in point (Moyo, 2008). The ongoing struggle for land in Southern Africa, therefore, has critical implications for the future of Africa as a whole.

African Potentials in History

African Potentials should be considered in terms of both spatial and temporal dimensions, reflecting the continent's integration into the space of world capitalist system, and its continued exposure to forms of severe personal and structural violence that centre around land and agrarian inequalities occasioned by different modes of European colonial penetration. Extending the time horizon a little further back to pre-colonial times enables us to "rediscover" the continuity of African agency. While going along with the "reinvention" of traditions thesis, we ought not to romanticise the African past. Nonetheless, elements of past practices for possible conflict resolution did not die out but persist into today's Africa, even though such potentials have been constrained by colonial and post-colonial politics.

Multifarious African societies have been consolidated into a larger polity that might face serious fission again, rendering the overall shape of African society extremely amorphous. There has not been a linear development of homogeneous "tribes" in Africa but a continuous rise and decline of heterogeneous societies and polities. Therefore, African "traditional" societies have largely been characterised by mobility, fluidity, flexibility and openness. These

13

traits of African societies seem to have affected the modalities of resolving everyday micro conflicts pertaining to the allocation of land and resources, succession struggles, family feuds, homicides, and skirmishes with neighbouring societies over livestock and so forth. In such a fluid and flexible society, boundaries of identities tend to be blurred; a person may keep dual ethnic identification with both the original community and the present settlement, switch over between them, or create a new identity platform. People often patiently let time pass before an implicit consensus is reached among diverse members by means of egalitarian, horizontal communication, sometimes called *Palaver* (see Neocosmos, 2016). Innovations brought by outsiders are experimented selectively before they take root as "indigenous." Traditional rituals to heal the wounds of society are constantly reworked to accommodate the needs of the present moment.

As evidenced in the new resettlement areas after the land reform of Zimbabwe, people with diverse backgrounds make use of marriage, burials, totemic ties, chief's authority and other traditional and modern tools to redefine the notion of autochthony and create a new sense of belonging (Mkodzongi, 2016). In the countryside facing land grabbing, the collective will of villagers prevails and effectively checks the undemocratic deviation of traditional leaders. Although some colonial scholars have marvelled at the sophistication of African contemporary practices and even attempted to codify them (Schapera, 1938), the modalities of conflict resolution and transformation have always been changeable and of an ad-hoc nature in the African peasant world. The experience of South Africa's TRC demonstrates the power of undetermined, open ventures aimed at social healing in Africa.

However, these historically rooted practices have been neglected, distorted and manipulated by colonial administrators, and then, by authoritarian rulers of African states after independence. Today, the relative fluidity of frontiers is making African societies vulnerable to larger-scale conflicts. The institutional vacuum in the periphery of existing nation-states sometimes serves as the hotbed of predatory militant groups, as well as the stage of large-scale land grabbing by global and domestic capital, thereby forcing African peasants to face insecurity over land more than ever before. On the other hand, cages of "modern nations" grafted to onto African soil are giving rise to hierarchical regimes of citizenship and belonging, thereby stoking xenophobic violence, ironically, in the regional centres of capital accumulation such as the African champion of "liberal democracy," South Africa (Neocosmos, 2006; Nyamnjoh, 2006).

As eloquently described by Frantz Fanon, in the colonial extremity of the dichotomy of absolute good and absolute evil, violence exerted by the colonised would function as a necessary momentum to liberate them. However, Fanon also believed that such cleansing violence of the masses should be given an appropriate direction by a dedicated leadership that would be willing to work among them. While engaging in the Algerian liberation struggle, he clearly foresaw the rule of a neo-colonial "national bourgeoisie" in independent African states and their hostility to the peasant majority (Fanon, 2004). This alienation seems to have cast a long shadow over contemporary African politics.

Categorising post-colonial African states, Thandika Mkandawire (2008) forcefully argued that the "rentier" states that depend on rents from the mining sector have been more prone to violent conflicts than the "merchant" states that rely on the taxation of peasants. In the former, the wealth tends to concentrate in economic enclaves and cities. Extreme forms of rising inequalities, which are becoming all the more visible today, thrusted the frustrated urban youth into radical and yet ideologically premature rebellion. Then, after being defeated, some of these groups were pushed out of the capital cities, roving and seeking support in the countryside, where they encountered indifference and even hostility among local peasants, whose worldviews were largely unfamiliar to the young rebels. This is considered a major factor behind the atrocities in the countryside, committed by the revolutionaries-turned-rogues who desperately tried to "capture" the peasantry in West and Central Africa (Mkandawire, 2008). It must be noted that the possibility of repetition of this type of conflict is becoming real, given the convergence of accumulation trajectories with the creation of more enclaves in many more African countries.

The antagonism between the urban and the rural spaces in Africa brings home the importance of learning from everyday practices for settling disputes and transforming conflicts in the world of the peasantry as a part of our collective endeavours to release historically grounded African Potentials. The modalities of micro practices of conflict resolution in the countryside, which have developed in African historical settings, should be nurtured carefully so that lessons can be adapted to other communities, including the space of urban dwellers, through mutual learning. African Potentials ought to address both personal and structural violence by connecting micro village practices with a larger attempt at structural transformation, so as to put an end to capitalist exploitation and super-exploitation and bring about the co-existence and flourishing of multiple communities in Africa.

Our book on African Potentials in the context of Southern Africa presents a powerful set of case studies that sheds light on various aspects of people's experiences with conflict resolution and transformation on the ground, avoiding the hasty generalisation and formalisation of such cases (Moyo & Mine, 2016).

Conclusion: Future Collaboration with Regard to African Potentials

The "African Potentials" Forums have certainly led to a variety of productive intellectual exchanges not only around the notion of African Potentials but also in terms of provoking discussion on epistemological issues and raising questions on the practical challenges of knowledge production in Africa with a global intellectual context. The Forums have initiated an opening up of many participants to the varied paradigmatic and intellectual practices of non-Western scholarship. There has been a widening of the research and learning vistas for many of those involved, as well as the creation of a space for imagining alternative ways of thinking about Africa's social and political transformations.

The "African Potentials" Forums have also been accompanied by other forms of academic collaboration between Japanese and African network members. This includes the inception of new forms of joint training of post-graduate students, various research exchange visits, the initiation of book publication projects, and the promotion of new publishing fora.

The scope for further deepening these intellectual spaces, exchanges and networking is substantial, but the potential is yet to be fully realised. The investments made so far in the African Potentials Network need to be leveraged immediately in order to broaden their impact on the autonomous and innovative intellectual projects ongoing among African and Japanese scholars and students.

The key initiatives that this combined Forum may consider for further discussion include how to:

1)   Establish new ways of strengthening the current networking system, including the reinforcement of key member nodes to enhance intellectual research and training within Africa;

2)   Support wider African publishing institutions and new publishing practices, including increasing the translation of works by various network members;

3)   Establish and institutionalize a systematic research programme with specified themes over a long-term period (i.e., five years and beyond);

4)   Develop a more structured and broader-based joint PhD training and scholarship programme in Japan and Africa;

5)   Link and broaden the African Potentials network to connect with other existing South-South and Pan-African networks which members of the Forum are part of; and

6)   Imagine new, feasible and adaptive ways of financing autonomous intellectual spaces in Africa and Japan.

Notes

(1) The project website is: http://www.africapotential.africa.kyoto-u.ac.jp/en/index.html. The second phase of the project was launched in April 2016: http://www.africapotential. africa.kyoto-u.ac.jp/mms/en/

Acknowledgements

This article is based on our paper presented at 'Land, the State and Decolonising the Agrarian Structure in Africa: A Colloquium in Honour of Professor Sam Moyo,' organized at the University of Cape Town, South Africa, on November 28–29, 2016. This colloquium was sponsored by the Japan Society for the Promotion of Science, Grant-in-Aid for Scientific Research (S) '"African Potential" and Overcoming the Difficulties of Modern World: Comprehensive Research That Will Provide a New Perspective for the Future of Humanity' (KAKENHI 16H06318 headed by Motoji Matsuda, Kyoto University), as well as by the University of Cape Town's Research Office (URC).

References

Amin, S. 1976. *Unequal Development: An Essay on the Social Formations of Peripheral Capitalism*. Monthly Review Press, New York.

— 1990. *Maldevelopment: Anatomy of a Global Failure*. United Nations University Press, Tokyo.

— 2011. *Ending the Crisis of Capitalism or Ending Capitalism?* Pambazuka Press, Cape Town, Dakar, Nairobi and Oxford.

Bach, D.C. & M. Gazibo 2012. *Neopatrimonialism in Africa and Beyond*. Routledge, London. Bernstein, H. 2002. *Agrarian Reform after Developmentalism?* Presentation at the Conference on Agrarian Reform and Rural Development, Taking Stock, Social Research Centre of the American University in Cairo, October 14–15, 2001. Cairo, Egypt.

Clark, P. 2010. *The Gacaca Courts, Post-Genocide Justice and Reconciliation in Rwanda: Justice without Lawyers*. Cambridge University Press, Cambridge.

Collier, P. 2009. *Wars, Guns, and Votes: Democracy in Dangerous Places*. Harper Perennial, New York.

Crowder, M. 1968. *West Africa under Colonial Rule*. Hutchinson, London. Denoon, D. 1972. *Southern Africa since 1800*. Longman, London.

Fanon, F. 2004. *The Wretched of the Earth*. Grove Press, New York.

Galtung, J. 1969. Violence, peace, and peace research. *Journal of Peace Research*, 6(3): 167–191.

Hayner, P.B. 2001. *Unspeakable Truths: Confronting State Terror and Atrocity*. Routledge, New York.

Hobsbawm, E. & T. Ranger 1983. *The Invention of Tradition*. Cambridge University Press, Cambridge.

Mafeje, A. 2003. *The Agrarian Question, Access to Land, and Peasant Responses in Sub-Saharan Africa: Civil Society and Social Movements Programme Paper Number*

6. United Nations Research Institute for Social Development (UNRISD), Geneva. Magubane, B.M. 1979. *The Political Economy of Race and Class in South Africa*. Monthly

Review Press, New York.

Mamdani, M. 1996. *Citizen and Subject: Contemporary Africa and the Legacy of Late Colonialism*. Princeton University Press, Princeton.

— 2012. *Define and Rule: Native as Political Identity*. Harvard University Press, Cambridge.

Mine, Y., F. Stewart, S. Fukuda-Parr & T. Mkandawire 2013. *Preventing Violent Conflict in*

Africa: Inequalities, Perceptions and Institutions. Palgrave Macmillan, Basingstoke.

Mkandawire, T. 2008. The terrible toll of postcolonial rebel movements: Towards an explanation of the violence against the peasantry. In (A. Nhema & P.T. Zeleza, eds.) *The Roots of African Conflicts: The Causes and Costs*, pp. 106–135. Ossrea, James Currey, Ohio University Press and Unisa Press, Addis Ababa, Oxford, Athens and Pretoria.

— 2013. *Neopatrimonialism and the Political Economy of Economic Performance in Africa: Critical Reflections, Working Paper 2013:1*. Institute for Future Studies, Stockholm.

Mkodzongi, G. 2016. Utilising 'African potentials' to resolve conflicts in a changing agrarian situation in central Zimbabwe. In (S. Moyo & Y. Mine, eds.) *What Colonialism Ignored: "African Potentials" for Resolving Conflicts in Southern Africa*, pp. 75–101. Langaa RPCIG, Bamenda.

Moyo, S. 2008. *African Land Questions, Agrarian Transition and the State:*

Contradictions of the Neo-liberal Land Reforms. CODESRIA, Dakar.

Moyo, S., P. Jha & P. Yeros 2013. The classical agrarian question: Myth, reality and relevance today. *Agrarian South: Journal of Political Economy*, 2(1): 93–119.

Moyo, S. & Y. Mine 2016. *What Colonialism Ignored: "African Potentials" for Resolving*
Conflicts in Southern Africa. Langaa RPCIG, Bamenda.

Moyo, S. & P. Yeros 2005. *Reclaiming the Land: The Resurgence of Rural Movements in Africa, Asia and Latin America.* Zed Books, London and New York.

Moyo, S., P. Yeros & P. Jha 2012. Imperialism and primitive accumulation: Notes on the new scramble for Africa. *Agrarian South: Journal of Political Economy*, 1(2): 181–203.

Neocosmos, M. 2006. *From 'Foreign Natives' to 'Native Foreigners': Explaining Xenophobia in Post-Apartheid South Africa: Citizenship and Nationalism, Identity and Politics.* CODESRIA, Dakar.

— 2016. Thinking an African politics of peace in an era of increasing violence. In (S. Moyo & Y. Mine, eds.) *What Colonialism Ignored: "African Potentials" for Resolving Conflicts in Southern Africa*, pp. 309–349. Langaa RPCIG, Bamenda.

Nyamnjoh, F.B. 2006. *Insiders and Outsiders: Citizenship and Xenophobia in Contemporary Southern Africa.* CODESRIA, Dakar.

Nyerere, M.J.K. 2000 Foreword. In (Y.K. Museveni ed.) *What Is Africa's Problem?*, pp. ix–xvi. University of Minnesota Press, Minneapolis.

Schapera, I. 1938. *A Handbook of Tswana Law and Custom: Compiled for the Bechuanaland Protectorate Administration.* Oxford University Press, London.

Soto, H. de 2000. *The Mystery of Capital: Why Capitalism Triumphs in the West and Fails Everywhere Else.* Basic Books, New York.

Corresponding Author's mail: ymine@mail.doshisha.ac.jp

Chapter 2

The Land Question and the Economy: Cues of an Incomplete Decolonisation Project in Africa

Horman Chitonge

Introduction

Since the university student protests in 2015, which occurred across South Africa, debates on decolonising the African continent have become a central topic in the media and academia. One of the demands students were making during the protests was the decolonisation of the university curriculum. But calls to decolonise the African continent are not new; nationalists leaders across Africa made decolonisation a rallying point during the struggle for and after independence. In this chapter, I argue that while the nationalists embarked on the project to decolonise Africa, which saw many African colonies become independent during the 1960s, the decolonisation project has remained an incomplete one, and there are many reminders of this. In this chapter I use the land question and the economy to show that decolonisation is an unfinished project in Africa.

Although the concept of decolonisation encompasses a wide range of ideas, there is a general sense that decolonisation is intended to draw attention to the fact that the dominant modes of thinking and production of knowledge across Africa are defined and dominated by a Western world view. In this debate, it is often argued that this represents the failure to fully decolonise the African continent, even if colonial occupation ended 60 years ago in most countries. By arguing that decolonisation has remained incomplete, this chapter is not arguing that there has been no attempt to decolonise; but that these efforts have not been radical enough to see the project to its logical conclusion. This is partly because the project of decolonisation was narrowly framed within the nationalist project, which tended to equate decolonisation with political liberation.

The land question has always been at the centre of the political decolonisation project during the struggle for independence in Africa. African peoples across the continent fought the colonisers because they took away the land, which is vital to self-determination and sovereignty. Sam Moyo (2007), who dedicated much of his life to the study of issues around land in Africa, has for instance argued that economic development for the continent would be difficult to achieve without resolving the land and agrarian question. In Sam Moyo's work, the land question was very central to the point that he saw the land and agrarian questions as constituting a *national question*, with direct connection to economic growth, development and national sovereignty (see Moyo & Yeros, 2011). In all this, the current state of the land and agrarian questions (the national question) and economic structural transformation in *most* African countries remains a clear reminder of an incomplete decolonial project. The incompleteness of decolonisation is partly evident in the post-colonial African states' failure to deconstruct the colonial social engineering and the subsequent power matrix (the *coloniality of power*) which continues to shape the land and agrarian structure and as well as African economies.

Completing the decolonisation project, would require a critical engagement with the subtle forms of the coloniality of power which continue to dictate not only the activities of most Africans, but also their modes of thought and being. Using examples from the land and agrarian issues, and also from the structure of African economies, this chapter illustrates that the decolonial project, embarked on in most African countries during the 1960s, has only partially dislodged the colonial rationality and hegemony. The importance of the land question and the structure of African economies in decentering colonial hegemony and modes of thought cannot be over-emphasised. The decolonial discourse in this chapter applies to the entire continent for two specific reasons. First of all, the decolonisation project was embarked on by all countries in Africa including countries which were not physically occupied by colonial powers; for example, Ethiopia and Liberia. Second, the colonial project was not merely a physical process of occupying certain territories; it was much deeper than that, involving the reclassification of the human race into *us* and *them*, the civilised and uncivilised, the developed and the underdeveloped, the industrial and pre-capitalist societies, the Christians and the pagans, literate and the illiterate, etc., (see Mamdani, 1996). It is indeed a dangerously superficial reading of colonialism to exclude Liberia and Ethiopia (and sometimes Morocco and Egypt) from the process of decolonisation simply because these countries were not 'fully colonised!' The colonial rationality and modes of thought applied to all countries in Africa, and as such, the process of decolonisation remains incomplete in all these countries.

This chapter is organised in five sections. In the next section, I discuss the importance of the land question in the colonial and decolonial projects. This is followed by a discussion of the concept of decolonisation and what this means in the African context today. In section three a brief discussion of African post-colonial states and the status of the decolonial project is presented. The next section illustrates the incompleteness of the decolonial project drawing from the land and the economy. The last section sums up the discussion.

Land in the Colonial and Decolonial Projects

Form the earlier encounters with imperial and colonial forces in Africa, the control over land proved to be at the heart of the colonial project. Colonialism became a viable project only after the colonial forces secured control of the land through various means including armed invasion, ruthless dispossession of indigenous communities, signing of dubious/fraudulent treaties with the African ruling elites, and the negotiation of loose mining concessions. The introduction of colonial rule in both settler and non-settlers colonies in Africa did not only lead to the introduction of a foreign system of land tenure, but it fundamentally altered the way Africans think and relate to land as illustrated below. Most of, if not all, the policy and administrative changes introduced through colonialism were tailored to protect and advance the interests of the minority European settlers, with little or no regard to the local African people who were, directly and indirectly, turned into tenants of the imperial Crowns, on their mother's land (Okoth-Ogendo, 1989). Given the humiliation and

23

violence to which Africans were subjected during colonialism, when most African countries became independent, there was great expectation that the nationalist leaders, who fought for the land against foreign occupation, would not only reconstruct the agrarian structure, but also remove the distortions which colonialism introduced around land and the economy. Not surprising, the decolonisation project, which started with the liberation struggle, was rooted in the land question as far as the land defined the polity and the sovereignty of the nation-state which the nationalist aspired to (Mkandawire, 2011). But, almost six decades after most African states gained independence, the decolonisation of the land and agrarian structures, and the accompanying administrative systems remain an incomplete, if not, abandoned project. Just as the securing of control over land was central to the colonial project, the resolution of the land question, in all its various dimensions across Africa, remains key to a complete decolonial project.

In this chapter, I use examples from land and the economy to show the continuity of the *colonialilty of power*, which is a reflection of the failure on the part of post-colonial African states to decolonise the land and the economy. This is not to argue that there has been no attempt to decolonise; early African nationalists recognised the need to decolonise (see Mkandawire, 1999; 2011). But their efforts were not sustained long enough to see the project to its logical conclusion. This is partly because the project of decolonisation was narrowly framed within the nationalist project by equating decolonisation with political liberation (see Ndlovu-Gatsheni, 2012); focusing mainly on the physical withdraw of colonial regimes and the centralisation of power there after (Mkandawire, 1999). In other words, decolonisaion has been restricted to merely seeking the "political kingdom." But a complete decolonial project has to go beyond the imperatives of political independence to include economic, cultural, and epistemological sovereignty, for the simple reason that the colonial project was not merely a political project, it was much more than that. A narrow conception of colonialism tends to equate it with the physical presence of a colonising force, such that once the colonial powers withdraw, colonialism should not be an issue, since there are no more colonisers on African soil. But the colonial hegemony and rationality is very much alive today in all parts of Africa in the education sector, in the economy, in the way knowledge is produced and validated, and indeed in the dominant modes of thinking and the sets of aspirations. In political economy literature, this unrelenting colonial hegemony is widely referred to as neo-colonialism.

Because of the narrow conceptualisation of the decolonial project, it has been difficult to extend the reconstruction of the African thought and society beyond the political expediencies of the day, and as such, there are many aspects of African societies that still operate under the colonial grip, which has largely been invisible. But now it is gradually becoming apparent that colonialism was a much more complex phenomenon with far deeper effects on African societies beyond the physical presence of the coloniser on African soil. Thus, colonialism, in different ways, is very much alive today even in the absence of a physical coloniser on the continent. Consequently, a total decolonisation of the continent would require much more than simply dislodging colonial regimes from the continent; it requires a radical reorientation of the African worldview to something fundamentally *African*, which ultimately entails decolonising the African mind (see Ngugi, 1986), and modes of *knowing* and *being*. Tuck & Yang (2012) refers to this as a process of "decentring" colonialism.

Decolonisation and Coloniality

The concept of decolonisation is increasingly becoming popular in academic circles in Africa, particularly, in the last half decade or so, to the extent of becoming a cliché. But there is much more to the concept of decolonisation than what is often conveyed in popular debates. Despite the lack of clarity on the exact meaning and practical implications of this concept, there is undoubtedly a revival of the radicalism of the 1960s; perhaps, representing a going back to the roots of sorts, may be an African renaissance of the 21st century. Prior to the current revival of media and scholarly interest in the decolonial discourse, the term decolonisation was used only by a few scholars in the global South, mainly the Latin America and Asian

Subaltern Studies Group of scholars (see Grosfoguel, 2007). In South Africa, the term has been lifted into the national consciousness largely by the student movements: "#Rhodes Must Fall" and later, "#Fees Must Fall," which have embarked on a specific campaign calling for the decolonisation of the higher education curriculum in South Africa (see Nyamnjoh, 2016).[1] For many scholars, the two big questions which arise when discussing decolonisation are: What does decolonisation mean? What does it entail in practical terms?

It is important, from the start, to note that, up to this point, the term decolonisation has not been sharply articulated, and as such no single definition exists. Several definitions have been offered, and in some discussions, no attempt is made to define what is meant by decolonisation; there seem to be an assumption that the term is self-explanatory. But a cursory glance at the decolonisation debates, reveals that the term can mean different things to different people. Depending on what meaning one adopts, decolonisation evokes a wide range of sentiments in different people. For instance, Suren Pillay (2013) reports that some esteemed professors have dismissed the term as "a dangerous call to participate in 'applied nationalism.'" For those who adopt this view, decolonial discourse evokes anxiety about the changes that such a project may bring. Understandably, genuine decolonisation involves a radical re-orientation of entire epistemologies and systems of power which can lead to anxiety and resentment for those who fail to see the violence of colonialism. A good example of this is Bruce Gilley's (2017) article in which he argues that colonialism was not only a legitimate project, but hugely beneficial to the colonised peoples.

For some scholars, decolonisation is conceived as a critique of modernism, while for others it denotes a "critique of eurocentrism from subalternized and silenced knowledges" (see Grosfoguel, 2007). For Fanon (1963) decolonisation is not just a critique, but a process and programme of de-centring (disordering) colonial rationality, structures, institutions, knowledge systems and world view. In the Fanonian framework, decolonization is a process of recovering oneself from the derangement which colonialism induced in the colonized; a recovery that unveils the myth that colonialism came to lighten the burden of the colonized. In that sense, we see Fanon in

Wiredu (1998), who defines decolonization as simply a call for the colonized to know themselves better—as in the maxim, "African, know thyself."

For Tuck & Yang (2012) decolonization is a project of 'decentring settler perspectives' and dominant theories of social change, which are presented as the only way to explain the world everywhere. While Tuck & Yang (2012) acknowledge the importance of decolonization, they are critical of the now popular calls for decolonization which, according to them, fail to grasp the deep implications of decolonization as a project that seeks to "decentre settler perspectives," leading to perceptions of "decolonization as a metaphor" (Tuck & Yang, 2012). Decolonisation is sometimes conceptualized as something comparable to de-westernisation, meaning that "the rules of the game" are no longer set by "Western players and institutions." If decolonization is seen from that angle, it inevitably leads to a "definitive rejection of 'being told' from the epistemic privileges of the *zero point* what we [the colonized] are, what our ranking is in relation to the ideal of *humanitas* and what we have to do to be recognized as such" (Mignolo, 2009: 3, emphasis in original).

When applied to the African context, the plurality of views on what decolonisation means is apparent. For instance, while Thomas Sankara conceptualised decolonisation as a revolutionary movement that sets the restoration of the dignity of African people as its goal (Sankara, 2005), Sabelo Ndlovu-Gatsheni (2012) sees decolonization as primarily an epistemological undertaking that seeks to systematically "unpack" not only the genealogy of colonialism; but its ethical and ideological dimensions and assumptions. Similar to Ndlovu-Gatsheni (2012), Nyamnjoh (2012: 129) sees decolonization as a process of unveiling the hegemonic nature of the "epistemological paradigm of the conqueror." For Ngugi Wa Thiongo (1986) decolonization in an African context essentially entails a process of overcoming the *alienation* of an African from her/his-self, caused by the colonial devaluation of African culture, life, art, religion, geography, education, literature, and most importantly, languages and modes of being.

There are several other ways in which decolonization has been defined and approached, and it is not my intention here to exhaust the list of such definitions. My main aim in discussing the different meanings assigned to the term is to highlight the point that there are different views on what decolonization means, and that every meaning is contested.

However, while decolonization is viewed from different perspectives by different scholars, as shown above, most of these views point to two fundamental aspects. The first is that colonialism was built on the assumption that there was only one valid way of *knowing*, one authentic way of *being*; one valid history, language, system of education, culture, etc.; and that authentic way, was (and still is) that of the colonizing powers'. Whether we take decolonization as decentring settler perspectives or overcoming the alienation of the colonized, the underlying point which these views bring out is that the colonizing powers devalued and dishonoured other ways of *knowing* and *being*; other histories, other lives, cultures, languages, religions, etc. What this essentially means is that colonialism was a project infused with ontological, and as a consequence, epistemological violence. The physical violence, which is frequently associated with colonialism such as land dispossession, slavery, forced labour, unequal exchange of material goods and ideas, is underpinned by the ontological and the epistemological brutality it embodies. Thus, a decolonial project, by virtue of being a counter discourse, seeks to expose the violence by showing the disregard of other forms of *knowing* and *being* that colonial epistemologies constitute. In this sense, decolonization is a radical discourse that has the enlightenment of both the colonized as well as the colonizer as its objective (Mignolo, 2009).

The second fundamental feature that the different views on decolonisation discussed above bring out, albeit implicitly in some, is that colonialism is ultimately about power relations. It is the seemingly powerful (coloniser) who imposes his or her cosmology, epistemology, culture, language, and being, as '*the*' world view, '*the*' culture, '*the*' knowledge, etc. This hegemonic posturing by the colonizer has evolved into what has been called the *coloniality of power* after the end of formal colonisation. Coloniality of power signifies the "Eurocentrification of the new world power" leading to "a new social classification of the world population on a global scale" (Quijano, 2007: 171). This power matrix, on the side of the colonizer, was not only constructed through the barrel and gun powder, but through a systematic narrative that entrenches ontological and epistemological violence. Although often overlooked in the popular discussions of colonialism, the latter form of violence is much more harmful than the barrel and gun powder, and gives more power to the aggressor, in that it enables the colonizing powers to control how the colonized think, not just about the world, but also about themselves. As Lukes (1974) argues, the most powerful way of exercising power is by controlling people's perceptions, system of values, wants, aspirations, views, beliefs, shared meaning and choices. It is this form of exercising power which is subtle and is often deeply entrenched in processes that apparently seem to be done in the interest of the powerless.

Colonisation was justified on exactly such grounds as evident in the civilising missions (Pax Britanica, and now Pax Americana) narrative; and Christianisation (saving the infidels/pagans from going to hell), as a favour to the colonised. Such sentiments are not buried with the end of colonial occupation, they are still being entertained, for example, in a recent article that argues for the replication of colonialism through the good governance agenda and the recolonization of weak states in the former colonised world (see Gilley, 2017). Through such views the colonisers continue to amass power in subtle ways that enables them to keep influencing what the colonised want, think and aspire for—holding the coloniser as the ideal, the ultimate example of a perfect humanity, civilisation, culture, development, economy, education, system of land tenure, etc. This has been the most enduring dimension of colonialism which still has a lot of sway in the minds, actions and dreams of the colonised even after physical occupation of colonies ended. Thus, decolonisation at this level requires much more thinking in order to unmask the subtle forms of power which enables the colonialists to continue controlling the colonised's minds and actions.

Understanding these two core elements of colonialism (the ontological and epistemological violence, and the power to control what the colonised want) is very central to understanding the decolonisation project, and the different forms in which coloniality[2] survives today (Maldonado-Torres, 2007). Seen from this perspective, decolonisation is not about reversing what colonialism has done so far; that would be not only an impossible, but also an unnecessary mission. A reversal of colonialism would imply going back to the static moment of encounter with the coloniser (see Nyamnjoh, 2012). For instance, decolonising the land tenure system in Africa does not mean that we go back to where African land tenure systems were before the colonial/imperial encounter; that would validate a static view of Africa, which in the end reinforces the colonial narrative.

However, this does not mean that decolonisation is an impossible undertaking; it means that a decolonial project undertakes to understand and expose the distortions, the violence and the power imbalances at play, and to find ways to re-orient the thinking, aspirations, perceptions, knowledges and the being of the colonised. It entails the unmasking and overcoming of the "widespread and stubborn misrepresentation of African cultures as static, bounded and primitive, and Africa as needing the benevolence and enlightenment of colonialism and Cartesian rationalism or their residue to come alive" (Nyamnjoh, 2012: 136). It involves, for example, unmasking the violence and power play entrenched in privileging statutory tenure over customary tenure; it requires rejecting the privileging of colonial epistemologies over endogenous systems of knowledge (Nabudere, 2006; Maldonado-Torres, 2007). Mkandawire (1997) frames this as the "demand to be heard" in a world where knowledge about Africa has not been produced to improve the welfare of Africans, but to better control them.

From this perspective, decolonisation is a call to a critical awareness of the fact that knowing is influenced by the location of both the *known* and the *knower*. Once this awareness is realised, it is inevitable that the locus of decolonisation should be on the 'terms of the conversation,' and not just the 'content' (Mignolo, 2009). Paying attention to the location of the knower brings out what Mignolo (2009: 4) has referred to as the 'geo-politics of knowledge,' which makes clear the main task of decolonial thinking as the "unveiling of the epistemic silences of western epistemology and affirming the epistemic rights of the racially devalued."

When the colonised are at this level of engagement, instead of prematurely celebrating the withdraw of the colonial regimes from colonised territories as the real moment of decolonisation, the focus shifts to the surviving influence of the *coloniality of power* that shapes not only the power relations, but also the way the colonised think, the way knowledge is produced, and what is validated as *"the"* knowledge. This is a more radical way of breaking ranks with colonial hegemony and rationality. A decolonial thinking therefore embraces a broader view of colonialism beyond the physical imposition of a foreign rule, to include the reality of ontological and epistemological violence which entrenches a deeper form of control among the colonised. It embraces the broader vision which creates room for a diversity of epistemologies and cultures beyond the western paradigms (Grosfoguel, 2007; Nyamnjoh, 2012).

The Postcolonial African States and the Decolonial Project

A close look at decolonisation from the ontological and epistemological point of view violence makes it clear that the post-colonial African states are sitting on an incomplete project. One does not have to go far to realise that the decolonial project in Africa so far has been restricted to the physical withdraw of the colonialist. But as illustrated above, this is only one dimension of a genuine decolonial project, and perhaps the easiest to accomplish. Any celebration of this dimension of decolonisation as the end game of the liberation struggle, "obscures the continuing operations of coloniality of power and hides the myths of decolonisation and illusion of freedom in Africa" (Ndlovu-Gatsheni, 2012: 71). It is such narrow conceptualisation of the decolonial project that explains the incompleteness of the project on the African continent and in other colonised countries. Colonialism as elaborated above, was not just about the imposition of foreign rule; it also encompassed the denial of the humanity of the colonised by degrading them to primitive people needing civilisation, and humanisation. Linda Thuwai Smith, speaking from the experience of the indigenous people of New Zealand, captures the degrading effects of colonialism succinctly

31

when she argues that:

> One of the supposed characteristics of primitive peoples was that we could not use our minds or intellects. We could not invent things, we could not create institutions or history, we could not imagine, we could not produce anything of value, we did not know how to use land and other resources from the natural world, we did not practice the 'arts' of civilisation. By lacking such values, we disqualified ourselves, not just from civilisation but from humanity itself. In other words, we were not "fully human;" some of us were not even considered partially human. Ideas about what counted as human in association with the power to define people as human or not human were already encoded in the imperial discourses prior to the period of imperialism... (cited in Mignolo, 2009: 13–14).

From what Smith is saying, there is no doubt that colonialism is much deeper than just an act of physical occupation of foreign territories; it involves a complex process of inferiorising and dehumanising other people. Inferiorising others created power for the colonisers to decide not only who is to be counted as human, but what is good for the colonised, whether they know something or not, and more importantly that their knowing was second-rate. This power configuration (see Maldonado-Torres, 2007; Ndlovu-Gatsheni, 2012), continues in a subtle way (often branded as neo-colonialism), to influence not only the production of knowledge in the colonised societies, but also the modes of thought and the manner in which knowledge is validated.

The implication of this is that although the withdrawal of colonial regimes from African soil was accomplished during the 1960s, that did not mark the end of colonial influence; it was the first step on the long road to complete decolonisation. In Africa, decolonial thinking of the nationalists has, so far, not gone beyond this first step, to deconstruct the power structures of coloniality which perpetuate subservient and dependent relations with Africans, not only in matters of trade, but also culture, art, language, education and more importantly, the way knowledge is produced and validated. While post-colonial African states have been content and bent on wrestling the political kingdom from the colonialist (Fanon, 1963), they have forgotten that the real power lies in the colonial designs that control not only the way the colonised think, but what they want and the agenda they set for the future. Seemingly, this part of the decolonial project was assumed to follow naturally after achieving political decolonisation. But today, it has become quite clear that without unveiling and challenging the ontological and epistemological violence and the power matrix of colonialism, political independence actually means very little (Ndlovu-Gatsheni, 2012). Moyo & Yeros (2011) frame this as the return of the national question in which nations begin to assert their autonomy, seeking to extricate themselves from the hegemonic structures of neo-colonialism. In trying to undo the colonial structures of power and influence, the revival of the national question is a manifestation of the search for alternatives to colonialism, which is popularly framed as decolonisation—the need to overturn the coloniality of power.

With the colonial matrix of power remaining intact, Africa remains "a product of active operations of colonial matrices of power" (Ndlovu-Gatsheni, 2015: 15). Without critically engaging the power matrix of colonialism, the biased ontological and epistemological dualism which puts the colonised in an inferior, less rational, less civilised, less developed, less objective, less human, less modern, under-developed, position, will continue.

In this way, the colonisers will continue to put themselves up as,

> ...the mirror of the future of all societies and cultures, as the advanced form of the history of the entire [human] species. What does not cease to surprise, however, is that Europe succeeded in imposing that 'mirage' upon the practical totality of the cultures that it colonised; and, much more, that this chimera is still so attractive to so many (Quijano, 2007: 176).

A complete project of decolonisation would not ignore the mirage and leave it masked as the universal truth, the only truth; it would lay bare its geo-political positionality and seek to broaden the epistemological scope that allows for a genuine interchange of experiences and knowledges. Such a decolonial project will not be content with achieving a "mere modicum of juridical freedom… which has been mistakenly conflated with achievement of popular freedom for the ex-colonised African peoples" (Ndlovu-Gatsheni, 2012: 72–73).

To be fair, the nationalist project in Africa, through which the decolonial project was articulated, showed some commitment to decolonisation, and succeeded in achieving political decolonisation. Mkandawire (1999) observes that the nationalists in Africa allocated themselves five key tasks: 'complete decolonisation,' economic and social development, nation-building, democratisation, and regional cooperation. Out of these five, "only the first one—decolonization—has been completed, now that South Africa has at last won its arduous battle for non-colonial status" (Mkandawire, 1999: 75). From this, it is apparent that decolonisation has been restricted to the dislodgement of foreign rule from African soil, and this is one of the reasons why it makes perfect sense for the nationalist to assume that the achievement of political independence implied that the decolonisation project is accomplished; there was nothing more to fight against. This narrow approach to decolonisation explains why the project has remained largely incomplete, if not, totally abandoned today.

However, even if one takes the nationalists on their own terms, it is apparent that the self-allocated tasks remain incomplete to a large extent. While issues of economic and social development have remained on the radar (often thrust on the agenda by the former colonial powers), it is not clear if nation-building, democratisation and regional cooperation are still projects under construction today (Mkandawire, 2011). Soon after independence, the nationalist ideology itself became problematic as the project was reduced to that of nation-building, and eventually state-building, focusing on narrowly defined goals aimed at concentrating power and control in a few big men. This has become a pre-occupation of most of Africa's political elite. At the moment, there are no indications that African leaders are even thinking about decolonisation in the broader sense discussed above. It is students' demands, particularly in South Africa, for a decolonised curriculum, which have inadvertently reminded them about the incompleteness of the decolonisation project on the continent. It is not surprising that decolonisation as a process of disrupting colonial rationality; the re-orientation of African societies to alternative modes of being, knowing and relating with the world, has remained an unfinished business in many respects. In this sense, even the notions of a nation-state as an autonomous social and political formation has been largely hollowed out as most African states continue to operate under the coloniality of power, which dictates, in subtle ways, what institutions to establish and how to run them. That dream of establishing genuine African systems and institutions built on the African world view and values has largely faded away. It is the colonial value system in all sectors of life which has been prioritised, giving rise to a situation where the African systems and values are valued less. To illustrate this, I use two examples from the land and the economy.

Decolonisation and the Land Question in Africa

Like many other aspects of African life, the colonial encounter drastically changed not only the relations around land, but the way Africans think about land. There are several ways in which the colonial encounter significantly altered land relations and tenure arrangements in Africa. One of the most fundamental changes is the introduction of an entirely foreign land tenure system, based on European conception of land, and property in general. The large body of literature on land and land tenure in Africa is almost unanimous on the view that the dominant conception and approaches to land tenure and management in Africa today are largely a product of colonial construction (Okoth-Ogendo, 1989; Bassett, 1993; Agbosu, 2000; Akuffo, 2009). In the context of decolonial thinking, it is important to note that this change has always been portrayed as a positive change (for the better), since customary land tenure systems in Africa were seen as the ones responsible for blocking progress to more productive use of land (see Bassett, 1993; Peters, 2009). This is one area where the coloniality of power is quite evident.

The introduction of a completely foreign way of thinking about land has not just led to tenure dualism (customary and statutory tenure); it has also been a source of tension between the two systems, and this sometimes has given rise to conflict over land. Sam Moyo (2007; 2008) in is work, consistently wrote about this as a sign of an incomplete process of decolonisation; a failure to address the colonial imprints on the land and agrarian question in Africa. Agbosu (2000: 13–14) captures the tension that ensues when the two systems exist side by side, leading to "an ideological struggle reflecting the ideas of the two systems of production in which the dominant capitalist ideas held sway over the traditional. The most significant areas in which these conflicts become manifest can be found in the transfer of interests in land." Since the introduction of the European tenure system in Africa by the colonial governments, customary land systems have had an uneasy co-existence with the European system. In this disquiet cohabitation, customary land tenure has always been seen, by both the colonial and post-colonial African policymakers, as something backward, inferior, unproductive, inefficient, insecure, old-fashioned, and a barrier to investment and economic growth (see Peters, 2009; Bassett, 1993).

This should not be surprising, in the context of the discussion above, that the colonial discourse has always operated on a binary logic that inferiorises the experiences of the colonised. Colonisation by its nature is a direct confirmation of this binarism, which justifies the imposition of a foreign world view on another, on the pretext that one is better, more effective, more civilised than the other. It is this logic that does violence to the *being* and the *knowing* of the other. In this logic, statutory tenure is seen as more superior, more secure, with great potential to promote investment, increase productivity and contribute positively to economic growth and development. Here we have an example of a colonial experience presented as the ideal to which the colonised should aspire. The entire system is built around a biased dichotomy in which anything indigenous is seen as inferior, backward and inefficient (see Mamdani, 1996). With specific reference to land tenure, the "early colonial and missionary attitude toward what they saw as 'communal' forms of landholding was deeply entrenched in longstanding cultural preconceptions that set individual, private ownership as superior to communal or collective forms of tenure" (Peters, 2009: 1317). The continuation of these preconceptions in post-colonial Africa is a reflection of the reality of the coloniality of power and the incompleteness of the decolonial project.

Distorted Conception of Land

To understand the coloniality of power around land relations in Africa, it is important to identify the drastic changes or distortions that colonialism introduced in the African land systems. The first and most important distortion was around the conception of land itself. From a European perspective, land was largely conceptualised as a property like any other properties (Agbosu, 2000). As a property, all land had to have an "owner," with absolute ownership (property) rights, such that land tenure was conceived as a set of clearly delineated rights and claims that one holds in the land. On the other hand, in the traditional African tenure system land was never thought of as a property that someone can exclusively own. As Akuffo (2009) explains, the concept of land in traditional African society was deeply embedded in the complex social relations which defined access to land and the exercise of power over land. In this regard, a clear distinction was made between the *soil* (*solum*) and the things that grow on it; "there was a clear separation in African thought and law between the *solum* and any *manifestation*, such as crops, trees and buildings which symbolises human interaction with it" (Okoth-Ogendo, 1989: 8). This separation was not present in the Dutch-Roman conception of land where the solum was fused together "with water and air in a compact, recording the claims of individuals rather than social labour upon it" (Okoth-Ogendo, 1989).

What this difference in the conception of land highlights is that land in the two systems mean different things. While in the European system it was the norm for the individual to have exclusive rights to land, in the traditional African system, ownership of the soil was only a reserve of the collective; only the things attached to the soil could be owned individually. The collective (which is often referred to as communal ownership) was understood broadly to include the past (ancestors), those living at the time, and those yet to come (future generation). This intergenerational conception of land in Africa, transcends the immediate imperatives of individual ownership of the *solum*, at any particular moment, since the land was intricately connected to the past and the future, not just the present. This is why it was only the collective (community in the broader sense) that could own the land; no single individual, not even the chief had ownership rights to the *solum* (Okoth-Ogendo, 1989; Mamdani, 1996; Agbosu, 2000). Thus, when the concept of ownership is transported from its European context to the African context, it creates not only confusion, but tension and conflict as well:

> ...the transposition of Western (Roman-Dutch/civil law and Anglo-American) property concepts and terminology in the analyses of African processes is a veritable source of confusion. The characterisation of property concepts and legal relationships using Western analogies and paradigms is perhaps understandable but has nevertheless, led to an unnecessary degree of confusion with wholly negative practical consequences such as destructive litigation over land titles and land alienation (Akuffo, 2009: 62).

Earlier on, Meek (1946) issued a warning on the dangers of applying the European terms to understand land relations in Africa:

> [A]frequent source of error has been a presupposition that native conceptions of ownership must be basically the same as those of Europeans. English terms such as 'rent,' or 'lease' have been employed to denote practices which bear only a superficial resemblance to those denoted by these terms. The gift given to chiefs as administrators of land have been assumed to be 'rent', and the chiefs to be 'landlords' (Meek, 1946: 11).

Meek's caution above is critically important in highlighting the violence that a colonial imposition of a European experience, meaning and knowledge does to the colonised. However, instead of looking at these as misunderstandings of the local context, the assumption that the terms should mean the same reflects the coloniality of power where the experience of the colonised must be monotonically mapped onto the experience of the coloniser, since the later represents the ideal, the real, the rational, the advanced, the standard against which everything else should be measured. Anything that does not fit the European norm is dismissed as primitive, traditional, uncivilised, and barbaric. When seen from this perspective, the violence of colonialism becomes more palpable, and the incompleteness of the decolonial project becomes conspicuously evident.

The implications of this conceptual distortion of land is that land then becomes a commodity which can be sold and bought like anything else. In an African setting, this creates numerous conceptual and practical challenges which led to three basic distortions: that land should have an owner; that only members of a given tribe should own land in a particular community, and that the person responsible for the administration of land is effectively the land owner (see Mamdani, 1996). By presenting the European system as superior to the African, the colonialists created an imbalanced power relation where their system becomes the sought after, and the traditional system is something that had to be abandoned. This has continued even today when statutory tenure is not only preferred, but is emphatically endorsed by many African governments, with the aim of replacing customary tenure.

As illustrated later, most African political elite still believe that customary tenure has no place in modern Africa, and at various times, frantic efforts have been made to do away with customary tenure. Here again we have an example of how coloniality of power continues to shape not just the way the colonised think, but also what they aspire for. There is nothing more powerful than having the power to control what someone thinks and wants, as Lukes (1974) argues. By affirming the colonial claim that customary land represents backwardness and a barrier to progress, the colonised have forfeited power to the coloniser who then has an advantage because his or her ideas become dominant, become the leading ideas. This has resulted not only in the distortion of the African experience but has also stifled the efforts to understand land relations in Africa after the colonial encounter, as Bassett (1993: 5) observes:

The tendency of colonial apologists to project their own (European models and concepts onto African societies has hindered our understanding of development and change in this area. …ethnocentric and ideological biases and their attendant agenda distort much of the literature.

Colonial DNA on Africa's Land

Privileging colonial ideas is also evident in the structure and institutions surrounding land administration in Africa's urban and rural areas. As Home (2012: 62) argues, the "legacy of colonialism is still etched on the landscape and practices of Sub-Saharan African Towns and cities." Many post-colonial African governments, immediately after independence, formulated laws and policies to respond to the challenges of land tenure and agrarian reforms introduced by colonial regimes (Adams & Turner, 2005). But most of these laws and institutions simply inherited and tinkered with the colonial social engineering to the extent that continuity has been the norm rather than the exception (Bassett, 1993).

Continuity in these reforms is evident in three aspects: the first is that "many post-colonial governments simply retained or revised colonial land rules." The second is that many of the African governments have continued to perceive customary tenure as something that hinders development and therefore inferior; and thirdly, the colonial idea that by merely reforming land tenure arrangements, the complex agrarian transformation issues will be resolved, has continued to define the official approach to land reform in post-colonial Africa, where land tenure reform is broadly seen as a panacea for everything (Bassett, 1993: 9; Moyo, 2007). Apart from these three, there have been continuities in the land administration institutions with only cosmetic changes introduced (Adams, 2003). For example, the centralisation of land administration is something introduced by the colonial governments prior to the 1960s, and yet in many countries these same structures have remained intact, with land administration concentrated in the capital cities, as was the case in colonial times.

This is a clear sign of the failure to deconstruct the colonial structure in the post-colonial context. If we start from the view that colonial institutions and legal systems around land were introduced to serve colonial interests (often without any due regard to the colonised), it would be expected that the post-colonial African states, because of their opposition to the colonial project as a whole, would re-orient and radically transform these institutions and laws to serve the interest of the African people. But so far, little has happened in that regard (Metcalfe & Kepe, 2008). To achieve this, a radical re-orientation of the colonial system is needed. This is more so because of the centrality of land in the liberation struggle, but also in the lives of many Africans today. Despite land being the key motive for the liberation struggle across Africa (Havnevik, 1997), the land and agrarian questions remain aspects of post-colonial African societies where decolonisation is poignantly incomplete (Moyo, 2007).

As noted above, we have seen many African governments privileging statutory tenure over customary tenure in no uncertain terms. For instance, the 2006 draft land policy in Zambia does not hide the fact that customary land tenure is not a suitable form of land tenure, in a manner that sounds like a rehearsal of the colonial narrative:

> Free access to resources provided by customary tenure has the disadvantage that the individual has no incentive to invest in common resources such as pasture improvement. This has the effect of encouraging overuse and can result in severe degradation of the environment. Rights derived from customary tenure are not registered and difficult to define. Private credit institutions do not recognise such rights as collateral. Furthermore, rights to land derived from customary tenure are subject to local practices and beliefs (The Republic of Zambia, 2006: 13).

Similar views can be found in the national land policies in Tanzania, Ghana, Zimbabwe, South Africa, Swaziland, Mozambique, Rwanda, Uganda, Malawi and Liberia, where the drive to formalise customary land through some form of statutory instrument has been promoted to attract foreign investment. While in many countries this is not stated so clearly, it is evident that policy makers have fallen prey to the colonial chimera that everything non-European is retrogressive and not desirable; they have surrendered their power to think independently, thereby losing control to determine their thinking and system of wants.

The other example of the failure to decolonise the land tenure in African lies is the maintenance of the colonial land ownership structures, especially in the former settler colonies where large portions of land were alienated from local communities by European settlers. Sam Moyo (2007) identifies the failure to redistribute land after independence as one example of incomplete decolonisation. He frames the debate broadly around reparation for "colonial land loses" which many African governments have not addressed. A decolonial thinking around land would follow the logic that the mass dispossession of indigenous people during colonial rule merits a massive land redistribution to re-orient the colonially designed land and agrarian structure.

As observed above, although many African countries gained independence 60 years ago, restructuring colonial land tenure policy and institutions is one area where decolonisation has remarkably failed, with most governments maintaining the colonial land administrative policies and institutions (Adams, 2003; Obeng-Odoom, 2012). As a result, the inability to expose the violence of colonialism and therefore the need to decolonise to create an environment where justice can be restored, is evident. Instead, just as the "colonial government found ruling the indigenous hinterland easier by co-opting traditional governance system, rather than deconstructing them...post-colonial, independent, African governments have more or less adopted the same approach" (Metcalfe & Kepe, 2008: 238).

Even in countries where some relatively radical reforms were undertaken by means of nationalising land and the abolishment of freehold title in Tanzania, Zambia, Ethiopia and Guinea, there has been widespread failure to reconstruct the colonial agrarian landscape. For instance, in Zambia, despite the seemingly radical steps introduced by the Kaunda government (to nationalise land in 1975 by abolishing freehold tenure), land throughout the post-colonial period retained the original colonial tri-modal structure of *crown land* (which was simply renamed *state* land at independence), and *native reserves* and *trust land*. Native and Trust lands comprised lands that were reserved for the native populations and were therefore administered by traditional authorities using local customary norms and traditional practices. It was only in 1995 when *native reserves* and *trust lands* were consolidated into one category—*customary land*. This consolidation of the two categories into customary land was merely cosmetic and did not in any way alter people's rights to customary land. Thus, even after the reforms introduced in 1995 in Zambia, land tenure dualism (customary and statutory) has persisted, with customary land tenure widely perceived as something retrogressive that needs to be done away with. As a result, customary tenure continues to awkwardly coexist with statutory tenure as evident in the practice of converting customary land into leasehold tenure which is promoted by the state (Chitonge et al., 2017). Land tenure dualism is so prevalent across Africa that it defines the continent's agrarian land scape. It is here where the failure to grasp the ontological and epistemological violence and the power matrix inherent in the colonial design becomes more obvious. A genuine decolonial project should aim to reconstruct and re-orient the colonial land and agrarian structure.

Decolonising African Economies

The other example I would like to use to illustrate the incompleteness of the decolonial project is the structures of African economies. The economic sphere presents another interesting example of how the colonial logic continues to operate today, conceptually and theoretically, to shape the economic and development agenda. A quick glance at the structure of most African economies today makes this very clear. Almost 60 years after colonial occupation ended, most African economies still have the same economic structure that was left by the colonialists; most of them are still predominantly extractive mono-economies. As Table 1 shows, most of the countries are involved in the extraction of raw materials as was the case during colonial rule. In many countries, only a few commodities account for the entire export earning; meaning that the economies have drastically failed to diversify the production and export base (see Chitonge, 2015).

In countries such as Angola, Chad, Congo Brazzaville, Nigeria, only one commodity accounts for more than 75 percent of total exports (Table 1). Most importantly, even in countries with more than one major exports, these exports are predominantly raw materials, sent to Europe and other developed countries, unprocessed. In the colonial economic logic, defined by the international division of labour, the African economies were set up to dig out minerals from the ground and grow agricultural products to feed the industries in Europe and America. This set up puts African economies at a great disadvantage in that the activities to which they are assigned add low value, leading to the situation where these economies only capture a tiny fraction of the value chains in which they participate (Chitonge, 2015). Walter Rodney, in his famous book, *How Europe Underdeveloped Africa*, captures the colonial design well when he observes that in the colonial division of labour, "Africans were to dig minerals out of the subsoil, grow agricultural crops, collect natural products, and perform a number of other odds and ends such as bicycle repairing. Inside Europe, North America, and Japan, workers would refine the minerals and the raw materials and make the bicycles" (Rodney, 1974: 177).

The platinum that is mined in South Africa and Zimbabwe is exported "raw" to Germany (and now China) where it is processed into metal alloy which is used in the manufacturing of cars and other heavy metal equipment. South Africa and Zimbabwe only captures 15–25 percent of the platinum value chain. Of course, this serves the colonialists interests well, and the expectation was that in post-colonial Africa, all African economies will be re-oriented to serve the interest of the African people. Yet, most economies in Africa have maintained the same economic structure; resulting in serious economic leakage to the former colonial powers.

The broader context to this is that African economies were immersed into the colonial global economy in an extroverted manner, such that African economies would produce raw materials which were exported for processing in developed countries and brought back for the consumption by a small elite population, which is now growing if we take the stories about the rise of Africa's middle class seriously (see Melber, 2016).

Hountondji (1997) and Nabudere (2006) draw interesting parallels between the structures of commodity and knowledge production, arguing that in both cases, Africa is geared to produce raw materials for processing in Europe into finished products, which are then returned for the consumption of a few. The production of knowledge and commodities is structured in such as a way that raw materials and raw data are extracted from Africa, processed elsewhere and exported back to Africa for consumption, but only for a few in both cases. The copper that is dug out of the Democratic Republic of the Congo (DRC) is processed in China just as the data collected in Mali or Kenya is processed in France and Britain respectively, and the copper products and the findings (and theories constructed) are then exported back to Africa. This again exposes the violence of the colonial design and social engineering to the extent that it becomes a social justice issue. Here decolonisation is not just a critique but uncovers the injustice of the entire system.

The other way in which decolonisation has remained incomplete in the economic sector is around the enclave nature of African economies (Moyo, 2008). Enclavity is a concept that captures well the colonial logic where economic activities in Africa were set up without any regard for the local population; the driving motive was to serve particular colonial interests (Mhone, 2001). It is common to find, even today, that a mine develops in an area where a lot of people are not connected to the activities of a mine in any significant way (and were they are, it is through the negative impact of the mine such as water pollution and land degradation). During colonial times, such activities did not take into account the plight of the people around the mine; the interest was only to dig the minerals out of the soil. As a result, pockets of modern infrastructure and economic activities developed in the sea of poverty and misery—hence the enclave nature of these activities.

Table 1. Top three exports and share in total export (2015) for selected African countries

	1st	share %	2nd	share %	3rd	Share%	Number of export products accounting for 75% of total export
Angola	Petroleum	97.3					1
Botswana	Diamond raw	43.7	Nickel Mattes	21.9	Diamond	8.9	4
Burundi	Coffee raw	70.2	Black tea	13.1			2
Chad	Petroleum	80.6	Petroleum oils	8.6			1
Cameroon	Petroleum	42.1	Cocoa bean	15.8	Wood	7.2	6
Congo	Petroleum	85.1					1
Ethiopia	Coffee raw	42.1	Sesame Seed	22.5	Shirts	8.6	19
Gabon	Petroleum	75.8	Manganese Oil	12.3	Cut	10.7	1
Kenya	Black tea	18.6	Cut flower	13.1	Coffee raw	6.1	48
Malawi	Tobacco	53.0	Black tea	6.9	Uranium	6.5	5
Mali	Cotton	35.6	Petroleum oils	29.1	Sesame Seed	7.8	4
Mauritius	Tuna	11.3	Shirts	11.0	Cane beet	6.8	43
Namibia	Uranium	26.8	Diamond	16.1	Zinc	13.4	6
Nigeria	Petroleum	85.9	Natural Gas	6.9			1
Rwanda	Coffee raw	30.4	Vanadium Ores	24.8	Black tea	13.8	4
Senegal	Petroleum	26.4	Cement	10.5	Phosphor-ic acid	9.8	18
South Africa	Platinum	7.6	Gold	6.9			92
Tanzania	Precious metal	14.5	Tobacco	8.7	Coffee raw	6.4	24
Togo	Cocoa Bean	26.7	Gold	12.8	Cement	10.1	8
Uganda	Coffee raw	32.8	Tobacco	9.9	Fish	9.3	13
Zambia	Copper Cathods	48.0	Copper anodes	26.7	Cobalt	11.2	2
Zimbabwe	Tabacco	20.5	Chromium	15.3	Nickel	7.1	17

Source: Author based on data from African Development Indicators 2012/13 (World Bank, 2013).
Note: Countries are selected randomly. For a full list of countries, see World Bank (2013: 72–73).

Kamarck (1967) gives an example of roads or railway lines which were constructed by the colonial governments in Africa as an example. He argues that these were meant specifically to transport the minerals form the mine to the point of export, with no due regard given to the local people living along the road or railway line. Most of these projects have continued today, characterised by new forms of enclavity, mimicking the colonial design. A decolonised economy is expected to re-orient the logic of these projects in ways that recognise and value the humanity of the people around. But because the dominant logic operative even today is still entrenched in the colonial matrix of power, the process of decolonisation has not translated into anything tangible in this respect. Enclavity is still a dominant characteristic that defines most African economies in one way or another, to such an extent that in some cases we have continued to use the same roads that were constructed during colonial rule.

The other area where decolonisation has not gone far is around the use of economic growth models. It is common within the economic mainstream scholarship to employ economic models developed in the advanced economies and expect these to explain and shed more light on the challenges of economic growth in Africa and other developing areas (see Chitonge, 2015). The problem with importing economic models was observed earlier by the pioneers of development economics such as Albert Hirschman who argued that these models developed to understand economic problems in advanced economies have little relevance in developing countries. Hirschman (1958) in particular argued that these models because they were constructed to understand economic challenges in advanced economies, they "will have minimum relevance in any radically different environment." He goes further to advise that the "economics of development [developing economies] dare to borrow too extensively from the economics of growth [advanced economies], like the underdeveloped countries themselves, it must learn to walk on its own feet, which means that it must work out its own abstractions" (Hirschman, 1958: 33). But in the colonial framework, valid knowledge is only that which is produced in the coloniser; the rest of the world produce wisdom and culture (Mignolo, 2009); and as such they rest of the world should rely on theories and models from the dominant economies. Use of such models in Africa and other colonised places only reflect the failure to decolonise the knowledge production system which continues to operate

Conclusion

There are other ways in which decolonisation can be demonstrated to be incomplete in Africa. In this chapter, I have focused on the land and the economy as examples and the discussion above has presented a number of ways in which the colonial logic and design continues to influence the thought and practice in colonised areas. From the discussion above, it is apparent that genuine decolonisation is not a simple project, it requires developing a critical decolonial thinking that unmasks the violence and lop-sidedness of colonialism. The first step to a decolonial thinking is a full understanding of the coloniality of power and what this entails for a process of decolonisation. A failure to grasp the deep rootedness of colonialism and its power can lead to premature celebration of an incomplete decolonisation as was the case in Africa where the dislodgment of colonial regimes from the continent was celebrated as if it were the ultimate goal.

It is also clear that a decolonial project does not entail reversing colonialism, but rather unveiling its violence, injustice and insensitivity and then re-orienting the societies of the colonised. This, as noted earlier is not a mean task; it calls for a radical engagement and commitment to changing the power matrix between the colonised and the coloniser.

This chapter has shown that although colonial occupation ended during the 1960s in most countries, the effects of colonialism are still very much alive today and manifest in different forms. In the case of land, the tenure dualism, with an outright preference of the statutory tenure system over customary tenure demonstrate the coloniality of power where the colonised is made to believe the coloniser's knowledge, systems of law, education, cultures, languages is more superior and therefore desirable. In the economic sphere, the failure to transform the extroverted structure of African economies, set up during colonialism, into diversified production and export bases also highlight the incomplete nature of the decolonisation project. The repeated calls from students to transform the curriculum in African universities is an indication that there is need to engage with the colonial realities in Africa, not just around education, but in other aspects of life including the economy.

Notes

(1) It is not clear if similar calls have been made in institutions of higher learning in other countries. But the sentiments of having an Africa-centred knowledge system are strong across the continent not just today (see Nabudere, 2006).

(2) Maldonado-Torres (2007: 243) distinguishes colonialism as political and economic relations between the coloniser and the colonised, while coloniality refers to the "long-standing patterns of power that emerged as a result of colonialism, but that define culture, labour, intersubjective relations, and knowledge production well beyond the strict limits of colonial administrations."

Acknowledgements

This article is based on my paper presented at 'Land, the State and Decolonising the Agrarian Structure in Africa: A Colloquium in Honour of Professor Sam Moyo,' organized at the University of Cape Town, South Africa, on November 28–29, 2016. This colloquium was sponsored by the Japan Society for the Promotion of Science, Grant-in-Aid for Scientific Research (S) '"African Potential" and Overcoming the Difficulties of Modern World: Comprehensive Research That Will Provide a New Perspective for the Future of Humanity' (KAKENHI 16H06318 headed by Motoji Matsuda, Kyoto University), as well as by the University of Cape Town's Research Office (URC).

References

Adams, M. 2003. *Land Tenure Policy and Practice in Zambia: Issues Relating to the Development of the Agricultural Sector.* Mokoro Ltd, Oxford.

Adams, M. & S. Turner 2005. *Legal Dualism and Land Policy in Eastern*

& Southern Africa: Proceedings of the UNDP-International Land Coalition Workshop. Land and Property Rights for African Development: From Knowledge to Action, October 31–November 3, 2005. Nairobi, UNDP.

Agbosu, K.L. 2000. *Land Law in Ghana: Contradiction Between Anglo-American and Customary Conceptions of Tenure and Practice: Land Tenure Centre Working Paper No. 33*. Land Tenure Center, University of Wisconsin, Madison.

Akuffo, K. 2009. The conception of land ownership in African customary law and its implications for development. *African Journal of International and Comparative Law*, 17(1): 57–78.

Bassett, T. 1993. Introduction: The land question and agricultural transformation in Sub- Saharan Africa. In (T. Bassett & T.J. Crummey, eds.) *Land in African Agrarian Systems*, pp. 1–27. University of Wisconsin Press, Wisconsin.

Chitonge, H. 2015. *Economic Growth and Development in Africa: Understanding Trends and Prospects*. Routledge, London.

Chitonge, H., O. Mfune, D. Kafwamba & G. Kajoba 2017. Hybrid land markets: Monetarised customary land transactions in Zambia. *Canadian Journal of African Studies*, 51(1): 123–143.

Fanon, F. 1963. *The Wretched of the Earth*. Groves Press, New York.

Gilley, B. 2017. The case for colonialism. *Third World Quarterly*. DOI: 10.1080/ 01436597.2017.1369037

Grosfoguel, R. 2007. The epistemic decolonial turn: Beyond political-economy paradigms 1. *Cultural Studies*, 21(2–3): 211–223.

Havnevik, K. 1997. Land question in Sub-Saharan Africa. In (I. Nils-Ivar, ed.) *Land Question in Sub-Saharan Africa*. Department of Rural Development Studies, Swedish University of Agricultural Sciences, Uppsala.

Hirschman, A.O. 1958. *The Strategy of Economic Development*. Yale University Press, New Heaven.

Home, R. 2012. The colonial legacy in land rights in southern Africa. In (B. Chigara, ed.) *Southern African Development Community Land Issues: Towards a New Sustainable Land Relations Policy*, pp. 8–26. Routledge, London.

Hountondji, P. 1997. Introduction: Centring Africa. In (P. Hountondji, ed.) *Endogenous Knowledge: Research Trails*, pp. 1–42.

CODESRIA, Dakar.

Kamarck, A.M. 1967. *The Economics of African Development.* Frederick Pager, London. Lukes, S. 1974. *Power: A Radical View.* Macmillan, London.

Maldonado-Torres, N. 2007. On the coloniality of being: Contributions to the development of a concept. *Cultural Studies,* 21(2–3): 240–270.

Mamdani, M. 1996. *Citizen and Subject: Contemporary Africa and the Legacy of Colonialism.* Princeton University Press, Princeton.

Meek, C.K. 1946. *Land Law and Custom in the Colonies.* Oxford University Press, London.

Melber, H. 2016. 'Somewhere above poor but below rich:' Explorations into the species of the African middle class(es). In (H. Melber, ed.) *The Rise of Africa's Middle Class: Myths, Realities and Critical Engagements,* pp. 1–16. Zed Book/Nordic Africa Institute, London.

Metcalfe, S. & T. Kepe 2008. Dealing land in the midst of poverty: Commercial access to communal land in Zambia. *African and Asian Studies,* 7: 235–257.

Mhone, G.C.Z. 2001. *Enclavity and Constrained Labour Absorptive Capacity in Southern African Economies.* A paper prepared for the discussion at the UNRISD on The Need to Rethink Development Economics, September 7–8, 2001, Cape Town, South Africa.

Mignolo, W.D. 2009. Epistemic disobedience, independent thought and decolonial freedom.
Theory, Culture & Society, 26(7–8): 159–181.

Mkandawire, T. 1997. The social sciences in Africa: Breaking local barriers and negotiating international presence: The Bashorun M.K.O. Abiola distinguished lecture presented to the 1996 African studies association annual meeting. *African Studies Review,* 40(2): 15–36.

— 1999. Globalisation and Africa's unfinished agenda. *Macalester International,* 7: 71–107.

— 2011. Rethinking pan-Africanism, nationalism and the new regionalism. In (S. Moyo & P. Yeros, eds.) *Reclaiming the Nation: The Return of the National Question in Africa, Asia and Latin America,* pp. 31–53. Chicago University Press, Chicago.

Moyo, S. 2007. Land in the political economy of African development: Alternative strategies for reform. *Africa Development*, 32(4): 1–34.

— 2008. *African Land Questions, Agrarian Transition and the State: Contradictions of the Neo-liberal Land Reforms.* CODESRIA, Dakar.

Moyo, S. & P. Yeros 2011. Introduction: The fall and rise of the national question. In (S. Moyo & P. Yeros, eds.) *Reclaiming the Nation: The Return of the National Question in Africa, Asia and Latin America*, pp. 3–28. Chicago University Press, Chicago.

Nabudere, D. 2006. Development theories, knowledge production and emancipatory practice. In (V. Padayach, ed.) *The Development Decade? Economic and Social Change in South Africa 1994–2004*, pp. 33–52. HSRC Press, Cape Town.

Ndlovu-Gatsheni, S. 2012. Fiftieth anniversary of decolonisation in Africa: A moment of celebration or critical reflection? *Third World Quarterly*, 33(1): 71–89.

— 2015. Genealogies of coloniality and implications for Africa's development. *Africa Development*, 40(3): 13–40.

Ngugi, T. 1986. *Decolonising the Mind: The Politics of Language in African Literature.* James Currey, London.

Nyamnjoh, F. 2012. 'Potted plants in greenhouses:' A critical reflection on the resilience of colonial education in Africa. *Journal of Asian and African Studies*, 47(2): 129–154.

—— 2016. *#RhodesMustFall: Nibbling at Resilient Colonialism in South Africa.* Langaa RPCIG, Bamenda.

Obeng-Odoom, F. 2012. Land reform in Africa: Theory, practice, and outcome. *Habitat International*, 36(1): 161–170.

Okoth-Ogendo, H.W.O. 1989. Some issues of theory in the study of tenure relations in African agriculture. *Journal of International African Institute*, 59(1): 6–17.

Peters, P. 2009. Challenges in land tenure and land reform in Africa: Anthropological contributions. *World Development*, 37(8): 1317–1325.

Pillay, S. 2013. Decolonising the humanities. *Mail & Guardian.* Online. https://mg.co.za/article/2013-04-05-decolonising-the-humanities (Accessed January 17, 2018).

Quijano, A. 2007. Coloniality and modernity/rationality. *Cultural Studies*, 21(2–3): 168–178. Rodney, W. 1974. *How Europe Underdeveloped Africa*. Howard University Press, Washington D.C.

Sankara, T. 2005. *We Are the Heirs of the World's Revolutions: Speeches from the Burkina Faso Revolution 1983–87*. Pathfinder Press, New York and London.

The Republic of Zambia 2006. *Draft Land Administration and Management Policy*. The Ministry of Lands, Lusaka.

Tuck, E. & K.W. Yang 2012. Decolonisation is not a metaphor. *Decolonisation: Indigeneity, Education & Society*, 1(1): 1–40.

Wiredu, K. 1998. Towards decolonising African philosophy and religion. *African Studies Quarterly*, 1(4): 17–46.

World Bank 2013. *African Development Indicators 2012/13*. World Bank, Washington D.C.

Author's E-mail: horman.chitonge@uct.ac.za

Chapter 3

Corporate Power, the State, and the Post-Capitalist Future

Peter Lawrence

Introduction

This article draws attention to the ways in which the State under late capitalism has been subject to capture by the increasingly concentrated, powerful, and predominantly financial, global corporates through such mechanisms as the 'revolving door,' the privatization of state services, the funding of political parties at election time and the increasing links between finance and private and state security agencies. It goes on to put these issues into the context of the broader developments in late advanced capitalist societies, and especially in advanced technologies, which could subvert its very logic and assist the process of popular resistance to state capture in Africa and elsewhere.

In an article in *Agrarian South* in 2012, Sam Moyo and his co-authors declared that the 'global competition for Africa's land and natural resources is in full swing' but that 'the existence of relatively autonomous capitalist states on the continent …. [has] the potential to resist and form effective alliances on regional, continental, and inter-continental levels' (Moyo et al., 2012: 182). This chapter sets out the ways in which the State in the current phase of capitalism has been subject to capture by the predominantly financial global corporates, thus blurring the boundaries between the State/public and the corporate/private. We argue here that the State, or alliances of States, can no longer be relied on or expected to lead resistance to these global corporate forces and in the case of Africa, prevent land capture either for commercial agriculture or for mineral wealth. Such resistance to these forces will have to come from the mobilization of popular movements both local and international, across Africa, but ultimately across the world.

Capitalism has undergone many changes since it emerged as the dominant mode of production, although its basis has been the need to accumulate capital through maintaining the necessary rates of profit. The capitalism of small firms owned by individuals in a system economists mythologised as 'perfect competition' is now the capitalism of global financial corporates. This has been a slow but accelerating process starting from early in the 20th century with increasing monopolisation of production, and later services, within nation states and developing into a concentration of enterprises across the globe. The process of what has been called 'the financialization of everything' (Harvey, 2015: 33) has produced an outcome in which financial corporates dominate the global economy. There was a short period of history during which the State exercised a degree of control over the activities of what used to be known as monopolies, then multinationals and now global corporations. However currently the power of those global corporates is such that they have effectively captured the State and the international financial institutions. Further concentration is likely. This in large part helps to explain why governments, especially radical ones which promise much, are unable to deliver.

This increasing concentration of control in the hands of very few global corporates is paralleled by rapidly growing global inequality, not only between nations but also within them. This is driven by the dictates of the dominant financial institutions whose demand for a rate of profit that matches that which they can achieve through the trading of the financial instruments ('products') they issue, forces enterprises in the non-financial sector to squeeze wages and salaries of all but the top executives and worsen conditions of work. This is the race to the bottom where many areas of production migrate to where labour is cheapest and the labour force is unorganised or politically suppressed. Recent research has drawn attention to the way wealth is increasingly concentrated in the hands of the few to the extent that 1% of the world's population owns approximately 50% of global wealth (Oxfam, 2016). Even within that 1%, there is a further concentration. In the US, for example, the wealth of the top 0.1% is now almost equal to that of the bottom 90% (Saez &

Zucman, 2014), something that, according to the authors, has not occurred since the beginning of the last century.

However, there are developments within the system that may make it unsustainable and lead to a new way of organising society and its production of goods and services. Marx's argument that capitalism would sow the seeds of its own destruction was largely forgotten in the wake of socialist revolutions in Russia and China before capitalism had fully taken root. However the evolution of capitalism as a hegemonic global system, and especially the abundance and cheapening of so many goods and services together with the development of the 'sharing economy,' has prompted a return to the notion of the evolutionary demise of capitalism (Mason, 2015).

This article draws together work on the concentration of capital, on the relationship between the State and Corporate Capital and on the future of capitalism all of which demonstrate the possibilities of different futures some less benign than others.

Corporate Concentration and Control

Capitalism is supposed to generate the most efficient outcomes in terms of minimising the costs of production and, given 'normal' profits, minimising the cost of consumption thus maximising consumer welfare. This is achieved by a large number of firms in an industry competing with each other for market demand, seeking continually to drive costs down in order to maximise profits. However, as is by now well known, this neoclassical economic picture of capitalism probably never existed and certainly does not now. What we observe in all products and services is their production by a small and ever declining number of producers. A good example is illustrated by the chart below which shows that 10 food companies own almost all the well-known brands of processed food many of which began their life as independent enterprises before the raft of mergers and acquisitions that produced these global conglomerates (Fig. 1). The process of concentration of capital continues and accelerates. In late 2016, global brewers SAB-Miller, an amalgamation of major South African and US brewers and a number of other small brewers around the world, merged with its main global rival,

Anheuser-Busch InBev, itself an amalgamation of three major national brewers in Belgium, Brazil and the US, to form a global brewer with over 30% of the world market in bottled and cask beer (Economics Online, 2014). Two of the major media companies in the US, Time Warner and AT&T have announced a plan to merge to create a giant corporation dominating US media and challenging that country's famed anti-trust laws, although a government suit to prevent this merger is delaying its implementation (Rushe, 2017). This process of mergers and acquisitions has been operating throughout the history of capitalism and looks set to continue. This suggests a further corporate stranglehold leaving the small percentage at the top with even greater power than they already have.

A Swiss team of researchers (Vitali et al., 2011) constructed a global corporate network starting from a list of over 43,000 transnational corporations. They found that 737 top holders accumulate 80% of the control over the value of all TNCs, 40% of the control of this network of corporates was held by a group of 147 TNCs in the core, which had almost full control over itself, 75% of the core were financial intermediaries, 75% of the ownership of firms in the core remained in the hands of firms of the core itself and finally, the top 50 (45 of which are financials) have 75% of the core.

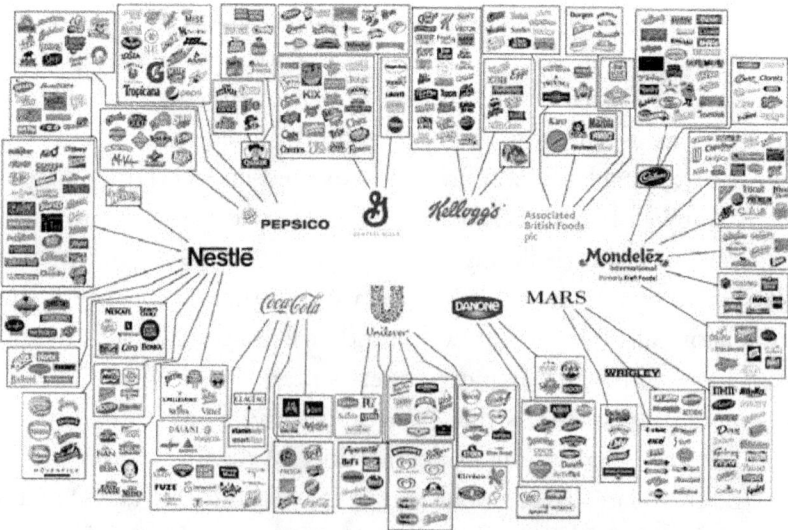

Fig. 1. Brands of 10 food companies Source: Oxfam (2013: 8)

The leaders of these corporations along with senior politicians from both centre-left and right, both in government and opposition, can be found at the annual World Economic Forum (WEF) held in Davos in Switzerland and at the meetings of the Bilderberg Group which now seeks to be more transparent with a website that, like Davos, tells us who was there. At the last meetings of WEF at Davos, of the top corporates mentioned above, over one-third were represented by executives at the levels of chair or CEO and just below. The IMF and World Bank heads were there as were several prime ministers, presidents and royal heads of state as well as various security interests—private firms, academic bodies and defence ministries, and senior members of military forces and alliances. Bilderberg is a more restrained event with a much smaller number covering much of the same sets of interests. This is less a conspiracy to maintain the existing power relations than an exercise in solidifying the 'groupthink' of those who attend and this effectively defines the limits of state power vis a vis the corporations. Given these relationships, it is hardly surprising that after the financial crisis of 2007–2008, governments rescued the banks and other financial institutions and have allowed them to continue as before by pursuing an economic policy of 'quantitative easing' which has allowed them to restore their capital base. As we shall see below, there are other ways in which these corporates ensure that their interests are protected at the political level.

The concentration of corporate power has accelerated a process of state capture which has itself aided the increasing corporate dominance of the system. The election of governments in the late 1970s and during the 1980s and after, which embraced the ideas of what has come to be called 'neo-liberalism' has assisted this process in many different ways, not least through limiting the ability of trades unions to protect their members and managing to divide the working population into different and opposing camps. The neoliberal ideology has been promoted in academia and the media and this has ensured that corporate power effectively runs government policy. This policy has accelerated state capture not least by allowing a creeping privatisation of traditionally state-run activities, such as health, education, transport, power and prisons, generally by selling off state-owned assets, or through a system of the sub-contracting of government services to the private-for profit- sector, or the licensing of private for profit companies to run public services in competition with the state sector. This practice has permeated local authorities so that there is no part of the public sector that is not commercialised except for the army and the police services, and even there, the rise of the private security companies is beginning to invade that space.

The State and the Corporates

The financial crisis and its resolution recalls the observation Marx and Engels made in 1846:

> With... the development of commerce and industry, individuals grew richer and richer while the state fell ever more deeply into debt... It is therefore obvious that as soon as the bourgeoisie has accumulated money, the state has to beg from the bourgeoisie and in the end it is actually bought up by the latter (Marx & Engels, 1998: 382).

Substitute financialisation for 'commerce and industry' and the banks for 'individuals' and this summarises neatly what happened after that banking crisis. This is not to say that individuals have not grown richer in the process, as noted above, giving rise to the widely held view that capitalism works for the 1%, or the 0.1% and that the modern state follows suit. Indeed, in spite of the apparently more sophisticated analyses of the State which appeared in the 1970s and after, it would seem that rather than this institution being 'autonomous' and independent of class, it has developed to the condition where it conforms to that famous remark about the State in the Communist Manifesto:

> The executive of the modern state is nothing but a committee for managing the common affairs of the whole bourgeoisie (Marx & Engels, 1962: 36).

The Revolving Door

Over recent years it is becoming clearer how corporate power has captured the State to the extent that the two have formed a symbiotic relationship in which government policy follows the interests of the corporates. The revolving door which sees politicians join the boards of corporates and corporate directors or senior executives recruited to the 'executive of the modern state' is now well oiled and has led Transparency International to conclude about the UK that:

> Surveys of public perceptions of the most corrupt sections of British public life revealed that a public official taking a job with a company that s/he was previously responsible for regulating was rated as potentially corrupt by 80% of respondents (Transparency International UK, 2010).

Indeed a survey conducted by the UK polling company, YouGov, in January 2012 found that 69% of respondents agreed that it was 'too easy for former ministers to get jobs that allow them to make improper use of their time in government' (Transparency International UK, 2012). Indeed it is. Fourteen former ministers set themselves up as consultants in 2010–2011 compared with just one in 2005–2006. One of those, a former Labour Defence Secretary, Geoff Hoon, has helicopter manufacturer Augusta Westland among his consultancy clients. In 2005, while Defence Secretary, he approved a £1 billion contract to this company, which was controversially declared a 'preferred bidder' despite claims that other companies could have provided better value-for-money helicopters in a shorter time-frame.

There are many examples of former ministers, civil servants and ambassadors going to well paid jobs or directorships in big banks or other corporates with interests in areas where former politicians might provide useful information from which the corporates might gain. In 2015, the former Health Secretary, Andrew Lansley, a newly elevated member of the House of Lords, and who actively worked towards the further privatisation of the National Health Service, took a job with a US consultancy firm working with healthcare clients.

Lansley's job is to advise corporate clients on healthcare reforms, as these clients become increasingly involved in bidding to run parts of the NHS (Syal & Hughes, 2015). In January 2013, the former head of the UK tax authority, Her Majesty's Revenue and Customs (HMRC) became an advisor to the Hong Kong and Shanghai Banking Corporation (HSBC)'s Committee on Financial Systems. Four months later the same man joined Deloitte's, a global accountancy corporate to 'advise overseas governments on how to implement "effective tax regimes" (Neville, 2013). The Director General of Commissioning at the UK Department of Health became the Global Head of Healthcare at the accounting corporate, KPMG, taking him from responsibility for designing new ways of commissioning healthcare to preparing bids for DoH contracts. His successor at the Department followed him to KPMG a year later. KPMG won at least three contracts following these moves (BBC, 2011). Some former ministers are prepared to act more directly in gain income to add to their substantial pension. Two former foreign ministers were secretly filmed offering their services for hire and naming their price. Although this was a newspaper 'sting,' it still revealed that these politicians were for hire, after they ceased to be MPs, as long as everything remained confidential (Perraudin, 2015).

The revolving door also sees people moving from the private sector to the civil service. It was reported that John Manzoni the new chief executive of the civil service, would be 'allowed to keep a £100,000-a-year position on the board of the drinks company SABMiller ….he takes his salary in company stock and holds shares worth more than £250,000 in the company.' The report continued: A government spokesman said: "The Cabinet Office is satisfied there is no conflict of interest."

Manzoni left the private sector to become chief executive of the Major Projects Authority earlier in the same year and worked in the Cabinet Office with Lord Browne, who was his boss when both worked at BP. Browne is the government's lead non-executive director and the chairman of Cuadrilla, the chief fracking company in the UK. He was one of six members of the appointment panel who chose Manzoni for the job (Mason & Campbell, 2014), demonstrating the role of networks and connections, both personal and political.

A more recent example of this revolving door is related to a government decision, after a delay of years, about which of London's airport should get an additional runway following the recommendation from the Airports Commission set up to look at the options. The chair of the commission, Sir Howard Davies, formerly the first head of the UK's Financial Services Authority, is also on the board of the Prudential, where he chairs a committee on investment risk.[1] Prudential has spent £300m spending buying properties around Heathrow. Its asset management business, M&G. bought in 2013 the Hilton hotel at Terminal 5 for £21m and received planning permission to build a hotel close the proposed third runway, and two years later bought more property close to Terminal 4. Davies also used to advise the GIC (Singapore), which owns 11.2% of Heathrow. Questions have been raised about the impartiality of the chair of the Commission given what appears to be a clear conflict of interest (Davies, 2015).[2]

There are many other examples of this close relationship between the supposedly independent civil service and the private sector (Wilks, 2015). Most recently this practice affected the leadership contest in the opposition Labour Party. One of the candidates had worked for Pfizer, the global pharmaceutical corporate and played an important role in its lobbying activities for NHS contracts. This compromised whatever he had to say about reducing the role of the private sector in public health provision, however strongly held his apparent left wing views appeared to be (Watt et al., 2016).

The criticisms of the various cases of the 'revolving door' hinge on the notion of a 'conflict of interest,' while the defence of such practices is usually that of vouching for the integrity of the person involved who is able to 'wear different hats' and resolve any conflict of interest by shutting out other personal interests while pursuing the public interest. However, this apparent conflict could be looked at in another way. The revolving door is about ensuring that the commercial interest becomes the public interest and so then there is no conflict of interest. The case of the UK is replicated in many other countries and groups of countries. The European Union (EU), has drifted from offering the opportunity to have greater control and regulation over the activities of international corporates to being captured by global capital through the same revolving door as evidenced in the UK. The most infamous recent example is that of former EU president Jose Manuel Barroso, who on retirement from that post, joined Goldman Sachs (one of those 50 global corporates) as an non-executive chairman (Dolan, 2016). Former EU staff move from gamekeeping to poaching on a large scale. One former lobbyist for the coal industry joined the EU staff as a coordinator of coal policy. A former MEP who was a supporter of carbon capture and storage, set up his own lobbying consultancy after he left the European Parliament, a consultancy that has as a client a firm that represents the major oil companies, keen on this technology because it safeguards their mineral production (Corporate Europe Observatory, 2015). The former German Chancellor, Gerhard Schröderwhile in office championed the Russian-German pipeline. Out of office, he became chairman of the board of the North-European Pipeline Company, majority owned by Gazprom, the giant Russian energy corporate, a post reportedly paying between €200,000 and €1m a year, though Schröder claimed those sums were exaggerated (Harding, 2005). These examples, and there are many more, suggest that the power of the large corporates over states and state groupings through the use of the revolving door is getting stronger. The revolving door and the power of corporate lobbyists has been prevalent in the USA for decades[3] and some of the flavour of practice in that country is given in the following discussion of election funding.

Election Funding

The funding of political parties, especially during election campaigns, has been subject to considerable scrutiny and criticism in many countries, not to mention accusations of the corruption of the political process. In the USA, for example, the US presidential campaign of 2016 saw billions of dollars raised in funding for each candidate. Limitations on individual donations directly to political parties and candidates is now overshadowed by the donations to 'super-PACS'—the political action committees that are prohibited from having direct ties with politicians or their parties but are able to support particular candidates through advertising in newspapers, on television and through electronic media. There is no limit on what they can spend but the money they raise has to be spent independently of the parties and candidates they support. Furthermore, although for-profit corporates are required to declare the source of their contributions to super-PACs, non-profit organisations do not have to do so. Donations from unknown sources, 'dark money,' to non-profit organisations allow corporates to donate through the back door and thus swell the coffers of candidates and parties. Up to the middle of October, over $1.5 billion had been raised by the presidential candidates, of which a sixth came from super PACs (Allison et al., 2016). Ironically given the result, Clinton raised twice as much as Trump overall, and three times as much from the super-PACs, which raises questions about the effectiveness of the expenditure of these sums (Open Secrets, 2016).

The funding of candidates for Senate and the House of Representatives raises issues concerning the direct influence of legislation. For example, the largest donors by far to members of the Senate Banking, Housing and Urban Affairs Committee are from the Finance, Insurance and Real Estate sector. Thanks to WikiLeaks, we now know that an executive of Citigroup, one of the four big US banks, played a major role in advising newly elected President Obama on his staff and cabinet (Martens & Martens, 2016). Citigroup had to be rescued by the US government in 2008, and as in many other cases of banking failure through corrupt practices, nobody was prosecuted. One of the explanations that has been given for this is the large amount of funding for election campaigns. One insider who became a whistle-blower and stood in the recent elections against a member of the above Senate Committee, has observed that,

> The banking and financial industry is the leading financial contributor in this election. Hands down. Banking has the most to lose, said Stern in an interview. So they are trying to buy as many politicians as possible. The banks are very smart. They know that if they get their

voices heard in Washington and they buy the politicians they'll be OK (Hill, 2016).

During 2015–2016, the Finance, Insurance and Real Estate sector contributed over $912 million to election funding, of which just over half went directly to the parties and candidates in the ratio of 58:42 to the Republicans and Democrats respectively. The other half went to 'Outside Spending Groups,' the super-PACs. This is by no means the only explanation for the failure to prosecute banking and finance executives for the failures of their institutions, but it is quite a persuasive one. Other explanations are of course plausible. Proving intent to defraud is difficult, proving that sophisticated financial institutions that purchased the toxic assets did not know the risks and relied on the sellers' honesty is also possibly difficult, and it is also possible that prosecuting senior executives would have further damaged the finance sector and therefore the economy. Prosecutors' having too much on their plate to investigate and ordering priorities to deal with cases that were easier to prosecute may also explain the senior executives' escape (Rakoff, 2014). Whatever the case, that politicians can be bought adds to the general discontent with the political systems that allow this kind of influence to be exerted on elected representatives and the governments they support.

The Financial-Security Complex and the 'Deep State'

The concentration of economic control in the hands of a small number of corporates, and especially financials, who appear to have the power to guide government policy in directions which suit their interests, together with the heightened levels of security concerns at home and abroad, has given rise to the concept of the *financial-security assemblage*, to complement the 'military-industrial complex,' as the driving force of modern capitalism. This relatively new term in the academic literature embodies both the phenomena of the financialization of the system and the increasing need for the securitisation of the system, not simply in its financial sense but also in the sense that global military and private security needs to expand to ensure that this process of financialization is not disrupted, especially by 'terrorist funding.' The effects of ensuring that informal money transfers worldwide, and especially by migrants sending money home, are not being used for funding terrorists, are to draw such transfer arrangements into the formal banking sector where they can be subject to security checks, as well as allow growth in financial activities (Gilbert et al., 2013).

The increase in the surveillance activities of state security agencies and of military interventions in pursuit of terrorists, or of regime change, has occurred alongside the growth of private security enterprises, not only providing services for the movement of money, the security of shopping malls, sports events and universities, but also working with the military forces involved in the various 'wars on terror.' Private security is big global business with one of the best known corporations, G4S, operating in well over 100 countries, and in any one country, a major employer (Abrahamsen & Williams, 2011). Private security now outnumbers the traditional suppliers of personal and public security services, the police force, by ratios of between 2:1 and 10:1 (Abrahamsen & Williams, 2007).

The research suggests that security against terrorism, security for the plutocracy that lives in gated mansions, and security for the financial institutions now underpins the dynamic of global capitalism in which the State is colonised by finance and the military and provides profitable activities for global finance capital. Emerging too from these developments is the 'Deep State.' The concept originated in Turkey under military rule and has more recently been broadly defined as representing:

> ..... the political interplay between unacknowledged or unrecognized factions inside and outside the regular government. The deep state is not an entirely monolithic entity that shadows the bureaucracy, military, or civil society. Rather it is an eclectic, ever-evolving political theatre of competition, one that includes elements both explicitly legal and outlaw in nature. Paramount to the operation and survival of the deep state is the extreme emphasis placed upon state security, a need that places both law enforcement and clandestine agencies in the forefront of both the formulation and execution of state policies (Gingeras, 2011).

This development will further inhibit the possibility of any State policies to counter corporate capture.

The Future out of the Present[4]

The concentration of economic power and its capture of the State raises the question of where this is all leading and what is to be done to change the direction of travel. The increasing levels of inequality, the proliferation of low paid jobs and zero hours contracts alongside the huge senior executive salaries and bonuses, the pressure from the private sector to roll back the State's ability to protect people at the lower end of the pay scale and maintain the quality of public services thus forcing a move to increase privatisation, have all resulted from the pursuit of the neoliberal political economic model over the last four decades. The 2007–2008 financial crisis occurred in spite of the widespread belief among proponents of the system, that such crises could never occur, and that the boom and bust of the system had seen its last as a consequence of the neoliberal revolution. The crisis has further exacerbated the condition of large proportions of the population in late capitalist societies but has not created the classic revolutionary conditions which accelerate the demise of the system and the rise of its successor, socialism.

The failure of social democratic parties to reverse this process, and their effective co-option by the corporate interests that have colonised the State, have fuelled the now abundant cynicism about governments' ability to do anything about a system in which they have a vested interest. Lower voter turnout and voter rebellion as manifested in the UK vote to leave the EU and the election of a political outsider to the US presidency, accompanied by a shift to supporting populist parties, mainly of the right, but some of the left, recalls an earlier era of the 1920s and 1930s which ended in a world war.

However, the capitalism of the early 21st century is not the same as that of the 1930s and its development since 1945 and especially after the micro-electronics revolution has prompted the use of the concept of 'post-capitalism' to describe the ways in which late capitalism is morphing into something else. Proponents of this thesis argue that the neoliberal model is effectively broken. The assumption that there can be a return to the model that was based on the growth of financial markets is a flawed one as the financial system is fragile and prone to further crises. In any case, the model prior to the crisis depended on private more than public borrowing financed by bank credit. Wage growth was suppressed except for those at the top of private and state enterprises and public bodies. The debt problem became a global one with creditor nations financing borrowers, China lending to the US and Germany to Greece being two examples of these debt relations. Most importantly the rapid development of information technology made many consumer and capital goods much cheaper.

The financial crisis demonstrated that, contrary to the view of 19th century economic liberalism, and 20th century neo-liberalism, markets allowed to operate freely would self-correct, but they clearly did not. The response to the financial crisis and the subsequent increase in state expenditure to rescue the banks and mitigate the economic and social consequences of the crisis, was austerity, driving down wages so that at some point in the future they would match those of countries in the Far East as those countries' wages rose. Mason refers to a report of a speech by the then CEO of Prudential, Tidjane Thiam, now CEO of Credit Suisse (no 14 in the league of those 50 corporates listed above), in Davos in 2012. Thiam argued that 'Unions are the 'enemy of young people' and the minimum wage is 'a machine to destroy jobs.' Minimum wages made 'the workforce more precarious' and reinforced the protectionist nature of trade unions which "represent people already in jobs so they always support minimum wages. That crowds out the unemployed. People can't get full time employment'" (Mason, 2015: 4). A liberated labour market would no doubt find market clearing wages where everyone would have a job, though what those wages would be is another matter.

Postcapitalism is not socialism as in the classical Marxist trajectory in which capitalism sows the seeds of its own destruction and the proletariat effect a revolution, although the process postcapitalism theorists describe bears a strong resemblance to that Marxist trope. It could lead to socialism, but it is beyond capitalism.

However, it is a process which arises out of the contradictions of capitalism and contains the seeds of a new relationship between social relations and an economy dominated by information technology. While capitalism's persistent tendency to crisis, such as the financial one of 2007–2008, encourages the belief that the system is unsustainable, postcapitalist theorists accept the system's unsustainability because there is a disjunction between the changed social relations (no longer characterised by a capitalist class and an industrial proletariat) and the changed technological level (forces of production in Marxist terminology) which has created free goods, zero prices and zero work.

Going beyond this critique postcapitalist theorists argue that that the latest technological developments are going to create an abundance of goods whose production costs tend to zero and whose prices tend to zero. Markets in the sense of institutions which fix a price that satisfies both producers and consumers, cannot operate at a zero price. Furthermore, markets cannot deal with climate change, nor with the current migrant and refugee crisis. Increasing automation now using robots is reducing the amount of work that needs to be done by human beings. Ironically, given the potential of IT, Mason argues that 'instead of rapidly automating work out of existence, we are reduced to creating bullshit jobs on low pay, and many economies are stagnating' (Mason, 2015: 242). However, information technology is also driving down marginal costs, and prices, towards zero and thus together with other non-market developments, 'corroding market mechanisms, eroding property rights and destroying the old relationship between wages, work and profit,' 'leading towards a post-capitalist economy' (Mason, 2015: 112). As it now well recognised, advanced capitalist economies have seen the decline in the relative importance of manufacturing as the economy of retail and financial services has rapidly developed. Financial services no longer simply provide credit to the other two sectors, but develop a life of their own with an array of financial 'products,' some of which were a direct cause of the 2007–2008 crash. Automation accelerated by developments in IT has accentuated the decline in the relative position of manufacturing by reducing the size of the manufacturing labour force. The labour force

70

in general is better educated and has seen the emergence of what Mason calls 'the universal educated person' who now works in networks, not factories.

The emergence of the 'knowledge economy' is another key development. A good part of it is free to access. Wikipedia operates on the basis that the information it contains is free to access and is produced (and corrected) for free by those with the knowledge. Free open source software can be improved by those who use it. Indeed it would seem that charging and thus restricting the use of this software makes it less valuable. IT software is now added to the content of physical goods thus reducing the costs of production towards zero and creating 'a world of free stuff' (Mason, 2015: 142).

If this is really the way capitalism is developing in a way which will see it destroyed by the 'world of free stuff,' then how do we get there? Mason schematizes the following paths. First, we should and will engage in more collaborative work which would involve the creation of more cooperatives coordinated by an Office of the Non Market Economy, the socialization or suppression of monopolies, the gradual disappearance of market forces, as the myth of the free market is exposed through its erosion, the socialization of finance as it is returned to its original purposes of holding accounts and lending money, and last but not least, the institution of a basic income for everyone. To achieve all this it is necessary to 'unleash the network' (Mason, 2015: 286): IT enables the production of an abundance of goods, everyone has a basic income which allows them to access these goods, while they contribute to society freely in exchange.

The abundance of production and the sharing of consumption according to need and on the basis of the contribution to society being based on ability is of course not new and an outcome envisaged by Marx after the transition from socialism to communism. Mason has effectively updated this vision in the light of the possibilities which IT offers to make what appeared to be a Utopian fairy story into a reality for the future. A future in which work to earn the means of subsistence is no longer the central purpose of living is now possible. A combination of a universal basic income and the option of a reduction in working hours to zero would mean that people could choose how much work they wanted to do and the boring and mundane jobs could increasingly be done by robots.[5] However the question of exactly how this transition can occur and through which human agency remains. How are people to believe that society is moving in this direction and that they have to push it that way? If the agent of change is to be the State, as Mason suggests, then the State has to be liberated from the corporates and the famous 1%, or even 0.1% have to be liberated too, and not just of their wealth. Srnicek & Williams (2016) offer a more detailed discussion of who might be 'the active agent of a post-work project' (p. 156). They opt for a populist movement organised around 'an ecology of organisations' (p. 163) to counter the hegemonic 'common sense' of neo-liberalism with a hegemonic common sense of a vision of a post-work society. The organisations could encompass political parties and campaigning organisations, local and national with the common vision of a post-work society given the unsustainability of capitalism as it now exists.[6] Much of this discussion of the transition to a postcapitalist world does not raise the issue of the place of the Global South in relation to the automated global North with zero work, and is yet another question that needs more thought than yet given to it by the postcapitalist theorists.

State Capture in Africa

Although this article has been concerned with State-Capital relations at the centres of late capitalism, the evidence of a process of state capture in the Global north will no doubt resonate with citizens of African countries who have witnessed similar connections between corporate capital and the State. The publication of a report, on alleged links between a particular corporate and government ministers, by South Africa's former Public Protector (Madonsela, 2016) raises issues not unfamiliar to citizens of many other African countries, even if it only deals with one very public case, rather than the more pervasive issues of revolving doors and political connections.

More widely in South Africa, there is evidence of a revolving door which takes former ministers into senior positions in major corporates and in the case of the new President of the country, Cyril

Ramaphosa, from politician to corporate business and back. He was leader of the National Union of Mineworkers, chief ANC negotiator with the apartheid government and Mandela's preferred choice as deputy. After losing out to Thabo Mbeki, he went on to develop business interests before re-entering politics, by which time he was the 12th richest person in South Africa, and brother in law of the sixth richest (Bracking, 2016). These business interests included being a director of Lonmin at the time of the massacre of striking miners at Lonmin's Marikana mine in which he reputedly played a role in instigating the police action, although he was exonerated by the Commission of Inquiry (Smith, 2015). The former Finance Minister, Trevor Manuel, became deputy chair of Rothschild South Africa and later acquired a non-executive directorship of Old Mutual, South Africa's largest insurance company, later becoming chair of its emerging markets business.[7]

Elsewhere in Africa there is increasing evidence of the merging of state and private interests and the mutual enrichment of a political and business elites. This process of enrichment is particularly evident in countries with high value minerals. So for example, Angolan and Namibian ruling parties have set up a myriad of offshore bodies (Bracking, 2016) which channel the vast profits from mining away from much needed investment in national productive activities into the pockets of the elites. Bracking cites the example of Namibia Finance, set up in the Dutch tax haven of Curaçao in 1990 and moved in 1997 to the Portuguese tax haven of Funchal, Madeira, comprising 'over 100 entities of Namibian mining trading companies at Banif Bank alone, and 2178 companies with "African roots" registered by Madeira's fiduciary trusts' (Bracking, 2016: 10). It would seem that the blurring of the boundaries between private and public in favour of the private is resulting in vast outflows of funds from Africa. The Paradise papers give the example that $3bn of Angola's sovereign wealth fund has been given to a company owned and controlled by a Swiss-Angolan from which he personally and his company will benefit (Pegg, 2017).

The blurring of the boundaries between the State and private interests can take other, more classically corrupt forms, and even when exposed, reinforce the position of what can only be called a kleptocracy. There is evidence that the Museveni regime in Uganda has not only tried to cover up the misuse of public funds but has punished those who blow the whistle. Bracking, citing work by Asiimwe (2013) reports the case of the current Ugandan Prime Minister and the current Finance Minister who together with a private businessman, all benefiting from the National Social Security Fund's (NSSF) purchase of land owned by the businessman's company and held by the National Bank of Commerce, in which they all had shares. When the NSSF managing director blew the whistle on this deal, President Museveni intervened with the result that the Ministers went free and the whistle-blower went to jail (Bracking, 2016).

There is a growing literature on the ways in which 'land grabs' in Africa such as the one above are facilitated by African governments or by private sector interests with good government connections through ex-politicians coming through the revolving door. For example there is the case of AgroMoz in Mozambique, a reportedly joint venture between the Grupo Américo Amorim of Portugal, a holding company of Portugal's richest man Américo Amorim, and Intelec, again reportedly, former President Guebuza's investment vehicle. AgroMoz is part of AGS Moçambique, SA., a Mozambican company owned by two Portuguese subsidiaries of Grupo Amorim (Solfim SGPS and Sotomar—Empreendimentos Industriais e Imobiliários, S.A.) and ESF Participaçoes, a subsidiary of ESF Investimentos. This latter is owned by Intelec and SF Holdings and Guebuza's main business partner Salimo Abdul heads both of them. It is not difficult to see how with those connections the company quickly acquired land rights in the Nacala corridor from the authorities resulting in the eviction of more than a thousand peasants from their lands thus potentially creating a source of supply for company workers. The company expanded form the initially stated 200 ha to over 2,000ha a year later, cultivating soyabeans and rice. Compensation was derisory though other land was made available elsewhere for those displaced. The promised clinic and school was not constructed, while crop spraying affected the health of the workers and destroyed their crops. In spite of these experiences with AgroMoz, the Government authorized a DUAT (Direito do Uso e

Aproveitamento da Terra) for another 9,000 hectares—this was while Guebuza, one of the investors in AgroMoz, was still president of the country (GRAIN, 2015).

Perhaps the most significant revolving door in the case of African governments pursuing economic policies likely to aid corporate investment, is that between them and the International Financial Institutions (The World Bank, the International Monetary Fund and the World Trade Organisation). In 2012, it was found that 20 per cent of the Finance Ministers of the 47 African countries then aided by the World Bank, had previously worked for the Bank or the IMF (Bretton Woods Project, 2014), returning to their countries to implement policies that would promote the interests of the corporates—privatisation and the alienation of land for prospecting for minerals or for growing industrial or high value food crops (the 'land grabs'). How far in African countries, corporate power and political connections have pushed policy in the interests of corporate capital, or how far this is a systemic consequence of neoliberalism will always be a matter of some debate and in any case requires further research.

Another Future?

The increase in inequality and the concentration of capital has resulted in what has become a global plutocracy with increasing control over what governments can do. More especially there are increasing limits to what governments are able do for the growing numbers of people in precarious existence without upsetting 'the markets.' This is also the case in Africa which now has its billionaires, too, with equally growing power over governments as they occupy the State's space, and live in protected communities, while a large proportion of the population becomes part of a growing 'precariat.' All of these aspects of capitalist disorder show no signs of being dealt with and look like they might get a lot worse.

Where are the movements seeking to reverse this process? There are now radical left movements in western Europe such as Syriza and Podemos as well as radical libertarian movements, who might shift popular opinion in the direction of the change to a post-capitalist future that Mason and others predict. However, there is also the parallel rise, in Europe especially, of right wing populism, including elements of fascism, which offer a challenge to this IT-inspired collaborative, dare one say, socialist future. Indeed this is a reminder that morphing into socialism is not the only direction that capitalism can take. There are an increasing number of examples of a 'disordered future' (Streeck, 2014). The current refugee crisis in Europe and the Middle East, the EU crisis which is not simply about 'Brexit,' but about its very existence, the various political crises of around the world, the failure of the United Nations to become an institution of world governance, and now with Donald Trump in the White House, the certain US withdrawal from the various proposed free trade treaties which corporate power needs for its economic health but which also embody provisions which ensure it gains even more power. The era of growth which characterised the neoliberal renaissance of the late 20th century has given way to a decline in growth, even negative growth at some points, the increasing concentration of oligarchic power, and the rolling back and disempowerment of the State and its provision of public services. The State in this scenario becomes solely the provider of security for the private sector as more and more of its service activities become privatised. The rise of neo-fascist parties could well provide the repressive state security backdrop to the maintenance of the power of the plutocracy. While the future is uncertain the present corporate capture of the State is clear and we are no closer to dealing with it or its consequences.

Acknowledgements

This is a revised version of a paper presented at 'Land, the State and Decolonising the Agrarian Structure in Africa: A Colloquium in Honour of Professor Sam Moyo,' organized at the University of Cape Town, South Africa, on November 28–29, 2016. This colloquium was sponsored by the Japan Society for the Promotion of Science, Grant-in-Aid for Scientific Research (S) '"African Potential" and Overcoming the Difficulties of Modern World: Comprehensive

Research That Will Provide a New Perspective for the Future of Humanity' (KAKENHI 16H06318 headed by Motoji Matsuda, Kyoto University), as well as by the University of Cape Town's Research Office (URC). An earlier and shorter version was published in the South African magazine, *The Thinker* 71. An outline was first presented at the Second European Blue Sky Conference: Global Transformations Consequences and Alternatives, Budapest, October 29–31, 2015.

Notes

(1) This is another example of the revolving door. After chairing the Airports Commission, Davies moved on to chair the Royal Bank of Scotland, technically state-owned after being bailed out in the financial crash of 2008.

(2) Ironically, the one member of the Commission who was forced to resign because of a conflict of interest was the former chief executive of Manchester Airports Group, which owns the third London airport at Stansted, and which seems to have been out of the running very early on.

(3) See for example the work in this area of Open Secrets: https://www.opensecrets.org/ revolving/index.php (Accessed January 15, 2018).

(4) The following account of postcapitalism and its future is heavily based on: Mason (2015) and Srnicek & Williams (2016).

(5) See Srnicek & Williams (2016: 120–127).

(6) The reduction in the working week and the emancipation of people from 'psychologically unproductive labour time within necessary labour time' was part of the East German thinker, Rudolf Bahro's vision of a different future (Bahro, 1978).

(7) See Bloomberg. Online. https://www.bloomberg.com/profiles/people/1515553-trevor-andrew-manuel (Accessed January 15, 2018).

References

Abrahamsen, R. & M.C. Williams 2007. Securing the city: Private security companies and non-state authority in global governance. *International Relations*, 21(2): 237–253.

— 2011. *Security Beyond the State: Private Security in International Politics.* Cambridge University Press, Cambridge.

Allison, B., M. Rojanasakul, B. Harris & C. Sam 2016. Tracking the 2016 presidential money race. *Bloomberg Politics*. Online. http://www.bloomberg.com/politics/graphics/2016-presidential-campaign-fundraising/ (Accessed January 15, 2018).

Asiimwe, G.B. 2013. Of extensive and elusive corruption in Uganda: Neo-patronage, power, and narrow interests. *African Studies Review*, 56(2): 129–144.

Bahro, R. 1978. *The Alternative in Eastern Europe.* New Left Books, London. BBC 2011. *File on Four.* Transcript.

Bracking, S. 2016. *The Financialisation of Power: How Financiers Rule Africa.* Routledge, London.

Bretton Woods Project 2014. *Revolving Doors: Staff Turnover Between IFIs and African Governments.* Online. http://old.brettonwoodsproject.org/art-570796 (Accessed January 15, 2018).

Corporate Europe Observatory 2015. *Brussels, Big Energy, and Revolving Doors: A Hothouse for Climate Change.* Online. https://www.corporateeurope.org/revolving-doors/2015/11/brussels-big-energy-and-revolving-doors-hothouse-climate-change (Accessed January 15, 2018).

Davies, H. 2015. Independence of airports commission questioned over chair's prudential role. *The Guardian*. Online. https://www.theguardian.com/uk-news/2015/aug/05/independence-airports-commission-chair-prudential-howard-davies-properties-heathrow-report (Accessed January 15, 2018).

Dolan, C. 2016. How to fix the EU 'revolving door.' *EU Observer.* Online. https://euobserver.com/opinion/134484 (Accessed January 15, 2018).

Economics Online 2014. Online.
http://www.economicsonline.co.uk/Business_economics/
Brewing_merger.html (Accessed January 15, 2018).

Gilbert, E., M. Atia, M.B. Salter & M. de Goede 2013. Reading
Marieke de Goede's speculative security. *Political Geography*, 32:
52–60.

Gingeras, R. 2011. In the hunt for the "sultans of smack:" Dope,
gangsters and the construction of the Turkish deep state. *The
Middle East Journal*, 65(3): 426–441.

GRAIN 2015. *The Land Grabbers of the Nacala Corridor: A New Era of
Struggle against Colonial Plantations in Northern Mozambique*. GRAIN,
Barcelona.

Harding, L. 2005. Schröder faces growing scandal over job with
Russian gas giant. *The Guardian*. Online.
https://www.theguardian.com/world/2005/dec/13/russia.ger
many (Accessed January 15, 2018).

Harvey, D. 2015. *A Brief History of Neoliberalism*. Oxford University
Press, New York. Hill, D. 2016. Billions in damage, but no
charges: How U.S. banks pay for protection. *The Star.com*. Online.
https://www.thestar.com/news/world/uselection/2016/11/07
/billions-in-damage-but-no-charges-how-us-banks-pay-for-
protection.html (Accessed January 15, 2018).

Madonsela, T. 2016. *State of Capture: A Report of Public Protector*.
Republic of South Africa, South Africa.

Martens, P. & R. Martens 2016. WikiLeaks bombshell: Emails show
Citigroup had major role in shaping and staffing Obama's first
term. *Wall Street on Parade*. Online. http://
wallstreetonparade.com/2016/10/wikileaks-bombshell-emails-
show-citigroup-had- major-role-in-shaping-and-staffing-
obamas-first-term/ (Accessed January 15, 2018).

Marx, K. & F. Engels 1962. Manifesto of the Communist Party. In
(K. Marx & F. Engels, eds.) *Selected Works Vol 1*. Foreign
Languages Publishing House, Moscow.

— 1998. *The German Ideology*. Prometheus Books, Amherst.

Mason, P. 2015. *Postcapitalism: A Guide to Our Future*. Allen Lane,
London.

Mason, R. & D. Campbell 2014. Civil service chief under fire for keeping job at drink manufacturer. *The Guardian*. Online. https://www.theguardian.com/politics/2014/ oct/28/civil-service-john-manzoni-job-sabmiller (Accessed January 15, 2018).

Moyo, S., P. Yeros & P. Jha 2012. Imperialism and primitive accumulation: Notes on the new scramble for Africa. *Agrarian South: Journal of Political Economy*, 1(2): 181–203.

Neville, S. 2013, Deloitte appoints official criticised over 'sweetheart' tax deals. *The Guardian*. Online. https://www.theguardian.com/business/2013/may/27/deloitte- appoints-dave-hartnett-tax (Accessed January 15, 2018).

Open Secrets 2016. *2016 Presidential Race*. Online. http://opensecrets.org/pres16 (Accessed January 15, 2018).

Oxfam 2013. *Behind the Brands: Food Justice and the 'Big 10' Food and Beverage Companies, 166 Oxfam Briefing Paper*. Oxfam GB, Oxford.

— 2016. *An Economy for the 1%: How Privilege and Power in the Economy Drive Extreme Inequality and How This Can Be Stopped, 210 Oxfam Briefing Paper*. Oxfam GB, Oxford.

Pegg, D. 2017. Angola sovereign wealth fund's manager used its cash for his own projects. *The Guardian*. Online. https://www.theguardian.com/world/2017/nov/07/angola-sovereign- wealth-fund-jean-claude-bastos-de-morais-paradise-papers (Accessed January 15, 2018).

Perraudin, F. 2015. Straw and Rifkind deny wrongdoing amid 'cash for access' claims. *The Guardian*. Online. https://www.theguardian.com/politics/2015/feb/23/jack-straw-malcolm- rifkind-deny-wrongdoing-cash-for-access-claims (Accessed January 15, 2018).

Rakoff, J.S. 2014. The financial crisis: Why have no high-level executives been prosecuted? *New York Review of Books*. Online. http://www.nybooks.com/articles/2014/01/09/ financial-crisis-why-no-executive-prosecutions/ (Accessed January 15, 2018).

Rushe, D. 2017. AT&T's Time Warner takeover: Justice department aims to block $85bn deal. *The Guardian*. Online. https://www.theguardian.com/business/2017/nov/20/justice-department-aims-to-block-atts-85bn-takeover-of-time-warner (Accessed January 15, 2018).

Saez, E. & G. Zucman 2014. *Wealth Inequality in the United States since 1913: Evidence from Capitalised Income Tax Data, NBER Working Paper Series 20625*. National Bureau of Economic Research, Cambridge.

Smith, D. 2015. South African deputy president cleared over Marikana massacre. *The Guardian*. Online. https://www.theguardian.com/world/2015/jun/25/south-african-deputy-president-cyril-ramaphosa-cleared-responsibility-marikana-massacre-miners (Accessed January 15, 2018).

Srnicek, N. & A. Williams 2016. *Inventing the Future: Postcapitalism and a World Without Work*. Verso, London and New York.

Streeck, W. 2014. How will capitalism end? *New Left Review*, 87: 35–64.

Syal, R. & S. Hughes 2015. Ex-health secretary Andrew Lansley to advise firms on healthcare reforms. *The Guardian*. Online. https://www.theguardian.com/politics/2015/oct/20/ andrew-lansley-advise-firms-healthcare-reforms (Accessed January 15, 2018).

Transparency International UK 2010. *Corruption in the UK Part One: National Opinion Survey*. Transparency International UK, London.

— 2012. *House of Commons Public Administration Select Committee Inquiry into the Role of the Operation of the Business Appointment Rules and the Advisory Committee on Business Appointments*. Transparency International UK, London.

Vitali, S., J.B. Glattfelder & S. Battiston 2011. The network of global corporate control. *Plos One*, 6(10): 1–6.

Watt, H., D. Pegg & M. Weaver 2016. Owen Smith backed big pharma over use of cheaper drugs by NHS in 2010. *The Guardian*. Online. https://www.theguardian.com/ politics/2016/jul/20/owen-smith-i-have-never-advocated-privatisation-of-the-nhs (Accessed January 15, 2018).

Wilks, S. 2015. *The Revolving Door and the Corporate Colonisation of UK Politics*. High Pay Centre, UK.

Author's E-mail: p.r.lawrence@keele.ac.uk

Chapter 4

Policy-Oriented Rural Development in China and its Potential Influence on Rural Development in Africa

Zhenke Zhang & Jianqin Li

Introduction

In most developing countries, large populations live in rural areas and rely heavily on the agricultural economy. Rural development has attracted much attention from the United Nations (UN), governments in developing countries and rural development researchers. Both China and the countries of the African continent have vast areas of rural land, and numerous farmers. In this chapter, the authors review rural development in China since 1978, and summarise stages of development and actual experiences. In the past 40 years, poverty reduction has been a key feature of regional planning and rural development in China, and rural development policies have played a crucial role in the success of rural poverty reduction. In 1978, some 250 million Chinese citizens, approximately 30% of the national population, were classified as living in poverty. With rural development and poverty reduction, the number of Chinese citizens in poverty decreased continuously to 125 million in 1986 and 80 million in 1993. In 2013, the population living in poverty in rural areas was about 70 million. The poverty reduction strategy in China has become much more precise and the central government hopes to solve the rural poverty problem before 2020. The three core components of China's rural development in recent decades have been policy, investment and technology. With government policies as a firm foundation, investment and technology have significantly accelerated the rural development process in China. China's rural development could potentially influence rural development in African countries, although there is a need to carefully consider the specific social systems of the different rural regions in the African continent. China's influence on African agriculture has been limited, but there is the potential for this to increase in the future.

China is the largest developing country in the world, with more than 600 million farmers across the nation. In the past few decades, rural development has not only been one of the main goals of the national government but has also been a focus of both international and domestic researchers (Perkins &Yusuf, 1984; Fan, 1991; Shen, 1996; Long et al., 2010; Chen & Scott, 2014; Cheremukhin et al., 2015). Rural development in the United States has been supported by the United States Department of Agriculture (USDA) Office of Rural Development (RD), which operates over fifty financial assistance programs for a variety of rural applications (USDA, 2017). Over the course of the Obama Administration, USDA made targeted federal investments in rural areas to create jobs, generate economic opportunities and strengthen rural communities. The USDARD has invested in rural America's remarkable comeback, with key economic indicators continuing to show that rural America is rebounding from past economic decline. Rural unemployment has continued to fall, dropping below 6% in 2015 for the first time since 2007, and rural poverty rates have also fallen in the past decade. Median household incomes in rural areas increased by 3.4% in 2015, and rural populations have stabilised and are beginning to grow (USDA, 2017). In the European Union (EU), the rural development policy has enabled the rural areas to meet the many economic, environmental and social challenges of the 21st century (European Commission, 2013). In India, a roadmap of rural development has been established and is strongly supported by the national government (Rajvanshi, 2016). Rural development has become an important domestic policy in the US, India and the EU.

In the early years of the 'new China' (established in 1949), private land ownership was replaced by public or collective ownership. From the late 1950s to the late 1970s, rural development proceeded slowly and was controlled by socialist policies. There were no economic or other subsidies for farmers, and investment in rural development was limited. In Africa, most countries gained independence before the 1970s, but their national economies still relied on the international market and international aid. Rural poverty and rural development are still serious problems for most African countries. In the period of 2010–2012, the prevalence of undernourishment in the total African population was about 20.7%, and exceeded 70.0% in Burundi and Comoros (African Development Bank et al., 2015). The high youth unemployment rate in Africa is also a problem that needs to be solved (African Development Bank et al., 2015). In 1978, the Communist Party of China began to implement economic reforms. Rural development has subsequently entered a new era and has experienced rapid growth in the past few decades. Several researchers have contrasted the rapid rural development in China with the slow pace of rural development in Africa. There are two lessons for Africa from China's success in rural poverty alleviation. The first is the initial importance of productivity growth in smallholder agriculture, which requires both market-based incentives and public support. The second is the role played by strong leadership and a capable public administration at all levels of government (Ravallion, 2009). This study focused on China's policy-oriented rural development, and has considered actual experiences from China, and the significance of African rural development in the future.

Changes in Rural Development Policies in China

For a long time in China the pace of rural development was slow, even after the People's Republic of China was established in 1949. In the early 1950s China reformed the system of rural land ownership. In rural regions, land that belonged to the local community was placed under collective ownership. Rural development was not a high priority for the central government during the period of 1949–1979. There were few subsides or investments in rural development in the 30 years prior to the 1978 reform period. Agriculture was one of the main contributors to the national economy, providing cheap food for urban residents and materials for industrial enterprises. However, the policy of collective land ownership did not generate reasonable benefits or enough food for the farmers. In rural regions, many farm families starved because of food shortages, especially during the Great Leap Forward (GLF) (1958–1962). The lack of farming incentives and policy-oriented agricultural activity resulted in the total factor productivity (TFP) falling by 41% from the peak in 1958 to a low in 1962. In the years prior to 1979, TFP remained low (Cheremukhin et al., 2015). In the period prior to the 1978 reform, the *Hukou* system, a system used to manage the population in urban and rural regions, restricted the mobility of rural labour (Song, 2014). Scarce investment, a strict market, non-mobile labour, and policy-oriented incentives, as well as the collective ownership of land, restricted agricultural and rural development in China prior to the 1978 reform.

After the 1978 reform, the household responsibility system was introduced as a new institutional innovation in China. This allowed farmers to determine farming practices themselves, and led to a desire to produce larger volumes of agricultural products, solving the food shortage and increasing the activity of farm labourers. The reformed agricultural market also enabled farmers to sell some of their crops. As industrialization and urbanization advanced in China, business enterprises and urban developers needed more labour. Farmers were encouraged to move to the cities and earn money for a living. Under the open agricultural policy and with market innovation, land ownership accelerated rural development.

Policy change was the main factor affecting rural development in China. For example, during the GLF (1958–1962), TFP in agriculture fell by 41% from its peak in 1958 to a low point in 1962. TFP in manufacturing fell in 1958 by 23% and again in 1961 by 26%. One important factor that affected TFP in both the agricultural and non-agricultural sectors was the worsening of policy incentives (Naughton, 2007). Material incentives, monetary rewards, and bonuses were prohibited, free markets in the countryside were curtailed, and restrictions were introduced on productive private farming plots. The fall in manufacturing TFP was attributed to several factors. First, the collapse of agricultural production led to a severe shortage of agricultural materials for the textile and food-processing industries. Second, many small-scale plants, such as backyard steel furnaces, were exceptionally inefficient. The productivity growth during the post-GLF period before 1978 was 2.4% per year in agriculture. After the 1978 reform, agricultural productivity increased rapidly. For example, annual TFP growth was

4.7% in 1978–1985, and in the period of 1985–2012 TFP growth was 3.9% per year (Cheremukhin et al., 2015).

Rural Development in China after the Rural Economic Reforms

Growth in Agricultural Production Solved the Food Shortage

After the 1978 reform, production of the main agricultural products increased rapidly and satisfied the needs of the population and the agricultural-based industrial sectors. Total grain production increased from 300 million tons in 1978 to 600 million tons in 2015, which completely solved the food shortage. Production of grains, vegetables, fruits, various types of meat and fishery products fulfilled the domestic demand and some products were exported to overseas markets.

The Mode of Agricultural Development Changed Rapidly

After the 1978 reform (especially after the mid-1980s), the mode of agricultural development was transformed from extensive to intensive cultivation. Technology contributed more than 50% of the overall advances in agricultural development. Agricultural mechanisation has improved significantly in recent decades. In 1978 the level of agricultural mechanisation was 20.2%, while in 2008 the level increased to 45.0% and in 2013 it reached 60.0% (National Bureau of Statistics of the People's Republic of China, 2015). Agricultural mechanisation reduced the need for labour force and the surplus labour in rural regions became available for industrial activity.

The Economic Structure in Rural Regions Changed Rapidly

Before the 1978 reforms, the economy was dominated by agricultural production. In recent years in rural regions, agricultural industry and agricultural services have developed in conjunction with each other. After the 1978 reforms, township and village enterprises boomed because of the open policy, improved investment environment and technological inputs. In 2008, the economic growth of township and village enterprises accounted for 28% of the national gross domestic product (GDP). In 2013, China's private economy accounted for more than 60% of the GDP (National Bureau of Statistics of the People's Republic of China, 2015). In more than 19 provinces the private economy accounted for more than half of their GDP. In Guangdong Province the private economy accounted for 80% of the GDP. The agricultural industry developed continuously, and the number of large-scale farming enterprises increased substantially.

Farmer's Incomes Increased Continuously

After the 1978 reform, the Chinese people progressed from being barely fed and clad to a more comfortable life. Famer's lives changed as they became wealthier. From 1978 to 2008, the net income increased from 133 RMB (or 20 USD) to 4,761 RMB (or 680 USD) per capita. In 2013 the average farmer's income was 8,896 RMB (or 1,271 USD) per capita. The population in poverty decreased from 250 million in 1978 to 70 million in 2013, and the UN millennium development goal was achieved in China (Agricultural Yearbook Editing Committee, 1979; 2009; 2014). The increase in work opportunities in urban areas or factories had an impact on population control in rural regions, with less children being born due to the opportunities to work outside the region. Family incomes increased as industrialisation and urbanisation increased nationally.

Great Changes in the Rural Economic System

In China the rural economic system has changed substantially since the 1978 reform. Self-sufficient farming has been transformed into an agricultural market economy. The current rural economy is based on both a household responsibility system and the mixed management system, which suggests that the collective ownership economy and family unit economy coexist. No strict agricultural product market and price system have been established in recent decades. In 2005, the central government issued legislation rescinding the agricultural tax and other taxes on special agricultural products. A system of agricultural subsidies has also been gradually established over the past 20 years. With support from central government, rural development policies such as the agricultural macroeconomic regulation and control system, the administrative system, the legal system and the protection policy system have been established.

Increased Public Finance to Support Rural Development

China has a typical urban and rural dual social structure and economy. After the 1978 reform, the central government introduced policies to move away from the dual social and economic structure to an integration between urban and rural areas. Public finances and services were used to support rural development, and infrastructure such as a clean water supply, electricity supply, road improvements and gas supply in rural regions improved rapidly. The overall quality of rural life has improved in recent decades. Prior to the 1978 reform, agriculture and rural regions contributed more to the national economy than industry and urban development. After the 1978 reform, rural development policies such as 'enlivening the rural economy' gave the right of self-management to farmers, enabling them to implement a household responsibility system and engage in industrial and agro-product processing. This has completely opened the rural market and, together with several poverty reduction campaigns, has resulted in significant rural development. Before the 1978 reform, there were few cement or asphalt roads in rural regions. With financial support from the central government, the total length of cement and asphalt roads in rural regions has reached 3.58 million km. In addition, rural education and hospital conditions also improved rapidly after the 1978 reform, especially in the past decade. These improvements indicate that policy-oriented rural development has been successful.

Some Problems on China's Rural Development Experience

The Effects of Urbanisation on Rural Development

Urbanisation has been the main trend in China's development. The number of cities in the country increased from 132 to 658 during the period from 1949 to 2013. According to the national census in 2010, there were six cities with a population of more than 10 million, whereas there were no cities of this size in 1978. The number of cities with a population of 3 to 5 million people increased from 2 to 21 between 1978 and 2010. During the same period, the number of cities with a population below 500,000 increased from 129 to 380. The urbanization rate was 17.92% in 1978, and 53.73% in 2013 (National Bureau of Statistics of the People's Republic of China, 2015). Urbanisation has attracted more labourers to work in urban regions. The proportion of all employees working in urban areas increased from 12.0 to 49.7% over the period from 1952 to 2013 (National Bureau of Statistics of the People's Republic of China, 2015). In contemporary China, many rural labourers have moved to cities to earn money and participate in city life. As a result, labour shortages in rural regions have become a key problem for rural development. Elder farmers and children have remained as residents in rural villages. Family relationships have, therefore, faced many challenges. For example, the level of care and family education provided to children in rural regions from their parents has declined (Xianzuo & Qingyang, 2015). Overall, the effect of urbanisation in China has improved the economic condition of farming families. As a consequence of the one family one child policy in China, many rural residents have remained on family farms throughout their lives. The rural labourers working in cities have experienced the difference between rural and urban regions for the first time. The willingness of rural labourers and others from the new rural generation to move to cities has been a noticeable trend and an indicator of the decline of rural regions. The national government has encouraged the combination of small communities or villages in the past decade, with the result that farmers living in the new larger communities must travel a relatively long distance to work on their farmland.

Environmental Problems: Wastes, Plastic and Soil Pollution

With urbanisation and rural development, solid waste management has become a problem in rural areas, especially in the suburbs. Large amounts of construction and household wastes are usually transported to the suburbs. According to the 2016 national report on solid wastes in 246 cities, the volume of industrial solid waste, dangerous industrial solid waste, hospital solid waste and household solid waste has reached 1.91 billion, 28.02 million, 689,000 and 185.64 million tons, respectively (Ministry of Environment of China, 2016). Rural regions, especially the suburbs, are the main disposal destinations for the city's solid wastes. Cities other than the 246 reported in the census do not have accessible solid waste disposal information; hence, the exact amounts of waste arriving in rural regions could not be calculated.

In the past decade, plastic films have been widely applied to farmland across the nation to increase grain production. China is now the largest country using plastic film mulching and consumes 1,200,000 tons of plastic film annually. Much of the plastic film degrades into plastic fragments and pollutes farmland. Some studies have shown that plastic fragments can change soil features and reduce grain production (Yan et al., 2014).

Maintaining crop production to feed a growing population is one of the greatest challenges faced by human society. The increased crop yields during the last century, and especially during the Green Revolution, were achieved through breeding for an increased harvest index and disease resistance, as well as by applying more irrigation water and agrochemicals. In terms of agrochemical pollution, fully developed farmland is usually treated with large amounts of agrochemicals, and the residues in soil can then enter the food cycle. In China's developed industrial regions, the plains of the Yangtze River Delta and the Pearl River Delta are facing severe soil pollution problems partly due to agrochemical applications (Chen & Ye, 2014).

Water Irrigation Systems: Reservoir and Pond Siltation and Damage to Ditches Water irrigation systems play an important role in maintaining crop production.

In China, the extensive construction of reservoirs and ponds occurred between the late 1950s and early 1970s. Because of the monsoon climate and deforestation, in extensively developed agricultural regions soil erosion has become an environmental problem that is extremely difficult to solve. Reservoirs and ponds are important parts of the water irrigation system that face the threat of siltation, while in farming land, irrigation ditches have been damaged by unreasonable usage. According to Tian et al. (2006), siltation data from 115 reservoirs indicate that 20% of the reservoir volume has been lost, with medium to small reservoirs being silted more than large reservoirs. In Anqiu City in Shandong Province, about 30% of the irrigation systems have been damaged over the past 20 years (Gao & Feng, 2004).

The Potential Influence of China's Rural Development on African Countries

China's experiences of rural development are of interest to African countries. In the huge continent of Africa, rural development could become a widespread business and is a national developmental target. Africa contains more than 50 countries, with different languages, cultures, climates, politics and economies. Within the various African countries there are different configurations of socialism, capitalism and traditional rural social structures. However, there are few examples in African countries of consistent efforts to improve rural infrastructure, implement population controls and develop rural industries. Rural development in most African countries has not been given the importance it has received in China. The authors believe that this is the result of differences in social institutions between China and African countries

Rural development in China after the 1978 reform has received the attention of many researchers. For example, Fan (1991) considered the effects of technological change and institutional reform on production growth in Chinese agriculture. However, few studies have concentrated on policy-oriented rural development in China. In African countries there are many people facing the challenge of food shortages. Statistics show African poverty has shown a declining trend over the past fifteen years. Nevertheless, compared to other developing regions such as South and East Asia, Africa's progress toward poverty reduction has been consistently disappointing. When compared to a typical Asian country, the growth in Africa's GDP per capita has generated only half the reduction in poverty of that experienced in Asia (African Development Bank et al., 2015). In general, China's rural development has the potential to influence rural development in African countries.

Policy-oriented Rural Development in China

The central government implemented a series of policies that stimulated the agricultural economy after the 1978 reform. These policies included institutional reform, the development of strict markets in rural regions, the cancelation of agriculture tax and taxes on special agriculture products, as well as financial support for agricultural mechanisation and rural infrastructure construction. In addition, there was also financial support provided for the education of the younger generation in rural areas. The above policies have encouraged China's rapid rural development in recent decades. China is a socialist country and all rural development has occurred in one country, with one national language and a unitary system of governance. The national and local government have strong decision-making powers and can easily implement rural development policies based on the social and economic status of regions as well as their changing trends. Since the late 1970s, the national population control policy has been one family one child, but this has changed rapidly among rural families, with parents moving to urban areas in search of part time employment. As a consequence, the economic conditions of many families have improved, with benefits for rural development.

The different African countries have their own unique national conditions. A series of policies are needed for the future rural development of the continent. African governments should have their own specific policies for supporting rural development. Learning from China's experience of rural development, a roadmap of rural development in African countries could be developed in advance. African countries should consider the different stages of China's rural development. The first stage involved land-use policy changes, which started in the late 1970s; this stimulated farmers to produce more grain. The second stage was the opening of agricultural markets and the rapid industrialisation experienced in the 1990s, which attracted more rural labourers to work in the cities and towns. Government policies played an important role in the changes experienced by rural areas.

China's Open Policy and Industrialisation Stimulated Rural Development

After the 1978 reform, the open policy has been the basic strategy of national economic development. Foreign investment and the import of foreign technology have stimulated industrialisation in China. More labour is needed to support industrialisation in urban areas. The surplus labour in rural regions have migrated to work in factories after receiving general training. Most of the construction projects in Chinese cities were completed by trained surplus labour from rural regions. Given the background of the open policy and ongoing industrialisation, farmers have more opportunities to make money. In the globalised era, African countries should adopt open policies for sustainable development. Foreign investment and industrialisation will partly solve the unemployment problems and boost rural development, especially in agro-based industries. During the changes experienced in China, the country maintained a stable social condition and adopted a continuous open market policy, which provided the best social and economic conditions to attract more foreign investment and foreign technology imports.

Rural Education is Important for Rural Development

Prior to the 1978 reform, China established a rural education system, with all children required to enrol in school for elementary education. In the past 20 years, occupational education and industrialisation have intensified in China. The current rural generation has had more chance to receive an occupational or university level education than their predecessors, which has enabled them to increase their employability and has encouraged rural development. In most African countries, the residents of rural areas usually lack an elementary level or occupational education, which restricts their employment and family income. According to the African Statistical Yearbook 2014 (African Development Bank et al., 2015), the adult illiteracy rate in Africa was 37.6% and the female adult illiteracy rate was 46.1% during the period 2005–2012. In rural regions the adult illiteracy rate is even higher. Therefore, education is a limiting factor for rural development in some African countries. For future sustainable rural development, the education of the rural population must be strengthened across the African continent, especially in rural regions.

China Should Help to Improve Decision-making with Regard to Rural Development in African Countries

Africa is a huge continent with obvious diversity among its rural societies and cultures, as well as in relation to its agricultural production and rural development levels. The realities of agricultural and rural development are not usually recognised by foreigners (Christiaensen, 2017). In recent decades, close relationships have been established between China and most African countries. China has invested in African countries, not only in infrastructure but also in other economic sectors since the 1990s. For example, with support from the Chinese Ministry of Agriculture, 24 demonstration centres of China-Africa agricultural technology have been established since 2007. Recently, some Chinese researchers have conducted field surveys and reported several obvious inadequacies of these centres. After three years, the centres were no longer in receipt of financial support from the Chinese government, and some centres then faced the problem of operational sustainability, with no suitable connection to the habits of local agricultural producers (Li, 2015; Zhu et al., 2015; Xu et al., 2016). For example, some centres demonstrated rice planting technologies, whereas the local people in the surrounding rural areas regularly consumed potatoes and were not motivated to operate a rice planting, growing, management, harvesting and grain market system. Centres in such areas soon became disused because they did not consider the real needs of local communities. However, there were also some good examples, such as the Chinese infrastructure companies that became involved in the reclamation or improvement of farming lands for local communities. For example, in November 2015, one Chinese infrastructure company reclaimed farmland for 20 people in a small village in southern Botswana, which met the needs of the local community in that particular rural region.

The China-Africa relationship has been developing very rapidly and is important to regions. Despite this, there are few examples of African countries that have made consistent efforts to improve rural infrastructure, implement population growth controls and develop rural industries. China's influence in African agriculture is limited and should be improved in the future.

Conclusion

Moyo (2003) reported that the land question and land reforms in Africa have a long history spanning the colonial and post-colonial period. Most studies of land reform have been poorly disseminated and have tended to neglect the emergence of various land questions, as well as the structures and processes that drive them, land conflicts and the growing deep-rooted demand for land reform. The land question that Moyo (2003) considered includes rural development, and an assessment of the evolution of the land question, as well as the class dynamics and social movements that such development is grounded upon, to provide an understanding of the political and economic context in which the farmers, agrarian capitalists and external market influences function to shape the land question in the different regions of Africa (Moyo, 2003; Moyo et al., 2013). The Fast Track land reform in Zimbabwe and its impacts on rural development have been investigated by many researchers (Cliffe et al., 2011), and is a complex issue. China's potential influence on rural development in African countries should be grounded upon the specific social systems of the different rural regions across the African continent.

China's rural development in the past few decades has been impressive and has attracted the interest of African governments and researchers. Policy is an important factor determining the pace of rural development and poverty reduction. Rural development in China has been one of the most important tasks undertaken by central government since the 1978 reform. From 1982 to 1986, the No.1 document issued each year by the Central Committee of the Communist Party of China (CPC) focused on agricultural development and rural reform. From 2004 to 2015, the No.1 document issued every year by the Central Committee of the CPC focused on agriculture, farmer wellbeing and rural development. In recent years, the central government has implemented policies providing financial support to encourage farmers working in cities to return to the countryside as part of a new village improvement campaign. In China, a series of rural development policies, an open market policy, and industrialisation, as well as rural education have stimulated the agricultural economy and rural development in recent decades. Similar actions will be invaluable for rural development in African countries. In addition, the socialist institutions and their efficient administration ensured that policy-oriented rural development and rapid agro- economy growth were realised after the 1978 reform. The one family one child policy and increasing urbanisation and industrialisation against a backdrop of the open market policy were other factors affecting rural development in China.

Acknowledgements

This article is based on our paper presented at 'Land, the State and Decolonising the Agrarian Structure in Africa: A Colloquium in Honour of Professor Sam Moyo,' organized at the University of Cape Town, South Africa, on November 28–29, 2016. This colloquium was sponsored by the Japan Society for the Promotion of Science, Grant-in-Aid for Scientific Research (S) "'African Potential" and Overcoming the Difficulties of Modern World: Comprehensive Research That Will Provide a New Perspective for the Future of Humanity' (KAKENHI 16H06318 headed by Motoji Matsuda, Kyoto University), as well as by the University of Cape Town's Research Office (URC).

References

African Development Bank, African Union Commission & United Nation Economic Commission for Africa 2015. *African Statistical Yearbook 2014*. Scanprint, Denmark.

Agricultural Yearbook Editing Committee 1979. *China Agricultural Yearbook*. Agricultural Publishing House, Beijing.

— 2009. *China Agricultural Yearbook*. Agricultural Publishing House, Beijing.

— 2014. *China Agricultural Yearbook*. China Agriculture Press, Beijing.

Chen, A. & S. Scott 2014. Rural development strategies and government roles in the development of farmers' cooperatives in China. *Journal of Agriculture, Food Systems, and Community Development*, 4(4): 35–55.

Chen, R. & C. Ye 2014. Land management: Resolving soil pollution in China. *Nature*, 505(7484): 483.

Cheremukhin, A., M. Golosov, S. Guriev & A. Tsyvinski 2015. *The Economy of People's Republic of China from 1953, NBER Working Paper No. 21397*. National Bureau of Economic Research, Cambridge.

Christiaensen, L. 2017. Agriculture in Africa-telling myths from facts: A synthesis. *Food Policy*, 67: 1–11.

Cliffe, L., J. Alexander, B. Cousins & R. Gaidzanwa 2011. An overview of fast track land reform in Zimbabwe: Editorial introduction. *The Journal of Peasant Studies*, 38(5): 907–938.

European Commission 2013. *Overview of CAP Reform 2014–2020*. DG Agriculture and Rural Development, Unit for agricultural Policy Analysis and Perspectives, Brussel.

Fan, S. 1991. Effects of technological change and institutional reform on production growth in Chinese agriculture. *American Journal of Agricultural Economics*, 73(2): 266–275.

Gao, P. & Y. Feng 2004. Problems and its countermeasures of the four reservoir irrigation regions in Anqiu City. (in Chinese). *Shandong Hydrology*, 7: 14.

Li, J.L. 2015. Some problems and countermeasures of Sino-African China-Africa agricultural technology demonstration centres. (in Chinese). *World Agriculture*, 1: 148–149.

Long, H.L., Y.S. Liu, X.B. Li & Y.F. Chen 2010. Building new countryside in China: A geographical perspective. *Land Use Policy*, 27(2): 457–470.

Ministry of Environment of China 2016. *National Report of Solid Wastes and Management in 246 Cities (2015)*. (in Chinese). Environmental Science Press, Beijing.

Moyo, S. 2003. *The Land Questions in Africa: Research, Perspective and Questions*. Paper presented at the CODESRIA Conference 'The

Agrarian Question and nationalism' in Gaborone, Botswana, October 18–19, 2003 and in Dakar, Senegal, December 8–11, 2003.

Moyo, S., P. Jha & P. Yeros 2013. The classical agrarian question: Myth, reality and relevance today. *Agrarian South: Journal of Political Economy*, 2(1): 93–119.

National Bureau of Statistics of the People's Republic of China 2015. *New China in the Past 65 Years*. Online. http://www.stats.gov.cn/tjzs/tjbk/201502/t20150213_683631. html (Accessed January 15, 2017).

Naughton, B.J. 2007. *The Chinese Economy: Transitions and Growth*. MIT Press, Cambridge. Perkins, D. & S. Yusuf 1984. *Rural Development in China*. The Johns Hopkins University Press, Baltimore.

Rajvanshi, A.K. 2016. Roadmap for rural India. *Current Science*, 111(1): 39–43.

Ravallion, M. 2009. Are there lessons for Africa from China's success against poverty? *World Development*, 37(2): 303–313.

Shen, J.F. 1996. Rural development and rural to urban migration in China 1978–1990. *Geoforum*, 26(4): 395–409.

Song, Y. 2014. What should economists know about the current Chinese hukou system? *China Economic Review*, 29: 200–212.

Tian, H., Z. Zhang, Y. Li & H. Meng 2006. Differences of reservoir sedimentation in mainland of China. (in Chinese). *Advances of Science and Technology in Water Resources*, 26(6): 28–33.

United States Department of Agriculture (USDA) 2017. *About Rural Development*. Online. https://www.rd.usda.gov/about-rd (Accessed January 15, 2017).

Xianzuo, F. & G. Qingyang 2015. Review and reflection on the rural left-behind children education problem. *China Agricultural University Journal of Social Sciences Edition*, 32(1): 55–64.

Xu, X., X. Li, G. Qi, L. Tang & L. Mukwereza 2016. Science, technology and the politics of knowledge: The case of China's agricultural technological demonstration centres in Africa. *World Development*, 81: 82–91.

Yan, C.R., E.K. Liu, F. Shu, Q. Liu, S. Liu & W.Q. He 2014. Review of agricultural plastic mulching and its residual pollution and prevention measures in China. *Journal of Agricultural Resources and Environment*, 31(2): 95–102.

Zhu, Y., D. Zhou & P. Wang 2015. The present status, problem and measures for the Sino-African China-Africa agricultural technology demonstration centres. (in Chinese). *World Agriculture*, 9: 64–69.

Corresponding Author's E-mail: zhangzk@nju.edu.cn

Chapter 5

Agricultural Land-Delivery Systems on Zimbabwe: A Review of Four Decades of Sam Moyo's Work on Agricultural Land Markets and their Constraints

Rangarirai Gavin Muchetu

Introduction

Rights to land have changed hands several times across Zimbabwe's racial, class, socioeconomic, and political divides over the past century. This has occurred through greatly varying mechanisms, depending more on sociopolitical power dynamics and less on the supply and demand of land. Discussion of agricultural land-delivery systems in Zimbabwe requires an understanding of the deeply embedded socioeconomic and political factors that have driven supply and demand of agrarian land. This chapter examines Professor Sam Moyo's work on the evolution of land markets from the pre-independence era through the 2000s to the development of the new emerging land-market transactions in the countryside. Moyo's work shows how the state-led land-delivery system reconfigured the agrarian structure, changing it from a bimodal to a trimodal system. Giving due consideration to the different economic models that have been pursued by the Government of Zimbabwe since independence, and investigating how these have shaped power relations with regard to land, we attempt, from a political economy perspective, to develop an understanding of the land-reform program. Moyo's work on Zimbabwe's land markets shows how market-based approaches to land redistribution will always be inadequate for addressing social and historical injustices, because they favour capital at the expense of the peasantry. This article utilizes a tri-modal agrarian structure to analyse recent data from a 2013–2015 survey conducted by Sam Moyo Agrarian Institute for Agrarian Studies (SMAIAS). These data support Moyo's arguments: for example, that the pressure for Fast Track Land Reform Program (FTLRP) emanated from below, and that a spectrum of beneficiaries, outside the usual political elite, accessed land. Data analyses revealed continued demand for land from both local (informal markets) and international (large land deals) players, further substantiating Moyo's claim that there remains an unresolved land question in Zimbabwe.

Land markets are sensitive and complex because land is immovable, which problematizes its commodification. Land is a social good and a human right. Therefore, land markets deal in the methods, nature, and extent of transferability of rights to a piece of land. A number of different types of land markets exist, such as agricultural and non-agricultural, urban and rural, and formal and informal land markets. These markets continuously intersect and overlap, meaning that the existence of one market does not supersede the existence of others. In this chapter, land refers to rural agricultural land. Descriptions of land markets and/ or land-delivery channels over the past four decades, therefore, describe the methods, processes, and trajectories of the claims of different groups of people to agricultural land rights. This chapter accounts for the effects of inequitable land access, landlessness, and differentiated control of quality land on the different land-delivery systems utilized in Zimbabwe. National land markets are thoroughly politicized, forming the basis for mainstream national agendas. Trade in land, in Zimbabwe as elsewhere, constitutes direct trade of people's means of production, wealth, and source of sociopolitical influence and status. Governments have thus always tried to control land and protect it from the vagaries of unfettered global markets. Land reform and land redistribution have been at the forefront of the Zimbabwe national agenda dating back to the liberation struggle itself. The discussions of the pre-independence Lancaster House Conference (LHC) almost broke down because of disagreements on the land question.

One of the first scholars to write on these issues was the former President of CODESRIA (2008–2011) and former Executive Director of the Sam Moyo African Institute for Agrarian Studies (SMAIAS) (2002–2015), the late Professor Sam Moyo (1954–2015). His arguments, whether through assimilation or opposition, have found their way into discussions of agrarian-land markets and reform. His work covered food production and productivity, food security and sovereignty, rural poverty and underdevelopment, agricultural input and output markets, and agrarian land reform and markets. Moyo was an academic guru whose influence and research transcended political, economic, and academic boundaries. This chapter takes up his preferred theoretical framework, the political economy approach, to understand the evolution of agricultural land markets in Zimbabwe. We aimed to understand the economic, political, and social factors that have driven demand and supply in land and land-related policies from independence to the FTLRP and beyond.

Moyo's writing on land markets elucidated the land question in Zimbabwe and how it has been affected by 1) the characteristics of the people demanding land and 2) the economic model adopted by the state, which has implications for the land tenure system (security or insecurity) to be followed. In his rural and agrarian development studies, which span four decades, Moyo viewed land reform as a necessary but not sufficient condition for agrarian reform and national development, thus viewing the land question (and the agrarian question even more so) as being far from being resolved (Moyo & Matondi, 2004). In theoretical discourse, therefore, Moyo hypothesized that land reform was not enough to create an inclusive development of rural spaces. Without complementary support for the agrarian market, simultaneously increasing rural development and reducing poverty would remain problematic. Moyo wrote extensively on how market-led land reforms would always favour the wealthy and achieve inefficient redistribution outcomes. Issues such as historical race and class-based land ownership imbalances could not, in his view, be addressed through market-led land reform. Moyo argued that social equity in land access was best achieved through state-led land reform, which had to be radical in nature, given the pervasiveness of neo-liberalism in post-colonial Zimbabwe.

One of Moyo's major contributions to Zimbabwean agrarian studies was the proposal of a state-led reform to dismantle the existing bimodal agrarian structure in favour of a trimodal one. The former consisted of inequitable relations of land ownership, with large-scale farmers possessing private property rights, while peasants held communal tenure rights. Integration into the input and output markets differed immensely between these two. Prior to the new agrarian structure, differentiation was polarized, with the large-scale farmers being in complete control of the land markets and well-integrated into export markets for lucrative cash crops (Moyo, 2011a: 202–204). Moyo (2014) argued that market-led land-delivery systems perpetuated this dualism, because large-scale landowners would have better chances over peasants in purchasing land if such systems were adopted. Thus, the resultant tri-modal agrarian structure, incorporating large-scale farmers, numerous small-to-medium capitalist farmers, and an expanded peasantry, could only be brought about through non-market-led land reforms. The tri-modal agrarian framework ideally supports arguments of re-peasantization and semi-proletarianization, which have serious implications for post-reform class and accumulation analysis (not discussed in this chapter). Thus, it is imperative to draw lessons from Moyo's works, which covered the trajectory taken by land markets (and land policy) under the various national economic production models adopted in Zimbabwe. The span of his work extends from the time before the land-market phases of the LHC agreement, through land market liberalization (late 1980s to 1990s), and land reform (2000s) to the emerging land market deals in the agricultural sector (2010 and beyond). This chapter approaches land markets through the lens of the research of this great land and agrarian expert.

Land in Context

Zimbabwe's economy fundamentally depends on agriculture, as do most economies of southern Africa. Approximately 70% of the population derives their livelihood from it directly, and it accounted for an average of 16% of the GDP over the last five years (World Bank, 2017). Understanding land access goes beyond understanding agricultural land values and the prices that it attracts on the supply and demand schedules, as it encompasses a variety of other factors that are difficult to quantify and that have a bearing on agricultural land markets. Before discussing the evolution of the land markets, it is important to conceptualize the terms used, specifically with regard to the complexities of trading agricultural land on the open market.

Land as a Commodity

Market-led redistribution of land requires land to be tradable, that is, to be considered as a commodity. The ease or difficulty of commodifying agricultural land hinges on the definition of land. There are a number of definitions of land in the literature, depending on the field of study. In economics, land, together with labour and capital, form the basic factors of production. It is associated with an economic value, expressed in price per hectare at ownership, transfer or when paying for its use (rent). Modern scholarship has broadened the definition to reflect other non-productive uses. Land has become any delineable area of the earth's terrestrial surface, encompassing all attributes of the biosphere immediately above or below this surface (rivers, swamps), the plant and animal populations of that area, settlements and physical results of past and present human activity on that part of the terrestrial surface (UN, 1994; FAO, 1995). How we define land has implications for our understanding of demand and supply and, inevitably, on its value in the 'market.' Moyo & Skalness (1990) argued that it was inadequate to define land in an economic context only, and that struggles for land and the political economy of land reforms should also be considered.

In this respect, viewing (agricultural) land as a commodity becomes problematic for the simple reason that its market value is not merely affected by production costs. Supply and demand schedules on their own cannot explain the value attached to a piece of land that has a river flowing through it, trees, minerals underneath it, and the graves and memories of a particular group of inhabitants. Land values in economic principle are determined by the demand of land, which in turn is affected by the intended use of that land relative to the supply of other lands for that particular use. This type of analysis of land markets reveals a disarticulated market system for land, where two attached pieces of land can have different prices or values.

Moreover, the land question in Africa needs to be examined in the wider context of struggles over land rights "embedded" in the control, by external capital and the state, of extensive lands, which harbour minerals and other valuable natural resources (Moyo, 2007).

Market-based transactions are considered to be efficient, equitable, environmentally sound, and compatible with other sectors of the economy. While this is easily applicable to markets for real commodities, it does not apply to agricultural land markets. From a political economy perspective, Moyo showed how complex it is to assign a value to any piece of land, because it can be linked to alternative land uses, which change over time. The discovery of a precious mineral or the intention of constructing residential or industrial infrastructure can drastically change land values. In addition, two different land values may exist for peri-urban and non-peri-urban agricultural land with similar land uses. In some pre-Zimbabwe land valuations (1965 to 1990s), the racial category of the user and the size of the land were used to determine the value. The exclusive use of supply and demand schedules to determine land values resulted in the commodification of land, a commodity that can be traded regardless of its sociocultural dimension. The commodification of land had serious exclusionary effects on socioeconomically vulnerable groups (the downtrodden), such as women and children. The downtrodden have an insatiable desire for land but do not have the means (resources) to purchase it on the free market; thus, they lack effective demand. They do not have the means to purchase land unless it is provided to them for free. The essence of a market-led land-delivery system is that it seeks to permanently transfer land from less efficient producers to more efficient users. This land-delivery system would exclude the downtrodden, with their limited educational skills and access to capital and credit.

Conceptualization of Land Markets in Zimbabwe

As noted, if land were a commodity, its price would be affected by factors of 1) supply (price of the complementary or substitute goods, number of sellers in the market, and production costs) and 2) demand (incomes, consumer tastes and preferences, number of consumers, and potential future prices). Although this chapter does discuss the behaviour of the suppliers of land, it dwells more on the behaviour of the demanders and how they eventually triggered a

106

paradigm shift in the land-delivery system. Soon after independence, neo-liberal policies forced land seekers to access land through market-led land-delivery systems. Pressure for the creation of market-based land access in Zimbabwe mainly originated from international capital, the LHC agreement, and the Economic Structural Adjustment Program (ESAP) (Moyo & Matondi, 2004; Shivji, 2009; Moyo, 2010). However, this approach, which depended on responding to market supply and demand, was problematic, for the following reasons:

(1) There were too few sellers: these were less than 5000 white settlers who had control of over 15 million hectares of prime arable agricultural land (Utete, 2003). Markets are inefficient when the supply of a good is concentrated in the hands of a few (monopoly).

(2) The behaviour of these few sellers was highly unpredictable, as they were not responding to demands for land by the majority of the Zimbabweans.

(3) The buyer of the land, the state (on behalf of the people) was financially crippled and unable to drive effective demand.

(4) There is no substitute for agricultural land.

(5) In a purely competitive market, the government plays a regulatory role, guaranteeing fair practices in the market. However, according to the LHC agreement, the government was required to take an active role, as it had the first right of refusal for all agricultural land that was presented by white commercial farmers. From 1980–1990, the government received funds from Britain, bought land, and redistributed it to its people, albeit at a slow pace (see section 3). This then presented policy and ideological inconsistences.

Moyo disagreed with Bojo (1993) and other scholars who argued that direct state participation in land markets distorted land-use values. African land markets do not respond only to market forces but are also affected by the history of land appropriations during the settler regimes. They are marred by class, gender, racial, and ethnic inequalities that can never be addressed by market forces; thus, the participation of the state is required. In this regard, understanding land markets requires a political economy approach to answer various national land questions. The land question that has been the focus of much of Moyo's work is concerned with the following:

> [...] the adequacy of the quantity and quality of land [...], the method and costs of land acquisition and redistribution, the efficiency of land use in both the large farm and resettlement areas, the suitability of those benefiting from land redistribution, the fairness and equitability of procedures for dealing with land demands, and the economic impact of land reform (Moyo, 1994).

Land Supply and Demand

Agricultural land markets have seen a myriad of characteristic changes, from peasants to white settlers (appropriation and colonization), to the slow market-based land reforms of the 1980s and 1990s, and the more recent FTLRP (white settlers to the peasants). Thus, land markets have been determined by who controlled the land, the type of tenure by which it was controlled, and the level or intensity of demand for the land by those who did not have land.

These three variables formed the basis for the supply and demand functions for land in Zimbabwe (Moyo, 2005a). Furthermore, to understand land demand, an analysis of the social dimensions (connections, agency, and organization level) of the land seekers, and their place in a broad economic model and property rights regime had to be determined. The demand for land needs to be understood before we can understand how land markets evolved. This demand has taken various forms and emanated from various sources since the birth of the country (Fig. 1).

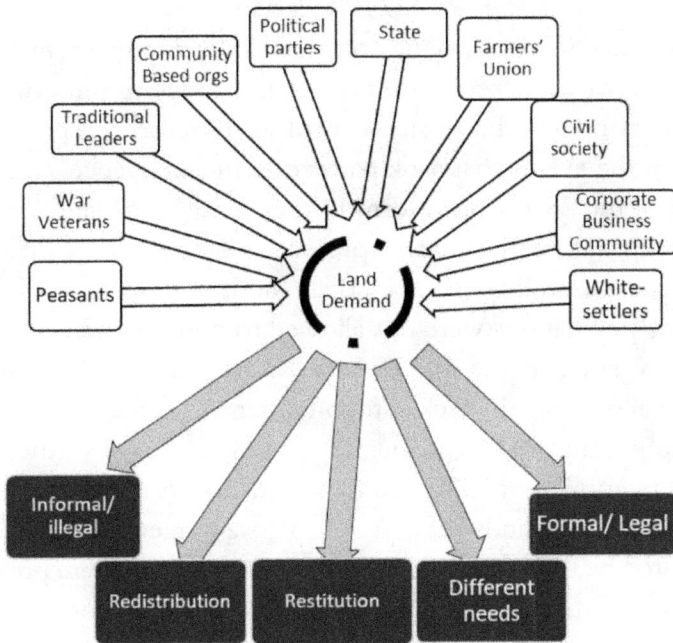

Fig. 1. Forms and sources of agricultural land demand in Zimbabwe Source: Adapted from Sam Moyo, various writings.

Moyo highlights how each source of demand has a different power or influence in the land markets. Different forms of demand can be linked but cannot be tied exclusively to one source. For example, traditional authorities may be heavily linked to demands for restitution, but it may also apply pressure for redistribution. The social, political, and economic dimensions (goals and ideology) of each particular grouping determine the type and extent of demand thereof (Moyo & Matondi, 2004). Before the reforms, land markets in Zimbabwe were dominated by a minority of white settlers exercising private property rights. Moyo discusses the different degrees of power and goals of the above-mentioned sources of demand within the context of 1) the socialist policies initially adopted in Zimbabwe (1980–1990), 2) the liberalization of the economy, and 3) the adoption of the FTLRP.

Structure of Land Markets from 1980 to 1997

The FTLRP was not a static policy but a continuum set in motion by the arrival of white settlers in the 1890s through to the 1960s (the land alienation period). A number of land reform experts have focused on the events that took place after independence, and some even isolate the 2000 land reform in their analysis of land reforms. After Europeans had settled in present day Zimbabwe, their new government controlled land markets and, in most cases, local indigenous populations were not allowed to purchase freehold land. It was only later, in the 1930s, that Native Purchase Areas were created to allow a small black elite to participate in the land markets. Beginning in the 1930s, through a number of laws (the Land Apportionment Act of 1930, the Land Husbandry Act of 1931, and the Tribal Trust Lands of 1965), oversize tracts of land were appropriated by the white settlers and converted to private property, creating a dualistic agrarian structure. This means the contemporary land question in Zimbabwe originated in geo-political, economic, social and demographic factors as well as in the current widespread global imperative (Moyo, 1992).

In 1980, the government faced the task of trying to correct the existing imbalance, which was deeply imbedded along racial and class lines. Approximately 70,000 white settlers controlled 70% of the agricultural land, while a group of black indigenous people 100 times as large had access to 15% of relatively less-productive lands (Moyo, 2000a). In this section, we discuss the pre-FTLRP attempts to redistribute land under different economic models and, hence, separate the discussion into two sections: 1980 to 1997. Later years are discussed in next section.

Economic model and sources of land demand (1980–1990)

In the first decade following independence, the government sought to access and control land within the framework set by the 1980 LHC agreement. From 1980 to 1985, the sovereign state of Zimbabwe was still a fledgling state, so understanding the land tenure system it had inherited proved to be a Herculean task (Herbst, 1987 in Moyo & Skalness, 1990). Government policy was heavily skewed toward supporting large-scale commercial production, even though it was buying land and redistributing it to black families; this formed a contradiction in policy (Mandaza, 1985). During this period, according to some scholars, the LSCF had power and influence through the state (which was upholding the LHC constitution) and through the historically institutionalized myths of the superiority of large-scale over small scale producers (Weiner et al., 1985; Musimbo, 2005). Moyo (1992) refuted this, because small-scale farming was not being supported in the same way. In addition to the Communal Lands Act of 1981, the government passed the Land Acquisition Act (1985) to speed up market-based land reform. This act secured the right of first refusal on any land to the government; thus, before any land was put up for sale in Zimbabwe, it first had to be offered to the government. This had only a limited effect, as the few lands supplied through this means was of poor quality and priced artificially high. Land redistribution in the unfettered markets was profiting the white settlers even more, even while it delayed land redistribution and re-established white settler control in both land markets and financial markets.

More white settlers, the white elite, and foreign companies who had the funds, also bought huge tracts of land through the government for wildlife and tourism. These groups of people presented themselves as a powerful source of effective demand for land in the 1980s (Table 1). In the period from 1980 to 1996, only a small black elite managed to purchase land from the market through private loans secured from such institutions as the Agricultural Finance Cooperation (AFC). However, other black Zimbabweans, traditional authorities, and the Zimbabwe National War Veterans Association (WVA) were excluded from the land markets. The force of their agency to access land was not yet radicalized. It is noteworthy that the access of women to land at this stage was extremely low. Even in the white settler farms, women only owned less than 5% of the title deeds, and land markets were extremely male dominated. However, Moyo pointed out that even though the resulting political pressure was not enough to radicalize the land question, it did manage to keep it the agenda through the ESAP era. Furthermore, the would-be salient voices of the WVA were muted, and Civil

Society Organizations (CSOs) were also in a dormant stage during these times (Table 1).

The black elite were also suppressed to some extent, although the majority purchased land outside the land redistribution program (Moyo, 2002a).

Table 1. Source, type, and effectiveness of land demand 1980-1997

Period	Source	Demand type	Influence/Power
1980-1990 (Later SAP)	White settlers	Tenure security	Low
	State	Redistribution	High
	Peasants	Redistribution	High
	ZNWVA	Redistribution	High
1990-1997 (ESAP)	White Setlers	Tenure security	High
	Foreign capital	Leases, Purchase	High
	State	Redistribution	High
	Peasants	Redistribution, Tenure security	Medium
	ZNWVA	Redistribution, Tenure security	Medium

Source: Adapted from Moyo (various writings)

Consequently, the state led the demand for market-based land reform, but it was limited by the LHC until its expiration in 1990. The government was expected to gain control of the land-delivery channels once LHC had passed. By 1990, only 70,000 families had been resettled, out of a target of 160,000, on 7% of arable lands. Funding from the UK, Germany, and the United States of America did not flow to the government, as agreed in the LHC. By 1988, the flow of funds had been drastically reduced, with only £44 million being received amid tighter restrictions set by the conservative UK government. In addition to allowing the white settlers to set the price of the land they wished to sell, the LHC agreement gave them the right to choose what currency they preferred to be paid in. This further complicated and delayed the land market transactions, given the shortages of foreign currency that were rampant at that time. The result was stunted progress in land redistribution from 1980 to 1997.

Economic model and sources of land demand (1990–1996)

The turn of the first decade saw the expiration of the LHC agreement and adoption of a new economic production model, as the government announced that it had adopted the WB-funded ESAP. Under pressure to reduce economic stagnation and rising unemployment, the GoZ erroneously opened up the economy and reduced public spending and subsidies, which worsened social infrastructure and gave the private sector complete control of the economy. The effect of this in the land market was a 180° shift of focus from redistribution to purely market-based transactions, which was even worse than under the LHC agreement. At this stage, the government was unclear about the implications of continued land redistribution (the Land Acquisition Act of 1992-LAA, which sought to acquire land through compulsion); at the same time, they followed a market-based economy mode of production. On paper, the LAA granted the ability to expedite redistribution. It gave the government powers to compulsorily acquire land, pay compensation on non-market basis, limit the size of large-scale farms, introduce a land tax, and introduce a system of land designation (to enable systematic land acquisition). Dube & Midgley (2008) argue that the LAA would have had the potential to hasten land reform had it been supported by the local farmers, donors, and the international community. Instead, it was ridiculed and, following the recommendations of the IMF and World Bank, support was re-focused on large-scale commercial production. Land redistribution was shelved during ESAP as the focus shifted to the implementation of the economic reforms, under supervision from the Bretton Woods institutions (Moyo, 2014: 2). We also note the effect of this policy on land use, as more land-use options presented themselves through tourism, wildlife, and preservation of bio-diversity (leading to land-grabbing).

Moyo & Skalness (1990) stressed three more factors acting against an increased focus on radicalized land markets: 1) the influential party elite who were purchasing land at an alarming rate, such that adopting land reform policies would go against their interests, 2) the coming together of the two parties ZANU and ZAPU in 1987 (institutional/structural forces) de-radicalized the land reform movement, and 3) the continued economic crisis extinguished any thoughts of state-led radical land reform. By 1995, the prospects of a state-led reform looked grim. By 1996, agency from below emerged, increases in the rates of peasants squatting on commercial farms, land occupations, popular protests, armed confrontations, and resource poaching as a form of agency against a state unwilling to do redistributive land reform became widespread (Moyo, 2000a).

By 1997, ESAP had torn through the land markets, causing disaster and untold mayhem to the lives of the rural poor by increasing differentiation in land use, labour, and commodity marketing (disregarding the 1992–1995 drought) (Moyo, 2000b). The state withdrew from the land markets, reduced extension and subsidies. The opening up of the economy unlocked access to the land markets for foreign capital and the white elite, alienating land further from the general populace. More black business capitalists joined the white settlers in their quest to access land. CSOs and CBOs were still silent at this stage (Table 1). The farmer organizations also failed to incorporate the peasants' voices, as in most cases these were formed by white master-farmers who opposed land redistribution. Suddenly realizing the limited options available through neo-liberal markets, the state and various stakeholders in the land markets began discussing other ways of rapidly redistributing land, including land restitution and state-led land reform.

Land Markets and Reform Policies, 1997–2010

Although ESAP was officially abandoned in 2001, the government began to move away from it in 1996. Budgetary support from the UK had officially expired. The Labour Party, newly arrived in power, made it clear that it was not going to support further land reform programs through the infamous Clare Short letter (Secretary of State for International Development). The intensity of land squatting, inversions and occupations grew. The WVA, which had been formed in 1989, took it upon themselves to initiate the restructuring of land markets.

Consequently, a number of conferences and meetings were carried out including, inter alia, the well-known 1998 Harare Land

Reform Donor Conference. Prior to the conference, a land task force was established, which saw the implementation of the program and that it adhered to the agreed guidelines. These included identifying farms and publishing a list of them in the Financial Gazette to give time for the farm owners to challenge the process. The government identified 1,471 farms for resettlement. An array of variables, ranging from land under- utilization, multiple farm ownership, derelict land, absentee farm-owners and proximity to communal areas (CAs) were used to identify farms (Moyo, 2000b). This raised concern among a variety of stakeholders leading into the 1998 conference resulting in the concerned parties being brought together to discuss redistribution and resettlement options. At this stage, there were low-key land occupations by CA people as they occupied white farms near them. The state sent the police and sometimes the army to stop these "illegal" occupations.

Sadly, the program failed. It was implemented within a liberalized market that put emphasis on the private property rights of white settlers. Just as in the 1993 and 1995 court cases against the state's compulsory land acquisition program, the landowners challenged and won back 40% of these farms. After this, farm occupations intensified, beginning with the well-known one in the village of Svosve in 1998 and spreading to other areas such as Manicaland, Masvingo, and even Matabeleland (despite poor soils and rainfall for crop production in that area). This time around, the peasants (through the WVA) had amassed political connections and were no longer facing state resistance. While other scholars (Elich, 2002; Human Rights Watch, 2002) viewed this social movement as the work of the powerful elite of the ZANU PF party, Moyo (2000a) opposed it, arguing that the WVA had established itself with the influential elite. Moyo (2000a) maintained that the government, realizing the extent of the land occupations and pressure for land by the poor, had co-opted it into its land acquisition agenda.

Upon realizing this, the international community began to take the Zimbabwe situation seriously. A UK mission was dispatched to Zimbabwe (representing Europe and the United States) to negotiate with Mugabe. A report was created by this mission, which concluded, again, that the government of Zimbabwe was on the verge of appropriating land from white farmers without compensation, a move they had been trying to push through into the constitution ever since the Land Acquisition Act of 1992 (Moyo, 1994; 2000b; Moyo & Yeros, 2007). The 1998 donor conference was subsequently organized to try and mobilize funding to the Zimbabwe government so that it would pay compensation. The property rights that were defined in the constitution in 1980 were still being protected under law, which delayed the compulsory land acquisition process, much to the chagrin of the state, WVA, and elite political leaders, further fuelling radicalism. The WVA, peasants, and the state itself were starting to realize the impracticality of any land reform approaches that respected the private property rights of the white settlers. Moyo argued, in this context, that the intense resistance of the white settlers played a great role in the eventual radical land reform.

Thus, 1997 marked the threshold of land reform strategy in Zimbabwe, given that it raised the question of whether the ruling party and its government could muster serious political resolve to challenge the legacy of settler land and property rights as enshrined in existing legislation and the "rule of law" (Moyo, 2000b).

The 1998 donor conference took place in September. In attendance were representatives of 48 countries and other international donor organizations. The most significant outcome of this conference was the agreement to set up a task force for joint land reform (to launch the second phase of land reform), which the international community and donor agencies would fund. This was an attempt to find a balance between land acquisitions and market-based redistribution (Moyo & Yeros, 2005). Nevertheless, the UK agreed to join but the GoZ had to meet certain conditions, such as a reduction of human rights violations and improvements in the levels of democracy (Hanyama, 2009). However, in doing this, it failed to understand how these issues where part of the national land question. The donor conference crumbled.

By 1999, GoZ still was not able to smoothly redistribute the remaining 60% of farms, as more court challenges came. This unified the peasants, the state, WVA, party officials, and traditional authorities behind the land reform agenda. For the first time since independence, the WVA had effective power and was grounded politically, making it a very powerful agent for reform (see Table 2). However, the country was still officially following a neo-liberal economic model, which meant, to some extent, that the government was obliged to balance the interests of some key white and black capitalist farmers (Moyo, 2002a). Although more discussion with the international community ensued from 1998–2001, the prospects for a further market-led land-delivery system looked grim. Among other conferences, Mugabe met with then UN Secretary General Kofi Annan in September 2000, which saw the UN technical assessment team arrive in Harare.

Table 2. Source, type, and effectiveness of land demand 1997–2014

Period	Sources	Demand type	Influence
1997–2007 State controlled	White settlers	Tenure security	Low
	State	Redistribution	High
	Peasants	Redistribution	High
	ZNWVA	Redistribution	High
2008–2014 Re-liberalization	Foreign capital	Tenure security, Leases, Purchase	High
	State	Redistribution	High
	Peasants	Redistribution, Tenure security	Medium
	ZNWVA	Redistribution, Tenure security	Medium

Source: Adapted from Moyo (various writings)

Eventually, they concluded that the framework for land reform was in place, but the process faced huge legal challenges, which would slow down any reform (Moyo, 2002a). Further inquiries through Obasanjo culminated in the Zimbabwe issue being tabled in the Commonwealth, eventually coming to be discussed by a team of nine ministers from member states (including the UK) in Abuja. The result was the Abuja commitments, which, again were halted by UK as it refused to honour the agreed terms of the meeting. Eventually, the UN and all donors advised the Zimbabwe government to delay the FTLRP indefinitely. The Zimbabwe government refused.

To this end, the GoZ attempted and failed to push a referendum to amend the constitution to allow it to seize farms without compensation. Interestingly, NGOs and CBOs came to life here, on the opposite pole of the land reform agenda. Most NGOs failed to admit the reality of the need for land reform, and others criticized it without giving alternatives.

Fast Track Land Reform Program (2000–2010)

In the wake of the failed donor's conference, failed LRP P2, and a rejected referendum (1997–2000), small cases of land occupations, farm inversions, and squatting then developed into full-scale occupations that would last until 2003–2004. Once the peasants and WVA put the FTLRP into motion, the state responded with a new land acquisition law in 2000, which finally removed the need to pay compensation for the invaded farms. In this respect, a state-led economic model of production was adopted, which saw the GoZ reasserting authority throughout the agrarian markets from input distribution to output marketing. Between the first rejection of the referendum in February and July 2000, the GoZ engaged WVA, the elite of the ruling party, landowners and donors again (the UK in April and the UNDP in June) to find amicable ways of performing the inevitable land reform. This proved futile and resulted in an escalation of confrontation leading to the full-scale state led FTLRP by August 2000 (Moyo, 2002a). As highlighted, power and control over land markets was in the hands of the masses by May 2000. Even the GoZ and some in the elite of the party feared losing control over the situation (Moyo & Matondi, 2004). The WVA has been described by scholars as a toothless bulldog; however, it managed to keep the land question on the agenda. It radicalized the question by mobilizing grassroots support from the congested CAs (Table 2).

This highlights WVA's ability to engage with the general populace to garner support at the same time as developing political alliances with the political elite, thus guaranteeing the success of land reforms (Moyo, 2002b). The state later gained control by creating District, Provincial, and National Land Committees, composed of representatives of the land demand drivers (WVA, government officials, national security officials, party officials, and local traditional authorities), through which land seekers could apply for land.

Although the WVA was already carrying out land occupations, officially, the FTLRP was launched in July 2000 as part of the second phase of the land reform. It was a completely different creature from the previous land-delivery systems. It was ideologically different, in that it no longer respected the property rights of the white settlers. This reform was institutionally supported by the state, as seen through the addition of constitutional amendments that allow for no compensation, removed legal challenges to land occupiers, and provide protection for them from eviction (Rural Land Occupiers Act 2000). Some of these statutes relied on presidential decrees vested in the Presidential Powers Act to be passed. Additionally, the FTLRP was to be taken up in an accelerated manner, speeding up land identification, planning, demarcation, and resettlement of the people. This program, in a break with the past, had provisions to provide basic primary (access roads, dip tanks, and boreholes) and some secondary infrastructure (schools and clinics). It was launched countrywide to improve comprehensiveness and even redistribution in all provinces, using only locally sourced resources (Hanyama, 2009). However, as with the previous reform program, the FTLRP hinged on achieving equitable racial land ownership, poverty reduction, and increased productivity, which formed the socioeconomic objectives of the reform. Furthermore, it targeted the decongestion of CAs, improving their land access, and the formation of an indigenous commercial farming sector (Moyo, 2002a; Hanyama, 2009). The allocation procedures were affected by the land occupations, which started after the 1998 donor conference. The majority of the land seekers who took part in the land occupations were later officially given usufruct rights (permissive) under the A1 resettlement tenure model, with land sizes ranging from 1–30 ha, depending on the natural region (NR). The other resettlement tenure system was the A2 model, which was for those who proved that they had the means to utilize more land. In general, there are two forms of land holding in this model, the one exercised on lands with 30–150ha (subject to NR) and those on lands with 150–400 ha. The A2 model beneficiaries hold leasehold tenure title. The FTLRP also left some former white-owned LSCF and some large corporate farms untouched if they were deemed strategic farms. These are still held through freehold tenure title.

The results of the FTLRP have been the focus of debate for the past decade, as scholars and government policy makers grapple with the task of fully understanding its nature and implications. Moyo (2014) argues that the exclusive use of economic variables to measure the impact of the reform is inadequate and that there is a need for deeper social and class analysis in addition to economic analysis. He proposed the use of a tri-modal agrarian structure. Utilization of this tri-modal structure enables analysis of the land reform based on such variables as land size (adjusted to reflect differences in quality and the agro-ecological potential of the land), the tenure system that the land was under, the control of land holdings, access to markets (support), accumulation, labour, technical capacity, and organization of production. Analysis of these variables enabled the classification of the beneficiaries into peasants (1.3 million), small-to-medium capitalist farmers (30,000), and large-to-corporate capitalist farmers (250) (Moyo, 2005b: 42). As alluded to previously, differences in these have implications for the mobilization of labour and incomes. By 2010, around ten million hectares of land had been redistributed during the FTLRP to over 170,000 households under the A2 (commercially oriented, 13% of the land) and A1 (small scale, 70% of the land) settlement models. This was 10 times the land and 2.5 times the number of beneficiaries as in the 1980–1999 reform, all done in a quarter of the time. To understand the emerging tri-modal agrarian structure, we examine some approaches used to gain access to the land during this period, using data from a household survey conducted by SMAIAS (2013–2015). The data were collected in six districts, representing the five main agro-ecological zones or Natural Region (NR) in Zimbabwe, from NRI (wet region ideal for crop production) to NRV (dry region ideal for livestock production). Analysis explores this tri-modal approach, examining data collected from the three emerging settlement types after the FTLRP (A1, A2, and the CA). In the sections that follow, we present evidence to support Moyo's argument that the FTLRP and the pressure for land-market reform and property-rights reform for land emanated from below. The characteristics of the people who gained land resemble the characteristics of the groups of people who, as the bulk of Moyo's writing makes clear, were in the forefront of land demand before the FTLRP.

Land access approaches and patterns

The land markets are now dominated by peasants (on less than 10 ha per farm), who are settled on 73% of Zimbabwe's arable land, followed by small-to-medium capitalist farmers (30 to 150 ha), settled on 9% of the arable land. The level of land quality and quantity, off-farm income, class, influence, and gender and age structures differ among peasant farms, which indicates a further differentiated control of the land markets (Moyo & Matondi, 2004; Moyo et al., 2014). SMAIAS survey data showed that the land access method depended on the type of land demanded. Farm occupations were more common in the A1 sector (46.4% A1, 12.5% A2), while the A2 sector was dominated by official allocations (84.8% in A2, 48.7% in A1). The majority of the A1 beneficiaries took part in the land inversions before the official FTLRP started and they were eventually regularized. There were also beneficiaries in both the A1 (0.4%) and A2 (0.7%) sectors (Fig. 2) who claimed to have purchased the land during the FTLRP period, confirming the existence of informal agricultural land markets.

Therefore, across the two settlements, only 33.5% of the beneficiaries accessed land through occupation and the majority's land was formally allocated (62.5%). In general, for the majority of land seekers, access to land in the A2 was heavily linked to associational brokering, while that of the A1 was mainly participation-based, coupled with negotiations with local land authorities. However, participation in the land inversions, engagement with local land authorities and WVA did not guarantee land access. It took a great deal of dedication and commitment: beneficiaries often had to spend several nights camped in the forest in what became known as "bases," awaiting re-allocation from District Land Committees (Moyo, 2011a; Sadomba, 2011).

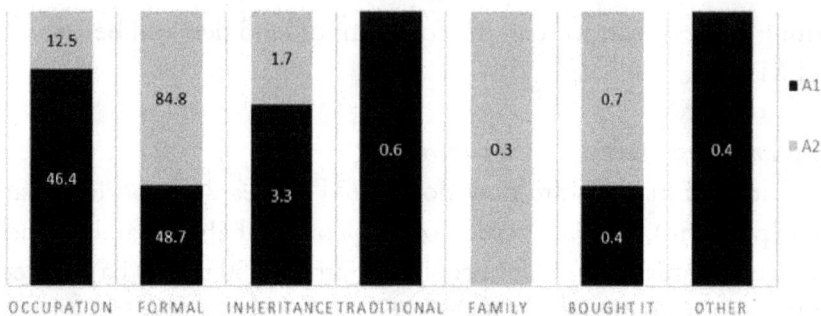

Fig. 2. Mode of land access for landholders by type of settlement Source: SMAIAS Household Survey (2013–2014).

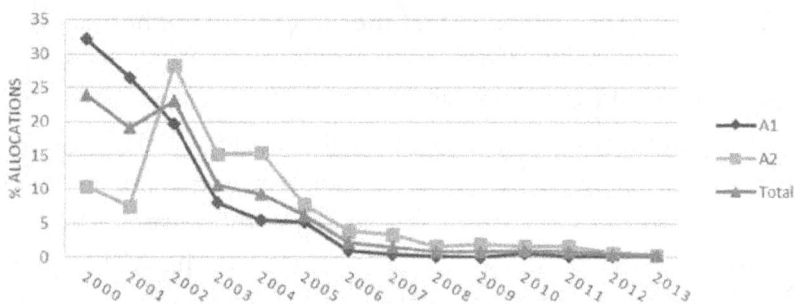

Fig. 3. Scale of land allocation from 2000 to 2013 Source: SMAIAS Household Survey (2013–2014).

Periodization of land access

The scale and magnitude of the land reform generally reveals the extent of the demand for land in the Zimbabwe land markets. From the SMAIAS data, it is clear that approximately 75.7% of the land redistribution occurred between 2000 and 2003, with the remainder taking place from 2004 to 2015. Interestingly, land demands were differentiated in different regions of the country, with some regions such as the Mangwe district, having completed 94.5% of its redistribution by 2005. Mangwe is in Matabeleland, which is NRV, and it receives very low rainfall. However, it was an area that was at the forefront of land occupations and land demands from 2000–2003 (Fig. 3). The same situation can also be said about the Kwekwe district, which is in Midlands province and is predominately NRIII. To a greater extent, these two districts were the base for the ZAPU party before the unity accord of 1987. This finding seems to confirm Moyo's (1992) argument that the unity-accord between the two political parties de-radicalized the land reform agenda in Matabeleland. Other regions came late to the party, as evidenced in the Midlands, where the highest number of land allocations occurred after 2004. A higher proportion of land allocations that took place from 2004 were in the A2 rather than in the A1 sector, a situation that obtained in all the districts surveyed (Fig. 3). The rate of land allocations per year was highest in the first three years of the FTLRP. The pace of land allocations between 2000 and 2002 was faster for A1 (inversions) and, later, the use of formal channels took centre stage from 2002 onwards. Although occupations or informal allocations persisted up to 2006, their scale was significantly lower.

Socioeconomic characteristics of land beneficiaries

Media reports and academic literature have suggested that the politically connected elite, WVA members, and their immediate families were the only beneficiaries of the land reform. A socioeconomic analysis of the beneficiaries is necessary to understand who they are beyond the war veterans or political elite rhetoric.

Geographic origins of land beneficiaries

The origins of beneficiaries played a significant role in the type and amount of land they could access. As Moyo (2000b) noted, the manner in which the 1,471 farms were chosen in 1997 and 1998 depended on their distance from CAs, to reduce the cost of relocation. Most land occupations occurred in farms close to CAs, as in the occupations of the villages of Masvingo and Svosve during the initial stages of the FTLRP (Cliffe, 2000; Moyo, 2000a). The FTLRP wanted to reduce overcrowding and poverty rates in these areas. For this reason, most land beneficiaries (53.6%) in the SMAIAS 2013–2014 survey came from the CAs (Table 3). Furthermore, the biggest number of land beneficiaries came from CAs within the immediate district (24.8%), followed by those from within the immediate province (19.6%), while those from other provinces were 9.2% of land beneficiaries within this group. Hence the distance from the area of origin to the desired or demanded piece of land bore heavily on the extent and the scope of land demand in land markets. These questions the widely held belief that most land was taken by the political elite, who predominately stayed in the diaspora.

Urbanites commanded a significant proportion of the participants in the FTLRP process, as 29.7% of those resettled originated from urban areas. Here, it is noteworthy to highlight the role of the tri-modal approach, since it was a deliberate state policy to create a new agrarian middle class. This state-led reform policy was able to articulate protests across the rural-urban spaces and simultaneously radicalize the working-class (Moyo, 2011a). The third-largest group of people came from former large-scale commercial farms, accounting for 9.3% of the land beneficiaries (90% of them coming from the same district). This group of people mainly included former farm workers in formerly white-owned farms.

Table 3. Place of origin by settlement type (2013-2014)

Place of Origin	No.	%	No.	%	No.	%
Total CA	311	63.9	102	36.0	413	53.6
CA in this district	147	30.2	44	15.5	191	24.8
CA in this province	114	23.4	37	13.1	151	19.6
CA from other provinces	50	10.3	21	7.4	71	9.2
Total LSCF	56	11.5	16	5.7	72	9.3
LSCF in this district	52	10.7	13	4.6	65	8.4
LSCF in this province	4	0.8	3	1.1	7	0.9
Diaspora	1	0.2	0	0.0	1	0.1
Urban area	88	18.0	140	49.4	228	29.7
Place of employment	14	2.9	15	5.3	29	3.8
Old resettlement	13	2.7	5	1.8	18	2.3
Other places	4	0.8	5	1.8	9	1.2
Total	487	100.0	283	100.0	770	100.0

Source: SMAIAS Household Survey
Note: CA: Communal Areas; LSCF: Large Scale Commercial Farms

Interestingly, some media reports suggested that the program only benefited rural dwellers who supported the ruling party. Furthermore, some studies argue that land could only be accessed around each individual's area of origin (this was only true for farm workers); on the contrary, people could generally apply for or take part in land occupations as was they saw fit.

Family structure (size and membership) of beneficiaries

The driving force behind the demand for land in the markets is also visible in the sizes of beneficiaries' families, as they sought to secure land to subdivide or bequeath to family. The plurality of households from the CA in the A1 sector generally had a family size range of 3–5 members per farm beneficiary (36.1%), while the second most common range was 6–7 members (26.7% of respondents), followed by 8–9 members per household (14.9%) (Fig. 4). Generally, A2 farms relied mostly on hired labour and had fewer members in their households than the CA and the A1 (SMAIAS, 2014). At the extreme end of the A2, in the CA there were larger families than in the resettled areas.

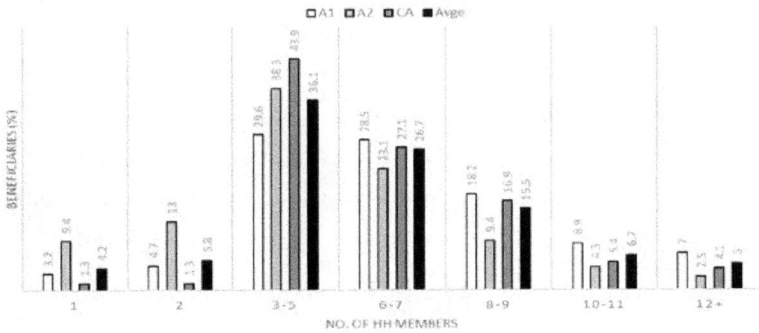

Fig. 4. Household size by model
Source: SMAIAS Household Survey (2013–2014).

Educational levels of land beneficiaries

Survey results revealed that the educational level of the participants of the land markets varied from no formal education to having a tertiary degree. A plurality (43.4%) of those who took part in land resettlement had a basic level of education (ordinary level), followed by primary education (33.1%), and tertiary education (13.9%). Approximately 7.8% of participants had no formal education (Table 4). Level of education also affects planning, power and influence in societal processes: that is, it can be a source of inclusion or exclusion (SMAIAS, 2014)

125

Table 4. Education levels attained by plot owner for newly resettled farmers

Education level attained	A1		A2		CA		Total	
	No.	%	No.	%	No.	%	No.	%
No formal education	45	9.6	8	2.7	32	10.2	85	7.8
Total primary	188	39.8	45	15.2	125	39.7	358	33.1
Some primary education	104	22.0	16	5.4	68	21.6	188	17.3
Completed primary education	84	17.8	29	9.8	57	18.1	170	15.8
Total 'O' level	205	43.4	118	39.9	148	46.9	471	43.4
Some secondary education	84	17.8	41	13.9	65	20.6	190	17.5
Completed secondary	121	25.6	77	26.0	83	26.3	281	25.9
Total 'A' level	5	1.1	14	4.7	0	0.0	19	1.8
Total tertiary	29	6.1	111	37.3	10	3.2	150	13.9
College education	21	4.4	42	14.2	8	2.5	71	6.6
University degree	7	1.5	69	23.3	2	0.6	78	7.2
Vocational training	1	0.2	0	0.0	0	0.0	1	0.1
Total	472	100.0	296	100.0	315	100.0	1,083	100.0

Source: SMAIAS Household Survey (2013–2014).

Employment profiles of beneficiaries

The 1980–1990 land reform targeted the unemployed, ex-combatants, and ex-farm workers in an effort to provide them with alternative sources of livelihood. This has been criticized by proponents of market-based approaches, who argue that the unemployed are not in a position to productively utilize the land, because they lack capital and the ability to access the capital. Moyo & Skalness (1990), however, argued that to restructure agrarian markets effectively, granting the general populace access to land was extremely necessary. However, land reform on its own was not sufficient; institutional, policy, and financial support were equally important.

Table 5. Previous employment status of landholders

	A1 No.	A1 %	A2 No.	A2 %	CA No.	CA %	Total No.	Total %
Never been employed	204	42.8	57	19.2	158	50.2	419	38.5
Total previously employed	201	42.1	155	52.2	86	27.3	442	40.6
Before 1995	33	(16.4)	16	(10.3)	21	(24.4)	70	(15.8)
Previously 1996 to 1999	33	(16.4)	17	(11.0)	10	(11.6)	60	(13.6)
employed 2000 to 2006	83	(41.3)	76	(49.0)	20	(23.3)	179	(40.5)
2007 to 2014	52	(25.9)	46	(29.7)	35	(40.7)	133	(30.1)
Currently employed	72	15.1	85	28.6	71	22.5	228	20.9
Grand total	**477**	**100.0**	**297**	**100.0**	**315**	**100.0**	**1,089**	**100.0**

Source: SMAIAS Household Survey (2013–2014).

In the SMAIAS household survey, a plurality of the respondents had been previously employed (40.6%) while a slightly lower number (38.5%) had never been employed prior to accessing land. Approximately 20.9% of the households were currently employed (Table 5). This gives an indication of the extent of demand for land as seen through higher proportions of people who took part in land resettlement programs despite being in employment. This analysis helps us to understand the levels of skill, size of networks, extent of habits built over time, and depth of the resource bases of the landholders. The largest proportion of farmers who had never been formally employed was found in the CA (50.2%) and A1 (42.8%); they were being given a source of livelihood by the land reform program.

On the other hand, the majority of the A2 land participants (52.2%) had been previously employed. Further disaggregation of previously employed households shows that a greater number of these stopped working in 2000–2006 in both the two resettlement models (A1 [41.3%] and A2 [49.0%]). This period was the farm establishment phase, when farmers were settling into their new land, which may indicate that a number of farmers left their employment to be full-time farmers, especially in the A2 sector.

Gender composition of land holders

Women's ownership of, and access to, land has been a contentious issue in the literature (Moyo et al., n.d.). Women's role in agriculture cannot be overstated, as they are at the forefront of virtually all farm activities, from household production to reproduction. However, there remains a mismatch between their role in the sector and their level of land access, a situation obtaining even during the era of the white settlers, when women owned just under 5% of the arable land (Rugube et al., 2003; Moyo, 2005b). In the old resettlement areas, 5% of the land was held by black women in their own right. Some studies have argued that women had access to land through their spouses (83% of women respondents in the SMAIAS survey, Fig. 5), since most men who have land have wives who have equal access to the land (new tenure laws require registration of the wife [wives] if a land holder is married). However, this is open to varied interpretations, as differences in rights exist between different households: one wife may have access to the land while another does not.

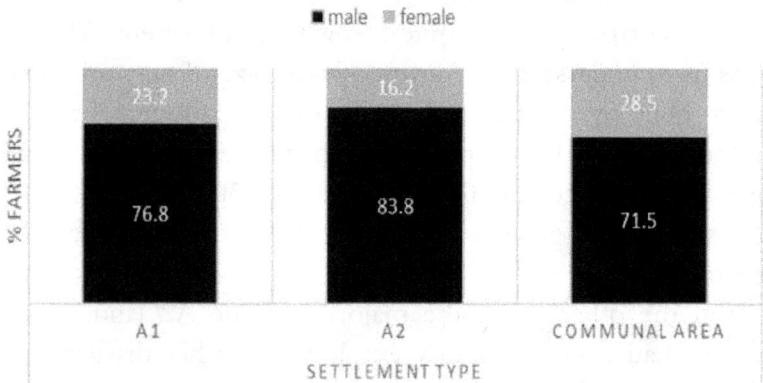

Fig. 5. Gender of plot owner by settlement type Source: SMAIAS Household Survey (2013–2014).

By 2010, women's access to land was estimated to be between 12% and 18% (Buka, 2002; Utete, 2003; GoZ, 2007). Furthermore, access to A2 land presented increased constraints, as beneficiaries needed proof of ability to produce before they could access the land. This discouraged the participation of women, who are historically disadvantaged and denied access. Some women entered their husband or son's names when applying for land to ensure access during the land reform (Buka, 2002; Utete, 2003; GoZ, 2007).

In the SMAIAS survey, women accounted for 19.7% of all land beneficiaries who received land in their own right in the resettlement areas. As expected, the percentage of women beneficiaries was higher in the A1 (23.2%) than in the A2 (16.2%). A greater number of women accessing land were widows (59.7%), followed by those who received land in their own right but were monogamously married (22.6%) (Table 6).

Table 6. Gender of landholder by marital status and settlement type

	A1 male		A1 female		A2 male		A2 female		CA male		CA female		Total male		Total female	
	No.	%	No.	%	No.	%	No.	%	No.	%	No.	%	No.	%	No.	%
Monogamy	288	79.1	31	28.4	223	90.3	18	36.7	184	81.5	7	7.8	695	83.0	56	22.6
Polygamy	44	12.1	5	4.6	12	4.9	1	2.0	21	9.3	3	3.3	77	9.2	9	3.6
Single	6	1.6	4	3.7	3	1.2	4	8.2	5	2.2	1	1.1	14	1.7	9	3.6
Divorced	9	2.5	9	8.3	4	1.6	5	10.2	1	0.4	12	13.3	14	1.7	26	10.5
Widowed	17	4.7	60	55.0	5	2.0	21	42.9	15	6.6	67	74.5	37	4.4	148	59.7
Total	364	100	109	100	247	100	49	100	226	100	90	100	837	100	248	100

Source: SMAIAS Household Survey (2013–2014).

Emerging Land Markets after the FTLRP

The demand for land from around 2007 onwards took a new twist, especially in light of the global food crisis, which saw global markets pushing for large-scale oriented food production systems to ensure global food security. There was still great demand for land among local people, as can be seen in the ever-growing list of applications for it. By 2009, the government had managed to identify 760,000ha, which was demanded by 100,000 land seekers. Post-FTLRP, there has been a resurgence of foreign capital into Zimbabwe land markets through collusion with government, the elite, CSOs, and MNC (land grabbing). These will be discussed in this section. Emerging markets are characterized by large-scale land deals as well as localized land sharing, leasing, and renting.

Agricultural Land Markets after FTLRP

The FTLRP nationalized all agricultural land; therefore, no land sales can occur under the currently available land tenure. However, new forms of local and international land deals emerged post-reform, signalling a new dimension in the land markets (Moyo, 2009).

Informal land market

The nationalization of land brought with it a new tenure system that allows no land transactions of any nature without state approval, thereby making any subsequent land transactions informal. However, these markets have persisted.

Table 7. Land sharing by Settlment Type

Is there anyone else with access to your land?

Settlement Type	A1		A2		CA		Total	
	No.	%	No.	%	No.	%	No.	%
Yes	36	7.5	21	7.1	7	2.2	64	5.9
No	442	92.5	274	92.9	309	97.8	1,025	94.1
Total	478	100	295	100	316	100.0	1,089	100

Source: Household Survey(2013-2014)

The extent of this market depends on a variety of factors, including inter-settlement class struggles.

SMAIAS (2014) underscores the difficulty of collecting data on informal deals and land sharing arrangements. However, approximately 5.9% of the respondents to the SMAIAS survey openly agreed that they were sharing their land, and the numbers were highest in the resettlement areas, A1 (7.5%) and A2 (7.1%) (Table 7). It is very important to note that these findings may grossly underestimate the occurrence of informal land markets post FTLRP. This is an area that requires further study.

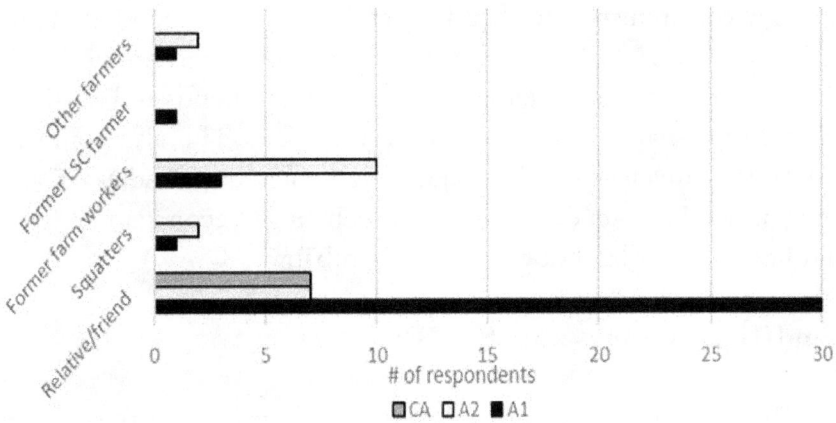

Fig. 6. Non-farm owners with access to land by settlement type Source: SMAIAS Household Survey (2013–2014).

In the A1 sector, most land sharing was done with relatives and/or friends (83.3%), followed by former farm workers (8.3%), a situation also obtaining in the land sharing deals in the CAs. In the A2 sector, with its larger amounts of land, 47.6% of land sharers were former farm workers, followed by relatives and/or friends (33.3%). In land sharing in the A2 sector, where the plurality of the landholders shares their land with their employees, access to land may be tied to the provision of labour on the same farm. Resettled farmers engage in these land deals to incentivize their workers. Consequently, A2 farmers were found to share land, mostly, with farmworkers, while A1 farmers mostly shared and leased out land to friends and relatives (Fig. 6).

Informal interviews show that a significant number of white former farmers and foreign capital owners (South African, Chinese, etc.) are working with black farmers on their allocated pieces of land to produce tobacco, wheat, and soybean. The presence of foreign capital in these markets had accentuated government fears of a reversal of the land redistribution process. The government has tried to re-gain control of these informal land market activities by formulating land-sharing policies that require that land-sharing deals be done through the Ministry of Lands. Although the rural lands act (20:18) has provisions for sharecropping and the leasing of land

131

through the ministry, further informal interviews found that the majority of these deals were informal (the ministry was not notified). Overall, 68.8% of those sharing land did so with friends and relatives, while 20.3% shared land with their farm workers. This also points to the feared, unanswered land question in agrarian studies. These informal land market deals necessitate debating a second land reform and LSCF-sector land downsizing in Zimbabwe.

Land Tenure Issues after FTLRP

The reform program drastically reconfigured property rights to land, which has had huge effects on the land markets. Contemporary tenure issues have mainly been driven by foreign capital pushing for the re-establishment of private property rights, as they argue that the reform rendered land as dead capital (De Soto, 2000). However, it is not a given that titling can automatically lead to success in the aftermath of the FTLRP, as it could also lead to increased class and racial clashes, which would depress economic and social development and trust in property titles once again (see Martin, 2008). Some farms are still held under freehold tenure, especially the farms that were termed strategic for the economy during the FTLRP. In the SMAIAS household survey, 83% of the resettled farmers held offer letters (permissive tenure) as ownership documents, while 13.3% and 2.6% are reported to have already-processed permits and 99-year leases, respectively (Fig. 7). From the initial stages of the FTLRP, the GoZ has tried to provide constitutional provisions to protect land beneficiaries and the process of land redistribution (e.g., constitutional amendment 97 of 2006, which removed the need for payment of compensation for repossessed land) as well as those who recognized the ownership rights of the land seekers who took part in the initial farm occupations.

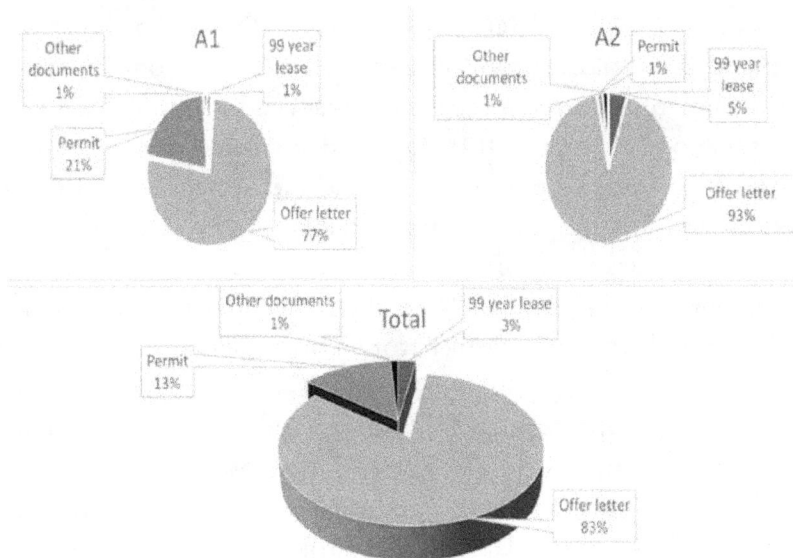

Fig. 7. Type of tenure document possessed by landholders Source: SMAIAS Household Survey (2013–2014).

Table 8. Type of tenure-related conflicts faced

Settlement Type	A1		A2		CA		Total	
	No.	%	No	%	No.	%	No.	%
Boundary dispute	26	51.0	47	65.2	7	38.9	80	56.7
Access to natural resources	1	2.0	4	5.6	4	22.2	9	6.4
Access to infrastructure	1	2.0	1	1.4	0	0.0	2	1.4
Inheritance	2	3.9	0	0.0	4	22.2	6	4.3
Ownership of farm/plot	20	39.2	19	26.4	1	5.6	40	28.4
Other types of conflict	1	1.9	1	1.4	2	11.1	4	2.8
Total who faced conflicts	51	100.0	72	100.0	18	100.0	141	100.0

Source: SIMAIAS Household Survey(2013-2014)

The anticipated illegal land-market deals have basically been the driving force for the GoZ's stance on issuing private property ownership rights to newly resettled farmers. It is feared that the demand for land by global capital will increase land values and, as a result of decreasing profits for small-scale producers, farmers might be forced to sell off their land (Pinckney & Kimuyu, 1994), thus reversing land reform. Land-tenure issues remain contested, especially between the GoZ and the private sector (the agricultural finance stakeholders), in terms of the level of security of tenure in current lease and offer letters in agricultural land markets. Although the majority of resettled farmers express confidence in the tenure documents they hold as proof of ownership, they are concerned that these documents are not accepted by financial institutions as proof of ownership (SMAIAS, 2014). Demand for land tenure has been pushed off to some extent by the middle and upper classes of land beneficiaries (Moyo, 2011b). Approximately 4% of respondents to the SMAIAS survey reported being threatened with eviction by government officials, while 0.8% of the respondents reported being actually evicted from one farm before being reallocated to another one.

Interestingly, approximately 95% of respondents to the survey had tenure documents, while 5% had no form of government documentation of ownership of land (SMAIAS, 2014). For farmers who faced land-tenure related land conflicts, these conflicts were largely boundary disputes (between farmers, reported by 56.7%) and disagreements over ownership of pieces of land (between farmers and GoZ, reported by 28.4%) (Table 8).

Informal interviews have also shown how class struggles remain at the forefront of certain farmer-to-farmer conflicts, with those farmers who have limited access to resources and no political influence facing more conflicts. Thus, land conflicts also have a gender dimension to them. More female than male farmers faced more conflicts as male neighbours believe they can increase the size of their land holdings by encroaching onto female-owned land. The A2 women landholders are more susceptible to land conflicts, reported by 34%, in comparison to the 10.8% reported in the A1 sector (see SMAIAS, 2014). Other issues raised relating to land tenure include a lack of clarity in the role of traditional authorities, who seem to have extended their authority from the CAs to the resettled areas, complicating the rights that leaseholders or permit holders have over a piece of land.

Large-scale land investments
The GoZ now controls the major part of all land. This gives ultimate power to the state, power that, if misused, may lead to undesirable outcomes. A number of scholars have written on the new

scramble for Africa and highlighted how the state was going to bed with foreign capital. Zimbabwe is no exception when it comes to this, with agreements ranging from tourism partnerships to mining and agriculture. Government-owned land has been leased to a number of foreign investors. Such agreements were in the tourism sector, or various Agricultural and Rural Development Authority (ARDA) farms leased out under the Build, Operate and Transfer Agreements (BOTA). However, the most recent example of this third wave for Zimbabwean land has been the concentration of land for sugarcane production aimed at bio-fuels production, whereby some farmers were moved to accommodate projects in Mashonaland west, Masvingo, and Manicaland. Concerns have been raised about the real motives for these large-scale investments. Some of the farmers affected had been newly resettled. Hence, large-scale land investments are already reversing land reform. Such investments have also come in, disguised as contract farming and/or out-grower systems, as evidenced in some cases in the Chiredzi district (Mazwi & Muchetu, 2015).

Conclusions

Land markets are, and always will be, politicized, consequently justifying government intervention. Moyo's work on land markets, spanning more than 40 years, offered explanations for the trajectory taken by agricultural land markets in terms of who demanded land, what type of demand it was, and how state economic production models affected its land-delivery mechanisms. State intervention has been constrained by LHC agreements and financial and legal systems, which frustrated the peasants, who took it upon themselves to correct historic injustices through extra-market approaches. Nevertheless, the success of these interventions from below depended heavily on collaboration with state apparatus. While it remains a fact that market land transactions should not be eliminated (only regulated), a state-led approach was appropriate and needed to be forged. Moyo's central argument was that market-led land reform, carried out under a market-oriented economic model, will always favour capital, the elite, and white settlers (a minority) at the expense of the peasantry (the majority). Land seekers had varied socioeconomic backgrounds, levels of education, family sizes, political influence, and employment histories determining their placement within Moyo's tri-modal agrarian structure. Land markets in Zimbabwe continue to be highly unpredictable, in part as a result of the re-emergence of demand for land by global capital from 2007 and 2008. This was stimulated by the global food crisis, which culminated in a new scramble for land (Moyo's term) or land grabs. At the household level, demand for land continues to be high, as seen by the rampant land sharing arrangements in the A1 and A2 sectors. There also exist informal land sales between beneficiaries. Beneficiaries derive security from their tenure documents, but this highlights the fact that the need for 99-year leases stems mainly from the need to use them to secure credit from financial institutions. Furthermore, farmers desired these new documents to reduce boundary conflicts.

Market-based land reforms and state-led reform approaches remain the major forms of land-delivery mechanisms in post-independence Zimbabwe. A limited number of beneficiaries have accessed land through informal markets, restitution, inheritance, and/or customary approaches. The Zimbabwe land-delivery markets have proved that a state-led approach flouts liberal political rights (settlers' property rights), reinvents the law, and scores less in terms of efficiency and democracy than market-led land reforms. While market-led reforms respect the existing system of law and property rights, they are extremely slow (the pace of redistribution 1980–1999) and serve the interests of the resourced at the expense of the downtrodden. We have further learned that state-led reforms are able to score higher on redistribution; decongestion of the CAs, women and youth participation, equity and social rights, correction of historical social injustices, and delivering land to the majority in a short space of time, while using minimum resources. For successful state-led land reforms, it is important to understand clearly the limitations and strengths of the economic production model in place, and the magnitude and potential of pressure from below to alter land-delivery systems. Furthermore, land reforms must be complemented with land registration and the provision of financial services to ensure increased productivity. Finally, the strength and limitations of the land delivery channel should be evaluated against the objective of land reform. That is to say, market-led land markets, if adopted, require regulation and, in cases where historical land injustices prevail, state-led interventions become more applicable.

Acknowledgements

This article is based on my paper presented at 'Land, the State and Decolonising the Agrarian Structure in Africa: A Colloquium in Honour of Professor Sam Moyo,' organized at the University of Cape Town, South Africa, on November 28–29, 2016. This colloquium was sponsored by the Japan Society for the Promotion of Science, Grant-in-Aid for Scientific Research (S) '"African Potential" and Overcoming the Difficulties of Modern World: Comprehensive Research That Will Provide a New Perspective for the Future of Humanity' (KAKENHI 16H06318 headed by Motoji Matsuda, Kyoto University), as well as by the University of Cape Town's Research Office (URC).

References

Bojo, J. 1993. Economic valuation of indigenous woodlands. In (P.N. Bradley & K. McNamara, eds.) *Living with Trees: Policies for Forestry Management in Zimbabwe*, pp. 227–242. World Bank Technical Paper, Washington D.C.

Buka, F. 2002. *A Preliminary Audit Report of Land Reform Programme*. Government Printers, Harare.

Cliffe, L. 2000. The politics of land reform in Zimbabwe. In (T.A.S. Bowyer-Bower & C. Stoneman, eds.) *Land Reform in Zimbabwe: Constraints and Prospects*, pp. 35–46. Aldershot, Ashgate.

De Soto, H. 2000. *The Mystery of Capital: Why Capitalism Triumphs in the West and Fails Everywhere Else*. Basic Books, New York.

Dube, M. & R. Midgley 2008. Land reform in Zimbabwe: Context, process, legal and constitutional issues and implications for the SADC region. In (A. Bösl, W. Breytenbach, T. Hartzenberg, C. McCarthy & K. Schade, eds.) *Monitoring Regional Integration in Southern Africa Year Book 2008*, pp. 303–341. Tralac, Stellenbosch.

Elich, G. 2002. Zimbabwe under siege. *Swans*. Online. http://www.swans.com/library/art8/ elich004.html (Accessed January 23, 2018).

Food and Agriculture Organization of the United Nations (FAO) 1995. *Planning for Sustainable Use of Land Resources: Towards a New Approach, FAO Land and Water Bulletin 2*. Food and Agriculture Organization of the United Nations, Rome.

Government of Zimbabwe (GoZ) 2007. *Provincial Land Audit Reports*. Ministry of Lands, Land Reform, Harare.

Hanyama, M. 2009. *Embassy of Zimbabwe in Stockholm*. Online. http://www.zimembassy. se/land reform document.html. (Accessed January 8, 2018).

Herbst, J.I. 1987. *Policy Formulation and Implementation in Zimbabwe: Understanding State Autonomy and the Locus of Decision-making*. Doctor Thesis, Yale University, New Haven.

Human Rights Watch 2002. *The Events of 2001, World Report*. Human Rights Watch, New York.

Mandaza, I. 1985. The state and politics in the post-white settler colonial situation. In (I. Mandaza, ed.) *Zimbabwe: The Political Economy of Transition, 1980–1986*, pp. 21–74. CODESRIA, Dakar.

Martin, J.C. 2008. Bringing dead capital to life: International mandates for land titling in Brazil. *Boston College International and Comparative Law Review*, 31(1): 121–136.

Mazwi, F. & R.G. Muchetu 2015. Out-grower sugarcane production post fast track land reform programme in Zimbabwe. *Ubuntu: Journal of Conflict Transformation*, 4(2): 17–48.

Moyo, S. 1992. *Land Tenure Issues in Zimbabwe during the 1990s*. Centre for Applied Social Sciences, University of Zimbabwe, Harare.

— 1994. *The Land Question in Zimbabwe*. SAPES Trust, Harare.

— 2000a. The political economy of land acquisition and redistribution in Zimbabwe, 1990–1999. *Journal of Southern African Studies*, 26(1): 5–28.

— 2000b. *Land Reform under Structural Adjustment in Zimbabwe: Land Use Change in Mashonaland Provinces.* Nordiska Afrikainstitutet, Uppsala.

— 2002a. The interaction of market and compulsory land acquisition processes with social action in Zimbabwe's land reform. In (I. Mandaza & D. Nabudere, eds.) *Pan Africanism and Integration in Africa*, pp. 1–50. SAPES, Harare.

— 2002b. *Land Reform and Transition in Zimbabwe.* Paper presented at EDGA conference, January 21, 2002, Cape Town, South Africa.

— 2005a. The land question and the peasantry in Southern Africa. In (A.A. Boron & G. Lechini, eds.) *Politics and Social Movements in an Hegemonic World: Lessons from Africa, Asia and Latin America*, pp. 275–235. CLACSO, Buenos Aires.

— 2005b. Land and natural resource redistribution in Zimbabwe: Access equity and conflict. *African and Asian Studies*, 4 (1–2): 187–223.

— 2007. Land in the political economy of African development: Alternative strategies for reform. *Africa Development*, 32(4): 1–34.

— 2009. *Agrarian Reform and Prospects for Recovery.* SMAIAS Monographs, Harare.

— 2010. The agrarian question and the developmental state in Southern Africa. In (O. Edigheji, ed.) *Constructing a Democratic Developmental State in South Africa: Potentials and Challenges*, pp. 285–314. HSRC Press, Cape Town.

— 2011a. Changing agrarian relations after redistributive land reform in Zimbabwe. *The Journal of Peasant Studies*, 38(5): 939–966.

— 2011b. Land concentration and accumulation after redistributive reform in post- settler Zimbabwe. *Review of African Political Economy*, 38(128): 257–276.

— 2014. *Land Ownership Patterns and Income Inequality in Southern Africa.* A paper presented at Conference of UN World Economic and Social Survey, Pan Africa Conference on Inequalities in the

Context of Structural Transformation. April 28–30, 2014, Accra, Ghana.

Moyo, S., W. Chambati, T. Chidavarume, N. Munyikwa, M. Nyakudya & E. Chigumira n.d. *Constitutional Provisions Regarding Women's Land Rights and Related Empowerment.* (unpublished).

Moyo, S., W. Chambati & S. Siziba 2014. *Agricultural Subsidies Policies in Zimbabwe: A Review.* SMAIAS, Harare.

Moyo, S. & P.B. Matondi 2004. *Land, Food Security and Sustainable Development in Africa.*

UNECA, SDD, Addis Ababa.

Moyo, S. & T. Skalness 1990. Land reform and development strategy in Zimbabwe: State autonomy, class and agrarians lobby. *Afrika Focus*, 6(3–4): 201–242.

Moyo, S. & P. Yeros 2005. Land occupations and land reform in Zimbabwe: Towards the national democratic revolution. In (S. Moyo & P. Yeros, eds.) *Reclaiming the Land: The Resurgence of Rural Movements in Africa, Asia and Latin America*, pp. 165–205. Zed Books, London.

—2007. The radicalised state: Zimbabwe's interrupted revolution. *Review of African Political Economy*, 34(111): 103–121.

Musimbo, C. 2005. *Land Reform in Post-Independence Zimbabwe: A Case of Britain's Neo- colonial Intransigencies.* Masters Thesis, Graduate College of Bowling Green State University, Ohio.

Pinckney, T.C. & P.K. Kimuyu 1994. Land tenure reform in East Africa: Good, bad or unimportant? *Journal of African Economics*, 3(1): 1–28.

Rugube, L., S. Zhou, M. Roth & W. Chambati 2003. *Land Transactions Monitoring and Evaluation of Public and Private Land Markets in Redistributing Land in Zimbabwe.* Centre for Applied Social Science, University of Zimbabwe and Land Tenure Center, University of Wisconsin, Harare and Madison.

Sadomba, W.Z. 2011. *War Veterans in Zimbabwe's Revolution: Challenging Neo-colonialism and Settler and International Capital.* James Currey, New York.

Shivji, I.G. 2009. *Accumulation in an African Periphery: A Theoretical Framework.* Mkuki na Nyota Publishers, Tanzania.

SMAIAS 2014. *Land Use, Food Security and Agricultural Production Survey Report, Survey Report.* Sam Moyo African Institute for Agrarian Studies, Harare.

United Nations (UN) 1994. *Convention of Desertification.* Information Programme on Sustainable Development, New York.

Utete, M.B. 2003. *Report of the Presidential Land Review Committee and Presidential Land Review Committee.* Government Printers, Harare.

Weiner, D., S. Moyo, B. Munslow & P. O'Keefe 1985. Land use and agricultural productivity in Zimbabwe. *The Journal of Modern African Studies,* 23(2): 251–285.

World Bank 2017. *Agriculture, Value Added Indicator.* Online. http://data.worldbank.org/ indicator/NV.AGR.TOTL.ZS?name_desc=true (Accessed November 1, 2016).

Author's E-mail: gavinmuchetu@gmail.com

Chapter 6

Cleaning the House, Greening the Farm: Reverse Thinking and "African Potentials" to Combat Desertification in Sahel Region, West Africa

Shuichi Oyama

Introduction

As their farmland deteriorates, the Hausa people improve its fertility by mixing household waste and urban waste into the soil. These wastes include excreta of cattle, leftover fodder, pruned branches, crop residues, worn-out cloths, plastic bag and metal pans. This local greening technique was developed by villagers in 1973 and 1974, during a time of drought and famine. Since 2003, the author has conducted repeated field experiments on the effectiveness and safety of the use of organic waste from urban and homestead environments. Shrubs grow from waste input after grassland is created, and herders foster forest growth in fenced experimental plots, using their livestock. The author has performed local techniques using external equipment. Although the lifestyle and production patterns of the residents in the Sahel exacerbate the desertification process, urban waste and livestock can restore the degraded land. This path of greening is considered reverse thinking and "African Potentials" based on the indigenous knowledge and day-to-day practice, which combats the desertification of the West African Sahel.

According to the United Nations Convention to Combat Desertification, which was ratified in 1994, the definition of desertification is land degradation. The 2030 Agenda for Sustainable Development Goal 15 is to protect, restore, and promote the sustainable use of terrestrial ecosystems, combat desertification, and halt and reverse land degradation and biodiversity loss. Desertification occurs through a combination of natural (irregular rainfall, drought, and poor soil fertility) and anthropogenic factors (overcultivation, overgrazing, and firewood collection). Many researchers and international organisations have reported that unsuitable cultivation, grazing, firewood collection, and urbanisation are the major causes of desertification (Anderson & Fishwick, 1984; Dregne, 1986; Turner, 1999; Gonzalez, 2001; World Bank, 2012).

The rapid increase in the human population of the Sahel, the southern fringe of the Sahara Desert, particularly in its urban population, is a fundamental driving force in desertification and land shortage (Reenberg et al., 1998; Wezel & Haigis, 2002). In recent years, famers and herders have both experienced hunger and poverty caused by desertification in the Sahel, which has led to armed conflict and terrorism (Ayantunde et al., 2000; Mortimore & Turner, 2005; Tschakert, 2007; Oyama, 2014). A downward spiral exists from desertification through hunger and poverty to armed conflict (Blench, 1996; Obioha, 2008), and the spectrum of terrorism is growing throughout the region.

Overcoming the problem of desertification is important not only for reducing poverty and maintaining and improving the quality of life but also for achieving regional political stability. In Republic of Niger, combating desertification is a crucial issue, and routine work is underway on tasks such as tree planting, dune stabilisation, catchment management, and erosion reduction. The national government promotes community participation in these initiatives, providing food for work and cash for work by making the distribution of food aid to villages conditional upon the engagement of their residents in tree-planting and the anti-erosion work. In 2004, the Nigerien government announced that from 2000 to 2002, trees had been planted in an area of 381 km2, 40 km2 of sand dunes had been stabilised, and surface runoff management and anti-erosion measures had been instituted across 384 km2 (Republique du Niger, 2004).

Programs to combat desertification in the Sahel were initiated at the international level in the 1970s, but their progress and outcomes have been unsatisfactory, and drought-induced desertification has continued, together with countless other related problems (Leisinger et al., 1995). The African Union, the European Union, and the Food and Agriculture Organization of the United Nations created the Great Green Wall Project for the Sahara and Sahel Initiative, promising in November 2011, 1.75 million Euro to tackle desertification in the Sahel and North Africa through revegetation projects (Europafrica.net, 2011). The planed greenbelt would be 15 km wide and 7,775 km long. In Senegal, the project planted trees over 50,000 acres. The current approaches to dealing with desertification tend to be directed towards technological development, involving expensive equipment and consuming vast quantities of energy and capital.

In 2012, for example, 5.5 million people in Niger were at immediate risk of starvation following a severe drought the previous year, and the United Nations World Food Programme requested that the international community provide US$800 million in emergency aid to deal with the crisis (World Food Programme, 2012). According to the Global Terrorism Index 2015 (Institute for Economic and Peace, 2015), terrorism and insecurity problems in the region are becoming increasingly serious.

Niger is also experiencing high rates of population growth, with an annual growth rate of 3.7%. This rapid pace has resulted in a doubling of its population in just 20 years. The fertility rate—the number of children each woman is projected to give birth to during the course of her life—has reached 7.4. When this author began research in Niger in 2000, the population was 10.92 million, and in 2015, it was 19.90 million. The United Nations (UN) predicts that it will continue to grow, reaching 83.92 million in 2055 and 137.94 million in 2075 (United Nations, Department of Economic and Social Affairs, Population Division, 2017). This rapid growth may lead to many problems in the near future including desertification, food shortages, and other forms of environmental degradation, as well as difficulty in allocating resources and energy. These problems are linked to violence, conflict, and terrorism due to resource scarcity. This chapter examines the consciousness of land degradation and day-to-day land restoration practices among the Hausa people residing in southern Niger. Rather than passively remaining at the mercy of their harsh natural environment, they use indigenous knowledge to address the land degradation. This chapter sheds light on these practices and the distinctive ways of thinking that underpin them. The author also discusses the trials of action research for developing new land restoration technologies based on the integration of indigenous knowledge and external equipment.

Hausa Society and the Natural Environment of the Sahel

Hausa Society

The Hausa are the largest ethnic group in West Africa. Hausa people dwell in an area extending from Filingue, Tahoua, and Zinder in central Niger to the north to as far south as Kano and Zaria in northern Nigeria. They refer to themselves as *Bahaushe* (sg.) or *Hausawa* (pl.), and the area in which they dwell is sometimes referred to in English as Hausaland. Major Hausa communities have formed in northern Ghana and northern Cameroon, and Hausa storeowners and artisans can be found in most of the cities of the Sahel. Most Hausa are Muslims, and it is possible to trace the history of this religion in Hausaland back to the 14th century. Islam spread as the Hausa migrated from one part of West Africa to another. In West Africa, Islam is now sometimes considered synonymous with the Hausa people, and in the spread of Islam, locals may see a kind of "Hausanisation" occurring (Adamu, 1978).

The Sahel once contained numerous kingdoms. Rather than being viable, stable nation-states founded on agricultural surpluses, these kingdoms were largely supported by livestock rearing and commerce. The true Hausa is the patrilineal descendants of the people who dwelled in the region controlled by the Hausa kingdom in the 15th century (Smith, 1971). This kingdom flourished as a centre of intermediary trade in produce from the coastal regions to its south, as well as of rock salt from the Sahara Desert and goods imported from the Mediterranean (Baier, 1980). The Hausa actively pursue commerce in urban areas of West Africa.

The region that is home to the Hausa is part of the Sudan–Sahel zone of West Africa. This zone encompasses a vast belt of land from the Atlantic coast of Senegal as far inland as Chad. The findings presented in this chapter are from a study of D village, a Hausa village, located in the southern part of central Niger (Fig. 1). When the author began the survey with a period of residence in D village in 2000, the village had 41 households and 280 residents; in 2010, it had

65 households and a population of 504. Thus the population increased by 6.0% per annum during the intervening decade. Most of the village's residents are of Hausa ethnicity, but it also includes one Tuareg and two Fulbe herder households. Most residents are Muslims, and at dawn and dusk each day, Muslim men attend prayers at a mosque in the centre of the village.

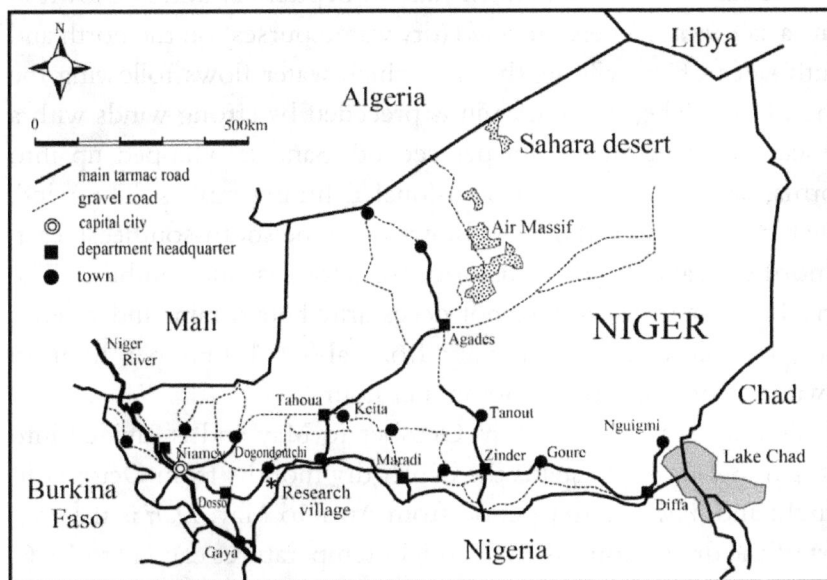

Fig. 1. Research site in southern Niger, West Africa

The Harsh Climate of the Sahel

The soil around D village falls into the Arenosols category (FAO/UNESCO, 1971). This oligotrophic soil type, characterised by extremely small volumes of organic matter, nitrogen, and phosphorus, is distributed across a large area from central Mali to southern central Niger and northern Chad. The village lies approximately 240 m above sea level and is surrounded on all sides by pearl millet fields. Running north–south on the east side of the village is a series of inselbergs or isolated rocky hills, reaching around 50 m tall. The inselbergs are covered in an iron duricrust, underneath which are deposits of sandstone, mudstone, and other sedimentary rocks dating from the Miocene to Pliocene eras, with stratifications visible on the surface. The inselbergs are topped with a type of vegetation known by scientists as tiger bush, which, when viewed

147

from the air, resembles the markings of a tiger (Galle et al., 1999; Malam Issa et al., 1999). It is difficult to cultivate crops on the duricrust, but the tiger bush is gathered for use as firewood, and the village women cultivate numerous small plots in which sand has accumulated, producing crops of Bambara nuts and groundnuts in the rainy season.

The rainy season lasts from June to September and is known in Hausa as *damana*. There are *wadis* (dry watercourses) on the north and south sides of the village, through which water flows following the time of rain. The arrival of rain is preceded by strong winds with a velocity of more than 10m per second. Sand is whipped up into storms, and there are also occasional lightning strikes. The wind, which can be followed by rain, blows from the south-southeast, east, or northeast, and brings sandstorms from the east and southeast. The arrival of a sandstorm does not necessarily herald rain, and when it does, rainfall volumes can vary from about 1 mm per hour to downpours in the order of 40mm per hour.

The dry season runs from October to May and is divided into two parts: *dari*, which spans the cooler dry months from October to March; and *rani*, a hotter period from April to May. *Dari* is the cool part of the dry season, when overnight temperatures can fall to 15°C, although daytime temperatures can exceed 35°C. *Rani* brings even hotter conditions. Overnight minimums are about 25–30°C; maximums in excess of 35°C are common, and days over 40°C Celsius are not rare. An oppressive heat prevails throughout *rani*. A hot, dry wind, generally known as the Harmattan, blows from the north and northeast with gusts of 10m per second or more. From May to June, the skies are filled with clouds promising the arrival of the rainy season; the days are hot and humid. This period is known in Hausa as *bazara*. Maximum temperatures often exceed 35°C, with a humidity ranging from 70 to 90%.

In the town of Dogondoutchi, 7 km northwest of D village, rainfall records have been kept since 1923, during the days of the French colonial government. The average annual rainfall for the three decades from 1981 to 2010 was about 460 mm, but there was considerable variance from year to year (Fig. 2). This variance is attributable to the activity of an intertropical convergence zone

148

(ITCZ), formed when warm, humid air from the Gulf of Guinea (the 'Guinea monsoon') meets the dry continental air mass. This ITCZ moves north from July to September, bringing rain to the Sahel. Around the northernmost edge of the ITCZ, however, rain is unreliable, and annual rainfall fluctuates dramatically (Mortimore, 1998). Thus, the influence of the Guinea monsoon wanes as it moves northward; in inland areas, the dry season tends to be harsher and the rainfall is less predictable the further north one goes. For these reasons, Niger is prone to drought and low rainfall. An annual rainfall of 350 mm is considered the minimum for cultivation of pearl millet. Since 2000, there has been no period of drought with lower rainfall than this, but such droughts occurred repeatedly from the 1970s to the 1990s, bringing severe food shortages. In 2011, the annual rainfall in the area surveyed was 389 mm. Rain was particularly scarce from mid-August through September 2011, endangering the pearl millet and cowpea harvest.

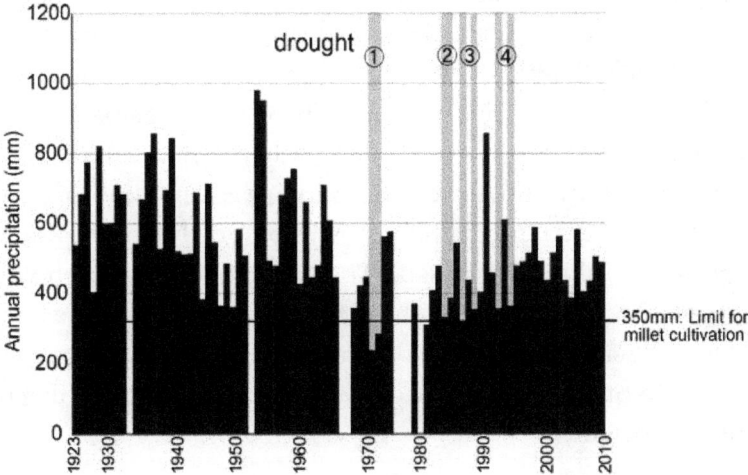

Fig. 2. Rainfall fluctuations and drought years in Dogondoutchi, Niger

Life in a Hausa Village

Extended Family Centred on the Household Head

The villagers' livelihood is based on the cultivation of pearl millet and cowpea; livestock are grazed as a subsidiary activity. Some villagers also earn extra cash income through side work as traders, butchers, blacksmiths, wood-turners, osteopaths and scribes, among others. The men of the village migrate to urban areas for work during the dry season when there is no farming work. In Hausa villages, due in part to the shortage of land, young men who have married and moved out of the family home tend to work on their father's land and take their meals together with their parents, siblings, and other members of their families. Below, the Bawa[1] household is presented as an example of the patterns of production and consumption in rural Hausa societies (Fig. 3).

In 2003, Bawa owned a 6.19-hectare plot of land, which was farmed by seven family members: Mohamad, the first-born son of Bawa's first wife Bangu; Yusuf, Zakari, Alio, and Djibulina, respectively the second, third, and fourth sons and a grandson of his first wife; and Tahil and Hasan, the second and third sons of his second wife Beiwa. Beiwa's first-born son, Asumana, is unable to work on the farm, due to a leg problem. Mohamad, Zakari, and Asumana also work alongside their father as blacksmiths, producing agricultural thrust hoes every day during the rainy season. Six of these family members tend the household's plot daily: Yusuf, Zakari, Alio, Djibulina, Tahil and Hasan. The head of the household, Bawa, struggles to make the household food supply last for the entire year, taking into account the fact that both the pearl millet harvested from his own plot and the income derived from his blacksmithing business are insufficient.

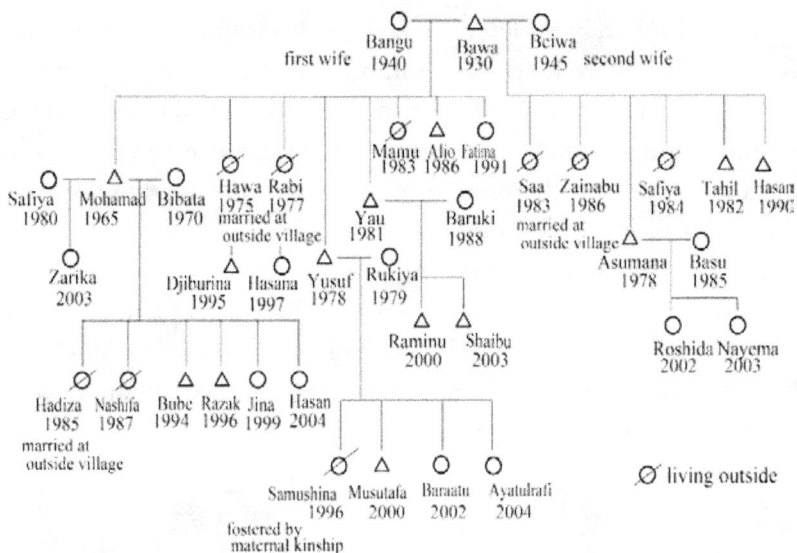

Fig. 3. Family Tree of Bawa In 2003

(All Names Of Individuals Are Fictitious.)

Hausa men see their ideal existence as one in which, as head of the household, they can balance food supply, cash income, and labour to achieve a comfortable existence for their wives and children, as well as their sons' families. Meals in the Bawa household begin with division of the millet porridge into five plates. The first plate is eaten by Bawa himself and his youngest son and grandson (Hasan and Djibulina), who are 10 to 15 years old, respectively; the second plate is for the older sons (Mohamad, Yusuf, Zakari, Alio, Asumana, and Tahil), both married and unmarried; the third is for Bawa's two wives (Bangu and Beiwa) and daughter (Fatima); the fourth is for Bawa's sons' wives (Bibata, Rukiya, Baruki, and Basu); and the fifth plate goes to the children under 10 years old. With a total of 22 mouths to feed, the household consumes approximately 100 kg of pearl millet grain weekly.

Ongoing Food Shortages

In 2005, the Bawa household's plot yielded 80 bundles of pearl millet (Fig. 4). Each bundle ranged in weight from 10 to 18 kg depending on the quantity and size of the grain therein, which was in turn determined by soil conditions and rainfall. Even if each bundle harvests yields the maximum grain volume of 18 kg, this is only 1,440 kg in total—barely enough to feed the household for 4 months of the year. The household's work in manufacturing and repairing hoes for other farmers in the village brings in an additional one-half to one bundle of pearl millet per farmer. The payment received from each farmer depends on the number of hoes repaired during the farming season. In all, this blacksmith business brings in about 40 bundles per year—enough for 2 months

The farmers make bundles of 300 to 500 millet panicles and place them at the front of the grain stockade to be counted. The head of the household formulates a 1-year consumption plan to prevent members of his family going hungry.

Fig. 4. Millet harvest

Even when the harvest is combined with earnings from the blacksmith business, the food supply of the household tends to run low as sowing time approaches. Such shortfalls are addressed by selling livestock. Approximately 10 goats and sheep are kept in the Bawa household compound, together with 1 donkey for carrying goods. There are also two cows, which the household tends for a Fulbe herder who lives in the same village. The Fulbe herders care for the farmers' cows, goats, and sheep. In March 2006, the Bawa household sold a 6-month-old calf born to one of these cows, and used a portion of the income from the sale, which totalled 40,000 CFA francs (US $80), to purchase 150 kg of pearl millet (at 18,000 CFA francs per 100 kg). This purchase met the household's staple food needs for 2 weeks. Cattle aside, goats, sheep, and poultry are also sold off to the village butchers or periodically at weekly markets to earn cash to purchase more grain. Cash income to offset food shortages can also be earned through the sale of firewood. Adult women and children gather firewood from the surrounding scrubland, and each morning carry it on their heads for 7 km to the town of Dogondoutchi, where a one-person load sells for 50–200 CFA francs. In recent years, some young villagers have also started collecting and selling building materials, such as clay and rock, in response to demand generated by a construction boom in urban areas. This is not a reliable source of cash income, however, as the arrival of trucks to collect the materials is unpredictable. The sale of items such as firewood and clay is considered a last resort for households unable to obtain food through other means.

If food runs out despite these extra efforts, villagers approach one of the rich households, known as *mai-kudi*, to request a cash loan with which to purchase more food. Because the price of pearl millet drastically increases in the sowing season, many villagers use this cash to purchase cheaper cassava instead. In its dried form, cassava is roughly crushed and sprinkled with salt for a makeshift meal. Debts are repaid through weeding work undertaken in the lender's plots during the following season. In the Bawa household, this labour is mainly performed by the unmarried sons—Alio, Djiibulina, Tahil, and Hasan. In 2006, the daily wage for this work was 1,150 CFA francs, but the amount varies depending on the food supply in the village each year, decreasing as food becomes scarcer. The workers weed the rich household's plots from just after 8:00 a.m. to after 4:00 p.m. in temperatures that can exceed 40°C. Wages are not usually directly paid to the labourers, but instead, are marked down against the household's debt to the wealthy family.

By mid-September, the pearl millet panicles are still not completely dry, but they are edible nevertheless. When harvested at this time, fresh pearl millet is known as *tumu* and is eaten either simply roasted or mixed with dried leaves of the Aduwa tree (*Balanites aegyptiaca*; a zygophyllaceous plant) known as *dubagara*, vegetable oil, sugar, and *bakuru*, a condiment made from groundnut oil meal. When household finances are running low, it is sometimes necessary to omit the sugar, oil, and *bakuru*. Thus, what the villagers eat varies depending on rainfall. Villagers reported that crop growth was particularly poor in 2004 and 2005, leading to food shortages in the subsequent years and making *dubagara* a precious commodity. When the author visited the village for research in July 2006, few residents had food left; they were thin, and the veins on their faces were prominent. This physical condition is known in Hausa as *yarami*. In the 2005 season, the villagers faced a poor millet yield; 27 households, representing about two-thirds of the total village population, had exhausted their stocks of pearl millet before the next sowing season (June 2006); and 24 of these households were using money borrowed from the three wealthy villagers to purchase food. In the Bawa household, and indeed in other households in the village, the last resort if food remains scarce after going into debt is to eat *dubagara* boiled in salted water. The *Balanites* leaves for *dubagara* are gathered when they are young and green in April and May by the women of the household, who decide how much to gather based on their household's food stores at that stage of the year. If the pearl millet harvest is good or if they have secured some wheat or maize flour through U.S. aid projects, they will gather fewer *Balanites* leaves; if conditions are tough, they will gather more. The leaves are dried and stored indoors. Other precious sources of food during the rainy season include leaves from the cowpea plants harvested at that time of year and herbaceous plants such as *Corchorus tridens*, *Cassia obtusifolia*, *Nothosaerva brachiata*, *Gynandropsis gynandra*, and *Amaranthus* spp., which grow naturally during the rainy season. These are mixed with small quantities of pearl millet, boiled in salted water, and eaten to tide the household over until harvest time. Sometimes pearl millet is not added to this mix if supplies have been exhausted, but villagers say that without any at all, the bitterness of the *Balanites* leaves burns the throat. The leaves are gently simmered for 7 to 8 hours, left overnight in the salted water to cool, and then consumed. In times of more severe famine, *Jacquemontia tamnifolia* and *Indigofera prieureana* leaves, which are apparently used as livestock feed under normal circumstances, may also be added. The author has personally sampled both of these plants; under no circumstances can they be described as appetising. The village women reported that they were reduced to eating livestock feed four times in the past 10 years: 2004, 2005, 2007 and 2011.

Severe Drought and Collective Memory

The people of the Sahel take various actions in response to crop failures caused by drought (Swinton, 1988). These actions are as follows: selling cattle, sheep, goats, and poultry; short-time migration to work in urban areas, both domestic and international; engagement in wage labour or procurement of supplementary food supplies; and borrowing money. Through these actions, people procure cash and food to provide for their daily needs. However, the Hausa people have experienced droughts so severe, that such actions were inadequate to address the food shortage.

In D village, each severe drought is given a name in Hausa and remembered by villagers, particularly the elders. The 1972–1973 drought, (1) in Fig. 2, is referred to as *nyunwa garin rogo*, the 'cassava flour famine.' During this drought, which is known in the Hausa society of northern Nigeria as *kakaduba* (Mortimore & Adams, 2001), no pearl millet was available for purchase, so people were forced to make do with cassava flour, the cheapest food available. Cassava is usually considered a famine food, to only be eaten when nothing else is available. Village elders recall that during the drought, their stocks of pearl millet were exhausted, leaving no seeds to sow for the next season even after the drought ended. Thus, this food shortage continued for 2 years.

The name given to the drought of 1984–1985,[2] in Fig. 2, is *nyunwa maizobe*: the 'ring famine.' In a ring of territory extending across West Africa, famine prevailed following drought-induced crop failures and livestock losses. Cattle grew so weak that their Fulbe and Tuareg herders were unable to move them south in search of pasture, and many perished as a result. There was no pearl millet in the markets,

155

so even those with cash reserves were unable to purchase food. *Nyunwa kanchikarage*, the 'famine of the food-seekers,' took place from 1987–1989,[3] in Fig. 2. Rainfall was unevenly distributed during this period; thus crop yields varied from region to region. Each locality experienced the famine differently. Where there were severe shortages, people could not purchase pearl millet even if they could afford it and had to make do with cassava flour instead. In other areas, crops performed well, but this did not mean that the residents were happy; they were inundated by people from less fortunate areas seeking food, and had no choice but to share their own valuable supplies with them. The 1993–1995 drought,[4] in Fig. 2, is known as *nyunwa mayahi* or the 'scarf famine.' Drought conditions extended across a wide area, with marked regional differences in food supply. People hid their food stores in scarves in a desperate attempt to protect them from beggars and job seekers.

Land Degradation and Restoration of Farmland

Growing Degradation of Farmland

Aerial photographs taken in 1950 show pearl millet plots dotting a grassy landscape of uncultivated and fallow land (Oyama, 2012). Elderly villagers recall that 40 to 50 years ago, there was still land to spare around the village, much of it untouched. Subsequently, however, the population grew rapidly, and an increasing area of land was farmed. Soon, all arable land was put to use for pearl millet cultivation. All of the plots are privately owned, although the government does not maintain official land ownership register. In recent years, land suited to cultivation has been in short supply, and it is difficult to find new land for farming. Village women have even attempted to cultivate Bambara nuts and groundnuts in the small sand hills found on the iron-crusted inselbergs. The land is not left to lie fallow; pearl millet and cowpea are grown in succession year after year. Under continuous cultivation, soil fertility drops, and the land drastically deteriorates. Pearl millet crops do not grow uniformly even within the same plot, and the differences among neighbouring plots is often striking.

Hausa villagers use three terms to classify the state of the soil in their plots: *kasa*, *leso*, and *foko*. *Kasa* denotes productive soil, and *leso* is the early stages of soil degradation when nutrients have leached out. *Foko* areas are in an advanced stage of degradation, as the fertile soil has been eroded and the base sedimentary rock exposed (Fig. 5). The Hausa people use the categories *kasa*, *leso*, and *foko* to express their assessment of the degree of decline in soil fertility and productivity (Oyama, 2009). *Kasa* areas have blackish sandy topsoil containing organic material mixed with what is known as 'termite soil.' This soil, which has a loose aggregated structure, is produced when termites combine their saliva with soil particles to create a material used in the construction of their nests. This type of aggregated structure is necessary for soil to support plant growth and root development. *Leso* soil, in contrast, consists of coarse, white, sandy particles; it has a high proportion of sand, little organic matter, and a non-aggregated structure. *Foko* denotes areas of exposed reddish sedimentary rock, which is so hard that it can only be broken by blows with a pick. *Foko* soil is poorly suited even to pearl millet; the seeds germinate but all of the plants eventually die. Soil that begins as *kasa* will be transformed through continuous pearl millet cultivation into *leso* within 3 to 5 years, and to *foko* in a further 3 to 5 years.

Two Approaches to Land Restoration

The villagers are not standing idle in the face of this ongoing degradation of their land. Two strategies are being employed to address land degradation and declining crop harvests: encampment contracts with livestock herders, and the use of household waste. The choice of strategy is determined by the condition of soil degradation.

Fig. 5. Rapid land degradation of millet fields
Leso is white sand, and it refers to the early stage of land degradation at which soil nutrition is decreased by plant growth and leaching. The composition of sand is high (more than 85%), and the sand can be easily eroded by rain water (top). The erosion of the topsoil results in exposure of the solid sedimentary rock beneath.

This rock is called *foko*, and it signifies an advanced stage of land degradation (bottom).

Encampment contracts with herders

First, let us examine the encampment contracts between farmers and herders. Hausa villagers enter into these contracts with Fulbe and Tuareg nomadic herders who move into the area with the coming of the dry season (Oyama, 2017). Under these contracts, the herders are invited to establish grazing camps on villagers' land where the soil has deteriorated (Fig. 6). Fulbe herders mainly raise cattle and Tuareg camels; other stock may include goats, sheep, and donkeys. The herders actively seek out farmers with which to enter into encampment contracts. The preference is naturally to contract with the wealthy villagers (*mai- kudi*) who are able to pay well. The herders will not deal with *talaka*, poor farmers who find it difficult to feed themselves and may end up not even paying for the enrichment of their pearl millet plots by the herders' livestock. To ascertain a farmer's wealth and financial circumstances, the herders use methods such as calculating harvest volumes based on the post-harvest stubble in the farmer's pearl millet plot and the size and number of grain sheds erected in the plot. Once they have estimated the financial resources of the farmers, the herders set up camp in plots that they judge to be owned by wealthy villagers. They sleep in these camps alongside their livestock. Soon, the villager who owns the plot, or one of his relatives, will come to check on the plot and will assess the situation upon seeing the Fulbe or Tuareg herder. At this point, the head of the household who owns the plot will begin to negotiate the terms of an encampment contract with the herder. The aim of the negotiation is to determine the encampment contract period and the price that the herder will be paid over this period. The herder will show his herd to the villagers, but will not under any circumstances disclose the number of animals. The owner of the plot must estimate the size and composition of the herd by visual inspection, and on this basis, negotiate the encampment period and fee, which is paid in pearl millet and cash. Negotiations are conducted in Hausa. Some herders cannot speak Hausa fluently, although they can engage in simple negotiations. When the parties have reached agreement on the terms of the contract, the Fulbe or Tuareg herder sets up his grazing

159

camp together with his family, herd, and household possessions at the agreed upon location. The villagers usually require the camps to be set up on sand-covered *leso* land, because livestock prefer to sit and lie on sandy ground at night.

Fig. 6. Encampment contract
The farmers make contracts with Fulbe and Tuareg herders during the dry season. The herders establish grazing camps on the farmers' millet stubble fields and their livestock provides dung to the farmland. The dung serves as crop fertiliser, but such contracts are limited to wealthy farmers (Oyama, 2017).

The following is an example of the contracting process. In February 2011, a villager named Yusuf observed that a Fulbe herder was grazing livestock around a camp set up on his land. The herder was about 30 years old, and his wife and children were also present at the camp. The herder told Yusuf that he had two wives, but only one was at the camp. Yusuf proposed that they enter into an encampment contract; the herder assented, and they agreed to negotiate the details that same evening. The herders' animals return to their camps in the evenings, which makes it possible to assess the size of the herds. When evening came, Yusuf assessed the herd visually and judged that were approximately 25 cows, 6 sheep, and 3 donkeys. Then he proposed to the herder an encampment period of 1 month, but the herder responded that there was almost no pearl millet stubble left on the plot to feed his herd and suggested a period of 1 week instead. Yusuf consented to this suggestion, and payment negotiations began. The herder requested payment in cash rather than pearl millet, so the negotiations focused on settling a cash price. The herder's asking price was 6,000 CFA francs, but on the basis of the type and number of animals in the herd, Yusuf believed that a fair price was 4,000 CFA francs. In February, when the negotiations took place, the volume of herbaceous plants and pearl millet stems on the plots dwindled, resulting in lower manure production by the herd, and as such, less effective fertilisation. Then the herder proposed a reduced price of 5,000 francs, and finally a price of 4,500 CFA francs was agreed upon—1,500 CFA francs less than the original asking price.

The villagers assess the fertilising effects of the manure as follows: camel 5 years, goat and sheep 3 years, cow 2 years. This means that cattle manure decomposes rapidly, providing nutrients for only 2 years, whereas camel manure provides up to 5 years of fertilisation. This notion of the effectiveness of different manures held by Hausa villagers is in accordance with the findings of an empirical study (Brouwer & Powell, 1998). That study found that sheep manure is highly effective for correcting soil pH, whereas much of the nitrogen and phosphorus in cattle manure is leached out by rainfall. In line with this assessment, villagers wishing to enter into contracts with herders who have many camels must pay a high price in cash and pearl millet. The animals nourish the soil in the vicinity of the camp by producing great quantities of manure. At the end of the contracted period, the herder receives his payment from the farmer in cash and pearl millet and then leaves the village. These contracted herd encampments are only conducted on sandy *leso* soil from which nutrients have been leached out or taken up by crops. Thus, farmers use the encampments to add nutrients back to the soil.

Addition of household waste to degraded land

The villagers accumulate composted household waste and transport it to their farming plots. The waste is placed in unproductive areas of the plot to rehabilitate *leso* and *foko* soils (Fig. 7). In *foko* areas, the villagers deposit plant residues of pearl millet stalks and crop residue; leaves and branches left uneaten by livestock; discarded clothing, cookware, baskets, mats and other items; all of which traps the sand blown in by the wind and facilitates the development of sandy topsoil. The amassed waste can be viewed as soil dressing for inferior, denuded areas of land, and can return deteriorated soil to productivity (Oyama & Mammam, 2010). Field experiments conducted by the author since 2003 have revealed that adding waste enables restoration of land through the combination of eight effects (Oyama, 2012; 2015): (1) trapping windborne sand; (2) preventing erosive wind and water; (3) attracting termites to feed on the waste and build nests, allowing rain water to penetrate the soil through termite tunnels; (4) mixing fine particles brought up by the termites with windborne sand; (5) developing an aggregated soil structure through the workings of the termites; (6) neutralising soil acidity (pH 4.5) of the degraded land; (7) adding nitrogen, phosphate, and potassium to the soil; and (8) enabling the germination of seeds of useful plants contained in the waste (Fig. 8). The process of adding waste to farming plots continues year-round, irrespective of the farming cycle. The volume of waste transported to the plots from each household varies, depending on the number of household members and the number and type of livestock kept in the household compound, but averages 10 to 40 kg per day. In households that own an ox cart, the men of the family load the cart with 200 to 400 kg once every 7 to 10 days; in households that do not have a cart, the men and/or women carry loads wrapped in cloth weighing about 10 to 15 kg each on their heads to their household plot.

Fig. 7. Indigenous knowledge and local practice for land restoration

When Hausa farmers recognise soil degradation in a portion of a crop field, they transport household and urban waste to the land. Farmers emphasise the importance of termite activity for land restoration. Plastic bags provide shelters for termites and prevent water evaporation from the ground. Metal dishes and pans are also important for trapping and accumulating blown sand (Oyama, 2012; 2015).

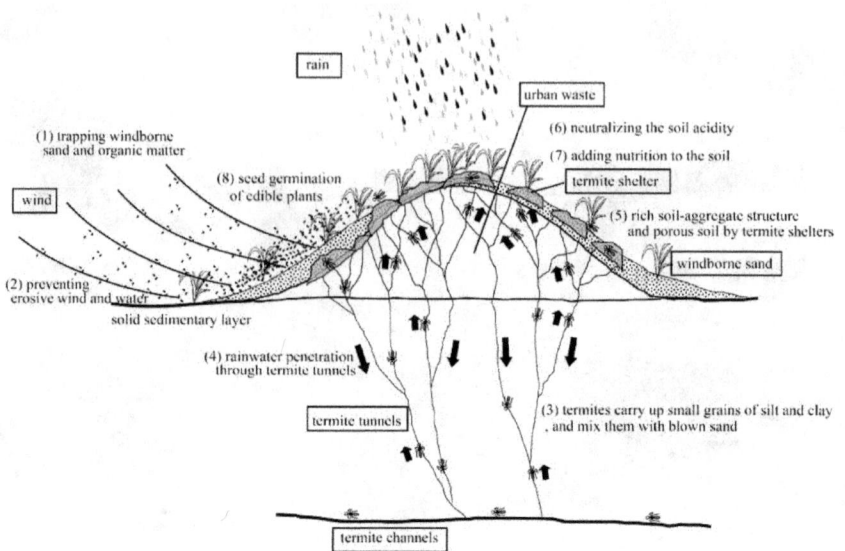

Fig. 8. Eight effects of urban waste input and methods of land restoration (Oyama, 2015)

Greening Techniques Born From the Hardship of Drought and Famine

As of 2012, the Hausa have mostly used waste generated within their household compound, primarily, leftover feed and manure from livestock and crop residue. However, those dwelling in villages on the outskirts of cities collect waste discarded in the cities for use on their own plots. The waste tends to be heavy, so it is mostly transported in ox carts; the maximum distance from where the waste is collected to where it is used is usually about 2 km. In recent times, particularly since about 2008, some wealthy city dwellers have started to load waste onto their tractors and trucks, and transport it to their farming plots to improve the soil. The idea of spreading waste on denuded land and farming plots is difficult for outsiders to comprehend, but it is a perfectly ordinary practice in Hausa societies.

Elder members of the community said that this practice, which is a distinctive aspect of Hausa life, began in the drought of 1973–1974. As previously noted in this chapter, that drought resulted in failure of the pearl millet crop. After the drought ended, farmers' stocks of seeds were exhausted, so they were unable to cultivate their crop in the following year. At that time, one man in the village took the waste that had accumulated in his household compound, namely animal manure and plant residue, and spread it over his farming plot. This man, named Sikaro, has since passed away, but his sons said that Sikaro reasoned that if pearl millet harvests improve in areas around Fulbe and Tuareg herders' camps, where livestock have left behind large quantities of manure and millet seed, then harvests should also be improved by adding manure and plant residue from his own compound to the soil. This strategy proved to be highly effective, because domestic animal manure contains many crop seeds, which the animals particularly enjoy, and because household waste contains large quantities of pearl millet seeds left over after hulling (Oyama, 2012). As he added the waste to his soil, Sikaro is said to have thought, 'I don't have any seeds left to sow, but if I spread my plot with waste that is full of seeds and nutrients, I am sure to get a harvest.' He did not own a cart at the time, so he wrapped the waste in cloth and carried it on his head. Repeating this chore daily was far from an easy task, but when the rainy seasons came, his plan came to fruition.

Aided by good rainfall, the pearl millet seeds in the manure germinated naturally, grew well, and seeded successfully. The harvest of pearl millet thereby obtained was not sufficient for meeting all of his household's needs, but it was a valuable source of food nonetheless. Observing Sikaro's success, neighbouring villagers, such as Andy, Chida, and Tankari, followed suit the next year, spreading household waste onto their plots and harvesting and eating the pearl millet that grew from the waste. Elders recalled that the famines following the droughts of 1973–1974 and 1984–1985 were particularly severe, and it was difficult to procure pearl millet seeds. They said that these famines prompted many villages to begin using household waste on their plots, and that some urban dwellers who owned land nearby also started to use urban waste in the same way.

Irrespective of whether the waste was sourced from villages or towns, adding it to the soil markedly improved the yields of crops such as pearl millet and cowpea. This realisation spread rapidly, and the use of waste quickly became routine practice. In recent years, an increasing number of farmers have begun collecting waste in urban areas and transporting it by ox cart to use on their land. Some wealthy households even transport urban waste by tractor to plots fenced in with wire, where it is used to help establish mango orchards. Urban waste contains many plastic bags, plastic containers, and metal scraps, but it is still considered an effective resource for revegetation in rural Hausa society.

Harkuki: Local Logic Backing Desertification and Revegetation

Land degradation, and the restoration of degraded land for farming, is known in Hausa as *harkuki*. Hausa–English dictionaries define *harkuki* as 'movement' or 'news.' The word thus denotes motion and change. Land degradation and restoration entail 'movement' in the condition of the land and are closely interconnected with the movement of humans. Let us look a little more closely at how the concept of *harkuki* is used in Hausa society. Hausa people, whether young or old, consider *harkuki* to be important. It is said that African greetings tend to be lengthy; this is certainly true in Hausa society. People question each other about how they sleep and how they feel, about the health of their wives, children, and families and about goings-on in their respective villages, and they also enquire about each other's *harkuki*. The Hausa consider it important to generate *harkuki* or movement in one's everyday existence and across the span of one's life. Local villagers not only farm the land, tend livestock, and travel to undertake seasonal work but also engage actively in a range of other pursuits, in the belief that these activities will give their lives purpose and bring wealth. They consider that both their daily existence and lives as a whole hinge on *harkuki*. This is one reason that people enquire about each other's *harkuki* in the course of greetings.

It is important to try many different things during the span of one's life. For example, it is common for 10-year-old Hausa children to operate stalls at the regular markets held within or near the village. From about 15 years old, they travel to work in unfamiliar cities, even beyond the national borders, selling goods, finding mentors to teach them skills in commerce or manual trades, and ascertaining their own aptitude for such work. They search for their own foothold in life (*bida*) and decide on the path they will follow into the future. In this way of thinking, it is through movement that people find their foothold and gain *harkuki* and wealth. As children grow into adults, they learn to farm the land, keep livestock, and help their fathers, brothers, and other people around them; they may go to the city to work and may even return with a fortune. They are educated at school and may go on to earn a salary in a stable city job. Children are considered the wellspring of *harkuki*. People who are ill, have few children, or are lazy are said to be lacking in *harkuki*, thereby being unable to find a foothold, a reason for living and future wealth.

Illness drains one's vitality and restricts one's movement. Having few children means there are less people to do the work that supports daily life and economic activity in one's household such as fetching water, collecting firewood, tending to livestock and gathering feed, making the household's capacity for movement (*harkuki*) limited. Therefore, in Hausa society, to acquire more *harkuki*, people proactively engage in adoption (*adani*) and raise adopted children as their own. Monogamy is not frowned upon, but it is considered better for men to have two or three wives, as a larger number of children will increase *harkuki* and bring more vitality. Movement will not always lead to success, but without movement, finding a foothold in life is impossible; this is the belief of most Hausa people dwelling in rural villages.

Livestock can also generate *harkuki*. Livestock produce offspring, and the offspring grow as they consume vegetation. Upon reaching maturity, they can be sent to market for sale. Cash from the sale can be used to purchase food for the household during dry season shortages, pay for children's education, or fund the marriage of a son. Such expenditure generates a new cycle of movement. Proceeds from livestock sales can also be used for repairs in the household dwelling and clothing for family members. Livestock manure, pearl millet residue, and waste accumulated in the household compound are taken to the farming plot by members of the household. The application of these compost materials to the soil, together with activities such as cutting vegetation and gathering livestock feed enable pearl millet and cowpea to grow, leading to a successful harvest the following year. This is considered *harkuki*, the movement that gives purpose to the lives of Hausa people.

Naturally, money can also be a source of *harkuki*. A young villager who goes to the city to work and earns a reasonable income usually returns home not with food, gifts, and other purchases, but with the cash he has earned. This cash does not lie idly in its owner's pocket or home for long; it is quickly spent on acquiring livestock, paying for encampment contracts, purchasing farmland, and other such investments. Since 2005, mobile telephones have rapidly gained popularity in the village. These can also be seen as a form of *harkuki*. By 2016, it was entirely normal for villagers to use mobile telephones to greet and talk with their friends and acquaintances. The use of telephones has enabled instant access to important information, although this does not mean that villagers are presented with a succession of attractive propositions, they are now able to communicate with relatives working in cities both within and beyond the country, and to ask how they are and obtain information on matters such as economic trends in urban areas. Men in Hausa society are expected to find a foothold in life and to use all means and capacities at their disposal to work for their families. Hausa men keep working and continue their 'movement' together with their wives, to build a fulfilling life for their families.

Land Restoration and Greening Trials Based on Local Practices

In 2011, due to an inadequate local government budget under the military regime in Niger, there was no civil waste-collection service in the town of Dogondoutchi. The author made an agreement with the Dogondoutchi mayor to collect some of the urban waste. This agreement was intended to support a civil waste-collection service in urban areas and land restoration using urban waste in rural areas. After understanding the effects of urban waste on land restoration, the author started a social experiment with local residents, which could be used to restore degraded land and prevent conflicts between farmers and herders in the future. With the co-operation of local residents, the author transported 150 tons of urban waste in hired tractors and piled it on a 50 × 50 m fenced plot of degraded land. Urban waste can improve soil fertility and plant growth productivity. In the 2012 rainy season, 42 plant species were found in the fenced area (Fig. 9). Most of these were crops or useful plants including pearl millet, cowpea, amaranthus and pumpkins growing from the urban waste (Table 1). We herded livestock onto the rehabilitated land, which fed on the grass within the fenced area during the crop-harvest season. This practice was intended to avoid proximity of grazing livestock and farmland and to prevent livestock-induced crop damage and farmer–herder conflicts. The Fulbe herders were pleased with the species of grass created from the urban waste. In southern Niger, livestock are owned by both herdsmen and farmers. Both groups can enjoy the benefits of new pasture land. We continued to keep the animals within the fenced area for at least 2 weeks, even after all of the grass had been consumed. The livestock dung maintains soil quality.

Fig. 9. Plant growth from urban waste
We piled 150 tons of urban waste on a 50 × 50 m fenced plot (February 24, 2012). We placed sand and stones politely onto plastic bags to avoid scattering (left) and found 42 plant species in the first year (September 5, 2012) (right).

In the second year, December 2013, surprisingly, we found 13 tree species germinating from the livestock dung and shrubs were growing within the fenced area (Table 2). These tree species could be used for livestock fodder, famine relief food for the residents, or in cooking local dishes. According to the Hausa people, baobab provides soup material and can be sold for cash, and *Balanites aegyptiaca* and *Zizyphus mauritiana* serve as food for people and livestock. The leaves of *Balanites aegyptiaca* are a well-known relief food for the local residents. *Phoenix dactylifera* (date palm) is produced in the Sahara region and is transported to local markets in the Sahel region. Dogondoutchi residents consume date fruits and the waste is added to the urban waste. According to Tybirk (1991), *Acacia* and *Tamarindus* seeds in the Sahel region are transported by livestock and readily germinate after being digested and ruminated by livestock. Therefore, the tree species germinated from urban waste and livestock dung were useful for both humans and livestock. The Fulbe herders worked to maintain straight tree growth. Trees can be used by the herders for shelter during storms and as a source of shade during hot days. In the fourth year, May 2016, trees continued to grow in the severe dry season. Shrubs also grew from urban waste input, and the herders fostered forest growth in the fenced area using their livestock.

Table 1. Plant species that germinated from urban waste in the first year (September 2012)

Family name	Scientific name	Hausa name	Plant coverage
Malvaceae	*Borreria radiata*	*kumuguduwa*	2
	Hibiscus sabdariffa	*sure*	+
	Hibiscus sabdarrifa	*ware*	+
	Sida cordifolia	*garumani*	+
Poaceae	*Andropogon gayanus*	*gamba*	+
	Brachiaria xantholeuca	*hatsin tsutsu*	+
	Cenchrus biflorus	*kalengia*	+
	Cymbopogon giganteus	*sabre*	+
	Cynodon dactylon	*halkiya*	+
	Dactyloctenium aegyptium	*atuku*	1'
	Digitaria longiflora	*birbirwa*	+
	Echinochloa colona	*garaji*	+
	Pennisetum glaucum	*hatsi*	2
	Pennisetum pedicellatum	*jambako*	+
	Schizachyrium exile	*kyasuwa*	1
	Sorghum bicolor	*dawa*	+
Cucurbitaceae	*Citrullus vulgaris*	*guna*	1'
	Cucurbita maxima	*kubewa*	1
Pedaliaceae	*Ceratotheca sesamoides*	*ramuti*	+
Tiliaceae	*Corchorus tridens*	*koku*	1'
Portulacaceae	*Portulaca oleracea*	*halusin sa*	+
Commelinaceae	*Commelina benghalensis*	*balasa kura*	+
	Commelina forskalaei	*balasa*	1'
Solanaceae	*Solanum lycopersicum*	*tomate*	+
Zygophyllaceae	*Trubulus terrestris*	*tsaida*	+
Amaranthaceae	*Amaranthus* spp.	*rukubu*	1
	Celosia trigyna	*nannafa*	+
Convolvulaceae	*Ipomoea vegans*	*walkindam*	1'
	Jacquemontia tamnifolia	*kukumbara*	+
	Merremia tridentata	*yambururu*	+
Capparaceae	*Gynandropsis gynandra*	*ranje daji*	+
Leguminosae	*Alysicarpus rugosus*	*gadagi*	+
	Arachis hypogaea	*korenshe*	+
	Cassia mimosoides	*bagaruwa kasa*	+
	Cassia obtusifolia	*tafasa*	+
	Indigofera prieureana	*kyamuro*	1
	Indigofera tinctoria	*baba*	+
	Zornia glochidiata	*maras*	+
Not identified	Not identified	*masun katangari*	+
	Not identified	*kasaura*	+
	Not identified	*gidagiri*	1'
	Not identified	*tonka daji*	+

Notes:
1) The plot was a 50 × 50 m fenced plot.
2) Plant coverage is rated as follows 4 for 4/4–3/4, 3 for 3/4–2/4, 2 for 2/4–1/4, 1 for 1/4–1/20, 1' for 1/20–1/100 and + for less than 1/100.

Table 2. Perennial and tree species that grew in the second year (December 2013)

Scientific name	Hausa name	Number of plants
Cassia obtusifolia	tafasa	1,122
Balanites aegyptiaca	aduwa	150
Borassus aethiopium	kaba	110
Indigofera tinctoria	baba	90
Antidesma venosum	magariya	55
Phoenix dactylifera	dabino	48
Adansonia digitata	kuka	15
Guiera senegalensis	sabara	15
Acacia nirotica	bagaruwa	5
Combretum nioroense	geza	5
Pergularia tomentosa	fataka	5
Detarium senegalense	takowasala madawa	4
Boscia senegalensis	anza	2
Piliostigma reticulatum	kalgo	2
Faidherbia albida	gawo	1
Bauhinia rufescens	dirga	1
Acacia laeta	akura	1
Tamarindus indica	tsamya	1
Calotropis procera	tumfafiya	1
Total		1,633

Note: 50×50 m fenced plot.

Conclusion

In the Sahel, farmers have been implementing traditional soil management practices such as the application of dry farmyard manure and household waste, livestock corralling, and fallows (Orr, 1995; Harris, 1999; Gandah et al., 2003; Shinjo et al., 2008; Suzuki et al., 2014). Hausa farmers' cultivation and grazing activity cause the soil to deteriorate, and also restore it to enable these activities to continue. Waste is transported promptly to denuded areas of farmland. In these areas, waste is the driving force for *harkuki*: the restoration of the land's productivity. Since 2002, when this author first developed an interest in the use of waste by the Hausa for environmental restoration, the practice appears to have become more widespread and frequent (Oyama & Mammam, 2010; Oyama, 2012; 2015). Natural conditions in the Sahel are changeable; these changes are known in Hausa as *harkuki*, or movement. The *harkuki* generated by humans causes the land to deteriorate, and also enables its

172

restoration. The Hausa people's practice of using waste for degraded land could be seen as emerging from their outlook on life in relation to the changeable natural environment around them, an outlook combined with a work ethic that involves actively generating *harkuki* to overcome difficulties and safeguard one's livelihood. According to Moyo & Mine (2016), the concept of "African Potentials" is defined as the capability Africans have to achieve solutions to contradictions among people utilizing indigenous knowledge of human relations that has been continuously transformed and has accumulated on the level of everyday life. This practice of urban waste input based on local concept of *harkuki* is a typical African Potentials, taking measures against the ways desertification is promoted in everyday life.

Current approaches to addressing desertification tend to be directed at technological development and permanent forest creation, involving expensive equipment and consuming vast quantities of energy and capital. Most of these approaches have failed due to shortages of finance, labour and suitable land, together with unstable foreign aid policies. The practices of the Hausa suggest the need for understanding the changeable natural environment induced by variable climate and human activity in the Sahel region. In densely populated areas of the Sahel, working against the popular belief that human activity and livestock destroy the land, for combating desertification, urban waste and livestock can instead be used to restore the degraded land, which makes this practice a kind of reverse thinking, which uses urban waste in an opposite manner to human activity and livestock that are exacerbating desertification.

Acknowledgements

This article is based on my paper presented at 'Land, the State and Decolonising the Agrarian Structure in Africa: A Colloquium in Honour of Professor Sam Moyo,' organized at the University of Cape Town, South Africa, on November 28–29, 2016. This colloquium was sponsored by the Japan Society for the Promotion of Science, Grant-in-Aid for Scientific Research (S) "'African Potential" and

Overcoming the Difficulties of Modern World: Comprehensive Research That Will Provide a New Perspective for the Future of Humanity' (KAKENHI 16H06318 headed by Motoji Matsuda, Kyoto University), as well as by the University of Cape Town's Research Office (URC). The author would also like to express my gratitude for the financial support of the Japan Society for the Promotion of Science, Grant-in-Aid for Scientific Research (KAKENHI 23221012, 25300011, 15H02591, 17H04506 and 17H02235).

Notes

(1) All names of individuals are fictitious in this chapter.

References

Adamu, M. 1978. *The Hausa Factor in West African History*. Ahmadu Bello University Press, Zaria.

Anderson, D. & R. Fishwick 1984. *Fuelwood Consumption and Deforestation in African Countries: World Bank Staff Working Papers No.704*. World Bank, Washington D.C. Ayantunde, A.A., T.O. Williams, H.M.J. Udo, S. Fernández-Rivera, P. Hiernaux & H. van

Keulen 2000. Herders' perception, practice, and problems of night grazing in the Sahel: Case studies from Niger. *Human Ecology*, 28(1): 109–130.

Baier, S. 1980. *An Economic History of Central Niger*. Clarendon Press, New York.

Blench, R. 1996. Aspects resource conflict in semi-arid Africa. *ODI Natural Resource Perspectives 16*. Online. http://www.odi.org.uk/sites/odi.org.uk/files/odi-assets/publications-opinion-files/2959.pdf (Accessed February 3, 2018).

Brouwer, J. & J.M. Powell 1998. Increasing nutrient use efficiency in West-African agriculture: The impact of micro-topography on

174

nutrient leaching from cattle and sheep manure. *Agriculture, Ecosystems and Environment*, 71: 229–239.

Dregne. H.E. 1986. Desertification of arid lands. In (F. El-Baz & M.H.A. Hassan, eds.) *Physics of Desertification*, pp. 4–34. M. Nijhoff, Dordrecht.

Europafrica.net 2011. *Great Green Wall for Sahara and Sahel: Combat Desertification, Improving Food Security and Climate Change Adaptation.* Online. http://europafrica. net/2011/10/10/africa-and-europe-joint-efforts-to-combat-desertification/ (Accessed January 25, 2018).

FAO/UNESCO 1971. *Soil Map of the World 1:5,000,000.* UNESCO, Rome.

Galle, S., M. Ehrmann & C. Peugeot 1999. Water balance in a banded vegetation patter: A case study of tiger bush in western Niger. *Catena*, 37(1–2): 197–216.

Gandah, M., J. Bouma, J. Brouwer, P. Hiernaux & N. van Duivenbooden 2003. Strategies to optimize allocation of limited nutrients to sandy soils of the Sahel: A case study from Niger, West Africa. *Agriculture, Ecosystems and Environment*, 94(3): 311–319.

Gonzalez, P. 2001. Desertification and a shift of forest species in the West African Sahel. *Climate Research*, 17(2): 217–228.

Harris, F. 1999. Nutrient management strategies of small-holder farmers in a short-fallow farming system in north-east Nigeria. *The Geographical Journal*, 165(3): 275–285.

Institute for Economic and Peace 2015. *Global Terrorism Index 2015.* Online. http:// economicsandpeace.org/wp-content/uploads/2015/11/Global-Terrorism-Index-2015. pdf (Accessed January 25, 2018).

Leisinger, K.M., K. Schmitt & ISNAR 1995. *Survival in the Sahel: An Ecological and Developmental Challenge.* International Service for National Agricultural Research, Hague.

Malam Issa, O., J. Trichet, C. Défarge, A. Couté & C. Valentin 1999. Morphology and microstructure of microbiotic soil crusts on a tiger bush sequence (Niger, Sahel). *Catena*, 37(1–2): 175–196.

Mortimore, M.J. 1998. *Roots in the African Dust: Sustaining the Drylands.* Cambridge University Press, Cambridge.

Mortimore, M.J. & W.M. Adams 2001. Farmer adaption, change and "crisis" in Sahel. *Global Environmental Change*, 11(1): 49–57.

Mortimore, M. & B. Turner 2005. Does the Sahelian smallholder's management of woodland, farm trees, rangeland support the hypothesis of human-induced desertification? *Journal of Arid Environments*, 63(3): 567–595.

Moyo, S. & Y. Mine 2016. *What Colonialism Ignored: 'African Potentials' for Resolving Conflicts in Southern Africa*. Langaa RPCIG, Cameroon.

Obioha, E.E. 2008. Climate change, population drift and violent conflict over land resources in northeastern Nigeria. *Journal of Human Ecology*, 23(4): 311–324.

Orr, B. 1995. Natural forest management in Sahelian ecosystems of southern Niger. *Journal of Arid Environments*, 30(2): 129–142.

Oyama, S. 2009. Ecological knowledge of Hausa cultivators for the land degradation process in Sahel, West Africa. *Geographical Reports of Tokyo Metropolitan University*, 44: 103–112.

— 2012. Land rehabilitation methods based on the refuse input: Local practices of Hausa farmers and application of indigenous knowledge in the Sahelian Niger. *Pedologist*, 55(3): 466–489.

— 2014. Farmer-herder conflicts, land rehabilitation, and conflict prevention in Sahel region of West Africa. *African Study Monographs Supplementary Issue*, 50: 103–122.

— 2015. Land degradation and ecological knowledge-based land rehabilitation: Hausa farmers and Fulbe herders in the Sahel region, West Africa. In (T. Reuter, ed.) *Averting a Global Environmental Collapse: The Role of Anthropology and Local Knowledge*, pp. 165–185. Cambridge Scholars Publishing, Cambridge.

— 2017. Hunger, poverty and economic differentiation generated by traditional custom in villages in the Sahel, West Africa. *Japanese Journal of Human Geography*, 69(1): 27–42.

Oyama, S. & I. Mammam 2010. Ecological knowledge of Hausa cultivators and *in situ* experiment of the land rehabilitation in Sahel, West Africa. *Geographical Reports of Tokyo Metropolitan University*, 45: 31–44.

Reenberg, A., T.L. Nielsen & K. Rasmussen 1998. Field expansion and reallocation in the Sahel: Land use pattern dynamics in a fluctuating biophysical and socio-economic environment. *Global Environmental Change*, 8(4): 309–327.

Republique du Niger 2004. *Troisieme Rapport National du Niger dans le Cadre de la Mise en œuvre de la Convention Internationale de Lutte Contre la Desertification (CCD) Document Final.* Online. http://www.case.ibimet.cnr.it/keita-niger/data/file/3_rep_niger.pdf (Accessed August 29, 2016.)

Shinjo, H., K. Hayashi, T. Abdoulaye & T. Kosaki 2008. Management of livestock excreta through corralling practice by sedentary pastoralists in the Sahelian region of West Africa: A case study in southwestern Niger. *Tropical Agriculture and Development*, 52(4): 97–103.

Smith, M. G. 1971. *The Economy of Hausa Communities of Zaria: A Report to the Colonial Social Science Research Council.* Johnson Reprint Corporation, New York.

Suzuki, K., R. Matsunaga, K. Hayashi, N. Matsumoto, R. Tabo, S. Tobita & K. Okada 2014. Effects of traditional soil management practices on the nutrient status in Sahelian sandy soils of Niger, West Africa. *Geoderma*, 223–225: 1–8.

Swinton, M.S. 1988. Drought survival tactics of subsistence farmers in Niger. *Human Ecology*, 16(2): 123–144.

Tschakert, P. 2007. Views from the vulnerable: Understanding climatic and other stressors in the Sahel. *Global Environmental Change*, 17: 381–396.

Turner, M.D. 1999. Labour process and the environment: The effects of labour availability and compensation on the quality of herding in the Sahel. *Human Ecology*, 27(2): 267–296. Tybirk, K. 1991. *Regeneration of Woody Legumes in Sahel: AAU Reports 27.* Aarhus University Press, Aarhus.

United Nations, Department of Economic and Social Affairs, Population Division 2017. *World Population Prospects 2017.* Online. https://esa.un.org/unpd/wpp/ (Accessed January 25, 2018).

Wezel, A. & J. Haigis 2002. Fallow cultivation system and farmers' resource management in Niger, West Africa. *Land Degradation and Development*, 13: 221–231.

World Bank 2012. *World Development Indicators 2012.* World Bank, Washington D.C. World Food Programme 2012. *Drought Affects*

Millions in the Sahel. Online.
http://www.wfp.org/stories/drought-returns-sahel (Accessed January 25, 2018).

Author's E-mail: \underline{oyama@jambo.africa.kyoto-u.ac.jp}

Chapter 7

Reactions of Peasants to Global Capital in Zimbabwe: A Case Study of Tobacco Contract Farming in Mashonaland East Province

Yumi Sakata[1]

Introduction

This study presents an empirical survey of the economy of peasant farmers against the backdrop of the penetration of global market forces into rural Zimbabwe. As shown in a series of works by Sam Moyo and the African Institute of Agrarian Studies based in Harare, the Fast Track Land Reform Programme (FTLRP), which was undertaken in the 2000s, reconfigured the agrarian structure in Zimbabwe. Tobacco is one of the sectors that clearly show that among the aims of the FTLRP was the peasantization of the country's agriculture. The reconfiguration of the tobacco industry has taken place in parallel with the FTLPR and the introduction of the contract farming arrangement fuelled the peasantization of the industry. Through the tobacco contract farming arrangement, the peasants have been more exposed to the global capital, and their tobacco farming has been much more internationalized. After showing the mode of business conducted by the global capital in the rural Zimbabwe, the study concludes by demonstrating the diversified rural tobacco market which the peasants take advantage of in the global economy.

This study presents an empirical survey of the economy of peasant farmers against the backdrop of the penetration of global market forces into rural Zimbabwe. As shown in a series of works by Sam Moyo and the African Institute of Agrarian Studies based in Harare, the FTLRP, which was undertaken in the 2000s, reconfigured the agrarian structure in Zimbabwe. The FTLRP was aimed at adjusting the racial land possession imbalance, and is characterized as

179

the means of drastic transformation of the agricultural structure.[2] The reform distributed land from the dominant white large-scale farmers to mass African peasant farmers. Mamdani (2008) highlighted that Zimbabwean land reform made the greatest transfer of property in Southern Africa since colonisation, and it has all happened extremely rapidly.

This highly redistributive land reform, which was supposedly 'democratic,' faced harsh criticism from around the world. The western media and some groups of academia argued that the reform caused gross violation of 'human rights' through the acquisition of 'private property' from the people (who 'owned' the land before), and the collapse of 'food sovereignty' (Hammer et al., 2003; Richardson, 2005). The media portrayed the reform as 'brutal,' 'undemocratic' or 'violent' since the white 'privately owned' lands were often forcefully expropriated.[3] While the fact that there were brutal violations of people's rights during the land reform process cannot be erased, Moyo's work showed how the FTLRP greatly distributed land to peasants and the racially imbalanced agrarian structure was adjusted to a great extent.

Tobacco is one of the sectors that clearly show that among the aims of the FTLRP was the peasantization of the country's agriculture. With the introduction of contract farming, the tobacco industry managed to absorb many peasants who had been allocated relatively small plots under the FTLRP, as A1 farmers (Moyo, 2011a; 2013; Chambati, 2013; Moyo & Nyoni, 2013; Moyo & Yeros, 2013). The research interest of this chapter is to explore how the tobacco industry became the major agricultural industry for peasants after the FTLRP.

The chapter also examines the arrangements that opened the industry to peasants through contracts with international companies. This development raises questions of whether the peasants should be exposed more intensely to global capital, whether they have been marginalised even more by global capital, and how they cope with the global market forces of the 21st century. After discussing the way business is conducted in rural Zimbabwe with global capital, the chapter concludes by showing how peasants have created an informal agricultural market and taken advantage of neoliberal capital.

The Peasantization of the Tobacco Industry

It was through the white settlers that the agrarian structure is characterized as a dualistic system under which blacks became a labour pool for white farming capitalists. At independence of Zimbabwe in 1980 the white population was less than 2% although it owned about 47% of the agricultural land; blacks constituted more than 95% of the population and occupied the remaining land (Moyo, 2011a). Until the beginning of the FTLRP, this racially dualistic system persisted. The FTLRP redistributed land through small-scale (A1) farms and medium-scale commercial (A2) farm schemes. The size of A1 farms varies depending on the condition and the environment of the agricultural lands. However, Moyo (2013) showed the average size of an A1 farm to be 20 hectares, including access to common grazing areas, and the average size of an A2 farm 142 hectares. The reform programme had produced about 145,800 A1 farms and 23,000 A2 farms by 2010 (Moyo, 2013: 43). Communal areas account for 42% of land in the country, and 74.2% of this land is in the poorest rainfall zones (Moyo, 1992: 9). Blacks were forced to live in communal areas during the colonial era, which ended in 1980.

Sam Moyo demonstrated how the agrarian structure shown in his tri-modal was reconfigured from 2000, as shown in Table 1 (Moyo & Nyoni, 2013; Moyo & Yeros, 2013). The tri-modal structure is composed of peasants, medium-to-large-scale farms and estates (Chambati, 2013; Moyo & Nyoni, 2013; Moyo & Yeros, 2013). While the tri-modal agrarian structure still favours the class of large-scale farms, the land occupied by the peasants has been greatly expanded after the FTLRP (see Table 1 below).

Table 1. Agrarian structure: Estimated landholdings from 1980 to 2010

Farm categories	Farms/households (000's)						Area held (000 ha)						Average Farm size (ha)		
	1980		2000		2010		1980		2000		2010		1980	2000	2010
	No	%	No	%	No	%	ha	%	ha	%	ha	%			
Group 1															
Peasantry	700	98.00	1,125	98.70	1,321	98.00	16,400	49.00	20,067	61.00	25,826	79.00	23	18	20
Group 2															
Mid-sized farms	8.5	1.00	8.5	1.00	30.9	2.00	1,400	4.00	1,400	4.00	4,400	13.00	165	165	142
Large	5.4	1.00	4,956	0.40	1,371	0.10	13,000	39.00	8,691.6	27.00	1,156.9	4.00	2,407	1,754	844
Sub-total	13.9	2.00	13,456	1.40	32,271	2.10	14,400	43.00	10,091.6	31.00	5,556.9	17.00	2,572	1,919	986
Group 3															
Estates	0.296	0.10	0.296	0.02	0.247	0.02	2,567	8.00	2,567	8.00	1,494.60	5.00	8,672	8,672	6,051
Total	714	100.00	1,139	100.00	1,354	100.00	33,367	100.00	32,726	100.00	32,878	100.00	46.7	28.7	24.3

Source: Adapted from Moyo & Nyoni (2013).

This new structure, a result of the FTLRP, is unique in that it is based on a clear demarcation in state policy: distinct land holding sizes, forms of land tenure, the social status of landholders, and dominant forms of labour used (Moyo, 2011a; Moyo & Nyoni, 2013; Moyo & Yeros, 2013). The peasantry, or the small-scale farming group, is dominant in aggregate number of farms, including communal, old resettlement and A1 farms (group 1 in Table1). Farmers in this category hold usufruct permits over their land and depend on family labour (Moyo & Nyoni, 2013; Moyo & Yeros, 2013). The second group consists of small-scale commercial farms (SSCFs), A2 farms and large-scale commercial farms (LSCFs) (group 2 in Table 1). The farmers in the latter category hold 99-year non-tradable leases and depend more on hired labour than on family labour (Moyo & Nyoni, 2013; Moyo & Yeros, 2013). This second category is remarkable among the other groups in the tri-modal disposition as a new class that emerged as a result of the FTLRP. Before the advent of the FTLRP this class was made up mainly of large-scale white commercial farmers. After the FTLRP the proportion of medium-sized black-owned farms increased and the class became more racially balanced. The third group comprises state-owned and privately owned estates (group 3 in Table 1). They hire large numbers of permanent and seasonal labourers and contract outgrowers (Moyo, 2011a; Moyo & Nyoni, 2013).

The FTLRP enlarged the peasantry and increased the number of medium-sized farms, while reducing the number of LSCFs, most of which were white-owned. With the addition of thousands more black

A2 medium- and large-scale farms, the land reform programme has created a 'de-racialised' tri-modal agrarian structure (Moyo, 2011b). While the estates retain about 5% of all agricultural land, the actors involved in their businesses, such as outgrowers and shareholders, are diversified in terms of race, nationality and class (Moyo & Nyoni, 2013: 203).

The tobacco sector has steadily aligned with the agricultural class transformation brought about through the FTLRP. With the land reform the number of small-to-medium-sized tobacco growers greatly increased, and the structure of the tobacco industry was 'de-racialised.' Since the arrival of the British South African Company column in 1890, land in Zimbabwe has had great potential for farming, especially for tobacco (Rubert, 1998).[4] Immigrants from Europe and South Africa led by the column started growing tobacco in the early 1920s, and tobacco had surpassed the revenue from gold among Southern Rhodesia's exports by 1945 (Rubert, 1998). Tobacco has been an important cash crop for both the country and the farmers. The colonial government also put a lot of effort such as subsidies to expand tobacco farming led by the commercial white farmers, and the tobacco industry during the colonial time was formed as a dualistic aspect, divided between white capitalists and black labourers (Rubert, 1998). The tobacco structure only configured after the FTLRP, in parallel with the new national-level agrarian tri-modal structure.

Table 2 shows yield and area planted for tobacco in the three classes. Small farms in the table consist of communal, old resettlement and A1 farms. Medium farms consist of SSCF and A2 farms. Large farms consist of LSCFs. The table shows how the tobacco industry has changed to another level of tri-modal, enlarging the presence of small-to-medium-scale farms, as can also be seen at the national level.

In 1995, before the land reform programme, the dominant large farms grew about 98% of tobacco, and about 94% of the tobacco fields were controlled by this class. By 2012 the share of national tobacco production of large farms had decreased to 21%, medium farms increased their share to 26%, and small farms had the largest share, growing 53%. The area under tobacco has also been transformed the racially balanced tri-modal, in which the dominant small-scale farmers have more than 50% shares in the production and the tobacco growing area. The FTLRP created an agricultural structure for small- and medium-scale farms to engage in the industry as tobacco growers.

The tobacco industry was also reconfigured by the introduction of contract farming. Until 2004 all the tobacco produced in Zimbabwe was sold at only three licensed auction floors: Boka Tobacco Auction Floors, Tobacco Sales Floor Limited and Premier Tobacco Auction Floors. With the advent of contract farming, however, growers have been able to choose their own markets, whether the auction floors or under a contract arrangement. With the latter, farmers receive inputs in advance and the contracting company deducts the costs from their sales. After the introduction of contract farming, the number of tobacco growers, the overall area of tobacco planted and the volume of tobacco sales all increased. The expansion of small-to-medium farm classes through the FTLRP and the introduction of contract farming in 2004 have popularized tobacco farming and greatly increased the number of tobacco growers. While there were only 1,547 tobacco growers at independence in 1980, by 2014 there were 87,166 farmers registered as tobacco growers (Fig. 1). Of this total, 31,487 (about 36%) were A1 farmers, and 39,094 (about 44%) were communal farmers (TIMB, 2014). Thus, more than 80% of tobacco growers were small farmers or peasants. Indeed, while the industry was traditionally led by white LSCFs, the peasantry is now the driver of the industry.

Table 2. Tobacco production by class

	1995				2000				2012			
	Production		Area		Production		Area		Production		Area	
	Tons	%	ha	%	Tons	%	ha	%	Tons	%	ha	%
Small-scale	3,598	2.0	3,760	5.2	9,258	4.8	11,204	14.6	73,656	53.0	58,317	62.9
Medium-scale	326	0.2	427	0.6	1,051	0.6	834	1.1	36,449	26.0	21,670	23.4
Large-scale	174,728	97.8	68,273	94.2	179,333	94.6	64,448	84.3	29,074	21.0	12,718	13.7
Total	178,652	100.0	72,460	100.0	189,642	100.0	76,486	100.0	139,179	100.0	92,705	100.0

Source: Complied by the author from Zimstat (2012) data.
Note: Large-scale comprises large-scale commercial farms, medium-scale comprises small-scale commercial farms and A2 farms, and small-scale comprises A1 and communal area farms.

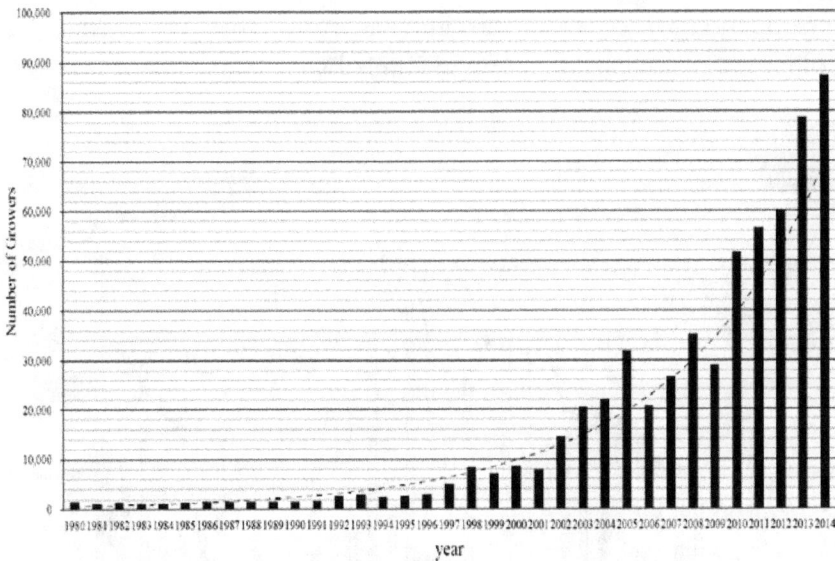

Fig. 1. The number of registered tobacco growers since 1980 Source: TIMB (2014).

Fig. 2 shows the area of tobacco planted and the volume of tobacco sales, which started to climb from an all-time low of about 49 million kg in 2008[5] to 216 million kg in the 2014 harvest. The area planted to tobacco has increased even more markedly. In the 2014 agricultural season, the area under tobacco reached its greatest extent since 1980.

Fig. 3 shows the volume of tobacco sold through contract arrangements and tobacco auction floors since the introduction of contract farming in 2004. In 2008, when the volume of tobacco sales was the lowest, around 49 million kg was transacted, of which 36%, or 18 million kg, was sold through the auction floors, and 63%, or 31 million kg, was sold through contract arrangements. In the 2014 season, when the volume of tobacco sales increased to around 216 million kg, about 23%, or 51 million kg, was sold through the auction floors and about 76%, or 165 million kg, was sold through contract arrangements. While the entire volume of tobacco sales grew fourfold between 2008 and 2014, tobacco sales through contract arrangements increased fivefold during the same period. Tobacco sales at auction floors also increased but did not reach as high a level as that produced through contract arrangements. It is obvious that

185

introduction of contract farming has substantially increased the volume of tobacco production in Zimbabwe.

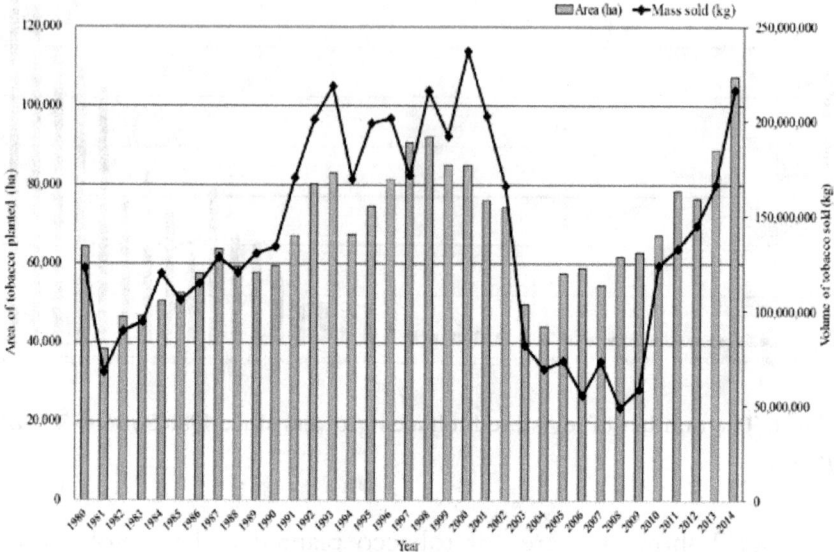

Fig. 2. Area of tobacco planted and volume of tobacco sold since 1980
Source: TIMB (2014)

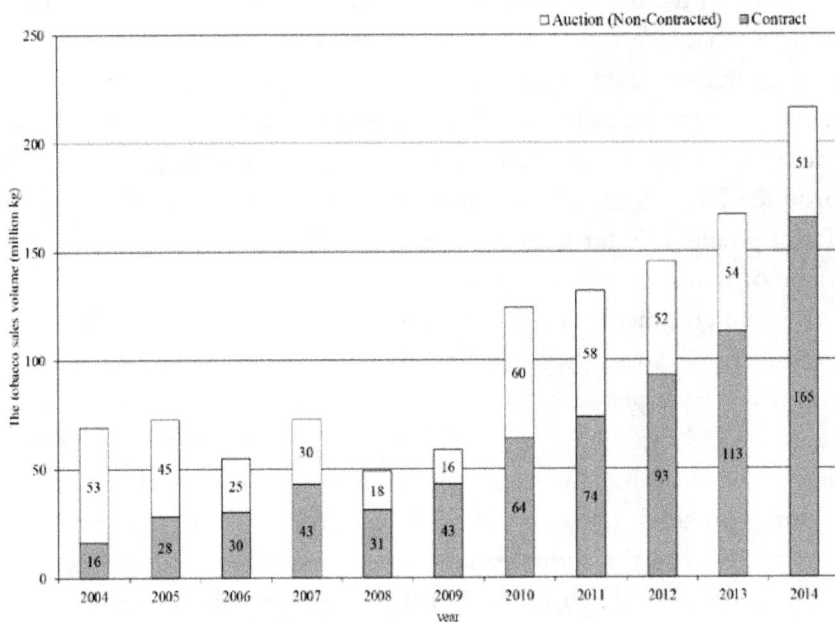

Fig. 3. Tobacco sales volume by different markets

Source: TIMB (2014).

Table 3. Contracted tobacco production by farming sector (2014)

	Number of Growers	%	Mass (kg)	%	Mass (Value, USD)	%
A1 Resettlement	17,918	36.5	42,197,031	26.0	128,656,613	23
Communal	21,641	44.0	38,452,893	23.0	115,667,801	21
Other	9,584	19.5	84,722,592	51.0	304,116,902	56
Total	49,143	100.0	165,372,516	100.0	548,441,316	100

Source: TIMB (2014).

Contract farming arrangements are open to all tobacco growers, from large- to small- scale. While many donors and think-tanks assume that land beneficiaries are inherently incapable of producing agricultural commodities commercially, and accordingly promote the privatisation of communal land tenure, ostensibly to improve access to credit (Moyo & Nyoni, 2013: 198), international tobacco companies have expanded their operations in resettlement and communal areas in Zimbabwe since the FTLRP.

Among the 87,166 farmers registered as tobacco growers (Fig. 1), 49,143 tobacco growers registered as contracted farmer in 2014. And among the contracted farmers, about 80% of them are small-scale farmers or the peasantry: 36% of them are A1 farmers, and 44% of them are communal farmers (Table 3). Contracted A1 farmers produce 26% of national tobacco crop and communal farmers 23%. These small-scale farmers contribute less than half of the amount or value of national tobacco production.

Some contractors prefer to deal with peasants and medium-scale producers because 'they are less able to resist lower price margins compared to larger-scale producers, who generally have higher social standing and fare better in procuring inputs using their own income, credit, and subsidies' (Moyo, 2011a: 957). While the impact of contract farming on small farmers will be discussed later in this chapter, their contribution in the industry increased considerably compared with their marginal role before the FTLRP. Thus, the tobacco industry has been transformed and has subsumed various classes and races since the advent of the FTLRP.

Since 2011, Zimbabwe has been the third largest tobacco exporter in the world in trade value, after Brazil and the United States.[6] The value of exported tobacco has increased since the mid-2000s and the export value surpassed the levels achieved before the FTLRP (Fig. 4). While the largest volume of tobacco was sold to European Union countries until 2010, China became the biggest buyer of Zimbabwean tobacco in 2011. In 2014, China imported 36% of national tobacco production (TIMB, 2014).

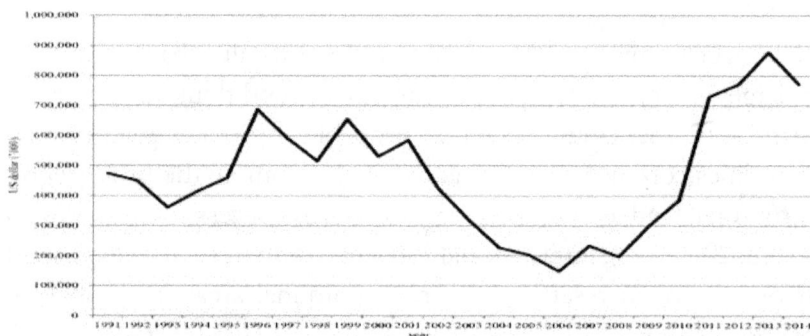

Fig. 4. Tobacco export value Source: TIMB (2014).

The FTLRP has brought about a revolution in the tobacco industry in Zimbabwe. The introduction of contract farming opened the door for the peasants to join as tobacco growers. The tobacco industry of Zimbabwe re-evolved in the 2000s, led by these peasants.

Contract Farming: The Agricultural Finance Solution?

Contract farming is not new in Zimbabwe but has been practised through tea, sugar, and cotton production since the mid-1950s (Jackson & Cheater, 1994). Especially after independence in 1980, the government supported contract farming to reduce the 'dualistic' agricultural structure, peasants versus commercial agriculture (Jackson & Cheater, 1994). Sachikonye (1989) studied contract farming from the cases of tea and sugar in Zimbabwe. And he concluded that 'contract farming is a crucial mechanism in the subsumption of growers to agri-business capital' (Sachikonye, 2016: 89). And he explained that while the contracted growers were much controlled by their contracting companies, the growers were not inferred as 'wage-labour equivalents' or 'disguised proletarians' since they still retained some measure of autonomy (Sachikonye, 1989; 2016: 89).

This survey shows how peasant growers conduct tobacco contract farming arrangements on the ground. A field survey was conducted in ward 7 of the Marondera district in Mashonaland East between July 2015 and June 2016.[7] The research area was chosen, first, for the author's historical interest, in that the land movement in the 1990s started from this ward. The FTLRP was carried out as a result of massive land movements occurred in several places, led by war veterans. And the research area, ward 7, is the first area where the movement was taken place among others.[8] A more practical reason is that the researchers found a number of global contracting companies operating in the ward.

In the study area the researchers interviewed 67 contracted farmers; all were A1 beneficiaries, all the farmers have 6 hectares arable land without irrigation systems. The researchers interviewed both contracted and independent farmers to compare their costs and revenues of tobacco farming. The researchers selected the

189

interviewees randomly among the farmers gathered at the public places, such as at communal tobacco barns, at village assembly points, or at shops. The interviews took place only with the agreed farmers at these public spaces or at their homestead upon their requests.

The study found four companies operating in the area (Table 4). These companies did not disclose their company profiles on their websites. However, according to an interview with an official of the TIMB,[9] two of the four are foreign companies and the other two are local. The former are financed from the U.S., and one of the local companies is apparently producing tobacco for a Japanese company.[10] The researchers collected information from 14 farmers contracted under company A, 11 under company B, 13 under company C, nine under company D, and 20 independent (non-contracted) farmers (Table 4).

The researchers inquired how the farmers had made their contract arrangements with the companies. Among the 47 contracted growers surveyed, 38 (or 80%) responded that the contractors came to their areas to recruit them. Seven (15%) said they themselves visited the companies in Harare seeking contract arrangements. One answered that he had been referred to the contracting companies by other farmers in the area. The interview results show that the tobacco companies take an active interest in recruiting small-scale farmers, making regular visits to the area. That seven of the contracted interviewees travelled to the capital, Harare, seeking contracts shows that farmers are not hesitant to work with global capital.

Table 4. Tobacco companies and independent growers in the study area

Company	Number (n=67)
A International (U.S.)	14
B International (U.S.)	11
C Local	13
D Local	9
Independent (non-contracted)	20
Total	67

Source: Author's survey data.

Every company has representatives working on the sites where they operate. The representatives use company cars to visit the contracted growers. Each representative is allocated a large area to supervise, for instance the whole of Marondera district, covering 100–150 growers. A representative from Company D said in an interview that the company assessed whether it was feasible to contract with a farmer before the contract was negotiated. Their assessment criteria included the applicants' assets—whether they had tobacco barns and scotch carts, for instance—whether they had debts with financial institutions or others, and the farm soil quality and tobacco productivity. According to the same representative, contracts were agreed only with farmers who could produce more than 1,000 kg per hectare and were not in debt to a bank.

The contracts signed for the 2014/2015 season with company B state that as of the date of signing the grower should have no outstanding debts or liabilities other than to the company (clause 8). Furthermore, the grower 'shall not, without the company's prior written approval, incur any debts or liabilities after the date of execution,' and in regard to the production of the tobacco on the farm, he should not sell, pledge or dispose of assets (clause 8) In clause 18 the grower is reminded not to dispose of or encumber any assets while any part of the debt to the company remains unpaid. The contract, which has 21 clauses, stipulates that the grower should keep his assets in reserve until he repays the debt to the company. In this way the company is sure to collect the debt from the grower's assets even if he cannot make payments from tobacco sales.

The debt in this context refers to the input costs borne by the company (clause 2). Clause 1 provides that the company may deliver inputs from time to time to meet the grower's requirements to produce tobacco. Clause 2 states that upon the supply of any inputs the company and the grower shall sign a delivery slip, which is the acknowledgement of receipt of the inputs and the agreed purchase price for the inputs. Clauses 1 and 2 confirm that the company has discretion to decide the kinds and amounts of inputs to deliver to the contracted farmers. Table 5 shows the inputs required for tobacco farming and those supplied by the four companies (A to D). All the growers needed to procure the items listed under the inputs column to grow tobacco, whether they were independent or contracted growers. The independent growers sourced the inputs themselves without incurring debts to the companies. All four companies supplied fertiliser, chemicals such as pesticides and fungicides, and tobacco baling materials. Company B arranged transport for the growers at a cost of $10 per bale. Companies C and D provided labour costs at $100 in cash per hectare. Company D supplied firewood as well.

The company's representatives are responsible for explaining the details of the contract arrangements when they sign contracts with growers. All 47 contracted growers who were interviewed agreed that the company representatives had explained the contract details, both in Shona[11] and in English. They all acknowledged that they fully understood their contracts—that the cost of the inputs, such as fertiliser and agricultural chemicals that they received upon signing, was to be deducted when they sold their tobacco. However, none had read the terms and conditions. One of the four companies did not make the terms and conditions available to its contracted growers.

Table 5. Inputs provided by the company

Company	Inputs						Operating costs	
	Seeds	Fertilizer	Chemicals	Firewood	Coal	Baling materials	Labour	Transport
A		●	●		●	●		
B	●	●	●	●		●		●
C		●	●		●	●	●	
D		●	●	●		●	●	

Source: Author's survey data.

Table 6. Whether the companies charge interest

Company	Yes	No	Unknown	Total
A	5 (36%)	9 (64%)	0 (0%)	14 (100%)
B	9 (69%)	2 (15%)	2 (15%)	13 (100%)
C	5 (56%)	3 (33%)	1 (11%)	9 (100%)
D	5 (45%)	6 (55%)	0 (0%)	11 (100%)
Total	24	20	3	47

Source: Author's survey data.

Contracted farmers were sometimes required to pay other costs to their contracting company. According to the terms and conditions of Company B, the firm provides that interest will accrue on the grower's debt 'at the rate of 3% per annum calculated from the date of each delivery slip on the total U.S. dollar figure reflected thereon' (clause 2).

The interviewees were asked whether they had paid any costs in accordance with their contractual arrangements. Twenty-four, about half, answered that they had been charged for some costs (as shown under the 'yes' column in Table 6), while 20 others said they were not (shown under the 'no' column). The remaining three farmers did not know whether they had been charged anything or not. The 24 were asked whether they knew what they were paying such charges for; 10 answered that they had paid penalties for shipping delays, and eight said they had paid interest on arrears from the previous season's debt. One answered that his input costs were subject to interest charges. The remaining interviewee did not answer the question.

The contract included the condition that the company will recover the money the grower owed it regardless of external circumstances. The contract does not acknowledge that the company and the farmers are collaborating in a tobacco farming venture. It is simply a loan agreement which is drafted by the company and is subject to interest charges. It is clear from the terms and conditions that the contract favours the company. Contracted growers cannot choose what inputs are to be supplied, and the company charges interest on the cost of the inputs. Most of the interviewed growers had only a rough understanding, if any, of the terms and conditions. While half of the interviewees understood that they needed to pay extra costs in accordance with their contracts, they did not know whether the costs were for interest, service fees or penalties, but they signed the contracts nonetheless.

Table 7 shows the motivations of the growers for contracting with the companies. About 90% of the interviewees said that they entered into contracts seeking access to finance to cover input costs without having to spend money themselves. Field data showed that tobacco growers lacking finances were more willing to sign contracts even with interest and other fees charged. Thus, in the absence of the tobacco companies these growers would be unable to access finance. Much less interviewees chose their motivation of being under contract as advantage of securing market. This is because tobacco market, auction floor, is always available for farmers, even if they are not contracted, as long as they are duly registered as tobacco farmers at TIMB. Thus, the peasant farmers often meet financial challenges to secure input costs tend to choose growing tobacco under contract arrangements.

Table 7. Motivation for contracting

	Advantage of income	Advantage of securing market	Other	Unknown	Total
No. of farmers	42	3	1	1	47
Percentage	89.4	6.4	2.1	2.1	100.0

Source: Author's survey data.

According to Moyo & Nyoni (2013), the volume of agricultural finance, such as loans and aid sourced domestically or internationally, fell sharply throughout the 2000s. The volume of government agricultural credit declined to below $3 million in 2007, whereas it had averaged around $25 million per annum between 2000 and 2007. In 2004 it peaked at $104 million (Moyo & Nyoni, 2013: 235). The volume of private agricultural credit declined from over $315 million in 1998 to about $6 million in 2008 (Moyo & Nyoni, 2013). Hyperinflation made agricultural credit much less feasible as the value of money declined daily, or even hourly. While hyperinflation ended with the introduction of a multi-currency system in 2009, it was still difficult for farmers, especially small-scale growers, to secure agricultural finance.

The growers interviewed had no access to agricultural loans from financial institutions such as banks. Table 8 shows that 26% of contracted and 15% of independent growers had family support. Most of them had borrowed money from family members; two growers received remittances from their sons working in South Africa. Table 7 shows that income from family and relatives was not a significant source of income for the study sample. Given the scarcity of agricultural credit for growers, the tobacco contract farming arrangement worked as an agricultural finance solution.

A key motivation for growers to become contracted to companies was simply to earn cash. While they needed to look for markets for other agricultural products they grew, the market for tobacco was always secure, whether on the auction floors or with the contracting companies.

Table 8. Whether growers have family financial support

	With family support	Without family support	Total
Contracted farmers	12 (26%)	35 (74%)	47 (100%)
Independent farmers	3 (15%)	17 (75%)	20 (100%)

Source: Author's survey data.

All the interviewees grew maize, some of which they sold to the Grain Marketing Board (GMB). AIAS interviewed a substantial number of growers who still chose to sell some of their maize to GMB, ostensibly to qualify for its input schemes, which require a record of sales (AIAS, 2015: 117). While the GMB offers higher prices for maize, it is largely unable to pay for grain deliveries on time (AIAS, 2015). A contracted grower, Mr Masango,[12] explained why he grew tobacco, albeit reluctantly:

> I grow a lot of maize but there sometimes is not a reliable market, since GMB does not pay on time. They still owe me a lot of money for the maize I dispatched last year. I also sell my maize through the local market. I sell maize to the people who visit my farm. I actually do not want to grow tobacco but want to concentrate on growing maize, since tobacco takes a lot of money and labour. It also damages a lot of the soil on my farm. But I still need to grow tobacco because of the secured market and reliable cash return (interview, November 7, 2015).

Mr Masango said the availability of a reliable market was another reason for growing tobacco. The contracts stipulate that tobacco sold will be paid for in two business days. In the absence of reliable agricultural markets for maize and other crops, contracted tobacco farming is an attractive option.

Peasants' Perceptions of Global Capital

The contract growers were also polled about their perceptions of the companies they worked with. Twenty-nine of the 47 said they found the agreements to be fair; 18 considered them to be unfair. Did the contracted companies strictly follow their agreements, they were asked, to which 27 replied 'yes' and 19 'no.' Twenty-five had complained to their companies and 22 had simply kept quiet. More than half of the growers thought that the agreements were unfair, while almost the same number said that the companies had complied with the contracts. About half of the interviewed growers said they had complained to the companies.

Table 9. Input satisfaction survey

Are the inputs provided by the company enough? (n=47)		
Enough	12	26%
Not enough	34	72%
No answer	1	2%
Total	47	100%

Source: Author's survey data.

Table 10. Average cost of growing tobacco (inputs, USD)

	Seeds	Fertilizer	Chemicals	Total
Independent	25	462	92	579
Contracted	25	1,009		1,034

Source: Author's survey data.

Inputs

The interviewees complained mainly about the inputs they received from the companies and the selling price of their tobacco. Table 9 shows growers' satisfaction with the inputs supplied by the companies. Thirty-four of the 47 answered that the inputs provided by the company were insufficient for growing tobacco. They explained that while they received enough chemicals, the fertiliser they received was about half the recommended amount.

The interviewees also complained about the cost of the inputs provided by the companies. The prices of fertiliser and chemicals vary according to amount and kind. Table 10 shows the average input cost of seeds, fertiliser and chemicals spent on one hectare of planted tobacco for contracted and independent growers. The average input cost is $579 for independent growers and $1,034 for contracted growers.

Selling Price

About half of the interviewees thought that the prices the companies paid for their tobacco were fair; the same number considered them unfair (Table 11). Approximately 66% of the interviewees said they would negotiate with the companies if they had not already agreed to the prices offered.

Fig. 5 and Table 12 show household-level median income of growers under the different categories of production: contracted growers under each of the four companies and independent farmers. In Fig. 5 the solid line shows the income of the contracted growers under each of the four companies (A to D), and the dotted line shows the income of the independent farmers. The numbers are based on their incomes, after deductions for inputs and other operational costs, such as levies and insurance. However, the figures do not include labour costs, because all the interviewed farmers paid their workers after they had been paid for their

Table 11. Peasants' perceptions of selling prices

(a)

Do you think the price given by the company is fair? (n=47)	
Fair	23 (49%)
Sometimes fair	1 (2%)
Unfair	23 (49%)
Total	47 (100%)

(b)

Will you complain to the company if you do not agree with the price? (n=47)	
Yes	31 (66%)
No	16 (34%)
Total	47 (100%)

Source: Author's survey data.

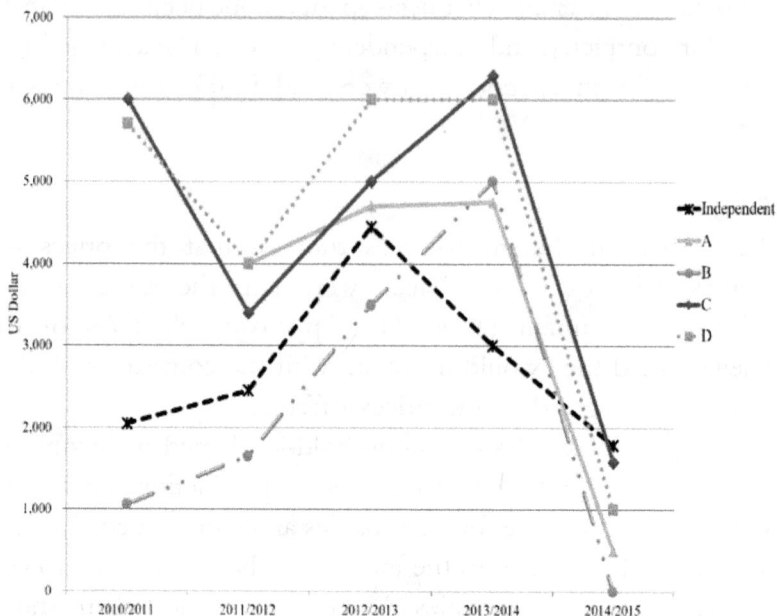

Fig. 5. Revenue from tobacco per household (median) Source: Author's survey data.

tobacco. Fig. 5 indicates that even though contracted farmers realised more income than independent farmers, their average income per household fluctuated widely over the seasons. The percentage change in revenue per season of the contracted growers ranged between -100% and 112%, while that of independent farmers moved in a narrower range, between -40% and 20% (Table 12). The revenue of the independent farmers was lower than that of contracted farmers in several years, except in the 2014/2015 season, where median revenue was the highest. That is, the contracted growers, despite facing high input costs, were able to earn a better income from tobacco in favourable seasons, while their income dropped sharply in poor seasons like 2014/2015.

Table 12. Revenue from tobacco per household (median) and the percentage change

	2010/2011	2011/2012	2012/2013	2013/2014	2014/2015
Independent	2,050	2,450	4,450	3,000	1,788
(% change)		(-20%)	(-82%)	(-33%)	(-40%)
A	N/A	4,000	4,700	4,750	500
			(-18%)	(-1%)	(-89%)
B	1,057	1,650	3,500	5,000	0
		(-56%)	(-112%)	(-43%)	(-100%)
C	6,000	3,395	5,000	6,290	1,579
		(-43%)	(-47%)	(-26%)	(-75%)
D	5,700	4,000	6,000	6,000	1,000
		(-30%)	(-50%)	(0%)	(-83%)

Source: Survey data

The 2014/2015 season was a difficult time, especially for small-scale tobacco growers with no access to irrigation. The revenue of all the interviewed farmers decreased in the 2014/2015 season, partly a result of the delayed rains and a lengthy dry spell. Some farmers planted at the beginning of the rainy season in November 2014 and their plants suffered damage when no substantial rains fell between mid-November 2014 and the beginning of January 2015. Erratic rainfall also resulted in severe leaching of nutrients from the soil (TRB, 2014). More fertiliser was required to address the problem, and there was premature ripening of the leaf, which required much more labour and thus increased production costs (TRB, 2014: 7). The Tobacco Research Board (TRB) noted that these problems reduced the quality of most of the crop, particularly in the case of small-scale growers, and inevitably affected prices (TRB, 2014). The unfavourable weather affected contracted growers in the research area particularly badly.

A substantial number of the interviewed growers failed to pay the companies for their inputs, which resulted in the termination of contract arrangements during 2014/2015. Some forfeited assets—such as cattle, scotch carts and ploughs—that they had used as collateral at the time of signing the contracts. Many said they had sold assets, such as cattle and goats, to meet their labour costs after failing to secure enough revenue from tobacco sales.

The survey showed that small-scale growers under contract arrangements could earn as much as, or more than, independent farmers when the weather was favourable. However, the income of contracted growers is less stable than that of independent farmers because of their greater dependence on the environment. Their input costs are markedly higher and their losses are correspondingly greater when there are unfavourable rains and poor tobacco prices. Independent farmers are flexible enough to adjust the volume of inputs in line with capricious weather changes.

The 47 interviewees were asked whether they would want to continue growing tobacco under contract arrangements in the future. Sixteen answered 'no' and 31 said 'yes,' despite the relatively high input costs and unstable revenue. As for the reasons for continuing under contracts, the interviews generally cited a lack of capital to pay for inputs themselves. Thirteen said they needed pre-supplied input materials and four said they had no alternative.

It is clear from the foregoing that contracts between tobacco companies and growers are simply a business arrangement that mainly favours the companies. The grower's income is neither guaranteed nor stable under the contract and many growers forfeited assets to cover debts to the companies or to pay for labour. Nevertheless, almost 66% of the interviewees said they would still want to remain under contract. The following section examines another aspect of peasants' approach to agricultural finance, an approach that helps them to make ends meet.

Dynamics of Rural Tabacco Market[13]

Makoronyera

The researchers interviewed Mr Makoni, an Agritex extension worker in ward 7,[14] about farmer survival tactics when not enough cash is earned from tobacco. He replied that A1 farmers resort to *makoronyera*, defined in the *Standard Shona Dictionary* (Hannan, 1984) as a 'place out of bounds for ploughing or building.' In practice the term is used to mean an arena where business is undertaken without licences or is illegal, or is conducted by crooks. The term refers both to informal activities and the people who conduct them. In the case of tobacco, *makoronyera* simply means side marketing. Mr Makoni said:

> Farmers undertake side marketing by selling their tobacco to *makoronyera*. *Makoronyera* buy tobacco directly from farmers outside the

formal markets, such as the auction floors or selling to their contracted companies. The side marketing transactions started just a few years ago. There was no such opportunity before. Side marketing was rampant, especially last year [the agricultural season 2014/2015] since tobacco prices, both at the auction floor and the ones given by the contractors, were very low. It is important to note, however, that any kind of side marketing activities is illegal. *Makoronyera* do business with farmers in this area [ward 7] at night to hide their illegal activities from us. I just saw a truck passing by my house last night, but I do not know where it came from. They were trying to buy tobacco from farmers in our area [ward 7]. I wanted to meet them but failed to do so. It is not allowed to sell or purchase tobacco outside the auction floors or contractor's market. But the farmers, sometimes, feel better doing business with *makoronyera*, since that way the farmer can earn cash apart from the sales they make at the auction floors or to their contracted companies. *Makoronyera* travel all over the country, wherever people grow tobacco. Since they travel all the way to our farm area, farmers can also save transport costs. It looks like a win–win situation for *makoronyera* and farmers, but side marketing is still illegal (interview, May 17, 2016).

As explained by Mr Makoni, *makoronyera* the TIMB requires growers to be 'properly registered' on its system and to submit statutory returns indicating whether they choose to sell their tobacco under contract arrangement or on the auction floors; they must keep to their choice of market (TIMB, 2016). Registration with the TIMB enables farmers to purchase seeds and is renewed every year.

Turning to the operations of the *makoronyera*, Mr Makoni said:

Makoronyera know where tobacco is grown, where to sell tobacco and whom to talk to at the auction floors. They can travel as far as Karoi to get tobacco. They cover all locations where tobacco is grown in the country and even come to our area! It seems they somehow have their own tobacco registration IDs, even though they do not grow tobacco by themselves. They do not spend a lot of money by growing tobacco. They may not have their own fields to grow it in. But they just buy it from farmers. So they save money and labour. Since they can buy low-quality tobacco from farmers and sell it at higher prices on the auction floors, they are disturbing the tobacco marketing system. Since they are connected with the insiders, they can get better prices for poor tobacco. The transactions run by *makoronyera* also discourage farmers to work hard to grow better quality tobacco (interview, May 17, 2016).

Growers view *makoronyera* as a financial opportunity. An A1 grower, Mr Chikukwa, said that while he delivers tobacco to the contracting company, he also sells tobacco scraps to *makoronyera*[15] because he does not expect a favourable price from the company. Another grower, Mr Mazodze, who is still in debt to a contracting company, also sells some of his tobacco to *makoronyera*.[16] Being indebted to the company means that he cannot get a cash return if he brings all his tobacco to the company because it would collect all his tobacco revenue to clear his debt. He sells some of his tobacco to the company to reduce his debt, but he also sells some to *makoronyera* to make cash on the side.

Besides making spot transactions on farms, according to two interviews,[17] some *makoronyera* also wait for farmers whose bales are declined on the auction floor.[18] A staff member of the Zimbabwe Farmers Union commented:

> *Makoronyera* wait at a certain point off the auction floors where farmers receive their declined tobacco bales. The bales carried to the tobacco auction floors get declined if they contain several grades of tobacco. Small-scale farmers definitely do not want to take such declined bales back to the farm, since they would need to pay the transport costs again. Farmers sometimes do not have any money left at the auction floors, because they have used all their money for their transport to come to the auction floors. If their tobacco is declined, farmers are willing to sell their tobacco to *makoronyera* even if they get very low price for their declined tobacco (interview, August 3, 2015).

None of the growers interviewed said they had sold declined tobacco to *makoronyera* at the auction floors, but a representative of the union disclosed that several kinds of side marketing were rampant in the tobacco market. The deals seemed to benefit growers and the *makoronyera* alike. However, the contracting companies find the practice unacceptable because they suffer losses when they fail to receive the expected amount of tobacco from their contracted growers.

Deals among Growers

The survey brought another kind of side marketing to light: transactions among farmers. For example, some contracted growers ask independent farmers to sell their tobacco on the auction floor when the auction price is higher than the contracted price. Likewise, some independent farmers ask contracted farmers to sell their tobacco if the contracted price is higher than what they expect to receive on the auction floor. A contracted grower, Mr Makuvaza, said:

> We always communicate with neighbouring farmers to check tobacco prices at several markets. We update the tobacco prices of several markets every day. For example, Company C is now buying tobacco between $1.20 and $1.30 per kg. I have not sold tobacco to Company C but I know their price. I am contracted under another company but deliver my tobacco to them only to cover the provided input cost. I can make more money sometimes on the auction floor or through other companies. I also communicated with *makoronyera* this year. I am expecting them to come tomorrow or the day after tomorrow to negotiate tobacco prices (interview, May 17, 2016).

Mr Makuvaza said he wanted to remain under contract for the sake of the inputs he received. However, he sold only enough tobacco to cover the debt he owed the contracting company. The rest was sold to another company, on the auction floor through an independent farmer, or to *makoronyera*. Thus, he used several tobacco markets to obtain the best prices.

Another contracted grower, Mr Mutenda, said:

> I ask my neighbour to sell some of my tobacco on the auction floor, since I do not want to give all my tobacco to the company. If I sell all my tobacco to the company, they just take all my profit and I am left with nothing. I still need cash. So what I do is to keep some of my

tobacco aside to get cash from selling it at the auction floor, which I ask my neighbour to do. I know what I am doing is not allowed under TIMB rules, but I still need to send my kids to school (interview, January 9, 2016).

Mr Mutenda said he diversified his marketing to make extra cash, because the costs deducted by the company were high and he would not receive an adequate return. However, he was also aware that such side marketing was not allowed.

Another grower, Mr Chirinda, said:

I am an independent farmer. I sell most of my tobacco to the auction floor, but sometimes I ask contracted farmers to sell my tobacco. Contracted farmers also ask me to sell tobacco on the auction floors. We talk daily about tobacco prices and know the daily price changes (interview, May 17, 2016).

Mr Makoni confirmed that contracted and independent growers communicated daily to find the best market:

Farmers daily get information from their neighbours on the tobacco prices. Farmers always talk with each other to find out the prices, or they can also call TIMB to find the average tobacco price of the day at the auction floors.

Cash transactions are involved when growers deal with their neighbours. Mr Chirinda and Mr Manwa, a contracted grower, stated that farmers wanting to sell their tobacco through a neighbour's market paid $25 per bale.[19] Mr Chirinda said the breakdown was $10 for administration, $10 for transport and $5 for food. The $25 is paid in advance.

Mr Chirinda said, 'This is a win–win transaction between us farmers since we can raise money by helping others. The farmers who want to sell their tobacco through another channel can also raise some more cash.'

While they take advantage of both formal and informal markets, farmers will not rely on the informal market alone. Mr Makoni noted that growers would not sell all their tobacco to makoronyera.[20] If they did, the TIMB system would notice that there were no deliveries of tobacco against the seed bought, which might lead to the withdrawal of the growers' licence. Farmers use their registration ID to buy seed, and the TIMB keeps records.

> I still sell several of my bales on the auction floor just to survive as a tobacco farmer, and I sell some to *makoronyera* or sometimes I ask my neighbour to sell my tobacco to a company. I want to continue growing tobacco and earn cash. To do that I need to continue to have my tobacco registration ID (interview with Mr Chikukwa, May 18, 2016).

Mr Makoni said, 'Selling tobacco to *makoronyera* seems to be a better deal for growers than shipping their tobacco to the auction floors or to the companies. But farmers are afraid of doing too much that is illegal.'

Fig. 6 shows the tobacco market channels the peasant farmers have in the ward 7. This includes both formal and informal channels. The solid arrows indicate the formal market both independent and contracted farmers maintain, and dotted arrows indicate the informal market they also utilize. There are at least three different kinds of tobacco markets the farmers have access to. The first market is the formal channel: the auction floors for the independent farmers and the contracting companies for the contracted farmers. The second market is the informal channel transacted between the farmers: the independent and contracted farmers utilize their own formal market for side marketing. Independent farmers would ask contracted farmers to sell their tobacco at their contracted companies, or contracted farmers would ask independent farmers to sell their tobacco at the auction floors. The third market is the informal channel with *makoronyera*, whom farmers would make spot transactions on the farm with. Fig. 6 shows that tobacco market on the ground is informalized but diversified, while they still maintain the formal market channels.

The diversification of agricultural market is also demonstrated by Scoones et al. (2010). With hyperinflation, economic and social instability, and the drastic agricultural transformation through the FTLRP, Scoones et al. (2010) expressed that 'the formal economy collapsed' and the local, rural informal economy play a significant role. This study showed that the peasants deal their tobacco with informal marketing practices does not mean that formal market went out completely. Whether we call it as collapsed or compromised, peasants rather take advantage of the diversified market to maximize their returns, utilizing both formal and informal markets. The rural tobacco market was much more diversified with the peasantization of the agrarian structure and the introduction of contract farming arrangement.

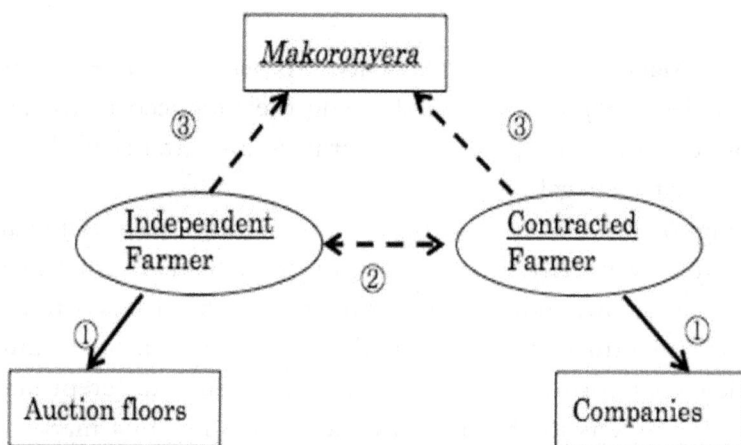

Fig. 6. Formal and informal markets Source: Author's survey data.

Conclusion

This study first described the tri-modal agricultural structure originally demonstrated by Moyo and colleagues. The examination of this system clarifies that the agriculture sector in Zimbabwe was peasantized during and after the FTLRP. The result of the FTLRP is shown clearly in the tobacco industry. And the peasantization of the industry was also the outcome of the introduction of contract farming. The peasants are now directly connected to global capital and their output of tobacco surpasses that of any other agricultural crop. While the industry was led by large-scale commercial farmers before FTLRP, the peasants now lead the industry.

Dealing with the contracting companies, however, does not generally benefit the peasants. There is no guarantee that they will achieve a stable income. Some of the contracted growers interviewed had not been able to make a profit because of high input costs raised by the companies and erratic rainfall. However, the peasants do not necessarily suffer under global capitalism. They also take advantage of global capital and are involved in side marketing. While they complete transactions on the auction floors and under contractual arrangements, they also exploit informal markets to maximize returns. Because of the benefits they can enjoy through these diversified but partly illegal tobacco markets, more peasants are willing to grow tobacco after the FTLRP. When they cannot access any other financial support, the contract farming arrangement with global capital at least ease initial costs for the peasants to start tobacco farming.

Many reports have described the current inflow of foreign capital into Africa as a 'new scramble' (Melber & Southall, 2010; Carmody, 2011; Moyo et al., 2012). The continent was once depicted as being in a crisis (Arrighi, 2002; Melber & Southall, 2010), suffering from a limited inflow of foreign investment. In the early years of the 21st century, however, the continent received more global investment than at any time in the previous five decades (Melber & Southall, 2010).

Inflows of global capital are reaching peasants even in parts of rural Zimbabwe, but far from being oppressed by unfavourable contracts, they exploit formal and informal market opportunities to their advantage. Indeed, the tobacco market has been to some extent informalized by the global economy.

Notes

(1) The author is a former research associate with the Centre for Applied Social Sciences at the University of Zimbabwe and is affiliated to the African Institute of Agrarian Studies. The research in this chapter was conducted under the auspices of these institutions and is not related to the

author's current occupation as an employee in the economic department of the embassy of Japan in Zimbabwe.

(2) While FTLRP was the most drastic and redistributive land reform, the country had implemented land reforms since its independent. Moyo (2013) has articulated its land reform programme which started after the independence, into three phases.

(3) The news reported then is found from the following site. http://www.zimbabwesituation. com/news/category/daily/ (Accessed December 30, 2017).

(4) Zimbabwe became independent in 1980. Until then the country was named Southern Rhodesia under colonial rule, which had lasted since 1923.

(5) At the peak of hyper-inflation in 2008, when the annual inflation rate reached more than 90 billion percent, it was extremely difficult for farmers to produce cash crops when they could not even use their money (Hayakawa, 2015).

(6) Data available from the UN COMTRADE database: http://comtrade.un.org/data/ (Accessed January 5, 2015).

(7) The ward is about 40 km south of Marondera, the capital of Mashonaland East, and about 100 km south-east of Harare.

(8) Masuko (2013) and Sadomba (2013) provide the empirical studies of the land movements taken place before the FTLRP by war veterans.

(9) Interviewed on May 10, 2015.

(10) Interview with a TIMB official on May 10, 2015. Japan Tobacco International signed a long-term agreement with Tribac in Zimbabwe for the supply of leaf tobacco on June 12, 2009 (JT press release, issued on June 12, 2009 and downloaded from www.jti.com/ download_file/395/410/, Accessed October 30, 2010).

(11) Shona is the local language spoken at the research site and widely in Zimbabwe generally.

(12) The informant's name has been changed.

(13) All the names used in this section were changed to protect the informants' privacy.

(14) Agritex is a department in the Ministry of Agriculture, Mechanization and Irrigation Development. Its main mission is to provide administrative, technical and advisory support to farmers (Zamchiya, 2011: 1095). In ward 7 of the Marondera district, there are four extension field

workers who provide agricultural knowledge to farmers and collect agricultural data from them.

(15) Interview, May 18, 2016.

(16) Interview, May 17, 2016.

(17) Interviews with a staff member of the Zimbabwe Farmers Union on August 3, 2015, and with Mr Masango in ward 7 on May 17, 2016.

(18) Auctioneers can reject tobacco because of its poor quality or in the absence of a buyer.

(19) Interviews at Mr Chirinda's homestead, May 17, 2016.

(20) Interview with Mr Makoni on May 17, 2016.

Acknowledgements

This article is based on my paper presented at 'Land, the State and Decolonising the Agrarian Structure in Africa: A Colloquium in Honour of Professor Sam Moyo,' organized at the University of Cape Town, South Africa, on November 28–29, 2016. This colloquium was sponsored by the Japan Society for the Promotion of Science, Grant-in-Aid for Scientific Research (S) '"African Potential" and Overcoming the Difficulties of Modern World: Comprehensive Research That Will Provide a New Perspective for the Future of Humanity' (KAKENHI 16H06318 headed by Motoji Matsuda, Kyoto University), as well as by the University of Cape Town's Research Office (URC).

References

African Institute of Agrarian Studies (AIAS) 2015. *Land Use, Agricultural Production and Food Security Survey: Trends and Tendencies, 2013/14.* African Institute for Agrarian Studies, Harare.

Arrighi, G. 2002. The African crisis: World systemic and regional aspects. *New Left Review*, 15: 5–36.

Carmody, P. 2011. *The New Scramble for Africa.* Polity Press, Cambridge.

Chambati, W. 2013. The political economy of agrarian labour

209

relations in Zimbabwe after redistributive land reform. *Agrarian South: Journal of Political Economy*, 2(2): 189–211.

Hammer, A., B. Raftopoulos & S. Jensen 2003. *Zimbabwe's Unfinished Business: Rethinking Land, State and Nation in the Context of Crisis.* Weaver Press, Harare.

Hannan, M. 1984. *Standard Shona Dictionary.* College Press Publisher Ltd., London. Hayakawa, M. 2015. *Anthropology of Hyperinfration.* (in Japanese). Jimbunshoin, Kyoto. Jackson, J. & A. Cheater 1994. Contract farming in Zimbabwe: Case studies of sugar, tea, and cotton. In (P.D. Little & M.J. Watts, eds.) *Living under Contract: Contract Farming and Agrarian Transformation in Sub-Saharan Africa*, pp.140–166. University of Wisconsin Press, Madison.

Mamdani, M. 2008. Lessons of Zimbabwe. *London Review of Books*, 30(23): 17–21.

Masuko, L. 2013. Nyabira-Mazowe war veteran's association: A microcosm of the national land occupation movement. In (S. Moyo & W. Chambati, eds.) *Land and Agrarian Reform in Zimbabwe: Beyond White-settler Capitalism*, pp. 123–155. CODESRIA, Dakar.

Melber, H. & R. Southall 2010. A new scramble for Africa? In (R. Southall & H. Melber, eds.) *A New Scramble for Africa? Imperialism, Investment, and Development*, pp. xix–xxvi. University of KwaZulu-Natal Press, Scottsville.

Moyo, S. 1992. *Land Tenure Issues in Zimbabwe during the 1990s.* The draft discussion paper presented for Centre for Applied Social Studies, University of Zimbabwe.

— 2011a. Changing agrarian relations after redistributive land reform in Zimbabwe. *Journal of Peasant Studies*, 38(5): 939–966.

— 2011b. Three decades of agrarian reform in Zimbabwe. *Journal of Peasant Studies*, 38(3): 493–531.

— 2013. Land reforms and redistribution in Zimbabwe since 1980. In (S. Moyo & W. Chambati, eds.) *Land and Agrarian Reform in Zimbabwe: Beyond White-settler Capitalism*, pp. 29–77. CODESRIA, Dakar.

Moyo, S. & N. Nyoni 2013. Changing agrarian relations after redistributive land reform in Zimbabwe. In (S. Moyo & W. Chambati, eds.) *Land and Agrarian Reform in Zimbabwe: Beyond*

White-settler Capitalism, pp. 195–250. CODESRIA, Dakar.

Moyo, S. & P. Yeros 2013. The Zimbabwe model: Radicalisation, reform and resistance. In (S. Moyo & W. Chambati, eds.) *Land and Agrarian Reform in Zimbabwe: Beyond White-settler Capitalism*, pp. 331–357. CODESRIA, Dakar.

Moyo, S., P. Yeros & P. Jha 2012. Imperialism and primitive accumulation: Notes on the new scramble for Africa. *Agrarian South: Journal of Political Economy*, 1(2): 181–203.

Richardson, C. 2005. The loss of property rights and the collapse of Zimbabwe. *CATO Journal*, 25(3): 541–565.

Rubert, S. 1998. *A Most Promising Weed: A History of Tobacco Farming and Labour in Colonial Zimbabwe, 1890–1945*. Centre for International Studies, Ohio University, Athens.

Sachikonye, L. 1989. *The State and Agribusiness in Zimbabwe: Plantations and Contract Farming, Leeds Southern African Studies, No.13*. African Studies Unit, Department of Politics, University of Leeds, Leeds.

— 2016. Old wine in new bottles? Revisiting contract farming after agrarian reform in Zimbabwe. *Review of African Political Economy*, 43(Sup1): 86–98.

Sadomba, Z.W. 2013. A decade of Zimbabwe's land revolution: The politics of the war veteran vanguard. In (S. Moyo & W. Chambati, eds.) *Land and Agrarian Reform in Zimbabwe: Beyond White-settler Capitalism*, pp. 79–121. CODESRIA, Dakar.

Scoones, I., N. Marongwe, B. Mavedzenge, J. Mahenehene, F. Murimbarimba & C. Sukume 2010. *Zimbabwe's Land Reform: Myths and Realities*. James Currey, Weaver Press and Jacana Media, Suffolk, Harare and Johannesburg:

Tobacco Industry and Marketing Board (TIMB) 2014. *TIMB Annual Statistical Report*.

TIMB, Harare.

— 2016. *Procedures for the Sale of Flue-cured Tobacco under the Dual (Contract and Auction) System in 2016 (BM/S.2)*. Online. http://www.timb.co.zw/downloads.php (Accessed December 5, 2016).

Tobacco Research Board (TRB) 2014. *Annual Report and Audit Accounts*. Tobacco Research Board, Harare.

Zamchiya, P. 2011. A synopsis of land and agrarian change in

Chipinge District, Zimbabwe. *Journal of Peasant Studies*, 38(5): 1093–1122.

Zimbabwe National Statistics Agency (Zimstat) 2012. *Compendium of Statistics 2*. Zimstat, Harare.

Author's E-mail: sakata.yumi@gmail.com

Chapter 8

Opportunities and Constraints for Black Farming in a Former South African Homeland: A Case Study of The Mooi River Irrigation Scheme, Msinga, Kwazulu-Natal, South Africa

Chizuko Sato

Introduction

The creation of a viable black farming sector has been one of the greatest challenges facing post-apartheid South Africa. While land reform was expected to become a cornerstone in achieving this, there is a growing consensus that it has not yet contributed to the emergence of viable black farmers. In this context, this study proposes the necessity of looking elsewhere and re-examining the current state and performance of black farmers in former homelands. Drawing on interviews with farmers who engage in crop farming at the Mooi River Irrigation Scheme in the Msinga district of KwaZulu-Natal, this study explores the opportunities and constraints for small-scale black farming. Irrigation schemes could stand out as exceptions to the general picture of former homelands which were largely equated with labour reserves for white business interests and consequent de-agrarianisation. This study has identified the availability of water and various informal markets as opportunities for small-scale black farmers to pursue agricultural livelihoods. However, there is differentiation among smallholders, not only in terms of the size of land and production, but also with regard to gender and generation. A number of constraints have also been recognized including shortage of labour, high production costs (especially hiring tractor services for land preparation), lack of or unreliable state support, and the increasing shortage of water.

The creation of a viable black farming sector has been one of the greatest challenges facing post-apartheid South Africa. The introduction of a programme with a three-pronged approach consisting of land redistribution, land restitution, and tenure reform was expected to become the cornerstone of land reform policy. The policy originally aimed to transfer 30% of white-owned farms to blacks within five years of the first democratic elections. The deadline for reaching this goal was deferred several times and, eventually, the government stopped mentioning it altogether[1] Moreover, the dismal performance of many land reform farms has become apparent, as illustrated by the Minister of Rural Development and Land Reform, who stated in 2010 that "more than 90% of land reform projects are dysfunctional" (quoted in Aliber et al., 2013: 92). While his statement is disputed by some academics, who believe that the failure rate for land reform farms is much lower (Aliber et al., 2013: 287), there is a growing consensus that land reform has not yet contributed to the emergence of viable black farmers.

Given that land reform policy is not producing the desired results, this chapter proposes that other perspectives should be explored to identify opportunities for small-scale black farmers in South Africa. In particular, I would argue that there is a pressing need to re-examine the current state and performance of black farmers in former homelands, which house approximately one-third of the population on only 13% of the country's land. Throughout most of the twentieth century, homelands were largely characterised by widespread poverty. These homelands were used as labour reserves for white business interests, such as mining and commercial farming. It has been argued that black farmers living in homelands worked on such small pieces of land that their yields were insufficient to meet even the lowest household subsistence requirements. The majority of residents were elderly, women, or children, who were widely considered unproductive farmers. Their dominant sources of income have long been remittances from migrant workers and social pensions (Wolpe, 1972; Platzky & Walker, 1985; Bundy, 1988; Beinart, 1994). While these characteristics may still be prevalent and even dominant across former homelands, real diversity among the homelands has not yet been examined extensively in the literature (Beinart, 2012).

One of the key elements influencing agricultural production in South Africa is the availability of water. During the twentieth century, a number of irrigation projects were created not only for white farmers but also for small-scale black farmers. By the early 2000s, the total amount of irrigated land used by smallholders had increased to 100,000 hectares, although this still represented less than one-twelfth of the total amount of irrigated land in South Africa (Van Averbeke & Mohamed, n.d.: 1–3). Despite the advantages that irrigation presents for farming, it was only since the beginning of the twenty-first century when a growing number of studies began discussing its use by black farmers in detail (Tapela, 2008; Cousins, 2012; Van Averbeke, 2012; Buthelezi, 2013; Van Averbeke & Denison, 2013; Van Averbeke & Mohamed, n.d.). This study aims to contribute to this emerging literature by looking at the characteristics of land tenure, agricultural production, and market interactions by black farmers in the Mooi River Irrigation Scheme in KwaZulu-Natal Province. This study specifically seeks to address the following two questions: What types of agricultural production do these farmers engage in; are they mainly subsistence farmers or market-oriented farmers? And, to what extent do they have the potential to become emerging farmers, and what are their primary constraints to doing so?

Constraints of Black Farming, the "Accumulation From Below" and Rural Differentiation in the Southern African Context

In spite of a highly commercialised agricultural sector owned and managed mainly by white farmers, South Africa is not necessarily blessed in terms of natural resources and climatic conditions. Lipton (1993: 362) states that less than 20% of South Africa's approximately 100 million ha of farmland are arable and only four million of these are high potential arable. Apart from poor soil in much of the remaining areas, low and erratic rainfall makes agriculture an unreliable and highly risky enterprise. While the history of the South African commercial farming sector essentially shows how white settler farmers have overcome these obstacles by organising themselves into politically-influential agricultural unions and by obtaining state support in various regards (Lipton, 1989), it also illuminates how black commodity producers who were once chief providers of staple foods in the country in the mid to late nineteenth century (Bundy, 1988) fell from that position and became labourers in mines and white-owned farms in the twentieth century. Consequently the South African agricultural sector has been characterised as consisting of two agricultures, one highly commercialised and capital intensive and the other subsistence-oriented and without access to finance and meaningful markets. The dualism in the agricultural sector is in fact common to African settler colonies like Zimbabwe and Namibia and dismantling it became one of the major political challenges after independence (Moyo & Yeros, 2005; Moyo, 2007). However, due to the length of colonisation and the extensiveness of land dispossession of African people, together with high degrees of capitalist developments in agricultural and industrial sectors, South Africa has been considered to be an "extreme and exceptional" case (Bernstein, 1996; 2005).

Indeed radical historians have argued that native reserves were essentially labour reserves where agrarian economies were only able to partially contribute to social reproduction of labour. The extreme processes of land alienation and oppression since the colonial period systematically undermined the conditions of peasant production. Since land was too small to maintain peasant production in native reserves, its residents were sooner or later destined to become labourers in the growing capitalist sector (Wolpe, 1972; Morris, 1976). While radical historians highlighted the oppressive nature of the South African states, their assumption that peasants had completely abandoned commodity production and are therefore destined to become a semi-proletariat or full-time proletariat is highly problematic. Because, as Neocosmos (1993: 6) argued, "[d]espite intense political oppression, extra-economic coercion and unequal exchange, capitalist relations have produced, however meekly, however mildly, however partially, class differences among the oppressed." Due to radical historians' tendency to view residents in native reserves as "overwhelmingly proletarianised" and to ignore "political economy of rural petty-commodity production," they failed to explain the origins of rising peasant production in post-independence Zimbabwe when it occurred (Neocosmos, 1993: 25–29). Drawing on Lenin's distinction of two types of agrarian accumulation that took place in history, namely accumulation "from above" in Prussia and accumulation "from below" in America, Neocosmos (1993: 50–52) argued that "a certain amount of 'accumulation from below' must have" occurred in the South African countryside. We should not be blind to the existence of "petty commodity producers" and rural differentiation that have been "caused by a shortage of means of production."

The problem of characterising native reserves as an overwhelmingly proletarianised population is not just theoretical or academic. This is a highly policy-related issue as well, because, come the end of apartheid, we need to explore where and how we could find black agricultural commodity producers in order to dismantle the dualism in the agricultural sector. This was one of the major policy questions in the early 1990s and at that time expectant eyes were cast on sugar-cane cultivation by small growers in KwaZulu and KaNgwane. In these homelands, sugar-cane cultivation has been introduced to small growers through contract farming with sugar mills since the mid-1970s. Secure access to market and the provision of inputs, financial loan and agricultural extension services to small growers on contract made it easier for resource-poor small growers to enter this sector and contributed to its growth (Bromberger & Antonie, 1993: 431–434). By 1992, small growers in KwaZulu produced about 8% of the industry's total sugar-cane production (Bates, 1996: 59). A similar contract farming of timber production was introduced to small growers in northern KwaZulu in the mid-1980s (Cairns, 1995). Although Bromberger & Antonie (1993: 434) expectantly stated that contract farming "is the only real option" for black farmers in former homelands, others are less optimistic cautioning that it is not a panacea (McIntosh & Vaughan, 1996).

Other potential origins of black commodity producers in post-apartheid South Africa could have been found in irrigation schemes in former homelands. However, in contrast to the importance of contract farming that was pointed out from the beginning of the transition to post-apartheid, it was only at the beginning of the twenty-first century when researchers began analysing small farmers in irrigation schemes in order to identify development possibilities (Tapela, 2008; Cousins, 2012; Van Averbeke, 2012; Buthelezi, 2013;

Van Averbeke & Denison, 2013; Van Averbeke & Mohamed, n.d.). By then the connection between agricultural and non-agricultural incomes was recognised and the diversification of livelihoods or the multiple livelihoods came to be seen as a common survival/ livelihood strategy for rural households in South Africa. This meant that rural households obtained income from various sources including agricultural production, informal sector employment, remittances and social security transfers (May, 1996). Thus, Van Averbeke & Mohamed (n.d.: 8), drawing on a case study of a smallholder irrigation scheme in Limpopo province, reported highly diverse livelihoods and farming of plot holders in the scheme. According to them, only 20% of the households "derived at least half of their income from agriculture. The others also farm, but they derived most of their income from sources other than farming."

If the rural population is no longer considered to be a homogenous entity, but has diverse households who may or may not derive considerable income from agriculture, the next question we need to ask is how we can break them down into different categories and to find out on what basis they are differentiated. Van Averbeke & Mohamed (n.d.: 8–11) classified plot holders at an irrigation scheme in Limpopo into four "farming styles"—"food farmers" who produce mainly for own consumption, "employers" who hire workers to grow crops because they are too old to farm or they engage in other livelihood activities, "profit makers" who farm to earn cash income and "others" who have a combined characteristic of food farmers and profit makers. According to them, these four types of farmers differed "in terms of choice of crop, crop husbandry, attitude towards risk, allocation of produce and marketing practices." Their choice of "farming styles" in describing rural differentiation is interesting, as it captures not only the distinction between those who grow crops for subsistence ("food farmers") and those who sell their agricultural produce ("profit makers"), but also it introduces two mixed or transitional categories. In fact they state that livelihood type and farming style were not only diverse, but very dynamic and could change rapidly "in a matter of one or two seasons."

Knowing the amount of income and income sources of rural households is not always easy, partly because they might be unwilling to disclose such information to researchers. Faced with this problem, Tapela (2008: 189–190) used assets (especially vehicle and tractor) ownership in order to measure socio-economic differentiation between and among plot holders and non-plot holders in three irrigation schemes in Limpopo. However, she states that "a number of householders among the subsistence food producers were found to own more of the expensive material assets, such as cars and electrical appliances than petty-commodity producer households." Thus she implies that income from agriculture may not be a determining factor in rural differentiation. On this issue of the sources of differentiation among rural households with irrigated plots in KwaZulu-Natal, Cousins (2012: 24) emphasises the importance of off-farm income "for successful accumulation in agriculture." In a later article, Cousins (2015: 258) differentiates "market-oriented black smallholders" who have plots in irrigation schemes based on whether they supply their fresh produce to "tight" supply chains such as supermarkets or "loose" supply chains such as informal and pension day markets. He estimates each number as 5,000–10,000 (the former) and 200,000–250,000 (the latter) in South Africa. Thus rural differentiation can be analysed in different ways based on farming style (Van Averbeke & Mohamed, n.d.), assets ownership (Tapela, 2008) or access to different markets (Cousins, 2015).

My own case study of black farmers in the Mooi River Irrigation Scheme in KwaZulu-Natal below also looks at diversity and differentiation among these farmers. However, instead of focusing on different farming methods or production size, this study will bring in a sociological perspective by introducing four categories of farmers based on gender and generation and describe concrete examples of each category of farmers. This was done partly because this study also encountered the same problem as Tapela (2008) and found it difficult to compute their income from agriculture when respondents used various parameters in their answers (see discussion below). But there is also a positive reason. The purpose of bringing in sociological categorisation is to give a better understanding of not only plot holders in the concerned irrigation scheme in particular, but also black small farmers in former homelands in general, by describing them not just as farmers, but also in familiar terms as grandfather, grandmother, migrant worker, and youth. If Cousins' (2012: 1) claim that "the paucity of reliable data on small-scale agriculture, and lack of clarity on the meaning of terms such as 'smallholder' and 'small-scale agriculture'" hinder the meaningful "debates on agrarian reform in South Africa" still holds water, it is my wish to contribute to deepening the understanding of black smallholders by bringing in a new perspective in describing black farmers.

Mooi River Irrigation Scheme and Research Methodology

The Mooi River Irrigation Scheme is situated in the southern part of the former KwaZulu district of Msinga in mid-western KwaZulu-Natal, South Africa. It currently lies in the local Msinga municipality and falls under *inkosi* (chief) Mchunu and the Mchunu traditional authority. The total area under irrigation is 601 hectares divided into 15 blocks and each block is demarcated by fences.[2] Most blocks lie along the Mooi River, which has historically served as a natural boundary between the white farming district of Muden/Umvoti and the black district of Msinga. This study was conducted with black farmers who used plots on Blocks 1–9, which fall under the authority of one *isigodi* (tribal ward) known as *Ekuvukeni*. *Isigodi* (pl. *izigodi*) is a territorial unit of traditional authority among the Zulu people. It usually refers to an area with boundaries that are physically defined by natural objects such as hills or rivers. An *induna* (pl. *izinduna*) is appointed by a chief (*inkosi*, pl. *amakhosi*) for each *isigodi*; however, an *isigodi* is not recognised as an administrative unit by any government entity in South Africa. *Ekuvukeni isigodi* is situated along a stretch of land about 10–19 km down a gravel road from the nearest village of Muden, and about 38–47 km from the nearby town of Greytown, where one can find modern supermarkets and banks.

The construction of irrigation furrows used to draw water from the Mooi River dates back to the end of the nineteenth century during the Natal colonial period. While archival research indicates that white engineers contracted by the Natal colonial government led its construction,[3] local oral tradition maintains that local men dug the furrows downriver to the flatland under the instruction of *inkosi* Mchunu. *Inkosi* Mchunu is also credited with securing assistance from the colonial government by obtaining implements and dynamite to remove large boulders during the excavation process.[4] The Mooi River Irrigation Scheme was part of a twin irrigation project in Natal at that time along with the Tugela River Irrigation Scheme, which is located along the nearby Tugela River in the same district (Cousins, 2012; Buthelezi, 2013). Once the canal was built, local black farmers cultivated plots on the irrigated fields. In the early twentieth century, farmers were required to pay rents to the authority, but they were frequently unable to do so and stopped paying at some point.[5] When the Tomlinson Commission conducted a research programme in 1952 on socio-economic development on native reserves, the Mooi River scheme was counted among 122 irrigation projects in place for small farmers at that time, including some that were still under construction (The Commission for the Socio-economic Development of the Bantu Areas within the Union of South Africa, 1955). In the late twentieth century, management of the irrigation scheme was transferred to the KwaZulu Department of Agriculture, which improved the construction by fortifying the canal with concrete supports and placing fences in the fields to protect crops from livestock.[6]

The data for this study were collected using semi-structured interviews with 94 black farmers who were using plots on Blocks 1– 9 in the Mooi River Irrigation Scheme in June 2014[7] In addition, follow-up interviews with 21 black farmers in Block 2 were conducted in August 2016 to get additional historical context and clarify some information that had emerged from the 2014 interviews. Aside from black farmers, the research also included information from interviews with a local *induna* and village elders, an extension officer in charge of the scheme based in Tugela Ferry, traders working at monthly pension day markets in Muden, and street traders selling vegetables in Greytown. Archival research on the scheme was also conducted from 2014 to 2016 in Pietermaritzburg, Ulundi, and Pretoria, South Africa.

In 2014 and 2016, the author together with local research assistants visited fields in the scheme and interviewed people who were working there. Therefore, the sample is not representative of all plot-holders or villagers in Ekuvukeni, Msinga. However, from a practical perspective it was necessary to approach the data collection this way, as the number of households in Ekuvukeni is far larger than the number of plot-holders and, at the time of the research, there was no central list available of farmers who owned or used plots on the scheme.[8] Furthermore, to collect the most useful data for the analysis, we decided to concentrate on people who cultivated land. Respondents were approached in the field and asked if they would be willing to participate in the study after a short introduction of the researcher and the project. The farmers often agreed to participate, but the interviews were sometimes conducted while the farmers were working on harvesting crops or weeding and not in a controlled environment. We interviewed all farmers who were actually working in their fields on the days when we visited as long as they agreed to be interviewed. Thus, our sample excluded those farmers who owned plots, but no longer came to work on the plots for whatever reasons. In this sense this study illustrates only the farming activities observed in the irrigation scheme on the days we visited rather than how plot-holders in general used their plots. We visited each block for a few days. The goal of this study was to find out how the farmers accessed land and other resources, what they produced, and where they sold their goods. In other words, this study investigated their land tenure arrangements and agricultural activities.

Characteristics of Black Farmers in the Mooi River Irrigation Scheme

Of the 94 black farmers interviewed on the Mooi River Irrigation Scheme in 2014, 74 were female and 20 were male. A majority of them (72%) were 50 years old or older, and 40% of them were pensioners who were living with their grandchildren and/or children. A majority of them were married/ cohabitating[9] (54%) or widowed (35%). Most of them were born locally or married locally. Those respondents who were not local had moved to the area through marriage. Almost all the respondents lived in one of the villages (*imihlati*, sing. *umhlati*) close to the irrigation plots at Ekuvukeni *isigodi*.

Nearly 60% of them had no formal education and could speak only isi Zulu. While 39% of respondents could speak, write, and read in isi Zulu, only 13% of them could do so in English.

In this part of Msinga, the population's basic rural livelihood comes from mixed farming. They grow vegetables on plots in the Mooi River Irrigation Scheme or in tiny gardens within their households' residential lands. The average plot size in the irrigation scheme is very small, usually 0.1 hectares or less.[10] As shown in Table 1, some farmers cultivate more than 10 plots, while most cultivate less than four plots.

Villagers also keep livestock, although ownership is unevenly distributed. At the time of the study, only one-third of the respondents owned cattle and about 60% owned goats; one-third owned neither cattle nor goats. Livestock farming in Msinga can be categorised as extensive. Cattle and goats graze around the mountainous areas and riverbanks and are not herded. Goats are either collected by the farmer or they come home on their own in the evening, where they are kept in the kraal overnight. Cattle are usually collected once per week or once every two weeks when their owners take them to a communal dipping facility. This kind of livestock practice clashes with crop farming unless the crops are protected by fences, as cattle and goats enter the fields and the gardens searching for food and eat all the crops, especially during the winter months when grass is scarce.

A large majority of respondents (82%) told us that they received some income from selling the crops they grew on their irrigated plots; however, it was difficult for us to compute their income from agriculture because they used various parameters to describe how much they earned. For instance, one respondent said, "R500 after three months," another said, "R1, 000 after the harvest," and yet another answered, "R5,000 for cabbage in 2013." Many of them also stressed that their income from selling crops differed depending on the harvest that year. Therefore, instead of estimating how much income the farmers made from agriculture, it is important to stress here that the majority of them received at least some income from agriculture, but the amount may be highly variable. While income from agriculture is unique to people in this area because of their access to irrigated plots, their other income sources were comparable to their counterparts in other former homelands in South Africa. Like many black people on former homelands, social grants were important income sources—nearly 40% received pensions, 46% received child support grants, and 7% received disability grants. On the other hand, only a limited number of respondents had other forms of income including salaries (6%), remittances from family members (6%), and proceeds from irregular work on white farms or smallholder plots (4%).

Table 1. Number of plots cultivated by farmers in the irrigation scheme (N = 65)

Number of plots	Farmers
One	10
Two	17
Three	12
Four	9
Five to Nine	13
Ten and above	4

Source: Author's interviews in 2014 and 2016.

Nonetheless, it is worth noting that most respondents (82%) had worked elsewhere in the past. The most common job (39%) was casual farm work on white farms in Muden. All the respondents who had done this type of farm work were women, most of whom reported that they accepted these assignments only when they were young. The second occupational category was government work (15%), which usually included men who had worked for the Department of Agriculture for the KwaZulu government. A similar number of men (14%) said that they had worked as migrant workers in the past, and had travelled to work in mines in Gauteng Province and factories in Durban. Most of them returned to Msinga as a result of retrenchment. Other respondents mentioned various jobs in Muden and Greytown including domestic work. To sum up, this study found that women typically worked on white farms in the neighbouring farming districts as casual workers, while men typically worked for the KwaZulu government or became migrant workers, returning to Msinga only once or twice a year until they were retrenched and came back permanently. Upon their return home, some men in Ekuvukeni decided to work on their plots in the irrigation scheme.

Land Access and Rental in the Irrigation Scheme

The land of former KwaZulu is officially known as "Ingonyama land" and is now legally owned by the KwaZulu-Natal Ingonyama Trust, a statutory institution set up by the KwaZulu-Natal Ingonyama Trust Act (1994) and its Amendment Act (1997).[11] The land tenure system on Ingonyama land is referred to as a customary land tenure, through which individuals and/or households obtain access to residential and arable lands and communal grazing land through their membership in a particular group. In former KwaZulu, this group was usually chieftaincy groups or "tribes" led by chiefs (*amakhosi*). Land rights under a customary land tenure system differ from those of legal ownership or possession under a freehold system. For instance, residential and/or arable land cannot be used as collateral for credit from financial institutions. However, once residential and/or arable land is allocated to an individual and/or a household, the land rights stay with them as long as the land is being used. They can also pass the land on to other family members through inheritance.

People in Ekuvukeni *isigodi* belong to the Mchunu traditional authority. *Inkosi* Mchunu was in his 90s and the oldest chief in South Africa at the time of interview in 2014.[12] Given the exceptionally long period of his reign in the chiefdom, he was well-known in the area and seemed to be highly respected among the local people. In theory, one needs permission from a traditional leader (*inkosi* or *induna*) to build a house or cultivate a plot under customary land tenure. However, our research indicated that traditional authority figures do not necessarily have exclusive rights to allocate residential land to build homestead in Ekuvukeni. When we asked 94 black farmers how they obtained their residential lands in Ekuvukeni in 2014, 51 of them answered that they were household plots. Sixteen of those respondents inherited their plots and 35 received land rights through marriage. Alternatively, 33 people said that they obtained their residential lands through a traditional authority, either *induna* or *inkosi*. In addition, five people said that they first asked their neighbours for permission to build a house, and were sent to *inkosi* or *induna* after the neighbours had accepted them into the community. Another three respondents said that they asked their neighbours if they could build a house, and the neighbours allowed them to do so without the involvement of any authorities whatsoever.[13]

Eight out of 43 respondents, excluding those who answered that they had household plots, said that they had obtained permission from neighbours to obtain residential land rights.[14] Proportionally, this may not seem substantial; however, an *induna* from Ekuvukeni *isigodi* further explained the procedure one had to follow to obtain residential land in his area in 2016. Someone who wanted to obtain residential land rights must first visit their potential new neighbours and introduce themselves. Then, the neighbours would direct him or her to an *induna*. After the *induna* had met the prospective owner(s), he would go to see an *inkosi* to report it and ask for permission to allocate the land. According to the *induna*, the inkosi had a list of the names of households in each village (*umhlati*). The *induna* also emphasised that anyone, regardless of gender, could ask for land in his area.[15] He also noted that in recent years there were hardly any outsiders moving to the area and demand for new residential land usually came from the sons of local families who wanted to establish independent households.[16]

As for the agricultural land in the irrigation scheme, Table 2 shows that 56 out of 82 respondents who owned plots answered that they held household plots that they inherited from their parents or other family members. Twelve people rented plots and thus didn't own their plots. Another 12 people received land rights to their plots from a traditional authority.

Table 2. How did you obtain your plots in the irrigation scheme? (N = 94)

Answer	Respondents
Household plot (inheritance)	56
From traditional authority	12
Renting	12
From previous owner	7
From government	5
Other	1
Unknown	1
Total	94

Source: Author's interviews in 2014.

Somewhat unexpectedly, 7 people answered that they obtained their plots from the previous owners. This demonstrates the existence of private transactions for plots in the irrigation scheme, albeit to a limited degree. However, the nature of these transactions differs from that of land purchases in the usual sense. In most of these cases, lease agreements preceded the transfer of ownership. When the previous owner became too old to continue farming, or when none of the previous owner's family members were interested in farming, the borrower was eventually able to take over the plot. As mentioned earlier, that Van Averveke & Mohamed (n.d.) introduced an "employers" category to describe those who are too old to farm or who engage in livelihood activities other than farming and therefore employ someone to use their plots in the irrigation scheme in Limpopo. The result from this study implies the possibility that those "employers" could eventually lose or give their plots to "employees."

In addition to 12 people who didn't own plots and cultivated only the rented plots as captured in Table 2, 11 more people borrowed plots. Thus, the total number of respondents who borrowed plots amounted to 23 (out of 94). This means that the land rental market in the Mooi River Irrigation Scheme was active to some extent. In almost all cases, the borrowing arrangements were quite informal and did not include any written agreement or specified duration. However, in many cases, tenants provided the owner with some of their crops. In some cases, they provided harvesting and weeding

227

labour to the owner in lieu of rental payments. The existence of de facto private transactions and informal land rental practices means that the tenure system in the irrigation scheme has not so far been an obstacle for people who wanted to farm. The number of plots each respondent used differed significantly, from one to over ten plots, and the constraints on production seemed to be a result of a lack of manpower and cost of production (as discussed later) rather than a lack of land. This was also illustrated by the existence of numerous uncultivated plots in the irrigation scheme. Many studies raised the issue of non-cultivation or under-cultivation of arable lands in the homelands without explaining the reasons behind it (Bromberger & Antonie, 1993: 420; Lipton, 1993: 376). This has a huge implication on the necessity and justification of land reform, as one could then argue that black people in the homelands are not in short supply of arable lands. However, this study argues that this is jumping to a wrong conclusion. What the existence of numerous uncultivated lands means instead is that land is essential but just one element in carrying out agricultural production. Other elements such as manpower, means of production and access to market are equally important as discussed in the following sections.

While the land rental market in the Mooi River Irrigation Scheme was active to some extent, it was also observed that customary influence over land tenure prevented the practice from expanding further. The KZN Department of Agriculture in Tugela Ferry has been keen to encourage farmers to expand their production, to use uncultivated plots. However, the Department of Agriculture stated that it did not have the authority to re-allocate unused plots to others because that responsibility fell to the chief.[17] However, the *induna* of the Ekuvukeni *isigodi* contradicted that statement, stating that it was the government that had the authority to allocate land in the irrigation scheme. It was, therefore, unclear who (or which institution) had the authority to allocate land in the irrigation scheme at the time of this study. However, the *induna* also said that they were in the process of transferring administration of the irrigated plots to the *inkosi*.[18] Even though South Africa's new land-tenure legislation, the Communal Land Rights Act (2004, CLaRA), has not been implemented because it was found to be unconstitutional, it seems that *inkosi*'s power over land allocation is increasing at the local level. This is also illustrated by the following comment from a respondent:

> I used to pay R300 per plot every three months, but I no longer pay. *Inkosi* says that people must not pay because people live together on *inkosi*'s land. I have been borrowing plots for five years. Mr S [owner of the plot] thinks that it is a problem that he does not receive payment, but he is waiting because negotiations are ongoing. [Negotiation with whom?] Between Mr S, the people renting land from him, and the *inkosi*. He [Mr S] also needs money.[19]

It seems that the strong social norm in the customary land tenure system, which has a tendency to emphasize equality among members of a group, doesn't like particular persons or families to overwhelmingly benefit from land. In a similar vein Cousins (2012: 22) argues that in spite of an informal land rental market he also observed in the Tugela Ferry Irrigation Scheme, "the nature of the property regime" is one of the "two key constraints on accumulation" by those who want to expand their production.

Production Processes and Market Forces

Next, let me turn to the production processes of black farmers in the irrigation scheme. What was clear from the interviews was that they relied on modern farming methods and technology. They used tractors for ploughing rather than oxen and bought seeds and fertilisers in town (usually in Greytown) rather than keep their own seeds from the previous season. However, very few farmers owned a tractor themselves. It was only four respondents who had previously worked for the KwaZulu Department of Agriculture that owned tractors. Those farmers who did not own tractors had to rely on tractor services by the government or by tractor owners. There were two types of governmental tractor services available for black farmers in the irrigation scheme. First, the KZN Department of Agriculture in Tugela Ferry, which manages the scheme, sometimes provided free or reduced-cost tractor services.[20] Second, depending on the *imihlati*, farmers could rely on the Msinga local municipality to provide, at times, cheaper tractor services in certain blocks. However, these governmental tractor services were highly unreliable and infrequent. Thus, many farmers hired tractor services from owners in the scheme. Respondents reported that private tractor owners provided better ploughing services than government tractors, but the cost of hiring them could be quite high.[21]

In terms of labour supply, as most farmers cultivated just a few plots, they relied on themselves, their families, and occasionally neighbours for various farming tasks like planting and watering. Nevertheless nearly one-third of the farmers employed additional workers on a part-time basis or during peak periods, especially for weeding and harvesting. Workers were often paid in kind, but cash payments also took place. The amount paid varied depending on the task, the relationship between the plot owner and the worker, and whether the workers were paid monthly or daily. For example, workers received between R150 and R250 per plot for weeding. Although the time required to finish weeding a plot has not been concretely determined, this amount seems reasonable compared with the daily wage farmworkers received on white farms in Muden. In March 2013, the minimum wage for farmworkers was raised to R105 from R69 per day because of strikes on commercial farms in Western Cape Province. Although the increase in the minimum wage caused an outcry from many white farmers nationwide, even pushing some to apply for an official exemption, white farmers in Muden were generally compliant with the new regulations. The amount of wages black farmers paid to their workers in Msinga were not dissimilar from those of casual workers on white-owned farms.

As shown in Table 3, the majority of farmers (82 out of 94 respondents)[22] in the irrigation scheme sold their crops. This was partly in order to recoup the production costs such as tractor services, inputs (seeds and fertilisers) and labourers. But which types of crops do they sell, and at what type of market do they sell them? Until recently these questions had not been fully explored (Cousins, 2012; Van Averbeke, 2012; Aliber et al., 2013; Van Averbeke & Denison, 2013), as black people on former homelands were traditionally believed to have engaged only in subsistence farming. In contrast, this study found that multiple types of informal markets are accessible and regularly used by farmers in the scheme. Table 3 lists the main markets where these farmers sell their agricultural produce. It is clear that most farmers sold their products to informal markets or "loose" supply chains (Cousins, 2015: 258) such as bakkie (pick-up trucks) traders, street traders/vendors, neighbours, and pension day markets, and only six respondents sold their products to supermarkets which is considered to be a "tight" supply chain.

Table 3. Where do you sell your agricultural produce? (multiple answers) (N = 82)

Main market	Respondents
Bakkie traders	57
Street traders/vendors	30
Neighbours	25
Pension day markets	7
Supermarkets	6

Source: Author's interviews in 2014.

Bakkie traders refer to the owners of pick-up trucks (commonly known as "bakkie" in South Africa) who come to the fields to buy agricultural products and sell them to wholesalers and retailers in town. Some bakkie traders also transport people as a means of local transport as well. Bakkie traders seem to have been around for some time in rural KwaZulu,[23] but it is only recently that their roles in connecting black small farmers with urban markets have caught the attention of researchers (Cousins, 2012). Many black farmers in the irrigation scheme sold their crops to bakkie traders, as it was one of the most convenient markets for a majority of respondents in this study who did not own a vehicle or have access to transportation. Unlike their neighbours, bakkie traders purchased crops in large quantities. Even if the yield for each black farmer was small, their concentration in the irrigation scheme made it worthwhile for bakkie traders to come and buy crops from them.

Another important market for farmers in the scheme was to sell their crops to street traders and/or vendors in the nearby towns of Greytown, Weenen, and Tugela Ferry. Street traders came to the Mooi River Irrigation Scheme from as far as Pietermaritzburg and Durban. Black farmers also hired transport individually or in groups and delivered their crops to street traders in nearby towns. Some even sold their crops as street traders in town themselves. Farmers understood that Greytown and other nearby towns offered them large markets to sell their goods. Street traders were also a good alternative in the event that the bakkie traders failed to come by when the crops were ready.

Other informal markets included sale to neighbours, who of course were easily accessible and this was especially important for those who had not been farming for very long, and the so-called pension day markets. The latter was held once a month in various localities and was also usually a site for local festivities. The size of the pension day market depended on the size of the locality and on how many people came to collect social grants. One of the biggest pension markets in the area was held in Muden, where numerous traders came and sold a wide range of goods including fresh food, vegetables, raw meats, snacks, *muti* (medicine), clothes, shoes, insurances, and small electrical appliances like radios.[24]

Crop Selection and Profitability

Farmers' crop choices also reflected their market orientation. Many of them grew beans, potatoes, tomatoes, spinach, sweet potatoes, cabbage, and maize. While some of these crops (especially beans and spinach) were grown mainly for personal consumption, others were sold. Although maize is a staple grain used to make *pap* and *putu*, which people eat on a daily basis in Msinga, many of them bought ground maize flour (*mieliemeal*) from shops and sold their own maize as green-mielie. These green-mielies are either sold in supermarkets as fresh corn, or boiled and sold by street traders in many towns in KwaZulu- Natal Province.[25] These fresh vegetables are considered commercial crops for black farmers in the irrigation scheme. The question is whether they are profitable, and to what extent?

As previously discussed, black farmers' income from crop sales could not be calculated using the data from the semi-structured interviews in 2014. Therefore, when the follow-up fieldwork was conducted in 2016, farmers were asked which crops they grew during

232

2015 and the first half of 2016 by using a calendar. The farmers were then asked how much they spent to grow each crop and how much they earned from it using an income and expenditure sheet for each crop they grew. This exercise indicated that the farmers could grow most vegetables twice per year in the irrigation scheme. However, not all farmers were willing to talk about money, while some were unable to remember how much they spent or earned from their crops, especially for the previous year (2015). The data limitations in this study regarding income calculation must therefore be acknowledged. Nonetheless, the data indicate that growing tomatoes was the most expensive activity, but it was also the crop that gave farmers the highest return.

Table 4 shows how much Ms S (female farmer in the scheme) spent on growing tomatoes and maize and how much she earned by selling these vegetables during the January to June 2016 season. She planted tomatoes on 2 plots and maize on 1.5 plots. Her agricultural expenses were broken down to tractor services, seeds or seedlings, fertiliser, pesticide and other items. During this season, she spent R4,595 in total to grow tomatoes on 2 plots, while it cost only R580 to grow maize on 1.5 plots. This shows that growing tomatoes is quite expensive due to the high price of seedlings and other expenses which do not occur if one grows maize. However, when we compare how much she earned by selling these vegetables, we are struck by the large amount of income tomatoes brought to her in that season. She earned R16, 000 from tomatoes, while maize brought her only R3, 500. Simple calculation of deducting expenses from income for each crop tells us that she made a profit of R11, 405 from tomatoes and R2, 920 from maize. Ms S was not an exceptional case. During the fieldwork in 2016, we did the same exercise with 14 farmers. Of these, 12 farmers grew tomatoes at some point during 1.5 years (2015 and the first half of 2016). Except for one farmer whose expenses exceeded her income from selling tomatoes, they made profits ranging from R700 to over R30, 000 from tomatoes for one crop season. Table 4 also indicates that apart from tomato cultivation which has various expenses unnecessary to other crops, the costs of tractor services pushed up the total cost of production and reduced the profit margins of other vegetables.

Table 4. Comparison of profitability between tomatoes and maize: Example of Ms S

Tomatoes: Jan–Jun 2016: 2 plots		Maize: Jan–Jul 2016: 1.5 plots	
Expenses (R)		Expenses (R)	
Tractor	860	Tractor	430
Seedlings	1,300	Seeds	150
Fertiliser	735		
Pesticide	600		
Other (pole, rope)	1,100		
Total expenses	4,595	Total expenses	580
Income	16,000	Income	3,500
Profit	11,405	Profit	2,920

Source: Author's interviews in 2016.

During the initial visit to the Mooi River Irrigation Scheme in 2014, we wondered why so many farmers grew tomatoes. Tomatoes are perishable vegetables and, therefore, farmers need to find markets to turn them over in a relatively short period. It was also thought that competition might bring down the price of the tomatoes; however, after calculating expenses and income, it was clear that tomatoes were the most profitable crop. Given the low level of literacy among farmers, especially elderly female farmers, and based on my impression of reviewing income and expenditure sheets with some of them, it seemed that they had never calculated these figures in detail.[26] Nevertheless, the farmers' crop choices made sense economically and it can be said that they were responsive to price differences.

This does not mean that competition among farmers in the irrigation scheme is non-existent. In 2016, some farmers in Block 2 told us that they agreed among themselves on the selling price per crate of tomatoes when they sold to bakkie traders and street traders in the fields. It is not difficult for farmers to share the price information as farmers who grow tomatoes live in nearby villages and see each other in the field almost on a daily basis especially during the harvest season. However, the number of growers far exceeds the number of bakkie traders and street traders, and the farmers' agreement is not binding in a sense that there is no punishment. A few farmers admitted that they had sold their tomatoes to bakkie traders at lower unit prices because they feared they would not be able to sell all their crops at the right time.

Farmers' Views on Agricultural Problems

In this section, the major constraints on farming will be discussed, especially those cited by farmers themselves. De La Hey & Beinart (2017) argues the importance of considering people's own perceptions of farming and reasoning in order to find out why arable lands have largely been left fallow in the former Transkei in recent years. They particularly highlight the shortage of family labour for agricultural work due to the younger generation's preference to look for a non-agricultural job as a constraint in farming in their researched village. This study also reported the existence of uncultivated plots in the irrigation scheme and how the shortage of labour facilitated land rental practices. Leasing a plot usually took place when a plot owner became too old to work and did not have a family member who was interested in farming. However, when we asked those farmers who were actually working on the plot in the irrigation scheme during our fieldwork in 2014 about their concerns and problems in farming, they raised other issues as their perceived problems in farming.

Table 5 shows that three problems dominated their concerns in 2014. The largest group of respondents (60) said that the biggest problem was livestock destroying their crops. Many farmers lamented that they had to go to their plots early in the morning to chase away cattle and goats. Interestingly, these farmers were often livestock owners themselves. The primary problem in Msinga was not, therefore, a conflict between agriculturalists and pastoralists. Many said that they tried to find solutions "as a community" by collectively fixing fences or organising meetings with livestock owners. The root cause of crop damage caused by livestock was inadequate fencing. The scheme's outside boundary was originally fenced by the KwaZulu government in the 1970s or 1980s. According to respondents, it had not been well-maintained. Although the farmers regularly repaired it themselves by using reed sticks and trees from the bush, the deterioration in the condition of fences was apparent and there were holes and gaps here and there.

The second largest group of respondents (24) complained of tractor-related problems. Some were unhappy about not being able to own a tractor, but most people grumbled about the high cost of hiring private tractor services. As illustrated above, hiring tractor services was a major cost of growing crops for them. Their problem was exacerbated by frequent delays and unreliability of cheaper governmental tractor services. Apart from ploughing by tractors, the government sporadically provides assistance to farmers in the irrigation scheme in the form of the provision of seeds (potato seeds, beans, or spinach seeds) and fertilisers.

Table 5. Farmers' own views on problems in farming in 2014 (multiple answers)

Problems	Respondents
Livestock destroying crops (lack of proper fences)	60
No tractor, cost of hiring it, or government tractor delays	24
Water shortage	21
Cost of inputs	8
Theft (crops and fences)	6
Lack of or unreliable markets	3
Lack of farming tools	3
Others	12

Source: Author's interviews in 2014.

Forty-one respondents (out of 94) answered affirmative to our question; "have you ever received any governmental assistance?" However, the provision of seeds and fertilisers by the KZN Department of Agriculture doesn't occur regularly and more importantly it doesn't reach every farmer in the scheme. Thus farmers would say to us "the government gave some farmers seeds and fertilisers, but I didn't get anything[27]" We don't know how the government decides to provide seeds to some farmers and not others.

Apart from the government, an agricultural and rural development NGO called LIMA offers credit services in the form of seeds and fertilisers to black farmers in the irrigation scheme, which they must pay back at the end of the harvest. LIMA staff based in Tugela Ferry also visit the irrigation scheme regularly and offer on-site training courses on proper crop care, soil preparation, and seedling cultivation. Considering that the provision of agricultural training and extension services by the KZN Department of Agriculture is limited in the irrigation scheme, LIMA's courses are a welcome intervention for farmers who want to improve the quality of their crops.[28] However, not all farmers are keen to join the LIMA scheme because of fear of debt, and only 14 respondents (out of 94) told us that they received assistance from NGOs in 2014. Thus not all farmers have the same level of risk-aversion. This brings us to the question of diversity and differentiation among black farmers in the irrigation scheme, which shall be discussed in the final section below.

The third largest group of respondents (21) mentioned the shortage of water as a constraint in farming. Perhaps this is the most worrying, as this area is no stranger to the regular occurrence of severe drought and there is no quick and easy solution to this problem. According to respondents, the KZN Department of Agriculture instructed them to introduce a water-saving and water-sharing measure. Under this system, the farmers in each block were allocated one day per week to retrieve water from the canal. This means that they could only irrigate their plots on a particular day of the week. The Department of Agriculture also employed a few local farmers as water guards to maintain water-related infrastructure in the irrigation scheme. The water guards also watch farmers to prevent them from breaking this local rule. However, not all farmers knew which days were allocated to their blocks and during the fieldwork we saw a water guard shouting down at farmers who drew water to their plots on the days when they were not supposed to do so.

Farmer Diversity

The aforementioned description of black farmers in the irrigation scheme confirms a historically held view that most farmers on former homelands are women, although it contradicts an equally popular view that they mainly grow crops for subsistence. A considerable number of black farmers in the Mooi River Irrigation Scheme sell their produce in various informal markets including local markets (neighbours), bakkie traders, and street traders in nearby towns. Land-rental practices also exist to a certain extent. Moreover, black farmers have also been integrated into the modern agricultural sector through their reliance on modern farming technology like using tractors and purchasing inputs like seeds and fertilisers. Nevertheless, not all of them can be categorised as emerging or capitalist-oriented farmers. There is considerable diversity among black farmers in the irrigation scheme in terms of the scale of their agricultural production, age, and gender. Since this study could not establish the income each farmer earned from agriculture, I would like to explore this diversity from a sociological perspective by introducing four different types of farmer in terms of gender and generation. Understanding the diversity of farmers is important to assess their diversified needs and policy prioritisation.

The most dominant type of farmer in the irrigation scheme is a *gogo* (granny) farmer. They are women of pensionable age or younger who have grandchildren living with them in Msinga. They are usually married/ cohabitating or widowed. For those who are married, their spouses are usually away. They normally cultivate 1–4 plots, but they are sometimes rented and not owned. Not all farmers in this group sell their crops for profit. Some use their plots for subsistence, although they will sell extra crops if a neighbour is interested in buying them. For example, Ms I, who was 67 years old, grew maize, butternut and spinach on two plots which she took over from her late sister. She grew these vegetables for mainly family consumption and only sold a small amount of them to neighbours if the latter asked her.[29] However, there are also *gogo* farmers who grow tomatoes for profit. One such example was Ms D, who was 58 years old and supported her grandchildren through agriculture. She started farming 20 years previously after returning to Msinga from Nkandla when her husband's parents died. She grew tomatoes, potatoes, green peppers, and onions on four borrowed plots. She employed three workers who worked together with her in the fields from August to December each year. She cultivated her crops only during the second half of the year, as she stated that she was busy looking after grandchildren during the first half of the year.[30]

The second type of farmer is a *mkhulu* (grandfather) farmer. These are men of pensionable age or younger who also have grandchildren. They are quite often former employees of the KwaZulu Department of Agriculture and own a tractor or two, with which they offer private tractor services to other farmers. These

238

farmers tend to own more plots than the others, some of which they had inherited from their fathers. One such farmer was a 72-year-old man named Mr A. He was a former employee of the KwaZulu Department of Agriculture and owned a tractor. He began farming on his own 30 years previously, but helped his father on the land when he was a boy. He grew numerous vegetables including maize, potatoes, peas, tomatoes, onions, green peppers, and butternut squash on 12 plots, four of which he had inherited from his father. He obtained the rest from other people in the area when they had stopped farming. He did not employ workers, as he could rely on his family members to assist him in the fields. Although his scale of farming was relatively large compared to the other farmers in the irrigation scheme, he did not know how much he paid for seeds and fertilisers, or how much income he earned from selling his crops. He said that this was because his wife (*gogo*) controlled the financial aspects of the farming operation.[31]

The importance of migration as a livelihood strategy for rural households has been discussed extensively in South African literature (May, 1996; Beinart, 2014). What is less known is their economic activities after they voluntarily or involuntarily return to their birthplace. Against this background, I call the third type of farmer a 'returned migrant farmer.' These are usually men in their 40s or older who have returned to Msinga after being retrenched in the city. The kind of work they did away from home varied, as does the amount of time they worked as migrant workers. However, I came across several men in their 50s or older who worked in the mines near Carletonville in west of Johannesburg, which seemed to be one of the most popular places for migrant workers among a certain generation of men from this part of Msinga. Younger men worked in the cities as taxi drivers or in other occupations rather than working in the mines. One example of such a worker was Mr B, who was 44 years old. By 2016, he had been farming for three years since returning from Pietermaritzburg and Johannesburg. Although his farming experience was not very extensive, he was elected as the Secretary of the Farmers Committee for Blocks 1–3. He grew tomatoes, cabbage, and onions on six plots that he had inherited from his mother. He said that he inherited all his mother's plots, as his siblings were "lazy",[32] suggesting that he was the only one in the family who was interested in taking up farming.

The last type of farmer is atypical in the irrigation scheme. These are young single or married female farmers whose spouses are either away working in the city as migrant workers or who have deserted them. One example was Ms N, who was 30 years old and began farming in 2016 after years of unemployment. She grew tomatoes, potatoes, and onions on three plots that she had inherited from her late father. In fact, her inheritance prompted her to take up farming. Her father had a total of eight plots: three were given to her, three to her stepmother, and two to her brother, although he leased them to other people since he worked in Vryheid, a town in northern KwaZulu-Natal. She also had a sister who was a bakkie trader and was not interested in farming and therefore did not get a plot.[33] This means that the inheritance was negotiated within the family and determined based on personal needs and preferences.

Conclusion

This study discussed current practices in black farming in the Mooi River Irrigation Scheme in the former KwaZulu district of Msinga, South Africa. Even though the income from farming may not be sufficient for most of them to be categorised as full-time or emerging capitalist-oriented farmers, it still represents an important component of their livelihoods. It is important to stress that many of them grow crops not only for subsistence purposes but also to earn an income. Farmers in the irrigation scheme no longer grow staple foods like maize for home consumption, but grow vegetables for sale instead, as the latter are in high demand in local towns. They buy their own *mieliemeal* from shops instead of living from their own production. The availability of water and various informal markets provided black farmers in the irrigation scheme with opportunities to pursue agrarian livelihoods. This finding itself is not new, as other studies on similar irrigation schemes also pointed out "reasonably high levels of crop productivity" among black farmers in such schemes (Cousins, 2012: 22). This study also explored diversity and differentiation among black farmers in the irrigation schemes and introduced four types of such farmers based on gender and generation. I used sociological criteria of gender and generation rather than the scale of production or asset ownership in order to show that not all black farmers in former homelands are old grannies and grandfathers. Among the younger generation, there are some people who would take up farming when the opportunity presents itself and they include those who have spent some time in the cities as a migrant worker. It is important to acknowledge that their needs, ambitions and constraints might be different from their parents or grandparents' generation.

The semi-structured interviews with 94 farmers in 2014 rendered a snapshot of the farming practices in the Mooi River Irrigation Scheme. The single survey round did not establish the length of time that black farmers in the irrigation scheme had been selling their products to wider markets outside their local neighbourhoods. Commerce in this sense may be a relatively recent phenomenon, especially since social grants have increased the availability of cash in rural areas. The increasing penetration of bakkie traders into rural areas and the regular occurrence of pension day markets seem to have provided an important stimulus for black farmers to become more market-oriented. The expansion of informal markets was necessary to protect them from competition with white commercial farmers with larger land plots and more resources. An attempt was made to supplement this snapshot from 2014 by asking farmers additional questions regarding historical changes in local agricultural activities during follow-up research in 2016; however, many farmers issued contradictory statements that hindered further analysis. Further research is required to understand the historical continuities and changes in local farming practices in the irrigation scheme properly.

Uncertainty exists not only with regard to the past but also in relation to the future of the irrigation scheme. There are at least three reasons for this. First, there is uncertainty in terms of land tenure. It is currently unclear which institution oversees land allocation in the irrigation scheme, the traditional authority or the KZN Department of Agriculture. The traditional authority's power over land allocation in the irrigation scheme seems to be increasing, but the consequences of this, in terms of tenure security for farmers, remain unknown. This study saw that while the KZN Department of Agriculture wanted to encourage capable farmers to expand their production by using uncultivated plots, the strong social norm in the customary land tenure system which has a tendency to emphasize equality among members of a group prevented it from happening. In this sense, it might be possible to say that customary tenure could provide security to relatively resource poor farmers like most *gogo* farmers, but hinder the expansion of agricultural production by ambitious farmers who are willing to take a risk like the ones who joined the LIMA scheme.

Second, the number of plots cultivated by each farmer is decreasing because of division by inheritance. Split inheritance seems to be fairly common among farmers in this irrigation scheme. Not only did the previous generation have more or larger plots than current farmers, but also current farmers with multiple plots are planning to divide them for their children when they become too old to grow crops themselves. The prevailing belief among the older farmers in the irrigation scheme is that young people are not interested in farming, so they do not perceive allocating inherited plots to multiple family members as a major problem. Taking the example of the young female farmer (Ms N), it is obvious that the number of plots each member of the family can inherit is getting smaller due to split inheritance. Although the viability of farming decreases when the inheritor receives a fewer number of plots, once the plots are divided among inheritors, they usually work individually on their own plots and don't farm cooperatively. However, Ms N is also an example of the younger generation who may take up farming when the opportunity presents itself through inheritance.

Third, the availability of water may become a more crucial factor than that of land in the irrigation scheme in the future. One century ago farmers on the irrigation scheme were required to pay for both land rental and water usage to the government, but this practice died out and none of the farmers we spoke to in 2016 recalled ever having to pay for the water. Given that water is getting scarce in the irrigation scheme, it is possible that the government might re-introduce the water use fee and those who cannot afford to pay it might eventually have to give up farming.

Therefore, the possibility for farming expansion in former homelands is limited by the customary land tenure system, by split inheritance among current plot- holder households and by the increasing shortage of water on the existing irrigation schemes. If black farmers want to expand their production, they need to look elsewhere, which would most likely be to land in formerly white-only farming areas. This scenario could be realised only by implementing more land reform policies. Moyo & Mine (2018) emphasise the importance of peasant production of the labour-absorbing type in order to make society more stable on the African continent. They convey a clear message that as long as a sense of injustice remains widespread as in the case of unequal land ownership in South Africa, we cannot hope to envision the formation of a more equal and stable society. Negative evaluation of many land reform farms by the Minister in charge of land reform that I quoted at the beginning of this article should not be used to discourage the implementation of more land reform. Many studies in fact blamed a lack of timely, adequate and consistent state support after land was transferred to the beneficiaries for their poor agricultural performance (Hall, 2007; Aliber et al., 2013).

Even though the future of black farming may not lie in former homelands, the fact that a general understanding of the rural economy is still limited justifies the necessity for this kind of research. This study on the one hand identified the availability of water and various informal markets as opportunities for small-scale black farmers to pursue agricultural livelihoods. On the other hand, a number of constraints were also recognised including shortage of labour, high production costs (especially hiring tractor services), lack of or unreliable state support, and the increasing water shortage. State support is important not only for beneficiaries of land reform, but also for residents of former homelands who also engage in farming. When we visited the Mooi River Irrigation Scheme in 2014, the most serious problem for farmers was livestock destroying their crops due to poor fencing. Subsequently the government decided to renovate and upgrade both the Mooi and Tugela River Irrigation Schemes. The renovation package included replacing old fences with new ones and installing underground water pipes and communal water valves to reduce water leakage. Although local farmers were not sure about how effective the new irrigation system would be to save water, they welcomed new fences. Unlike sporadic provision of seeds and fertilisers to a limited number of farmers, everyone benefited from new fences. It remains to be seen whether the government can introduce effective intervention such as this in more rural areas. Existing research on other irrigation schemes do not give us much hope (Tapela, 2008; Van Averbeke & Denison, 2013), but what we researchers hope is that a better understanding of the rural economy can serve as a guide to help policy makers assess the workable livelihood options for that 30% of the South African population who still reside in these areas.

Acknowledgements

This chapter is based on my paper presented at 'Land, the State and Decolonising the Agrarian Structure in Africa: A Colloquium in Honour of Professor Sam Moyo,' organized at the University of Cape Town, South Africa, on November 28–29, 2016. This colloquium was sponsored by the Japan Society for the Promotion of Science, Grant-in-Aid for Scientific Research (S) '"African Potential" and Overcoming the Difficulties of Modern World: Comprehensive Research That Will Provide a New Perspective for the Future of Humanity' (KAKENHI 16H06318 headed by Motoji Matsuda, Kyoto University), as well as by the University of Cape Town's Research Office (URC). A revised version of the chapter was presented at the Institute of Poverty, Land and Agrarian Studies (PLAAS) seminar, the University of the Western Cape, on September 8, 2017. I would like to thank the participants of both occasions for their insightful comments and discussions. I would also like to thank two anonymous reviewers for helpful comments while revising the paper for this final version. The financial assistance by the Japan Society for the Promotion of Science, Grant-in-Aid for Young Scientists (B) KAKENHI 24710300 to conduct fieldwork for this research is also duly acknowledged.

Notes

(1) The current estimate is that approximately 10% of farms were transferred to black people through land reform by 2016 (Zuma, 2017).

(2) However, one block is no longer in use due to severe soil erosion. Interview, Extension Officer of KZN Department of Agriculture, Tugela Ferry, February 5, 2015.

(3) 1906/292 Engineer Mooi River irrigation works, Muden, SNA I/1/334, Pietermaritzburg archive.

(4) Interview, Extension Officer of KZN Department of Agriculture, Tugela Ferry, February 5, 2015; Interview, Village Elders, Msinga, August 13, 2016.

(5) 1908/2706 W.R. Wilson, Resident Inspector Mooi River Works, Muden, SNA I/1/410; 1918/3461 Financial, irrecoverable revenue: Mooi River and Tugela irrigation works, CNC 343, Pietermaritzburg archive.

(6) Interview, Extension Officer of KZN Department of Agriculture, Tugela Ferry, February 5, 2015.

(7) These interviews were conducted jointly with Mr Mnqobi Ngubane, a doctoral student at the Institute for Poverty, Land and Agrarian Studies (PLAAS), University of the Western Cape, where I was based as a visiting research fellow from 2013 to 2015. We were assisted by two research assistants whom we recruited in Muden.

(8) According to an extension officer from the KZN Department of Agriculture, which oversees the Mooi River Irrigation Scheme, there were about 300 farmers in each block. However, the size of each block varies and he did not have a list of plot-holders.

(9) In traditional Zulu society, marriage is a process that can take time to complete. Thus, we found many older couples who had lived together for many years, but were not married. We combined married people with these "de facto" married (cohabitating) couples into a single category of "married/cohabitating."

(10) Since the land in the irrigation scheme is fenced and situated separately from homestead areas, this doesn't include the space for homestead. Gardens are usually made within the residential land (homestead area), but those who have a plot in the irrigation scheme rarely

have a garden. This is because of two reasons. First, people think that growing crops in gardens is not easy without access to irrigation water. Second, proper fencing is necessary in order to prevent livestock from destroying their crops in the garden and fencing can be expensive.

(11) *Ingonyama* means 'Zulu king.'

(12) Interview, Inkosi Mchunu, Mhlangana, July 18, 2014. He died in early 2015 and was succeeded by his son, who had been the acting chief of the Mchunu traditional authority for some time.

(13) Of the remaining two respondents, one said that he obtained his land from a previous owner and another said that he was brought to the land by a government truck known as a "GG truck" after being evicted from a white farm.

(14) Cousins et al. (2011) also discusses the role of neighbours in allocating residential lands in other areas of the Mchunu traditional authority as a "living law of land."

(15) This may not have always been the case historically. Some female respondents said that when they approached a chief to obtain a Permission to Occupy (PTO) Certificate for their residential land, they usually went to the chief with their father or male children. PTOs were issued in KwaZulu in the 1980s and 1990s.

(16) Interview, Induna, Msinga, August 17, 2016.

(17) Interview, Extension Officer of KZN Department of Agriculture, Tugela Ferry, February

5, 2015.

(18) Interview, Induna, Msinga, August 17, 2016.

(19) Interview, Farmer, Msinga, June 5, 2014.

(20) According to an extension officer of the KZN Department of Agriculture, the department's tractors are divided by *amakhosi*. *Inkosi* Mchunu has five tractors in total for his area (both irrigation and dry land farming areas), but only three tractors were in good condition at the time of interview in early 2015. Also, five agricultural advisors work in *inkosi* Mchunu's area and they must share these five tractors amongst themselves. This means that the extension officer of the Mooi River Irrigation Scheme can use the tractor services only on Fridays on Blocks 1–12 where he is in charge. Black farmers who have plots there have to be in the fields if they want their plots to be ploughed by the department's tractor (interview, Extension Officer of KZN Department of Agriculture, Tugela Ferry,

February 5, 2015). According to the respondents, whether the tractor service was free depended on the type of tractor used by the department. The modern tractor that can make lines was not free.

(21) One respondent stated: "Ploughing costs R150 per plot. Making soil smaller costs R120 per plot and making lines costs R120 per plot" (Interview, Farmer, Msinga, June 11, 2014).

(22) The discrepancy between the number of respondents here and those reported in the earlier section is because we asked farmers two separate questions during the interviews in 2014. In the early part of the interview, we asked them to list their sources of income (How do you make a living?) and 77 said that they grew and sold their crops. Then, after asking questions related to land tenure and the type of crops they grew, in the middle of the interview we again asked them whether they sold crops, and 82 answered affirmatively.

(23) According to farmers, bakkie traders have been coming to the irrigation scheme for at least the past 20 years. However, whether the number of bakkie traders has increased or decreased during this period could not be established because the farmers' answers were contradictory. Some said that it had increased, while others said it had decreased.

(24) During one pension day market in Muden in August 2016, I counted at least 151 traders selling various items. While some of them worked as professional traders moving from one pension day market to another, others were farmer-traders who brought their own vegetables to sell at that event.

(25) One of the reasons why farmers in the irrigation scheme do not consume their own maize at home is a lack of proper storage facilities. To address this problem, some black farmers in Limpopo have begun storing their maize in commercial silos, which used to be used exclusively by white farmers (interview, Prof. Wim van Averbeke, Tswane University of Technology, Pretoria, August 4, 2016). I have not come across a similar practice among black farmers in the Mooi River Irrigation Scheme, but there are such silos in Greytown, which may be used for the same purpose.

(26) We left a copy of the income and expenditure sheet with each farmer so that they or their family members could get a better understanding of the profitability of their crop farming.

(27) Interview, Farmer, Msinga, June 5, 2014.

(28) The KZN Department of Agriculture has a satellite office in

Kwanteneshane, which is situated in the middle of a long stretch of irrigation-scheme land right next to Block 6. The office is manned by an officer who works with water guards. There were about 5–7 tractors parked outside this office in 2014, but we never saw them operating in the fields. The extension officer from the Department in Tugela Ferry is supposed to visit this satellite office 2–3 times a week, but the irregularity of transport options from Tugela Ferry to Kwanteneshane seems to hinder him from doing so.

(29) Interview, Farmer, Msinga, August 15, 2016.
(30) Interview, Farmer, Msinga, August 12, 2016.
(31) Interview, Farmer, Msinga, August 12, 2016.
(32) Interview, Farmer, Msinga, August 12, 2016.
(33) Interview, Farmer, Msinga, August 18, 2016.

References

Aliber, M., T. Maluleke, T. Manenzhe, G. Paradza & B. Cousins 2013. *Land Reform and Livelihoods: Trajectories of Change in Northern Limpopo Province, South Africa.* HSRC Press, Cape Town.

Bates, R.F. 1996. *An Evaluation of the South African Sugar Industry's Small Cane Growers' Financial Aid Fund.* Doctor Thesis, Department of Agricultural Economics, University of Natal, Pietermaritzburg, South Africa.

Beinart, W. 1994. *Twentieth-century South Africa.* Oxford University Press, Oxford.

— 2012. Beyond 'homelands': Some ideas about the history of African rural areas in South Africa. *South African Historical Journal*, 64(1): 5–21.

— 2014. A century of migrancy from Mpondoland. *African Studies*, 73(3): 387–409. Bernstein, H. 1996. South Africa's agrarian question: Extreme and exceptional? In (H. Bernstein, ed.) *The Agrarian Question in South Africa*, pp. 1–52. Frank Cass & Co. Ltd., London.

— 2005. Rural land and land conflicts in sub-Saharan Africa. In (S. Moyo & P. Yeros, eds.) *Reclaiming the Land: The Resurgence of Rural Movements in Africa, Asia and Latin America*, pp. 67–101. Zed

Books, London and New York.

Bromberger, N. & F. Antonie 1993. Black small farmers in the homelands: Economic prospects and policies. In (M. Lipton & C. Simkins, eds.) *State & Market in Post Apartheid South Africa*, pp. 409–449. Witwatersrand University Press, Johannesburg.

Bundy, C. 1988. *The Rise and Fall of the South African Peasantry, Second Edition*. David Philip, Cape Town. (First edition was published in 1979).

Buthelezi, T.C. 2013. *Pro-poor Value Chain Governance in the Mtateni Irrigation Scheme at Tugela Ferry, Msinga, KwaZulu-Natal*. Mini-thesis, PLAAS, University of the Western Cape, Bellville, South Africa.

Cairns, R.I. 1995. *Small Grower Commercial Timber Schemes in KwaZulu, CSDS Research Paper No.6*. Centre for Social and Development Studies, University of Natal, Durban.

Cousins, B. 2012. *Smallholder Irrigation Schemes, Agrarian Reform and 'Accumulation from Below': Evidence from Tugela Ferry, KwaZulu-Natal*. Paper for a conference on "Strategies to Overcome Poverty and Inequality: Towards Carnegie III," University of Cape Town, September 3–7, 2012.

— 2015. 'Through a glass darkly': Towards agrarian reform in South Africa. In (B. Cousins & C. Walker, eds.) *Land Divided, Land Restored: Land Reform in South Africa for the 21st Century*, pp. 250–269. Jacana Media, Auckland Park.

Cousins, B., R. Alcock, N. Dlala, D. Hornby, M. Masondo, G. Mbatha, M. Mweli & C. Alcock 2011. *Imithetho Yomhlaba YaseMsinga: The Living Law of Land in Msinga, KwaZulu-Natal, Research Report 43*. PLAAS, University of the Western Cape, Bellville.

De La Hey, M. & W. Beinart 2017. Why have South African smallholders largely abandoned arable production in fields? A case study. *Journal of Southern African Studies*, 43(4): 753–770.

Hall, R. 2007. Transforming rural South Africa? Taking stock of land reform. In (L. Ntsebeza & R. Hall, eds.) *The Land Question in South Africa: The Challenge of Transformation and Redistribution*, pp. 87–106. HSRC Press, Cape Town.

Lipton, M. 1989. *Capitalism and Apartheid South Africa, 1910–1986*. David Philip, Cape Town. (First edition was published in 1985).

— 1993. Restructuring South African agriculture. In (M. Lipton & C. Simkins, eds.) *State and Market in Post Apartheid South Africa*, pp. 359–408. Witwatersrand University Press, Johannesburg.

May, J. 1996. Assets, income and livelihoods in rural KwaZulu-Natal. In (M. Lipton, F. Ellis & M. Lipton, eds.) *Land, Labour and Livelihoods in Rural South Africa, Volume Two: KwaZulu-Natal and Northern Province*, pp. 1–30. Indicator Press, Durban.

McIntosh, A. & A. Vaughan 1996. Enhancing rural livelihoods in South Africa: Myths and realities. In (M. Lipton, F. Ellis & M. Lipton, eds.) *Land, Labour and Livelihoods in Rural South Africa, Volume Two: KwaZulu-Natal and Northern Province*, pp. 91–119. Indicator Press, Durban.

Morris, M. 1976. The development of capitalism in South African agriculture: Class struggle in the countryside. *Economy and Society*, 5(3): 292–343.

Moyo, S. 2007. The land question in Southern Africa: A comparative review. In (L. Ntsebeza & R. Hall, eds.) *The Land Question in South Africa: The Challenge of Transformation and Redistribution*, pp. 60–84. HSRC Press, Cape Town.

Moyo, S. & Y. Mine 2018. Perspectives on "African Potentials." *African Study Monographs Supplementary Issue*, 57: 5–19.

Moyo, S. & P. Yeros 2005. The resurgence of rural movements under neoliberalism. In (S. Moyo & P. Yeros, eds.) *Reclaiming the Land: The Resurgence of Rural Movements in Africa, Asia and Latin America*, pp. 8–64. Zed Books, London and New York.

Neocosmos, M. 1993. *The Agrarian Question in Southern Africa and "Accumulation from Below": Economics and Politics in the Struggle for Democracy*. Nordiska Afrikainstitutet, Uppsala.

Platzky, L. & C. Walker 1985. *The Surplus People: Forced Removals in South Africa*. Ravan Press, Johannesburg.

Tapela, B.N. 2008. Livelihoods in the wake of agricultural commercialisation in South Africa's poverty nodes: Insights from small-scale irrigation schemes in Limpopo Province. *Development Southern Africa*, 25(2): 181–198.

The Commission for the Socio-economic Development of the Bantu Areas within the Union of South Africa (Tomlinson Commission) 1955. *Summary of the Report, Report U.G. 61/1955.*

The Government Printer, Pretoria.

Van Averbeke, W. 2012. Performance of smallholder irrigation schemes in the Vhembe District of South Africa. In (M. Kumar, ed.) *Problem, Perspectives and Challenges of Agricultural Water Management*, pp. 413–438. InTech, Rijecka, Croatia.

Van Averbeke, W. & J. Denison 2013. Smallholder irrigation schemes as an agrarian development option for the Cape Region. In (P. Hebinck & B. Cousins, eds.) *In the Shadow of Policy: Everyday Practices in South African Land and Agrarian Reform*, pp. 263–280. Wits University Press, Johannesburg.

Van Averbeke, W. & S.S. Mohamed n.d. *Smallholder Irrigation Schemes in South Africa: Past, Present and Future*. Mimeo.

Wolpe, H. 1972. Capitalism and cheap labour-power in South Africa: From segregation to apartheid. *Economy and Society*, 1(4): 425–456.

Zuma, J. 2017. *President Jacob Zuma: 2017 State of the Nation Address*. Online. http://www. gov.za/speeches/president-jacob-zuma-2017-state-nation-address-9-feb-2017-0000.

Author's E-mail: chizuko_sato@ide.go.jp

Chapter 9

An Assessment of the Cameroonian Government's Role in the Mbororo Land Struggle in the Northwest Region

Elizabeth Tabot

Introduction

The importance of land in Africa cannot be over emphasised as different groups struggle to gain access and secure land for one reason or the other. The strategies used to secure land by different groups depends on the social, economic and political dynamics of a given society. All these depends on the state and how its role in land management enables different land users to access and secure land. The violent land struggles in the Northwest region of Cameroon between the Mbororos and other groups mainly the farmers, private institutions like the Church and influential individuals have been blamed on the social relation dynamics of the different groups. I argue here that this struggle largely reflects the failure of the Cameroonian state in its role to manage and resolve land disputes which have provoked violent struggles over the years.

This chapter addresses the role of the Cameroonian government in the land dispute between the Mbororos and the Catholic Church. The chapter draws from secondary and primary data generated from focus group discussions and face-to-face in-depth interviews as part of my PhD fieldwork between November 2015 and April 2017 in the Bandzah village, in the North-west region of Cameroon. It aims to examine and analyse the role of the Cameroonian State in the land dispute drawing from the land struggle with the Catholic Church since 2012. To examine the role of the Cameroonian government, the chapter focuses on three main questions: What is the cause of the Mbororo land struggle with the Church in the Northwest Region? How has the government attempted to resolve problems surrounding this land struggle? And how has the state's intervention affected the Mbororos' access to land? The chapter shows that, the Cameroonian state's role has been more of an obstruction than that of facilitating access to land for the Mbororos. This finding confirms, Moyo's (2000a, 2005, 2008) assertion that land reforms in Africa need to deal genuinely with the inequalities in accessing land. He blames African governments for not putting in place genuine measures that can completely solve the land problems faced by the less privileged groups in Africa. Unfortunately, these suggestions are yet to be implemented, as most African states have politicised land problems and measures of redressing land problems only acknowledged on paper.

Moyo (2008) speaks to the contradictions of the African land reforms as they hardly solve the root causes of the land problems in the continent. He highlights the land struggles faced by different land users in Zimbabwe and Africa in general. The socio-economic and political causes are all blamed for the struggles, but the state shares the biggest blame because it is in the position to put in place favourable legislation which can eradicate the problems from their roots or minimise them. This chapter reiterates this point of view by exposing the poor facilitatory role played by the Cameroonian government in enabling the Mbororos access land. The chapter shows that the Cameroonian state through regional and divisional administrators has failed to put specific laws in place to enable the Mbororos who are considered strangers to acquire and gain access to secure land.

Chapter Outline

The chapter is divided into five main sections. The first section gives a background of land access and struggle in Africa. The second section describes the Cameroon land tenure system. The third section presents the Mbororo-Catholic Church land struggle to highlight the difficulties faced by the Mbororos in accessing land. The fourth section analyses the role played by the Cameroonian state in the above-mentioned land struggle and how land policies and land management procedures have acted as an obstruction to land access by this group. The fifth section offers the general concluding remarks.

Background: Access to Land in Africa

Land struggles are common in most African communities because land is more than just a commodity, as it has social, political and economic benefits attached to it. Thus, every group tries to access it using whatever strategy possible (Moyo 2005). Land struggles by different groups of people in Africa are persistent because of complex social relations and poor state management of the land. A cautious approach is required if one must prevent violent manifestations in future. The Southern African case which is characterised by the accumulation of land by the white minorities and the inequality to access such land is different in its dynamics from other African regions, but not different when it comes to inequality in access to land (Tong 2014). In the West African and Central African regions, such accumulations were perpetrated by the colonial administration and were later promoted and consolidated by the post-colonial African governments (ibid). Access to land has never been fair because the peasants and rural dwellers who need it more do not have the financial and the technical knowhow to pursue the necessary procedure put in place to acquire or have access to land.

The land struggle in Zimbabwe and Africa in general was captured by Moyo (2008, 2005, 1999) and he gave different suggestions as to how to solve land problems in the Southern Africa Region. Moyo (1999, 2005) condemned the accumulation of land by the white minority while the bulk of the Zimbabwean peasant population remained landless. He suggested that all lands that were acquired by white settlers under the guise of agricultural development should be recuperated and given to the landless who need land for their livelihood. Subsistence peasants were deprived of land because of commercial farmers. Development was used as an excuse to deprive these group of people. According to Moyo, (2003) development will be more effective if the subsistence peasants can access land, to guarantee their subsistence and use the excess for other financial commitments. Land struggles can never be prevented

255

because there are different land users with different interest. However, land conflicts can be minimized through legislation, dialogue and effective land governance.

Moyo (2005) was critical about what reforms needs to be put in place for the majority to access land in Africa, and he thinks such reforms could only be successful if land is reallocated by the state. Moyo (2005) argues that there is need for a land reform that will deal genuinely with the inequalities in the Southern Africa region. Unfortunately, these suggestions are yet to be implemented, as most African states have politicised land problems and measures to address land problems are only articulated on paper.

Other scholars have had similar opinion like Moyo in relation to the State being blamed for the land struggles experienced by their citizens. For instance, Hitcock (2011) examined the role of the Botswana government in the land struggle of the San. He blamed the laws put in place by the Botswana government which disregarded access and land rights to this group. The same state negligence and conspiracy in the land struggle is seen in the experience of the Pygmy population in Congo. The Congolese state acted against its own citizens' right to access land. In this case the Pygmies who are hunter-gatherers were stripped of their land rights in favour of timber exploitation for foreign markets. The state is an accomplice in the land struggles across the continent, and yet states are expected to prevent and manage these struggles (Ansome and Hillforts, 2014).

Unlike Sam Moyo, Richardson (2005) sees the land distribution policies as huge failures for a country like Zimbabwe which has ventured into land redistribution. He discourages any such land policies as he thinks land measures for redistribution were not based on merits, but on political affiliations and ethnic sentiments. While Moyo blames the Zimbabwean state for not doing enough to help the masses access land, Richardson blames the state for its incompetence in handling land reforms as it did not favour the commercial farmers who have occupied the lands for centuries. The case presented in this chapter is a good example of how the State has neglected putting in place genuine laws that will solve or minimise land struggles. The laws in place favour some groups over others. For instance, land certification as a means of securing land rights gave the

Church the advantage to secure the land unlike the Mbororos for whom the same laws restrict their ability to secure a land certificate through the chiefs.

Though not in the same context, I relate Moyo's stand point to the struggles of farmers and the poor majority in Zimbabwe who depended on land for their socio-economic survival and seek special land policies to address their situation. All the different groups of land users need land for one reason or the other, be it majority or minorities, indigenes or strangers, women or men etc. So, it is essential that access to land be secured for all, especially those who use land directly for pastoralism, subsistence crop farming and other related economic activities.

Access to land in Africa has been greatly politicised by African states and politicians, as well as lobbying groups for their specific interest. Moyo (2005) sees the Zimbabwean fast track land reform as the most effective way to solve the land inequality problem in Southern Africa which has been pending for long. That is why he dismisses the stereotype that such model and approach will lead to economic crisis and instead highlights the benefits of the fast track land reforms. He describes such assessment as "being static and to focus on the psychological effects that tampering with property relations may have on markets or investors" (Moyo, 2005:13). He contends that failure to address land inequalities would have had serious negative socio-political implications on African countries and so the government approach to solve this problem should be critical. In the case of Zimbabwe, the demand for the redistribution of land to the large- and small-scale black users was a way forward to curb the unemployment and poverty in the rural area as well as appeasing the long agitated and furious population (Moyo 2005).

Looking at Moyo, s (1999, 2005, 2008) line of thought, it is evident that it was the legislations that could change and solve the land struggles faced by most Zimbabweans, so the Fast Track Land Reform Programme (FTLRP) was put in place to solve this problem. It is along the same lines that this work holds that the Cameroonian government responsible for the land struggles faced by the Mbororos and suggests there is the need for a practical legislation to help them access land. Borrowing from Chitonge (2015a 2015b), rights over natural resources can be guaranteed only when legislation is matched with policy implementation. Thus, only good legislation and policy implementation can guarantee the Mbororo secure access to land.

For a better understanding of the main arguments and other sections of this chapter, an insight of Cameroon's land tenure profile is reviewed in the next section; with the main observation being that the main land laws and policies instituted or implemented during the colonial and post-colonial era disadvantaged the masses while favouring the colonial administrators. The Mbororos had certain opportunities to access land during the colonial era which is lacking in the post-colonial State. Their land right was guaranteed and protected by the colonial government even though the indigenes were retaliating against such favour and protection of the Mbororos.

Cameroonian Land Tenure Profile

The primary Land law in Cameroon was enacted on 6 of July 1974, namely Ordinance No. 74-1 and it established land tenure rules. Still in the same year, another ordinance was enacted to complement the land law, Ordinance No. 74-2 of 6 July 1974, to address how state lands were to be governed (Fisiy 1992). The implementation of these land laws has not been as helpful to land security as they ought to be. Most scholars contend that the land laws which are based on land registration failed to take so many realities of the country into consideration and so the laws are accepted just partially (Fisiy 1992, Nguiffo and Djeukam 2008, Sone 2012a, 2012b). All unregistered private pieces of land were considered national land (Unoccupied land and land held under customary law). The land laws were intended to attract foreign investments and so tried to differentiate private land from public and national land which could be allocated for foreign investment and development.

At this stage, it is crucial to discuss how the Cameroonian land tenure system is organized so as to understand the lapses in the management of land. From the colonial administration to present, there has been changes in the land tenure system in order to reflect the realities of society. These systems have worked in solving some of the land problems the citizens face while at the same time some scholars have analysed them as being problematic and irrelevant. (Fisiy 1992, Sone 2012a, Moritz 2006, Nguiffo and Djeukam 2008). Fisih (1992) for example observed that the land laws had loop holes and inconsistencies in them which gave room for state officials to implement the laws contrary to what they were supposed to be doing. In the same light of the laws being problematic, Sone challenges the discriminatory land laws as they are so biased against women who are the main food producers in the Northwest region (Sone 2012a). Using the same criticism Angwafor blamed the state for its laws which frustrated the female farmers more in that they made them to use ethnic rights to assume more rights over land in the region than the Mbororo herders (Angwafor 2014).

Land in Cameroon is classified as private, national or public. Private land can be owned by individuals, entities or the state, and it must be titled. Public land is lands used for public good like parks, roads and waterways. All other land which does not fall under the two categories above is considered as national land. That is land under customary law, informal settlements and grazing land. Land tenure types include ownership, usufruct, leasehold and profit or license. Looking at the three categories under which land has been classified in Cameroon, private ownership is guaranteed only with the availability of a land title. (Hobbs 1998). This is confusing and complex because communal land by nature does not have a land title. In most land struggles, it is common for the statutory land system to contradict the customary land system.

Land certification in Cameroon has three phases; the administrative phase which entails the assessment of land occupation and development, a technical phase which has to do with the physical description of the land, and a legal phase that analyses the conditions of access to property rights. Different administrative bodies are responsible for the different phases and this has made the process cumbersome and expensive. The Administrative phase is taken care of by the Department of Land Tenure and the Ministry of Territorial Administration for assessments, the Technical phase is handled by the Department of Surveys and the Legal phase is managed by the Department of State Property. The entire registration process takes 93 days and costs 18% of property value, compared to the average of

81 days and 10% of property value in most sub-Saharan African countries (World Bank 2009b; GOC 2009).

In 1974, a legal framework for land tenure and property rights was set up which served as a process for land rights registration and created a framework for private ownership of property. Fisiy (1992) argued that instead of the land policy put in place to protect citizens and increase land ownership security, it has instead exposed many citizens to loss of land because very few Cameroonians own titled land. Most of them still depend on the customary land ownership System. This has made the citizens vulnerable to the government which is supposed to protect them.

Most land rights in Cameroon have been secured through purchase, leasing, borrowing, inheritance, or allocation by traditional leaders (Nguiffo & Djeukam, 2008). Farmers, and particularly migrants, cultivate forest areas in order to gain rights to land under customary law. Under statutory law, Cameroonians occupying or using land from August 6, 1974 (30 days after the 1974 land laws were passed) could apply for formal ownership rights to the land (Hobbs, 1998). The implementation of land laws is contradictory because most times what obtains is not what is implemented. Farmers who are of the majority in the Cameroon's Northwest Region clash regularly with graziers who are in search of pasture for their cattle. The cattle destroy farmers' crops. That explains why farmer-grazier conflicts are common in the region (Fisiy, 1992).

Some African countries like Ethiopia, Tanzania, Niger and Nigeria had decentralised land management since 2005, and have state institutions created at local levels to manage land and resolve land related conflicts. In Cameroon, Article 16 of Ordinance No. 74-1 of the Land Law established Divisional-level Land Consultation Boards, and Decree No. 78/263 1978 established Divisional-level Commissions for Resolving Agro-Pastoral Conflicts. Decree No. 2005/481 governs land titling and registration (GOC Land Law 74-1 1974; GOC Land Law 74-2 1974; GOC Decree 481 2005; GEF 2006).)

Sone (2012a) highlights the deficiency and short comings of the Cameroonian land laws. Similarly, Orock (2005) examined an indigene-settler divide in the Cameroonian urban social space as an emanation of the land question, and hinges on the role which modernisation has played. Modernisation which is mostly used to dispossess and evacuate people from the land they have occupied for decades lack an effective legal framework. Thus, most victims of eviction hardly understand the process put in place to seek to compensation when they lose their land (ibid; 22). Orock argues that modernization as a policy has in place weak legal framework in Douala, and this has resulted into the fragmented urban social co-existence among stakeholders from the native and settler groups in Douala. According to his findings, within the context of such an indigene-settler dichotomy, social coexistence is being fragmented by rising animosity as the government and the various groups have resorted to the politicisation of the land question (ibid, 26).

The same land struggle still holds in other parts of Cameroon as is illustrated by the Mbororos for instance, who are still struggling to own land in both rural and urban areas in the Northwest region because of the native-settler divide. The general handicaps of the land law in Cameroon is reflected significantly in the land struggles between the different land users in the country. But this chapter has discussed only that of the Mbororo because they face more challenges in land struggles since they are considered strangers in the region. Also, the government promised to protect their minority rights in the international treaties they signed, but has not done so.

Mbororo Land Struggles in the Northwest Region

Analysts are arguing that the Mbororo have adapted to the normal socio-economic life of the majority and so should not be given special rights or access to land (Nyamnjoh 2013; Sone 2012a). Even after that I still contend that land is important to everybody, be it indigenes or non-indigenes, rich or poor, women or men, the minorities and the majorities alike because of its socio-economic values. Each of these groups thus tries to use any means to access and secure land.

There is a lot of literatures on herder-farmer conflict (Boutrais1995/96: 679-803, Chilver 1988, Fisiy 1992: 224-228, Sone 2012a, 2012b, Angwafor 2014) in the Northwest region which

261

sympathizes more with farmers because it is believed they have more rights to land as the first comers to the region and constitute the majority. In the colonial era, land was demarcated between farming land and grazing land. But with the post-colonial interest in promoting private land ownership, such demarcations have been abandoned and made irrelevant. Laws put in place to address herder-farmer conflicts have been compromised by corruption and so their applicability is not consistent (Sone 2012a; 2012b, Angwafor 2014)

Land struggles in the region date way back even before the colonial period, and they have continued with the -postcolonial period because the need for land and its value keeps increasing by the day. Dire need for land has led to struggles between different groups in the region like politicians, farmers and even the church. But the struggle for access for land is regulated and facilitated by the state. In this regards, it is important to ask, what has been the role of the Cameroonian state in managing Mbororo land access?

Farmer-herders land disputes are very common in the Northwest region. At times conflicts are very violent as was the case in 1973 in Wum where the Aghem women farmers abandoned land to lie fallow for years, and the Mbororo graziers occupied it thinking it was an unused land suitable for grazing. This led to a violent protest as the Aghem women boycotted market activities for weeks. The conflict was further aggravated by the state officials who sympathised with the herders and tried to prevent the women from accessing the land.

Farmer-herder relations have been characterised by competition and conflict over natural resources. However, there have been some complementary relationships as they share common space for their mutual benefit (Dafinger and Pelican, 2006). The relationship has been problematic in Cameroon just like the case of Cote d'Ivoire, Ghana and Nigeria (ibid). As noted by Pelican (2006, 2009), most farmer-herder disputes have been mediated by the colonial or post-colonial government administration to benefit the administration in place, thus the interest of the people was not taken into consideration. State agents who act as intermediaries to settle these conflicts have been guided by self-interest and corruption which have aggravated farmer-herder disputes in the region. (Ibid). The regional administrators have been at the centre of most land struggles, be they land legally registered land or not. The case under study below examines the Mbororo land struggle with the Catholic Church to unpack the role of the Cameroonian state in this struggle.

Mbororo-Church Land Dispute

Data

Data for this study were obtained from both primary and secondary sources. There were open interviews with interviewees on the problems they face in accessing land. A total of five purposely selected categories of people were interviewed including the Mbororo and their representatives; the government representatives, the church representative, the human rights advocacy organisation and non-Mbororos. Individual interview technique was used. There were different topics addressed by the different categories of interviewees. The research interviewed 25 people in total, 16 representing the Mbororo victims and their representatives, 2 representing the government, 1 representing the Church, 4 representing the non Mbororos and 2 representing human rights organisations.

The data collected were systematically analysed. The main challenges faced were those of mistrust and political instability in the region. This problem was minimised by working through the community leaders to instil trust. Primary data were complemented with secondary data. Secondary data were drawn largely from literature on land rights in Africa, minorities, indigeneity, citizenship, reports and government policies.

The dispute

In 2012, a land dispute broke out between the Mbororos at Mamada Hill in Bandzah Village under Mezam Division in the Northwest region and the Catholic Church. According to the narratives from both the Church and the Mbororos, the dispute was about land rights claim under customary law for the Mbororos and statutory law for the Catholic Church. The Church needed land to construct a university and they followed the formal procedure by requesting for land from the Chief of Bandzah. The Chief granted

263

the land request and the Church proceeded to the Divisional Office to certify the land. The land application was granted as a Concessional Land Grant and a certificate was issued to the Church by the *Minister of State Property* for 47 hectares of land. Compensation was said to have been paid to the Mbororos living on the piece of land secured by the Church, and the Mbororos were asked to leave the land. Their refusal to leave the land led to the demolition of their homes by the Church with the approval of the Divisional Officer of Mezam. A court action against the Mbororos was instituted for trespassing on land belonging to the Catholic Church.

The Mbororos on their part claimed land rights through inheritance and the development they had carried out on the land. They based their claim for this piece of land on the fact that they were Cameroonian citizens and indigenous minorities recognised by the state. The issuing of an eviction notice by the Church with the approval of the Regional Administrators sparked the violent manifestation of the land dispute. The Church obtained a demolition order from the Divisional Officer of Mezam Division and demolished all the houses of the Mbororos at the Mamada Hill. This rendered them homeless and led to the intervention of both international and national human rights organisations.

Analysis of the information collected for this study show that the regional government was in support of the Catholic Church against the Mbororos because they did not have a land certificate for the land which they were claiming to be theirs. Unlike the Mbororos, the Church had secured a Concessional Grant Certificate to the land, and this gave them the right to exploit the land. The procedure used by the Church to secure a land certificate was questioned because of some irregularities involved in how transactions around the land in question. As per the 1974 Land Ordinance, land that is developed and occupied physically (Category 2 land) cannot be selected for a Concessional Grant, it can only be expropriated with compensation paid to the owners. There was supposed to be no compensation because the land was considered by the law to be Category 1 Land (unoccupied and undeveloped land) which implies there was no development and people physically living on the land.

But the land in contention was actually occupied by the Mbororos and had developed the land with farms and houses. So, it was a Category 2 land whose owners were supposed to be compensated. However, since everything had been mixed up, the state officials and the Church claimed it was Category 1 land, yet it was handled as if it was Category 2 land since the Church paid compensation to the Mbororos through the State. There was so much contradiction as the Church claimed they were paying compensation out of good will because what is stated in the land law does not call for compensation on category 1 land. Moreover, the Mbororos did not have a land certificate and so by law they were not entitled to any compensation for the land. With the land struggle being violent, it is important to examine this case further to get some insight regarding the role of the state.

Intricacies of the land dispute

There are several reasons why the Mbororos face these land struggles. Generally, this land dispute is embroiled the broader social, political, economic and religious tensions between the different groups. Owing to these different dynamics, the social and economic dynamics of the land struggle faced by the Mbororos is of the utmost significance because all other dynamics revolve around these two. Firstly, the Mbororos are perceived and considered by the Northwest indigenous population as strangers in the Northwest region. Because of this, they are discriminated against by both the indigenes of the region and the state when it comes to accessing land. In the excerpt below, a non-Mbororo lawyer explains how the Mbororos are perceived in the region when land issues are concerned;

> The Mbororos normally in this region were considered as nomads, and therefore any area that they were moving into and occupying, nobody ever considers them as owning that land. Because as I described to you the ownership of the land belongs to the village and the chiefs. Since Mbororos were people who came from outside, nomads, the general concept among the natives was that the Mbororo did not own any land. They were just squatters (Interview by Researcher, 12 April 2017).

The Mbororos migrated into the region in the 19th centuries when other tribes had already settled, so they are considered latecomers. They are said to have settled after the colonial government was established in Cameroon. Their settlement in any village was approved by the chief of the village. This was maintained by the British colonial administrators who were accused by the natives of giving their land to the Mbororos. But this action by the British was a way of securing the economic benefits which they derived from the income generated from livestock (Awasum 1985, Njeuma & Awasum 1990).

In the post-colonial era, the Mbororos' struggles for land intensified because the value of land had not only increased, but Mbororos who were considered pastoralist had started settling down and creating permanent homes which was contrary to what the natives took them to be. So, the transition from being temporal to permanent occupants has changed the relationship with the natives and the claim to secure their land became even stronger with the laws put in place. This led to the politics of belonging and citizenship discourses which manifest in the dynamics around land rights between the indigenous groups and the Mbororos. Those who consider themselves citizens and autochthones of the region think they are entitled to land in the region, and those who are seen as strangers cannot claim land. This struggle has been ongoing for a long time, and the Mbororos have devised several strategies to claim and access land, and one of them is the use of indigenous minorities rights which has been contested by scholars and government officials. That is why the administrators do not make mention of any specific rights put in place to enable the Mbororos access to land. This is clearly evident in the land management policies put in place, which technically excludes the Mbororos from obtaining a land certificate without the signature of the Chief of the area in which they are settled. In the interview excerpt with the chief of Banzah below, he states that

If anybody has a plot here in Ndzah, I am the one that approved it. So, if you claim that a piece of land is your own and you have not demarcated it, and there is no land certificate, you don't own that land it is a government land' (Interview by Researcher. 9 March 2017).

In that regard, while an indigene or native of the village is assured to secure the chief's signature that enable one to obtain a land certificate (because the chief acknowledges their family and ancestral route), a Mbororo person will have to pay huge sums of money to get the chief to sign their application for a land certificate. A Mbororo representative revealed that;

> They know that Mbororo people are in desperate need to have this land, and occupy them permanently through getting land titles over them, and you know it is no news that Cameroon is corrupt. So most often they [local officials including chiefs] demand money, much more when it is a case of a Mbororo person than when it is a native of the region" (Interview by Researcher. 19 March 2017).

So, it means since the state has tied the application of a land title to the chief's consent, the Mbororo people are supposed to have a cordial relationship with the chief and the people of the community, without which their land application document will not be signed. So, had it been that they had to deal directly with the state and not pass through the chief, the struggle might have been different because the social relation as a determining factor would not be so compelling. The administrators thus take advantage of these preconditions which are difficult for the Mbororos to meet to extort money from them during the securing of a land certificate. It is because they cannot secure such a document that they lose land all the time to both private companies and public institutions.

In recent times, some Mbororos have used political connections and their economic strength to access land. But a common Mbororo person who does not have such influence and connection cannot access land because the procedure is expensive and difficult. Generally, the land certificate application procedure is a challenge to all groups of persons because of the unscrupulous behaviour of land management officials, but it is even more challenging for the Mbororos because they are perceived as being rich and at the same time strangers who do not have the right to claim land rights. If they must claim land, they have to pay large sums of money.

The Role of the State in Mbororo-Catholic Church Land Dispute

The state is supposed to be the facilitator of land access for all its citizens through practical legislations and civil administrative procedures. Different African States have put in place different strategies or laws to enable land access to land for all citizens. Some countries like Ethiopia, Gabon and Congo have even put in place specific laws to enable vulnerable groups like the Mbororos who are considered to be indigenous minorities to access land. But in practice such laws and legislations are still to be seen. In South Africa for instance, although the state set a target to transfer 30% of the total land to the black majority by 2014, little land has been transferred despite the numerous land reform programmes put implemented since 1994 (Tong 2014). Looking at the importance of the role of the state in managing land access, the case in this chapter shows that the role of the Cameroonian government has been more of an obstruction than a facilitation to land access and security for the Mbororos as will be seen below.

Failure to manage the dispute fairly
Firstly, the state is blamed for the role it played in provoking the dispute and in the way the dispute was managed. A human rights activist expressed his disappointment in the way the land dispute was managed in the interview excerpt below:

> I tried to make the case that the Mbororo land in Bandzah was developed, occupied by people, as opposed to the position of the Archbishop that the land was empty land. So I think the administration and the Church were playing wilful blindness. They were pretending not to see what was happening (Interview by Researcher, 10 March 2017).

According to him, the land category was different from what it was said to be by the Divisional Officer and the Church. The land was said to fall under Category 1 land which according to Cameroonian law was not supposed to be given out as a concessional grant. However, for development purposes the government had to expropriate the land after paying compensation to the owners and evacuating them from the land.

The state officials claimed the land in question was Category 1 land with no development and it was unoccupied because it did not have a land certificate. Accordingly, any form of compensation to the Mboroo inhabitants was done out of pity since the land was said to be undeveloped and unoccupied. The Mboroo inhabitants interviewed blamed the government for the land dispute with the Church. They think the State connived with the Catholic Church to seize land from them. A Mboroo representative explains:

> Let's look at it the other way around, the two communities have dispute over the community grazing land and the government has taken it away from the Mbororos, and now the government wants to take the Ardorate for development project again which means that the problem is caused by the administration. Which means since the Mbororos are a minority and their property becomes the property of everyone (Interview by Researcher. 8 March 2017).

Moreover, they blamed the state for not rejecting the application of the Church to acquire the land occupied by the Mbororos. The Mbororos think that the Chief of Bandzah and the Divisional Officer were bribed by the Church that is why they disposed them of land. A Mboroo respondent elaborates:

> What he [the chief] said is that the Catholic university is a very important project because of the might of the Catholic. But he does not see any important thing we can bring to his office. He told us openly. When we asked him, what was his position, he told us nothing goes with an empty pocket. From there we understood that there was some financial motivation behind his behaviour. That was the reason why he was saying all these things. He said we should stop all the talking

and we must leave the land issue, if not he will side-line us and we will go elsewhere and not in Cameroon ((Interview by Researcher. 8 March 2017).

In the excerpt an explanation is given of how the government preferred the Catholic project which is a university compared to the Mbororos occupying the land. That shows how the government has failed to be considerate of the Mbororos' land needs as seen in the way they have managed the dispute.

The ineffectiveness of land certificates

Another reason why the state is blamed for the land struggles of the Mbororos is its inability to regulate the land certification procedure in such a way that bottle necks and corrupt officials are adequately addressed. One of the main problems faced by the Mbororos in accessing and securing land is the lack of a land certificate. Several reasons have been given as to why the Mbororos cannot easily secure a land certificate for their land but most of the blame goes to the government because a favourable condition in the land certification procedure is an important step towards securing such a document. A Mbororo lawyer explained the difficulties involved in the land certification procedure for Mbororos:

In the rural areas, and it is in the rural areas that majority of the Mbororos live, it is very challenging to obtain a land certificate. First of all, the procedure to be followed to obtain the land certificate. This is because the Mbororo people are considered as strangers by their neighbours, farming neighbours. In the Land Consultative Board, there is supposed to be the Fon, or the leader of the village and two notables, so those two notables and the leader of the village are the people who consider Mbororo people as strangers" (Interview by researcher. March 22, 2017).

The Chiefs and administrative officials are not making land access easy for the Mbororos because they are benefitting from this group's struggles for land and the several disputes and conflicts they encounter in the region (Moritz 2006 :103; Kah 2009: 188; Dafinger

& Pelican 2006: 133.). In my opinion the state is to blame for allowing all these loopholes to persist in the land management procedures and practices. Despite the Divisional Officer being accused by the chiefs of taking bribe to resolve land disputes, the Chiefs are themselves not free from corruption as they make access even more difficult by refusing to sign the land title application form as required by the state to grant a Mbororo person a land title. If the conditions and procedures required for obtaining a land certificate are favourable, there is a possibility that all groups of persons can obtain a land certificate easily.

In the interview conducted with the Chief of Bandzah on the Mbororo land struggle with the Catholic Church in the Northwest Region, the Chief made it clear that the Mbororos cannot secure a land title on the land they occupy unless he signs the application form. He narrates,

> I asked the Ardo if he was giving any money to the council as he was occupying the land, he said it is his land. Does he have a land certificate? And if he had to get a land certificate, I had to be a signatory, and I will have to indicate I sold the land to him. Members of the commission are the chiefs, the DO of Bamenda 3, chief of lands in Mezam, and the quarter head need to approve on that land title" (Interview by researcher. 9 March 2017).

In the interview excerpt above which uses, the exact words of the Chief of Bandzah he confirms that the Mbororos cannot obtain a land certificate without his approval. He clearly boasts over the right and role chiefs play in land allocation and certification. By implication he thinks the Mbororos cannot challenge him over the land he gave to the Catholic Church for the construction of a university. The land was habited by the Mbororos and farms and houses had been built on the land, however, the lack of a land certificate made the case more complicated as the Mbororos know and claim that it is their land, but by law it is a state land, and in the opinion of the chief and the regional administrators, the land is state land.

The Chief of Bandzah who allocated the land to the Church is the same person who can grant the Mbororos the right to apply for a land certificate from the state; because, as earlier stated, any Mbororo living on a piece of land in the Northwest Region does so with the consent of the chief of the village concerned. The chief explained he preferred development in his village to the continuous stay of the Mbororo pastoralists who bring him very little or no benefit. In the interview with the chief, he made it clear that it is development he wants in his village,

> I have told you that eh, I had a vision then for a government university to be built on the land, but it failed. So, I decided to give it to the Catholics because I wanted to develop my village (Interview by researcher. 9 March 2017).

The university to be built by the Church will bring many other economic advantages with it. The procedure in place to obtain a land certificate makes it difficult for the Mbororos and its ineffectiveness favoured the Church against them.

Inability to regulate and implement land laws
Another role played by the state which obstructs land access rather than facilitate it is the inability of the state to regulate the different roles played by the statutory and the Customary land system. These two systems are the precolonial and the Colonial/post-colonial land systems. Because of the need for the State to benefit from the advantages of both systems, it decided to keep both systems. In the research carried out on the Mbororos' land dispute with the Catholic Church in the Northwest region, it was discovered that the Mbororos and the Church all had different legal frameworks under which they made claims over the land in question. While the Mbororos were claiming to have been the first people to occupy the land, the Church claimed they are the ones with the legal documents from the state to use the land. Both parties are right to some extent because the 1974 land ordinance accepts the first comer's right to land while at the same time it indicates that any uncertified piece of land is state land. So, both the Mbororos and the Church have a genuine claim over the land to some extent. If the government had

put in place well defined policies which do not clash with each other during implementation the case would have been different.

Worst still, this has caused more confusion. The customary law and the statutory legislation are at loggerheads when it comes to land acquisition, access and security. Customary land rights are accorded to indigenes only and those non-indigenes who have the money to buy plots. On the other hand, statutory land rights are for anybody who is a citizen and has the financial means to secure a land certificate. Some indigenes have lost their land because some rich non-indigenes were able to obtain a land certificate for the piece of land belonging to indigenes who could not obtain a land certificate. In the same manner the Mbororos lost the land they had developed to the Catholic Church because they did not have a land certificate. These conflicting rights accorded by the different systems have affected access to land seriously because people are confused and hooked between the two systems. The statutory system which mostly prevails over the customary system prescribes that people should fulfil certain conditions to acquire a land title and, at the same time it creates space for the customary system under the chiefs to play significant roles in land management, and some of them have used this role against some Mbororos to prevent them from accessing land, except they give large sums of money as a bribe. This affirms the contradictions created by the law which is supposed to be used to facilitate access to land for all.

Corruption

Another area where the state acts as an obstruction to land access instead of facilitating land access for the Mbororos is in the corrupt practices of land management. Its legal institutions are corrupt to the extent that money and political connections can influence land disputes and mediation in favour of the rich and those with political connection. In the research carried out on the Mbororo-Church land struggle, most of the Mbororos voiced their disappointment with the Divisional Officer and the Lands and Survey official as they think they were being bribed. First, they blamed them for giving their land to the Church, and later they masterminded the demolition of their houses by the Catholic Church when they started building the university. Moreover, the Mbororo representatives interviewed complained about the regional administrators soliciting bribes in order to be relocated to another area which the Chief gave. He explained;

> At that moment they wanted the Mbororo community to leave their land and that they should give them money to relocate them. That is what they have done to us several times. And if we had that money at that time, we would have given them because the pressure was too much. We had no means to farm on our land, we had no freedom on our land, we are with children going to school and so forth (Interview by author. 19 March 2017).

The human rights activist who assessed the intricacies of the land struggle between the Church and the Mbororos told me that the government officials had taken money from the Church to approve the land certificate given to the Church even when they knew the land was category 2 land which by law was not supposed to be given out for a land concession. The government did not verify the land category and it got to a stage where everything was mixed up as on paper it was said to be category 2 land and not category 1 land. Also, the extortion of Mbororos was voiced by a Mbororo lawyer:

> Because of the corruption of some government officials, some of the Mbororo people are hesitant to apply for a land certificate because they think that it is exploitative. And I will bet you, maybe two Mbororo people have land certificate over 10 over their lands" (Interview by researcher. 19March, 2017).

Looking at the circumstances surrounding how the Church and the government officials came to the agreement to take the Mbororo land, one could believe the corruption claims by the Mbororos. As per the stipulations of the Land Ordinance of 1974 as explained above, one could believe the narratives of the Mbororos about the bribe taken by the government officials and the Chief of Bandzah, even though they denied having taken any bribes to the researcher when they were asked to clarify the allegations. The law states that category 2 land which is developed and inhabited cannot be given out for expropriation. The Mbororos were living on the land and they had farms, houses and their cattle ranches on it which showed that there was physical presence. How then did the government claim they were not living on the land and there was no development there? Moreover, there were more than 12 households that were interviewed with an estimate of about 300 inhabitants, including both children and adults. The regional and divisional administrators like the DO, the Lands and Survey Delegate helped the Church to compile the required documents needed for the application for a concessional grant certificate from the government.

Furthermore, the state officials did not take responsibility for relocating the Mbororos to a new site after they were given an eviction notice. They took 54 acres of land from them and then wanted to relocate them on a piece of land which was not even 10hectres. What was paid as compensation was said to be small compared to the land taken from them. A Mbororo interviewee complained "They took our land and gave us so little in return. When we asked, they said we don't have a land certificate" Where they gave us to settle with our cattle in Bambili was very small to accommodate us and Bambili people were attacking us all the time". The Mbororos were relocated on a land that was owned by Bambili people and this led to constant harassment by the Bambili youths.

Looking at the dynamics of this case under study, it is worth noting that the land rights of the Mbororos is contested and so they are reminded that even though they occupied the land, it does not belong to them because they were given the land by the Chief of Bandzah in the past. This explains why the government administration claimed the development in terms of a university was very important and the laws do not recognise Mbororo presence on the land. So, without the approval of the state the Mbororos are said to be living on the land illegally. This could be another way of dispossessing them because they have some right to occupy the land, yet they cannot claim ownership and the government recognises only the certification procedure as legal ownership.

Conclusion

To conclude, it is very glaring that the Cameroonian state even though it has put in place measures to enable the Mbororos access and secure land it still has a lot to do to protect this group. There are no specific laws in place to help vulnerable groups like the Mbororos to access land easily, and the available laws disadvantage them because the reality on the ground is different from what the laws prescribe. This chapter has shown that the Cameroonian state has been an obstruction to land access by the Mbororos rather than a facilitator to their land access. The only law in place which guarantees Mbororo land access is the grazing permit which is full of stringent conditions and limitations in terms of how to use the land. If this group is supposed to be protected and considered to have a right to access land, then the Cameroonian government is supposed to play a very vital role such as putting in place specific laws pertaining to Mbororo land rights as was the case in the colonial days.

From the findings, some suggested solutions to the challenges discussed including creating good and trustworthy land commissions, corruption free institutions and creating effective government institutions. The Cameroonian state must match policies with legislation. For instance, there could be clauses that provide for a specific procedure for their land certification process which will be different from the procedure of the indigenes of the region. The state officials deliberately exploit them during land certification periods because the law does not state in its clauses that such distinctions should be made. Also, like Pelican (2009) earlier suggested, they should work on an amicable relationship with the indigenes of the Northwest region to access land even if the laws are in place. There should be a relationship of trust and collaboration. Let the laws speak to the different groups of land users, farmers, pastoralists, women, strangers, indigenes etc. to understand the challenges they face and the suggested solution to their land struggles to put in place specific laws to reduce the difficulties and challenges they face in accessing land.

Efficient state regularisation will make a difference in the land struggle in the Northwest region. All other groups like the farmers, women, and strangers are also struggling to access land, but the difference is that they are indigenes and their right to land is not questioned. Going back to Sam Moyo (2008)'s contention about the inability of African states to put in place measures that can solve land struggles, we see a replica of the same ineffective measures and institutions put in place in Cameroon to manage land. Instead of legislations that does not address the land problems, the government should get involved in studying how the laws in place have failed and how to come up with realistic policies to minimise the problem. This could be another research issue worth taking up. Also, Moyo (2005, 2008) revolved around issues of land distribution and land struggles because he realised land access was inequitable and unfair in Zimbabwean society. His writing showed that the state had a very significant role to play and that is why he blames the political and social manipulations tolerated by the state to keep in place such injustice in the name of economic development. This chapter reiterates Moyo's condemnation of the role of the Cameroonian state in land management as it failed to solve the root cause of the Mbororo land struggles. The measures put in place act as an obstruction to their land access instead of facilitating it. To bring about change, the Cameroonian state must pass legislation and policies which will facilitate access in a cordial manner with the indigenes of the Northwest region. More research needs to be carried out on how such a cordial relationship could be promoted on land related issues between the Mbororos and the Northwest indigenes.

Acknowledgment

This work would not have been possible without the funding from NIHSS (National Institute of Humanities and Social Sciences).

References

Ansoms and Hilhorst ed. (2014) Losing your Land: Dispossession in the Great Lakes. Suffolk: James Curry.

Arrighi Giovanni et al, Accumulation by Dispossession and its Limits: Copyrights Springer Science Business Media, LLC 2010, pg 410-438

Andreas Dafinger & Michaela Pelican (2006). Sharing or Dividing the Land? Land Rights and Farmer-Herder Relations in Burkina Faso and Northwest Cameroon. *Canadian Journal of African Studies / Revue Canadienne Des Études Africaines.* 40(1):127-151. Available: https://www.jstor.org/stable/25433869.

Angwafor, P.T. (2014). *Contesting land and identity: the case of women cultivators and Fulani cattle herders in Wum, northwest region of Cameroon.*

Awasom, Nichodemus (1984). 'The Hausa and Fulani in the Bamenda Grasslands1903–1960'. PhD thesis, University of Yaoundé I.

Boutrais, Jean 1984 Entre nomadisme et sédentarité: Les Mbororo à l'ouest du Cameroun. In Le développement rural en question: Paysages, espaces ruraux, systèmes agraires. Chantal Blanc-Pamard, éd. Pp. 225–256. Paris: ORSTOM. 1995–96 Hautes terres d'élevage au Cameroun. 2 vols. Paris: ORSTOM.

Chilver E.M (1988), 'The political economy of Cameroon: historical perspectives in women cultivators' cows and cash crops' *Phillis Kaberry's women of the Grassfields revisited,* African Studies centre, Leiden

Chitonge, H. (2015a). *Beyond Parliament: Human Rights and the Politics of Social Change in the Global South.* Boston: BRILL.

Chitonge, H. (2015b). *Beyond Parliament: Human Rights and the Politics of Social Change in the Global South.* Boston: BRILL. Available: https://ebookcentral.proquest.com/lib/[SITE_ID]/detail.action?docID=219689

Dafinger, A. & Pelican, M. (2006). Sharing or Dividing the Land? Land Rights and Farmer-Herder Relations in Burkina Faso and Northwest Cameroon. *Canadian Journal of African Studies.* 40(1):127-179.

Available: http://gateway.proquest.com/openurl?url_ver=Z39. 88-2004&res_dat=xri:bsc:&rft_dat=xri:bsc:rec:iibp:00377509.

Fisiy, C.F. (1992). *Power and privilege in the administration of law*. Leiden: African Studies Centre.

Hickey, S. (2011). Toward a Progressive Politics of Belonging? Insights from a Pastoralist "Hometown" Association. *Africa Today*. 57(4):29-47.
Available: http://www.jstor.org/stable/10.2979/africatoday.57. 4.29.

Hitchcock, R.K., Sapignoli, M. & Babchuk, W.A. (2011). What about our rights? Settlements, subsistence and livelihood security among Central Kalahari San and Bakgalagadi. *The International Journal of Human Rights*. 15(1):62-88.
Available: http://www.tandfonline.com/doi/abs/10.1080/1364 2987.2011.529689.

Hobbs, Mary. 1998. Cameroon country profile. Country Profiles of Land Tenure: Africa, 1996, ed. John W. Bruce. Washington, USAID.

Kah H. (2009), 'Governance and land conflict: the case of Aghem-Wum 1966-2005' in Fonchingong.T. S &Gemandze. J.B [eds] *Cameroon: the stakes and challenges of governance and development*, Langaa, RPCIG Mankon-Bamenda

Mbanaso, M.U. (2010). *Minorities and the state in Africa*. Amherst, NY: Cambria Press.

Michaela Pelican. 2006. *Getting along in the Grassfields: interethnic relations and identity politics in northwest Cameroon*.

Moritz, M (2006) 'The politics of permanent conflict: farmers-herder conflicts in northern Cameroon', CJAS/RCEA Volume 40 Number 1 pp 113

Moyo, S. 2000a. The Political Economy of Land Acquisition and Redistribution in Zimbabwe, 1990-1999. *Journal of Southern African Studies*. 26(1):5-28.
Available: http://www.tandfonline.com/doi/abs/10.1080/0305 70700108351.

Moyo, S. 2000b. The Political Economy of Land Acquisition and Redistribution in Zimbabwe, 1990-1999. *Journal of Southern African Studies*. 26(1):5-28.

Moyo, S. (2005a). Land and Natural Resource Redistribution in Zimbabwe: Access, Equity and Conflict. *African and Asian Studies.* 4(1-2):187-224.

Available: http://booksandjournals.brillonline.com/content/jo urnals/10.1163/1569209054547283.

Moyo, S. (2008). *African Land Questions, Agrarian Transitions and the State.* Oxford: African Books Collective.

Moyo, Sam, (2005) Land and Natural Resource Redistribution in Zimbabwe: Access, Equity and Conflict. African and Asian Studies, Vol 4, No 1-2. Brill, NV Leiden.

Moyo, Sam. (1999). The Political Economy of Land Acquisition in Zimbabwe, 1990-1999, JSAS, vol. 26, No. 1, pp. 5-28.neo-liberal land reforms. Dakar, CODESERIA.

Nguiffo, Samuel and Djeukam Robinson. 2008. Using the law as a tool to secure the land rights of indigenous communities in southern Cameroon. In Cotula, Lorenzo and Mathieu, Paul. Legal Empowerment in Practice: Using Legal Tools to Secure Land Rights in Africa. International Institute for Environment and Development (IIED), London.

Njeuma & Awasom. (1990). The Fulani and the Political Economy of the Bamenda Grasslands, 1940-1960. *Paideuma.* 36:217-233. Available: https://www.jstor.org/stable/40732671.

Nyamnjoh, F.B. (2013). The Nimbleness of Being Fulani. *Africa Today.* 59(3):105-134.

Available: http://www.jstor.org/stable/10.2979/africatoday.59. 3.105.

Orock, Roger. 2005. The Indigene-Settler Divide, Modernisation and the Land Question: Indications for Social (Dis) order in Cameroon,*). Nordic Journal of African Studies, 14(1): 68–78*

Pelican, M. (2008), 'Mbororo claims to regional citizenship and minority status in Northwest Cameroon', The Journal of the International African Institute, Volume 78 Number 4pp 550

Pelican, M. (2011). Mbororo on the move: from pastoral mobility to international travel. *Journal of Contemporary African Studies.* 29(4):427-440.

Available: http://www.tandfonline.com/doi/abs/10.1080/0258 9001.2011.607015.

Pelican, M. (2006). Getting along in the Grassfields: Interethnic relations and identity politics in northwest Cameroon. Halle, Saale: Universitats- und Landesbibliothek Sachsen-Anhal.

Pelican, M. 2009. Complexities of indigeneity and autochthony: An African example. *American Ethnologist.* 36(1):52-65. Available: http://www.ingentaconnect.com/content/bpl/amet /2009/00000036/00000001/art00005.

Pelican, M. (2009). Complexities of indigeneity and autochthony: An African example. *American Ethnologist.* 36(1):52-65. Available: http://www.ingentaconnect.com/content/bpl/amet /2009/00000036/00000001/art00005.

Pelican, M. (2013). Insights from Cameroon: Five years after the Declaration on the Rights of Indigenous Peoples (Respond to this article at http://www.therai.org.uk/at/debate). *Anthropology Today.* 29(3):13-16. Available: https://onlinelibrary.wiley.com/doi/abs/10.1111/14 67-8322.12029.

Richardson, C. (2005). The Loss of property rights and the collapse of Zimbabwe, CATO Journal 25. Available from: www.cato.org/pubs/journal/cj25n3/cj25n3-12.pdf [Date accessed: April 2011].

Richardson, C.J. (2004). The Collapse of Zimbabwe in the wake of 2000-2003 Land Reforms. New York: Mellen Press.

Sone, P. (2012b). Access to land in the Anglophone regions of Cameroon: Challenges and prospects. *Journal of Social Development in Africa.* 27(2):85-112.

Sone, P.M. 2012a. Conflict over landownership: The case of farmers and cattle graziers in the northwest region of Cameroon. *African Journal on Conflict Resolution.* 12(1):83-102. Available: http://gateway.proquest.com/openurl?url_ver=Z39. 88-2004&res_dat=xri:bsc:&rft_dat=xri:bsc:rec:iibp:00425807.

Tong, M. 2014. Decolonisation and comparative land reform with a special focus on Africa. *International Journal of African Renaissance Studies - Multi-, Inter- and Transdisciplinarity.* 9(1):16-35.

Documents

Decree No. 66-307-COR of 25th November 1966 on the registration of Traditional land rights

GEF 2006)

GOC 2009

GOC Decree 481 2005;

GOC Land Law 74-1 1974;

GOC Land Law 74-2 1974;

Land Reform Law 1974 Decree N0.76-165 of 27 April 1976 to establish the conditions for obtaining land certificates, amended and supplemented by Decree N0.2005/481 of 16 December 2005

Ordinance No. 74-1 to establish rules governing land tenure in Cameroon

Ordinace No.74-2 to establish rules governing state land

Ordinance No. 74-3 to establish expropriation procedures for 'public purposes' including the terms of expropriation passed in 1974, Preamble of the 1996 Cameroon Constitution

Constitution and Internal Regulations of MBOSCUDA, World Bank 2009b;

Mbororo acquittal from their ancestral land
http://www.un.org/apps/news/story.asp?NewsID=47545&Cr
=cameroon&Cr1#.WDFpmtJ97IW. Accessed 20/11/2016.

UN experts on minorities and indigenous peoples concerned about destruction of pastoralist homes -
http://www.ohchr.org/EN/NewsEvents/Pages/DisplayNews.
aspx?NewsID=14496&LangID=E . Accessed 20/11/2016

Mbororo appeal acquittal torture case.
https://www.culturalsurvival.org/news/lisa-
matthews/mbororo-appeal-acquittal-torture-case. Accessed 20/11/2016.

Email of author: tabotelizabeth@gmail.com

Chapter 10

From Friends to Strangers? Social Capital and the Fast Track Land Reform Programme of Zimbabwe

Senzeni Ncube

Introduction

Professor Sam Moyo was a renowned scholar who systematically studied land reforms not just in Zimbabwe, but across the continent. This chapter, which is influenced by some of his work, investigates the role of social capital in the outcomes of the A1 villagised model of the Fast Track Land Reform (FTLRP) in Zimbabwe. One of the A1 villagised model's main aims was to decongest overpopulated communal and urban areas and to expand the base for smallholder agriculture (GoZ, 2001). Beneficiaries were settled in village-like settlements divided into three portions: residential plots, arable plots, and communal grazing land (Moyo et al., 2009). Residents shared grazing land, social infrastructure and services. Thus, the model functions best when there are healthy relationships among beneficiaries that promote collaboration, also known as social capital. Although social capital is a multifaceted and contested concept, the chapter defines it as "features of social organisation, such as trust, norms, and networks that can improve the efficiency of society by facilitating coordinated actions" (Putnam et al., 1993:17).

The supporters of the FTLRP point to the A1 villagised model as the most successful component of the programme, with livelihood creation being the most visible outcome (Matondi, 2012; Hanlon et al., 2013; Moyo, 2011b). They further acknowledge the role of social capital in the realisation of livelihoods through the A1 model (Scoones et al., 2010; Murisa, 2011). What is missing in their analyses is the interrogation of the flaws of the A1 villagised model and their effect on hindering social capital. Yet social capital plays an important role in the realisation of livelihoods. This chapter responds to this gap, analysing the weaknesses of structure of the A1 villagised model, the imposition of government administration and its flexibility to absorb more beneficiaries on already allocated land. The chapter therefore argues that land reform models with a communal element can promote social capital. The chapter further argues that state-led land reform programmes should prioritise the context specific nature of social capital, particularly harnessing pre-existing relationships to strengthen local government initiatives. Insights are drawn from a study conducted on Rouxdale farm in the Bubi District, Matabeleland North Province, Zimbabwe between 2014 and 2015.

The chapter is divided into two broad sections. The first section covers the review of literature on the FTLRP and social capital. It is further divided into four sub-sections. The first sub-section deals briefly with theoretical debates of the concept of social capital and justification for its adoption as a framework for the chapter. The second section is a description of the A1 crop-based villagised model, its objectives, structure, and governance administration system in the context of the FTLRP. The third is a review of literature on the contested outcomes of the FTLRP, focusing on whether or not it was a success. The last is also a brief literature review on the role of social capital in the FTLRP, drawing from various case studies.

The second section of the chapter focuses on case study findings of Rouxdale (R/E) farm. It is subdivided into four sub-sections. The first provides a brief background of the case study and outcomes of the FTLRP on Rouxdale (R/E) farm. The second is a critique of the A1 villagised model that discusses weaknesses of the model and their effects on the social capital of beneficiaries. The third section is a broad discussion of factors that either enhance or hinder social capital, drawing insights from the case study. The fourth part concludes the chapter, highlighting its contribution to academic literature and overall argument.

Theoretical Debates about Social Capital

Social capital is a multifaceted and controversial concept in scholarly literature, with multiple definitions. According to Putnam et al. (1993:17), social capital is "features of social organisation, such as trust, norms, and social networks that can improve the efficiency of society by facilitating coordinated actions." Lin (2001:12) defines social capital as "resources embedded in a social structure which are accessed and/or mobilised in purposive actions." Field (2003: 1) defines it as the "connections of people through networks and sharing common values with other members of networks, to the extent that these networks constitute a resource." The common thread in these definitions is the importance of relationships within communities that manifest in the form of social networks whose resources benefit all members. Social capital is thus seen as a "public good," because of its benefits to a wider community (Putnam et al., 1993; Coleman, 1990). It is through social capital that communities tackle collective problems and build solidarity (Putnam et al., 1993; Coleman, 1990; Field, 2003).

Healthy social networks have an agreed code of conduct, values or beliefs also known as norms (Putnam et al., 1993; Coleman, 1990; Field, 2003). The most efficient norm is "reciprocity" or "obligations" (Coleman, 1990; Putnam et al., 1993). It entails an exchange of favours or items within social networks that builds togetherness and strengthens relationships (Putnam et al., 1993). Over time, stronger norms develop into trust, which is another essential component of social capital (Coleman, 1990; Putnam et al., 1993). Communities with high levels of trust are capable of achieving more common goals because trust "lubricates cooperation" (Putnam et al., 1993:171). In these social networks, members share ideas and experiences on particular issues, and this information facilitates the implementation of collective goals (Lin, 2001). However, access to what Lin (2001) calls "resources" of social networks, which are, in essence, their benefits, is only restricted to members.

The concept of social capital is contested in scholarly literature. Critics argue, *inter alia*, that it is a loose concept that is not clearly defined, and thus difficult to use as a tool for analysis (Durlauf, 1999). Some stress that social capital can be used by deviant groups to achieve goals that are destructive to society such as crime (Durlauf, 1999). Other critics argue that there is no connection between trust and the creation of a community collaboration and solidarity (Foley and Edwards, 1999). They highlight that it is through collaboration that communities build trust, not the other way round (Foley and

Edwards, 1999). Others argue that trust is delicate (Kay, 2006) and that social capital is context specific (Poder, 2011).

Despite the criticism of social capital, it has been used as a framework for this chapter for its invaluable strengths. The supporters of the concept have shown how social capital has largely delivered its promises (Field, 2003). According to Field (2003), "people who are able to draw on others for support are healthier than those who cannot...and their communities suffer less-anti social behaviour." Other scholars have demonstrated the input of social capital in various contexts, towards building community solidarity and addressing collective challenges (Coleman, 1990; Putnam, 2000; Bourdieu, 1986; Lin, 2001). Although the supporters of social capital admit that the concept has weaknesses, they have illustrated how these are far outweighed by its strengths. I welcome the views of the critics of the concept because some of them contribute to its improvement.

I take social capital to be a useful analytical framework because of the nature of the A1 villagised model. The communal element of the model where beneficiaries share resources and grazing land also elicit the need for cooperative action in order to coordinate sharing of resources and tackle communal problems. Social capital is that tool that facilitates such initiatives. A brief description of the A1 villagised model in the context of the FTLRP is the subject of the next section.

The Fast Track Land Reform Programme (FTLRP) and the A1 Villagised Model

Land reform in Zimbabwe started immediately after independence in 1980 under the Zimbabwe African National Union (ZANU) Patriotic Front (PF) government, to address colonial imbalances of land ownership. The first phase covered the first two decades, 1980 to 1999. The FTLRP is a second phase of land reform in Zimbabwe initiated by war veteran-led networks in 2000, through the occupations of white owned large scale commercial farms (Sadomba, 2013; Moyo, 2013b). The programme was formalised through a policy document in April 2001 (GoZ, 2001). The main objectives of the FTLRP, were, first, to "decongest overpopulated wards and villages" both in communal and urban areas (GoZ, 2001). Second, to ensure that indigenous black Zimbabweans controlled the Large Scale Commercial Farming Sector (LSCF) (GoZ, 2001). Third, to alleviate high levels of poverty among the rural population, including farmworkers (GoZ, 2001). Fourth, to "integrate smallholder farmers into mainstream commercial agriculture," with the intention of capacitating them to produce for the export market (GoZ, 2001:13). A careful analysis of these objectives reveals the intention of the government to allow beneficiaries access to the benefits of land.

The government designed two models of land redistribution, the A1 (small scale) and A2 (large-scale) models (Moyo et al., 2009). The A1 model, also known as the "decongestion model," targeted poor landless people from both urban and rural areas (GoZ, 2001:11; Moyo et al., 2009). The model had two variants, the villagised and self-contained models. The self- contained model allocated beneficiaries an exclusive piece of land that beneficiaries subdivided into residential, arable and grazing portions (Moyo et al., 2009). The villagised model on the other hand, was further split into two variants, the crop-based and livestock-based. The livestock-based variant was largely implemented in drier areas of the country where livestock rearing is the most suitable type of farming (GoZ, 2001). It focused on establishing commercial livestock through the provision of adequate grazing land to beneficiaries (GoZ, 2001). This chapter focuses on the A1 villagised crop-based model.

As noted earlier, the A1 villagised crop-based model settled beneficiaries in villages demarcated into three sections; household plots, arable plots and communal grazing land (Moyo et al., 2009:8). Beneficiaries shared grazing land, social infrastructure inherited from former landowners, and services. The official land tenure for this model was in the form of offer letters from the government (Matondi and Dekker, 2011). According to the FTLRP policy document (GoZ, 2001), the model's main objectives include the decongestion of overpopulated communal and urban areas. It sought to improve the base for productive agriculture in the peasant farming sector. It also aimed to provide the necessary post settlement-support in the form of infrastructure and services to beneficiaries. Tackling the problem of squatters and disorganised settlements in rural and urban areas was another objective of the model (GoZ, 2001:11). These objectives point to government's intention to promote smallholder agriculture through the empowerment of ordinary people. In the rest of the chapter, the model will be referred to as the villagised model, or A1 village.

As expected in a state-led land reform programme, the government was responsible for administration and service provision of villagised model beneficiaries, through its various structures. At village level, village heads were selected with the role of overseeing general development of the village and steering the Village Development Committee (VIDCO) (Murisa, 2009). The VIDCO is a group of representative beneficiaries tasked with coordinating specifically assigned development initiatives of the village and ensuring that social infrastructure is shared in a fair and cordial manner (Murisa, 2009). Various committees were assigned to the VIDCO members to cover specific development targets. A committee representative for women, for example, could oversee all matters affecting women in the village (Murisa, 2009). The village head is the first point of contact, also responsible for all village administration and paid by the government through the Rural District Council (GoZ, 1999).

All A1 villages are components of a larger rural administrative unit known as Wards, which are under the leadership of councillors, also representing the Rural District Council. Councillors oversee activities of Ward Development Committees (WADCO), composed of all village heads of the Ward and other responsible authorities. Councillors coordinate the implementation of WADCO development plans of respective Village Development Committees (Murisa, 2009). They also chair WADCO meetings where ideas from village heads are discussed and channelled to the Rural District Council (Murisa, 2009).

The Department of Agriculture and Rural Extension (AREX) has a mandate of providing extension services to A1 villagised model beneficiaries (Moyo et al., 2009). Extension officers and veterinary services are most visible, with the former playing a role of assisting farmers with matters related to agricultural training, knowledge and procurement of government inputs (Murisa, 2009; Moyo et al., 2009). The latter focus on providing livestock related assistance (Moyo et al., 2009). All the FTLRP beneficiaries fall under the jurisdiction of traditional leaders such as chiefs, who provided traditional oversight of their communities (GoZ, 1999).

The FTLRP started when Zimbabwe was undergoing retrogressive economic and political crisis (Bond and Manyanya, 2002; Raftopoulos and Phimister, 2004). Thus, government lacked sufficient capital to finance post-settlement support, as in the first phase of land reform (Moyo et al., 2009). Infrastructure and social services such as education and health care were either below substandard or entirely absent in A1 villages (Moyo et al., 2009). Therefore, government transformed infrastructure inherited from white farmers into schools, extension offices and clinics for use by A1 beneficiaries (Sukume et al., 2004). Even then, the government was aware that this would not adequately cater for all beneficiaries' developmental needs (Scoones et al., 2010). However, to ensure that existing but limited infrastructure was used in a cordial manner, government instructed beneficiaries to share infrastructure and services (GoZ, 2001). This would require beneficiaries' collective action, drawn from the establishment of strong relations, and is seen as social capital (Field, 2003).

Contested Outcomes of the FTLRP

The FTLRP received tremendous attention in academic scholarship, and outcomes are contested. Critics of the programme argue that government officials and their connections, benefited most from the FTLRP, while marginalising opposition supporters and poor farmworkers (Zamchiya, 2011; Sachikonye, 2003; Bond, 2008). This, according to critics, was contrary to the programme objective of decongesting overpopulated areas and alleviation of poverty (Sachikonye, 2003). They stress that a large percentage of the population was isolated by the programme, especially farmworkers who were "displaced and impoverished" (Sachikonye, 2003:37). It is against this backdrop that critics argue that most beneficiaries of the FTLRP were not ordinary people (Zamchiya, 2011).

A massive decline of national agricultural production in the commercial farming sector was seen as the most immediately visible failure of the FTLRP (Hammar and Raftolpulos, 2003; Bond, 2008). Critics also highlight the failure of the programme to produce "small and medium capitalist farmers" owing to limited post-settlement support to beneficiaries (Hammar and Raftolpulos, 2003:23). They stress that the chaotic nature of the FTLRP, and absence of systems of ensuring beneficiaries' security of tenure, led to minimal investment on the land (Sachikonye, 2003). Overall, the programme was described as was "an overwhelming failure" (Derman, 2006:24).

Sam Moyo is one of the major supporters of the FTLTP, who argue that outcomes of the programme were positive, although beneficiaries faced a plethora of problems. They point to the deracialisation of land ownership as a positive change in the agrarian structure resulting from the FTLRP (Moyo, 2011a). Various studies have shown that the new agrarian structure has empowered indigenous black Zimbabweans to being majority players of agricultural production processes (Mkodzongi, 2013b; Hanlon et al., 2013). They argue that the process of land acquisition was not overall chaotic, citing some parts of the country such as Mhondoro-Ngezi District where it was orderly and organised (Mkodzongi, 2013a).

Supporters of the FTLRP stress that the programme benefited mostly ordinary "unemployed people from rural areas" with the inclusion of urban dwellers (Moyo, 2011a:506; Scoones et al., 2010). They also highlight the inclusion of opposition political party supporters in the allocation of land, even in those provinces with a stronghold of the opposition (Moyo, 2011a; Matondi, 2012). While they admit cases of corruption by elite government officials on land allocation, they emphasise that this was not the dominant trend (Scoones et al., 2010; Moyo, 2011b).

A general sense of security of tenure in both A2 and A1 farms is seen as a positive character of the FTLRP by its supporters (Scoones et al., 2010; Hanlon et al., 2013). Thus, they refute the view that investment by beneficiaries on the land was limited by insecurity of tenure (Matondi, 2012; Mkodzongi, 2013a). Evidence of farm investment, drawn from various case studies has been presented (Mkodzongi, 2013a; Mutopo, 2014b; Murisa, 2013). Supporters add that most beneficiaries relied on their personal income to finance investment (Hanlon et al., 2013; Moyo, 2013a).

While admitting that national agricultural production declined due to the FTLRP, supporters point to evidence of improvement in production over time (Moyo, 2011b; Hanlon et al., 2013; Matondi, 2012). The most positive outcome is the contribution of the programme to livelihoods of beneficiaries (Mutopo, 2014b; Scoones et al., 2010). The A1 model (self-contained and crop-based villagised) of the FTLRP has been successful in livelihood creation, compared to the A2 large scale model. Scholarly evidence is provided in various nationwide cases, illustrating the success of the model, despite various challenges faced by beneficiaries (Mkodzongi, 2013b; Matondi, 2012). Some studies focusing on drier provinces, concur that beneficiaries of the model have attained much-needed livelihoods through the crop-based villagised model, although this is contested (Moyo, 2013a). The general trend has been that all positive outcomes are highly differentiated (Moyo, 2011b; Scoones et al., 2010).

The Role of Social Capital in the FTLRP

A careful analysis of academic literature has shown the pivotal role played by social capital in the realisation of livelihoods. Various social networks were created by beneficiaries of the A1 villagised model to combat multiple problems. These include, first, limited post-settlement support from the government. Second, the absence of close family ties owing to differences in the backgrounds of beneficiaries (Murisa, 2011). Third, the reluctance of Non-Governmental Organisations (NGOs) to provide support to beneficiaries due to the political nature of the programme (ibid). Fourth, the negative effects of a retrogressive economic crisis (Bond and Manyanya, 2002; Ndlovu-Gatsheni, 2006). Fifth, the communal element of the crop-based villagised model, that functions through collective action. Social networks therefore created a conducive environment for the attainment of livelihoods for the FTLRP beneficiaries in various parts of the country.

291

In Tavaka A1 village in Mwenezi District, various social networks among women were created to share resources such as labour, for example, assisted each other through collective groups during the harvest season in their fields (Mutopo, 2014b). Sharing ideas and insights on agricultural related issues based on previous experiences was another resource attained from women's social networks (Mutopo, 2014b). These networks, according to Mutopo (2014b), became strong friendships grounded in agreed norms and trust where women depended on each other even for emotional support (Mutopo, 2014b). The scope of social networks overlapped A1 village boundaries into nearby A2 farms and communal areas (Mutopo, 2014b).

In a case study of Zvimba and Goromonzi Districts, Murisa (2013) identified unstructured social networks operating at A1 village level. Their role included, *inter alia*, coordination of labour, sharing various agricultural inputs and specialised advice on agricultural production related issues (Murisa, 2013). These networks also encroached into A2 farms and communal areas (Murisa, 2009). Farmer groups were another type of networking with a different character (Murisa, 2011). These groups focused mainly on improving agricultural production, registered with extension officers as a means of lobbying for agricultural inputs from the government (ibid). Other farmer groups signed contracts with a tobacco company with the agreement to apportion part of their arable land for tobacco for sale to the company (ibid).

The character and composition of social networks was influenced by the various goals of beneficiaries. In Tavaka A1 village, for example, beef committees were established to manage the procurement and sale of beef (Mutopo, 2014b). Members of the groups contributed money for the purchase of cattle, which would be slaughtered and shared equally (Mutopo, 2014b). The Damvuri Development Association of Mhondoro-Ngezi District was another network of A1 villagers used as a channel of communicating beneficiaries' challenges with government authorities (Mkodzongi, 2013a). The Association also coordinated funds for the building of new infrastructure (Mkodzongi, 2013b).

Political participation, particularly the open support of the ZANU PF government was another area of collaboration, documented in Mhondoro-Ngezi District by Mkodzongi (2013a). While participation in political activities was a strategy to protect their tenure on the land, beneficiaries also used these networks to access particular services and favours from the government which could not be obtained elsewhere (Mkodzongi, 2013a). Evidence from Masvingo Province shows that most beneficiary social networks were strengthened in various gatherings organised by the government, such as political meetings and agricultural training events (Scoones et al., 2010).

These are just a few examples of social networks within the A1 villages of the FTLRP and beyond. Many scholars have also documented this outcome, such as Chiweshe (2011), Moyo et al.,(2009) and Scoones et al., (2010), which have not been discussed here. This chapter does not suggest that social networks have solved all problems of beneficiaries, since social networks also face various challenges (Murisa, 2011). However, social capital has, in the midst of these challenges, facilitated substantially the realisation of livelihoods among A1 villagised model beneficiaries. This emphasises the importance of relations of beneficiaries in a model with a communal element and limited post-settlement support. The next section discusses insights drawn from a research conducted in Rouxdale (R/E) farm of the Bubi District, Matabeleland North Province between 2014 and 2015.

The Rouxdale (R/E) Farm Case Study

Background

The chapter uses Rouxdale (R/E) farm of Ward 14, in Bubi District, Matabeleland North Province, Zimbabwe as a case study. The Province falls under Region 4 of the agro-ecological scale, fairly dry and suitable mainly for livestock production and drought-resistant crops (Weiner, 1988:66). The farm, 1 437 hectares in size, is located 30km north of the city of Bulawayo and previously utilised mainly for cattle ranching and minimal gold mining by white commercial farmers. In 2000, twenty-one beneficiaries acquired land through the A1 villagised model of the FTLRP, with one additional beneficiary in 2003, bringing the total to twenty-two beneficiaries.

Eighteen beneficiaries participated in this research in 2014 and follow-up fieldwork in May 2015. Sixteen of the participants originated from Bulawayo, and the other two from communal areas within the District. Thirteen of the beneficiaries resided permanently on the farm. Four beneficiaries resided in the city of Bulawayo and hired labour to run daily farm activities. The last beneficiary had just moved to an A2 farm at the time of fieldwork. Nine land officials representing various local government structures also participated. In August 2014, the District Land Office added twenty-two more beneficiaries on the farm. These occupied part of the communal grazing land. Additional beneficiaries were not part of this research because they acquired land towards the end of the major fieldwork period, and most were not yet permanently resident on the farm during the brief follow-up fieldwork visit in 2015.

Crop production

The villagised model on Rouxdale (R/E) farm was successful in the creation of livelihoods. Crop production was one of the major successful livelihood activities. Maize was the main crop planted by beneficiaries because it is a staple food in Zimbabwe. Other crops grown in smaller proportions were groundnuts, millet, sorghum, pumpkins and groundnuts. All beneficiaries relied on rain-fed farming. Production levels fluctuated in response to rainfall patterns, with more crops harvested in years of good rain. However, crop production levels were much less compared to high rainfall regions of the country, due to fairly dry agro-ecological conditions. Production levels also reflected the differentiation of beneficiaries.

Most beneficiaries used the harvested crop for subsistence. One beneficiary residing permanently on the farm expressed: "since I started to farm, I have never bought maize meal, I get mine from my harvest" (Fieldwork interview, 3 June 2014). Those beneficiaries residing in the city utilised their crop produce to feed their employees on the farm and supplementing food in the city. Another beneficiary narrated: "at least I carry crop produce to the city to feed people there, and leave some for those on the farm so that they will have something to eat, it helps to have a rural home" (Fieldwork interview, 9 July 2014). During years of good rains, a few beneficiaries produced surplus maize, and some of it was sold to people in the nearby farms. One beneficiary related: "we have been growing maize and selling to people who do not have food. Many people have been coming to buy maize from surrounding farms and former farmworker compounds." Crop production would not have been possible without access to land, even in a region with fairly dry aggro-ecological conditions. This livelihood cushioned beneficiaries from the economic crisis through access to subsistence for those living permanently on the farm and in the city.

The social capital of both government administration structures and beneficiaries facilitated the attainment of crop production in various ways. Although many government initiatives were incapacitated by lack of capital, some of the VIDCO committees such as the water committee were coordinated successfully. The water committee ensured that borehole water was shared cordially among beneficiaries. It also coordinated the financial contributions of beneficiaries towards electricity for the borehole pump.

Beneficiaries also relied on their own crop production related social networks. During Wednesday Ward communal projects organised by the VIDCO and WADCOs, beneficiaries shared agricultural information such as sourcing of affordable tractors services, location of grinding mills and purchasing of cheaper farm inputs. The scope of these networks was large, overlapping Rouxdale (R/E) farm due to interaction with other beneficiaries in the Ward. Other networks were created to facilitate the sale of agricultural produce. Beneficiaries sold produce within these networks that extended beyond Rouxdale (R/E) farm to people they had built relationships with over a long period of time. Other networks were created both within and outside the farm for labour procurement during harvesting and ploughing seasons. Those with cattle hired out draught power to neighbours within the farm while sometimes this service was offered free of charge where relationships were much stronger. This web of social capital within and outside the farm shows the importance of agricultural production to beneficiaries as a benefit of the FTLRP.

Livestock production

Livestock production was another livelihood activity and benefit of the FTLRP on Rouxdale (R/E) farm. Most beneficiaries did not own cattle prior to acquiring land while living in the city. Access to land therefore allowed them to venture into livestock production as explained by one beneficiary: "when I came here I did not own cattle, but through working hard and being motivated by having what I can call my own home, I bought cattle, three of them. As time went on they produced more cattle" (Fieldwork interview, 2 June 2014). Other livestock reared by beneficiaries were goats and poultry. Ownership of livestock also reflected the differentiation of beneficiaries.

Various benefits of owning livestock, cattle in particular, were reported by beneficiaries. Some regarded cattle as their savings bank because they were sold in the event of a financial need. One beneficiary related: "I sold a cow in January when schools were opening so that children could go to school. Every time I face challenges financially, I do not hesitate. I speak to my husband and we agree to sell a cow. Cattle are our bank, we draw from it" (Fieldwork interview, 3 June 2014). Other benefits of owning cattle were, *inter alia*, milk production, draught power and manure. Beneficiaries expressed that compared to communal areas, Rouxdale (R/E) farm had sufficient grazing land for their livestock. One beneficiary who grew up in Nkayi communal area explained: "in Nkayi, there is a shortage of grazing land because of overpopulation" (Fieldwork interview, 18 May 2015). The sufficiency of grazing land on the farm was also confirmed by land officials.

Social capital facilitated the rearing of livestock on Rouxdale (R/E) farm. Beneficiaries praised the cattle dipping committee of the VIDCO which successfully coordinated communal dipping. Beneficiaries established other networks; a cattle owners' network, for example, was formed to deal with cattle theft on the farm. Many beneficiaries had experienced cattle theft, as one beneficiary narrated: "there is a time when a cow was stolen from my kraal and when I woke up in the morning I immediately noticed that it was missing. So we looked for it and found that it had been slaughtered in the bush" (Fieldwork interview, 19 May 2015). After conducting night patrols to eliminate cattle thefts and being granted permission by the Provincial Commissioner of the police, beneficiaries built a police station located on Rouxdale (R/E) farm, servicing all areas in the Ward. This solved the problem of cattle theft as explained by one beneficiary: "ever since there was a police station here, thefts of cattle have become rare" (Fieldwork interview, 4 August 2014). Beneficiaries also alternated to keep watch on communal grazing land, to ensure that it was safe from veld fires. These networks made livestock rearing as a livelihood activity possible.

Gold mining

A few beneficiaries obtained certification from the Ministry of Mines to conduct gold mining on mines abandoned by the white farmers within Rouxdale (R/E) and nearby farms. This livelihood opportunity would not have been accessible without acquisition of land through the FTLRP because most beneficiaries originated from an urban area. Proceeds from gold mining were seasonal, dependent on the discovery of gold deposits. Whenever they found the gold, beneficiaries deducted all costs of processing after which gold was sold. All the money was shared by mine certified owners and their labour. Gold miners relied heavily on social capital for their activities. The first beneficiary registered the mine with his brother and friend from outside Rouxdale (R/E) farm. He had strong friendships with former farmworkers in the Ward, where he procured labour. The second beneficiary also registered his mine with three friends from outside the farm. They, likewise, procured labour from surrounding farms and former farmworker compounds. Two levels of networking are evident here. First, networks established for the formal registration of mines. Second, networks for labour procurement.

Critique of the A1 Villagised Model

Findings of the Rouxdale (R/E) farm discussed in the previous section are in line with the view of the supporters of the programme, who argue that the outcomes of the FTLRP were positive, with livelihood creation in A1 beneficiaries being most visible (Moyo, 2011a; Matondi, 2012; Scoones et al., 2010). This is despite various problems faced by beneficiaries. This finding is contrary to the views of the critics of the FTLRP who see the programme as a failure (Derman, 2006; Richardson, 2005). However, supporters, of the FTLRP, including Sam Moyo, do not discuss the weaknesses of the A1 villagised model, and their negative influence on social capital of beneficiaries, and their implications on livelihood creation in the future. This is discussed in the rest of the chapter.

Lack of privacy in residential plots

Rouxdale (R/E) farm beneficiaries acquired land through a war veteran-led social network, as in other parts of Zimbabwe. The network, responsible for land occupations at Rouxdale (R/E) farm consisted of people originating from the same township in the city of Bulawayo, most of whom were friends even before the occupation of the farm in 2000. War veterans, whose friendships dated back to the years of the liberation struggle in the 1970's, formed the core of the network, with much stronger social capital. Their friendships were strengthened in the township, where they all lived since independence in 1980 until the onset of the FTLRP in 2000. The network had, over the years, established its own norms and various levels of trust. This unique composition of beneficiaries is unlike most case studies in Zimbabwe where the FTLRP "brought together strangers from different backgrounds [communal areas, urban areas and former Large Scale Commercial Farms]" (Murisa, 2013:275). The strength of these urban originating beneficiaries would be tested by residing in a rural setting where, unlike in the city, they had to share grazing land, social infrastructure and services.

After land allocation, beneficiaries faced problems in their relationships, and some of these emanated from the physical structure of the villagised model. Residential plots on Rouxdale (R/E) farm were 0.5 hectares each, sharing boundaries with neighbours as illustrated in Figure 1. The plots were further divided into two sections: homestead and garden. Beneficiaries with residential plots positioned alongside the road built their cattle kraals in their gardens while the rest built theirs a few metres away from residential plots, in the south direction not far from passages. This means that all cattle exited through passages, into the road towards communal grazing land, located in the northern side of arable plots. Each beneficiary was allocated a 3 hectare arable plot. A single dusty road was the only physical feature separating the closest arable plots from residential plots as illustrated. Although arable plots had fence boundaries, these were not secure, according to fieldwork observation.

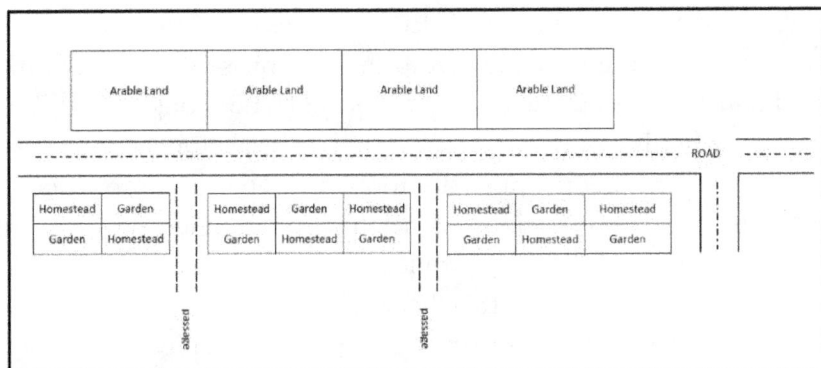

Figure 1: Structure of the A1 crop-based villagised model on Rouxdale (R/E) farm

Source: Rouxdale (R/E) farm fieldwork observation (Ncube, 2018).

Most beneficiaries criticised this structure of the A1 villagised model, highlighting various problems. Lack of privacy emerged as a serious challenge owing to lack of space between individual residential plots. In explaining this clustering of residential plots, land officials noted that this was a decision informed by the outcomes of the Model A of the first phase of land reform in Zimbabwe, from which the villagised model of the FTLRP was adopted. They explained that Model A residential plots were not subdivided, and were only used for household purposes. However, due to problems of lack of privacy expressed by beneficiaries, planners introduced the subdivision on the A1 villagised model of the FTLRP to include an orchard, which beneficiaries converted to gardens. One official narrated:

> ...the diagonal set up of orchards was meant to shield adjacent residential plots from each other using fruit trees. This idea was however alien to beneficiaries exacerbated by inadequate water for

irrigation of the orchards hence there was no buy-in. Instead, beneficiaries cleared the indigenous trees and developed rain-fed gardens where they plant their early crop. Note that residential plots were deliberately clustered so as to save money for laying water-pipes and electricity power-lines as the dream was to reticulate water and electrify each plot (Fieldwork interview, 22 May 2017).

The effort of the planners failed to address the issue of lack of privacy of beneficiaries, dating from the first phase of land reform. With limited post-settlement support, beneficiaries could not afford keeping orchards, as noted by the land official. One beneficiary related: "these residential plots are too close. There is no privacy; I end up hearing conversations of neighbours. Gossip and division amongst ourselves is a big problem in this set up" (Fieldwork interview, 21 May 2015). Other beneficiaries highlighted livestock-related problems emanating from sharing residential plot boundaries that soured relations soon after they settled on the land. Another beneficiary narrated that, "it was hard because we would have conflicts because of chickens. One would think that their chickens had laid eggs in their neighbours' homestead and the neighbour had eaten them" (Fieldwork interview, 3 June 2014). These problems caused a strain in the relationships of beneficiaries, and the weakening of once strong war veteran-led network responsible for land occupations.

Fieldwork observation revealed that if beneficiaries had adhered to planting orchards instead of clearing land for gardens, in line with the original plan of the model, this would not have solved the problem of lack of privacy because of various reasons. First, on Rouxdale (R/E) farm, located in a much drier agro-ecological region of the country with erratic rainfall patterns, maintaining an orchard would not have been possible. Second, as long as residential plots shared boundaries, they remained too clustered, given that 0.5 hectares is a very small piece of land, making the distance between households very little. The creation of a larger space between residential plots, such that they did not share boundaries would have alleviated this problem without derailing the "dream" of laying electric lines and water pipes highlighted by the land official. The possibility of this "dream" becoming a reality was hampered by lack of capital to finance post-settlement support by the government. Thus, during the fieldwork period, fourteen years after the onset of the FTLRP, residential plots had not yet been electrified, neither were they connected to water pipes. Therefore, the need for beneficiaries' input in the manner in which land reform models with a communal component are structured is important. This would assist planners to design land reform models that facilitate the growth and nurturing of social capital.

Livestock boundary conflicts

One of the challenges faced by beneficiaries was conflicts resulting from the mismanagement of livestock. Most beneficiaries complained that cattle from the neighbouring households invaded arable plots to feed on their crops. Vandalism of fence boundaries of paddocks upon acquiring land by beneficiaries was one feasible explanation that is common in other documented case studies such as Mazowe District (Matondi, 2012). The logic is that these boundaries would have blocked livestock from entering arable plots. Beneficiaries expressed that there were no strict measures enforced on owners of livestock who plundered neighbours' crops because of a general lack of respect for local authorities.

An analysis of the structure of the model in Figure 1 provides other explanations. The fact that a physical road was the only barrier between arable and residential plots is problematic. This means that the residential and arable plots were too close to each other such that cattle had easy access to arable plots to feed on crops. This was worsened by the fact that arable plot boundaries were not solid. This plan of the model was justified by land officials, and one of them said:

> The planner's wish would be to have arable lands as close to the village as possible. That would reduce the time taken by the farmer to travel to the field to work; guard his crops from destruction by domestic or wild animals; transport the harvest for processing or storage at home. (Fieldwork interview, 22 May 2017).

The above quote shows that the intention of model planners to protect crops from domestic animals was not successful on Rouxdale (R/E) farm. One beneficiary related: "every time I grow my maize, I never harvest much because when my maize has grown, someone's cattle will invade my arable plot and destroy my crop" (Fieldwork interview, 26 May 2015). This slowed the progress of attaining livelihoods from the land. The problem also soured beneficiaries' relationships as narrated by one of the beneficiaries: "I have had many fights with neighbours because of their cattle feeding in my arable plot" (Fieldwork interview, 27 May 2015). Model planners also did not consider how this structure of the model would weaken social capital of beneficiaries, yet it is an important asset for livelihood creation.

Some boundary conflicts revolved around the use of passages between arable plots, also illustrated in Figure 1. Beneficiaries struggled to maintain good relations with neighbours as a result of the conflicts. This resulted in the weakening of very strong relationships. One beneficiary who was involved in a boundary conflict with a neighbour, narrated:

> I fought with my neighbour because of cattle. So after ploughing with my cattle I would move them through the passage between our residential plots. He said he did not want my cattle to use that passage because they would dig a trench and cause water to move into his residential plot during the rainy season. He suggested that I move my cattle through my residential plot entrance (Fieldwork interview, 20 May 2015).

In a separate interview, the neighbour, a wife of a local government authority, confirmed the conflict, explaining that both families had not been on speaking terms for over five years. Although the local chief intervened because the other neighbour held a leadership position in the village, this did not bring a lasting solution. After the chief encouraged them to communally use the passage cordially, the other beneficiary argued that it was unsatisfactory. She narrated that "since we had a fight, my cattle started dying one by one, and my husband developed mental problems" (Fieldwork interview, 20 May 2015), stressing that their neighbours were bewitching them.

These two neighbours were war veterans that formed part of the core component of the network responsible for land occupations. Their friendship, which dated as far back as the 1970s, and survived the post-independence period of twenty years, was broken within the villagised model. Thus, while in other case studies, the FTLRP brought together people from various backgrounds (Murisa, 2013) who later became friends, on Rouxdale (R/E) farm, the programme gathered together friends and comrades. Conflicts resulting from the structure of the model disintegrated these friendships, and turned them into strangers. This shows the delicacy of social capital highlighted by its critics, that relationships established over a long time can be easily broken (Kay, 2006). Thus, the structure of land reform models with a communal element should be planned with the maintenance of social capital in mind to avoid the destruction of strong beneficiary relationships.

Imposition of government administration

The imposition of local government administration structures such as the VIDCO and WADCO also weakened the once strong network of urban originating beneficiaries after they settled on the land. The use of the word "imposition" is deliberate, given that governments should be actively involved in the administration of state-led land reform programmes (Sikor and Müller, 2009). However, on Rouxdale (R/E) farm, these structures had problems, although their intention had been to foster beneficiaries' collaboration and solidarity. The subdivision of members of the VIDCO into individual committees with different roles dismantled very strong relationships of the war veteran-led social network responsible for land occupations. It became difficult to cultivate relationships after the subdivisions thus weakening social capital. This does not mean that all VIDCO initiatives were unsuccessful, but some of its committees were efficient, as mentioned earlier.

The general dissatisfaction with VIDCO manifested in the lack of cooperation among beneficiaries with some absconding village meetings. These beneficiaries argued that village meetings consumed too much time and diverted their focus from agricultural and household activities. One beneficiary related: "if you live on the farm you should attend every meeting, but the rate at which meetings are called, people are not able to do their daily duties" (Fieldwork interview, 23 May 2015). Some beneficiaries residing in the city of Bulawayo felt that their contribution in village meetings was sidelined by the village head because they did not reside in the village on a permanent basis. This marginalisation contributed to their lack of commitment in attending all meetings. These dynamics work against social capital that is built primarily from collaboration among beneficiaries and is a negative consequence.

VIDCO problems were exacerbated by beneficiaries' perception of the village head and his role in steering development initiatives. While he was a friend to some for many years before the FTLRP, he was later seen as "an eye of the government" and an enemy of beneficiaries. One beneficiary also expressed her lack of respect for the village head, saying: "if you are the kind of leader who always does corrupt things, on the day that you discuss regulations with us, we will not listen to you" (Fieldwork interview, 2 June 2014). The negative sentiments about local leadership, lack of cooperation in village meeting attendance coupled with the general lack of capital for VIDCO initiatives created another kind of social capital weaker than that of the war veteran led network responsible for land occupations. While the developmental agenda of the VIDCO was noble, it was weakened by the lack of consideration by the government, of already existing social capital, and how it could be harnessed to strengthen government initiatives. This reveals the context specific nature of social capital, which discourages a one-size-fits-all approach to social organisation in post-settlement beneficiary relations.

Beneficiaries managed to navigate these problems emanating from the weaknesses of the A1 villagised model; lack of privacy, livestock related conflicts and imposition of government administration structures. The realisation that the communal element of model required cooperation saw the emergence of other networks discussed earlier, and these created a favourable environment for livelihood creation. At this stage, the model was still functioning, even in the midst of various problems. Whether this would be maintained after the addition of more beneficiaries on already allocated land and its severe impact on existing social capital is largely uncertain. This is the subject of the next section.

Addition of beneficiaries on already allocated land

Addition of beneficiaries on communal grazing land was a much bigger problem on Rouxdale (R/E) farm because it had a more drastic impact on the social capital of beneficiaries. As mentioned earlier, twenty-two beneficiaries were allocated land by 2003. These requested for their grown children to be allocated land within the village. After submitting required documents through the Village Head, the District Land Committee (DLC) approved the request, resulting in the addition of twenty-two more beneficiaries on communal grazing land. Although some beneficiaries opposed this request, the general expectation was that each selected child or person of choice would acquire land. However, this was not the case. The DLC sent a list of new beneficiaries, with very few children acquiring land on the farm. The rest were selected from outside the village. Their residential plots were pegged in 2014 on communal grazing land, and until the second brief field visit in May 2015, arable plots were yet to be pegged, also on communal grazing land.

This flexibility of the villagised model to absorb more beneficiaries had drastic implications on social capital. This created serious divisions among those who opposed the addition, parents of children who acquired land and those whose children did not. Parents of children that acquired land justified the process, as narrated by one beneficiary:

> Even if people get angry it does not change anything because land was allocated through a first-come-first-serve method; they did not discriminate using tribe or language differences. Those who responded quickly acquired land. Land is for all Zimbabweans which is why they took people from all walks of life (Fieldwork interview, 12 June 2014).

In the quotation above, the beneficiary's words deviate from the original agreement by most beneficiaries that only children and people recommended by beneficiaries were to acquire land on the farm. It is not possible that the beneficiary would have a similar view if their child had not acquired land. Those whose children did not acquire land were angered by the outcome. One beneficiary related:

> But when the list of people that acquired land came out, we discovered that there were names we did not know, which none of us had written. We asked whose names they were and where they came from and they said those people had applied for the land directly through the Ministry of Lands office in Bulawayo (Fieldwork interview, 22 May 2015).

These beneficiaries suspected corruption by local authorities, due to lack of a satisfactory explanation for the failure of their children to acquire land. In an informal conversation with one of the children that acquired land, the researcher gathered that one of the local authorities within the village had motivated for his access to land. What remains unknown is what happened to those who had no connections to motivate District authorities to allocate land to their children. Furthermore, it is not known whether this beneficiary provided a financial incentive to the local authority to access land. Land officials confirmed cases of corruption in similar cases. One explained that after the DLC receives authority from the Provincial Land Committee (PLC) concerning requests from village heads, "officials capitalise on such situations because of corruption to add their own people" (Fieldwork interview, 30 October 2014). Thus, the possibility of corrupt practices in the allocation of land to additional beneficiaries on Rouxdale (R/E) farm cannot be ignored. The fact that the model is flexible and open to manipulation by opportunists is itself a policy problem.

Earlier, the chapter discussed the complex nature of social capital on Rouxdale (R/E) farm, and how beneficiaries struggled to maintain collaboration in the midst of various problems. These efforts were further strained by the addition of beneficiaries, particularly weakening social capital. DLC officials overlooked the fact that for the model to produce successful results, social capital of beneficiaries should be handled with care. Therefore, it would be difficult to build positive communication and establish trust among beneficiaries, which, according to Putnam et al. (1993), is a vehicle for collective action. Without positive and regular communication, social networks dissolve (Putnam et al., 1993). Thus, on Rouxdale (R/E) farm, "strangers" did not meet at the onset of land allocation in 2000, as in other case studies. They were introduced fourteen years after land allocation, with no regard for their implications on existing social capital and its impact on the realisation of livelihoods. This will be discussed in more detail in subsequent publications.

The addition of beneficiaries on Rouxdale (R/E) farm caused problems likely to become visible in the near future. The DLC did not consider that those children that did not acquire land remained on the farm living with their parents. This would cause a stretch in available household and limited communal resources. In essence, they would, in the near future require land given that some had families. It would have been better if DLC officials had given land to children from within the farm, as this would have minimised tensions. The new beneficiaries would also bring their own families such that in the near future, problems of overpopulation could be a possibility. Worse still, overpopulation could be caused by very model with the aim of decongesting overpopulated communal areas. This remains an area for future research.

Discussion

Social capital is important for creating conditions that can promote the success of the A1 villagised model of the FTLRP. The chapter has shown how livelihoods both in Rouxdale (R/E) farm and in other case studies in Zimbabwe were attained in the context of various social networks. These networks tackle various challenges emanating from post-settlement support by beneficiaries. The fact that the model had a communal element where beneficiaries shared grazing land and resources made social capital an important resource. Social capital is the vehicle for collaboration and sharing support among social networks members. Thus state-land reform models of this nature should prioritise the creation and nurturing of relationships of beneficiaries as this promotes collaboration. While the functioning of social networks depends on the agency of beneficiaries, land reform models should also complement beneficiaries' efforts of building and maintaining social capital.

Land reform models should be structured in such a manner that they promote positive communication among beneficiaries, while limiting conflicts. Break down in positive communication hinders social capital thus hindering the creation of a conducive environment for the attainments of the benefits of land. Bourdieu (1986) stresses the need for social networks members to consciously make an effort to cultivate relationships through effective communication. Putnam et al. (1993) highlights that if these relationships are not nourished, they are easily destroyed. Coleman (1990:321) further explains that "expectations and obligations wither over time if not renewed, since norms depend on regular communication." Thus, while beneficiaries must exercise their agency in creating social networks, the planning of land reform models must enable such efforts.

Conclusion

This chapter benefited from the academic work of Professor Sam Moyo, a colossal leader of the supporters of the FTLRP and a seasoned scholar on land reform in Zimbabwe since independence in 1980. The supporters of the FTLRP went as far as discussing the positive outcomes of the programme and various problems faced by beneficiaries in nationwide case studies. They also articulate the role of social capital in the attainment of the benefits of land through the FTLRP, as discussed in this chapter, focusing on the A1 villagised model in the case of Rouxdale (R/E) farm. However, these scholars do not investigate the flaws of the A1 villagised model, their effect on the dissolution of social capital, and subsequent negative implications on the realisation of the benefits of land. This is an academic gap that was addressed by this chapter.

Lack of privacy in residential plots, livestock boundary conflicts, imposition of government administration and addition of beneficiaries on already allocated land were identified as weaknesses of the A1 villagised model using the case of Rouxdale (R/E) farm. These flaws had a negative effect on the building of social capital. A careful analysis of these flaws pointed to the need for model planners to seriously consider the complex dynamics of beneficiaries' relationships and how these directly influence the realisation of the benefits of land. First, that the structure of land reform models should ensure beneficiaries' privacy and the cultivation of positive communication that is essential for the creation and maintenance of social capital. This would limit conflicts among beneficiaries that negatively alter the environment for the attainment of the benefits of land. Second, that land reform models should not be open to manipulation, but have strict measures of adherence to original plans. Any addition of beneficiaries not previously planned would disrupt existing positive communication, norms and trust among original beneficiaries, thus destroying social capital. Third, that models planners should not introduce government administration initiatives without prior research on pre-existing social capital, as this would lead to its dissolution.

The chapter therefore argues that land reform models with a communal component and limited post-settlement support should promote social capital. It further argues that governments implementing state-led land reform should accommodate differences in the contexts in which models are implemented. Furthermore, governments should be aware of existing social capital before land allocation, and find means of harnessing it ensure the effectiveness of post-settlement administration. A consideration of these arguments would create a better environment for the attainment of the benefits of land.

References

Bond, P. 2008. Lessons for Zimbabwe: an exchange between Patrick Bond and Mahmood Mandani. *Links International Journal of Socialist Renewal.* [Online] Available: http://links.org.au/node/815 [5 September 2017].

Bond, P. & Manyanya, M. 2002. *Zimbabwe's plunge: exhausted nationalism, neoliberalism and the search for social justice,* University of Natal Press.

Bourdieu, P. 1986. The forms of capital. *In:* Richardson, J., G (ed.) *Handbook of theory and research for the sociology of education.* New York: Greenwood Press.

Chiweshe, M., K. 2011. *Farm level institutions in emergent communities in post fast track Zimbabwe: a case of Mazowe District.* PhD Thesis, Rhodes University, South Africa.

Coleman, J. S. 1990. *Foundations of social theory,* Havard University Press.

Derman, B. 2006. After Zimbabwe's fast track land reform: preliminary observations on the near future of Zimbabwe's efforts to resist globalization. *Colloque internatiopnal 'Les frontieres da la question fonciere/ At the frontier of Land issues.* Montpellier, France.

Durlauf, S., N 1999. The case "against" social capital. *Focus,* 20, 1-52.

Field, J. 2003. *Social capital,* New York, Routledge.

Foley, M. W. & Edwards, B. 1999. Is it time to disinvest in social capital? *Journal of Public Policy,* 19, 141-173.

GoZ. 1999. Traditional Leaders Act. Harare: Government of Zimbabwe Printers.

GoZ. 2001. Land reform and resettlement programme: revised phase 2. *In:* Ministry of Lands Agriculture and Rural Resettlement. (ed.). Harare: Zimbabwe: Government Printers.

Hammar, A. & Raftolpulos, B. 2003. Zimbabwe's unfinished business: rethinking land, state and nation. *In:* Hammar, A., Raftopoulos, B and Jensen, S (ed.) *Zimbabwe's unfinished business: rethinking land, state and nation in the context of crisis.* Avondale, Harare: Weaver Press.

Hanlon, J., Manjengwa, J. & Smart, T. 2013. *Zimbabwe takes back its land,* Sterling, Virginia, Stylus Publishing, LLC.

Kay, A. 2006. Social capital, the social economy and community development. *Oxford University Press and Community Development Journal,* 41, 160-173.

Lin, N. 2001. Building a network of social capital. *In:* Lin, N., Cook, K. & Burt, R., S (eds.) *Social capital: theory and research.* New York: Walter de Gruyer, Inc.

Matondi, P. B. 2012. *Zimbabwe's fast-track land reform,* London, Zed Books.

Matondi, P. B. & Dekker, M. 2011. Land rights and tenure security of Zimbabwe's fast track land reform programme. LandAc.

Mkodzongi, G. 2013a. *Fast tracking land reform and rural livelihoods in Mashonaland West Province of Zimbabwe: opportunities and constraints, 2000-2013.* PhD Thesis, University of Edinburgh, Scotland.

Mkodzongi, G. 2013b. New people, new land and new livelihoods: a micro-study of Zimbabwe's fast-track land reform. *Agrarian South: Journal of Political Economy,* 2, 345-366.

Moyo, P. 2013a. Urban livelihoods after the fast track land reform programme in Bulawayo, Zimbabwe. *Journal of Human Ecology,* 42, 25-32.

Moyo, S. 2011a. Changing agrarian relations after redistributive land reform in Zimbabwe. *The Journal of Peasant Studies,* 38, 939-966.

Moyo, S. 2011b. Three decades of agrarian reform in Zimbabwe. *The Journal of Peasant Studies,* 38, 493-531.

Moyo, S. 2013b. Land reform in Zimbabwe since 1980. *In:* Moyo, S. & Chambati, W. (eds.) *Land and agrarian reform in Zimbabwe: beyond white settler capitalism.* Dakar, Senegal: CODESRIA.

Moyo, S., Chambati, W., Murisa, T., Siziba, D., Dangwa, C., Mujeyi, K. & Nyoni, N. 2009. *Fast track land reform baseline survey in Zimbabwe: trends and tendencies, 2005/06,* Harare, Zimbabwe, African Institute for Agrarian Studies.

Murisa, T. 2009. *An analysis of emerging forms of social organization and agency in the aftermath of 'fast track' in Zimbabwe.* PhD Thesis, Rhodes University, South Africa.

Murisa, T. 2011. Local farmer groups and collective action within fast track land reform in Zimbabwe. *The Journal of Peasant Studies,* 38, 1145-1166.

Murisa, T. 2013. Social organisation and the aftermath of 'fast track': an analysis of emerging forms of local authority, platforms of mobilization and local cooperation. *In:* Moyo, S. & Chambati, W. (eds.) *Land and agrarian reform in Zimbabwe: beyond white settler capitalism.* Dakar, Senegal: CODESRIA.

Mutopo, P. 2014b. *Women, mobility and rural livelihoods in Zimbabwe: experiences of fast track land reform,* Leiden, Netherlands, Brill.

Ncube, S. 2018. *The role of social capital in the fast track land reform programme of Zimbabwe: a case of Rouxdale (R/E) farm, Bubi District,*

Matabeleland North Province. PhD Thesis, University of Cape Town, South Africa.

Ndlovu-Gatsheni, S. 2006. The nativist revolution and development conundrums in Zimbabwe. *ACCORD Occasional Paper*, 1-40.

Poder, T. G. 2011. What is really social capital? a critical review. *The American Sociologist,* 42, 341-367.

Putnam, R., D 2000. *Bowling alone: the collapse and revival of American community,* USA, Simon and Schuster.

Putnam, R. D., Leonardi, R. & Nanetti, R. Y. 1993. *Making democracy work: civic traditions in modern Italy,* USA, Princeton University Press.

Raftopoulos, B. & Phimister, I. 2004. Zimbabwe now: the political economy of crisis and coercion. *Historical Materialism,* 12, 355-382.

Richardson, C., J 2005. The loss of property rights and the collapse of Zimbabwe. *Cato Journal,* 25, 541-565.

Sachikonye, L., M. 2003. From 'growth with equity' to 'fast-track' reform: Zimbabwe's land question. *Review of African Political Economy,* 30, 227-240.

Sadomba, W., S 2013. A decade of Zimbabwe's land revolution: the politics of the war veteran vanguard. *In:* Moyo, S. & Chambati, W. (eds.) *Land and agrarian reform in Zimbabwe: beyond white settler capitalism.* Dakar, Senegal: CODESRIA.

Scoones, I., Marongwe, N., Mavengedze, B., Mahenehene, J., Murimbarimba, F. & Sukume, C. 2010. *Zimbabwe's land reform: myths & realities,* Great Britain, James Currey.

Sikor, T. & Müller, D. 2009. The limits of state-led land reform: an introduction. *World Development,* 37, 1307-1316.

Sukume, C., Moyo, S. & Matondi P, B. 2004. *Farm sizes, decongestion and landuse: implications of the fast track land redistribution programme in Zimbabwe,* Harare, Zimbabwe, Africa Institute for Agrarian Studies.

Weiner, D. 1988. Land and agricultural development. *In:* Stoneman, C. (ed.) *Zimbabwe's prospects: issues of race, class, state and capital in Southern Africa.* London and Basingstoke: Macmillan Publishers Ltd.

Zamchiya, P. 2011. A synopsis of land and agrarian change in Chipinge district, Zimbabwe. *Journal of Peasant Studies,* 38, 1093-1122.

Author's email: mancubes@gmail.com

Land Reform, Belonging and Social Relations: Probing the Linkages between Communal Areas and A1 Villagised Settlements in Zvimba District, Zimbabwe

Malvern Marewo

Introduction

In this chapter, I will build on insights from other studies on land reform and belonging, providing a detailed analysis of the linkages between A1[1] villagised settlements beneficiaries and households in adjacent communal areas.[2] The land reform programmes in Zimbabwe have implemented different versions of A1 models at different times. In this study, the focus is on the A1 villagised settlements. This chapter contributes to studies on FTLRP focusing on linkages between communal areas and A1 villagised settlements through an analysis of familial relations, religion, social networks and labour practices. Social relations in this chapter are delineated as the regular interactions of different individuals and households for socialisation, production, exchange, consumption and reproduction, as family, friends, neighbours and workers. Furthermore, these insights will contribute to ongoing debates on belonging from a point of view of land reform. I will engage with the concept of belonging as argued by (Nyamnjoh and Geschiere 2000). Within the context of FTLRP, this chapter notes that belonging does not only grant access to land but also ensures access to social benefits.

Most debates on land reforms and belonging have mostly focused on the dichotomy between autochthons (that is indigenes) and strangers (people from outside who come to settle in a particular community). In this chapter, I will explore how indigenes that received land through FTLRP within their districts of origin maintain connections with communities in the adjacent communal areas. Given that most studies on FTLRP have paid limited attention to connections between communal areas based on social relations and belonging, this chapter seeks to fill this gap using empirical data from Zvimba District. There is a need for both scholarship and policy to reflect on the linkages between land reform beneficiaries who moved to resettlement areas and those who remained in communal areas.

Beneficiaries of FTLRP and residents of communal areas still maintain certain linkages that demonstrate a sense of belonging and mutual relationship between the two models of agrarian settlements. Moyo explains that "most of these [FTLRP] beneficiaries have relatives and friends in the communal areas and retain associational links with these areas" (Moyo, 2009:125). These insights from Moyo generated interest for this study to explore the significance of linkages for A1 villagised beneficiaries and communal areas adjacent to A1 settlements. Land reform more often entails the relocation of families (beneficiaries) geographically (Sithole et al., 2003). Insights from post-Fast Track Land Reform literature indicate that households originated from various areas to settle on A1 farms including urban and rural areas (Murisa, 2009, Scoones et al., 2010). My focus here is on A1 villagised settler beneficiaries who relocated from adjacent communal areas.

In Africa, particularly in Southern Africa, land and agrarian questions were the creation of colonial administration policies (Adams et al., 1999). As Home (2013:62) cited in Chitonge (2018) notes, "the legacy of colonialism is still etched on the landscape and practices of Sub-Saharan African Townships". Decades after colonisation, Africa still struggle with the imprints of colonial governments and their policies. As Okoth-Ogendo notes, parallels with colonial agendas still exist in land ownership in Africa (Okoth-Ogendo, 1989). In Zimbabwe, communal areas still reflect colonial legacies. FTLRP was motivated to address uneven land distribution and will be reviewed within this context.

Considering this backdrop, this chapter will be divided into four sections. The first section looks at the land question in Zimbabwe, noting how the colonial land policies distorted belonging. The second section examines the Fast Track Land Reform Programme looking at the connections between communal areas and A1 villagised settlements. The third section uses qualitative narratives from the case study in Zvimba District to discuss how different aspects of belonging are manifested in this case study area. This last section concludes the chapter, arguing that land reform does not uproot people from places of origin rather enhances agency to remain connected and relevant in the broader social fabric which is anchored in their places of origin (communal areas).

Background

In order to understand the nature of the connections between communal areas and resettlement areas, it is important to locate this in the historical context of communal areas. Current day communal lands were a creation of colonisation by the Rhodesian settlers in 1890 (Moyana et al., 1984; Beach, 1986). During colonisation black people were forced to relocate to arid and poor land called tribal trust lands (later changed to communal areas) by force and various policy interventions (Palmer, 1990). These policies led to the creation of tribal trust lands (Moyo, 1995; Palmer, 1990). After attaining independence in 1980, the new Zimbabwean government continued with the same structure of communal areas. Communal areas historically functioned as residence, home, fall-back and food production areas for the majority of Zimbabweans, including those in urban areas (Makura-Paradza, 2010:19). Most communal areas are located in poor agro-ecological zones,[3] low-lying and in some cases infested with tsetse fly. The colonial allocation of land left regions with unreliable rainfall and less arable soil for black peasant farmers (Fink, 1981).

In order to address the uneven distribution of land, the Zimbabwean government, immediately after dislodging the minority government of Ian Smith, embarked on a land reform programme using a market-led approach. The first land reform was launched in September 1980 and was expected to run up to 1983 (Kinsey, 1982; Moyo, 2000). From 1983 to 1998, a series of resettlement programmes were implemented. However, these programmes failed to adequately address the issues of land congestion and the need for more arable land in communal areas (Masiiwa & Chipungu, 2004; Hanlon et al., 2012). Between 1995 and 1998, there was an increasing demand for land from people in communal areas, and the government was forced to resuscitate land reforms which had slowed down over the years (Kanyenze, 2011). In 1998, the Zimbabwe African National Union – Patriotic Front (ZANU–PF) sought to change the Constitution, which was rejected in a draft referendum in April 2000 (Moyo & Yeros, 2005). Frustrated war veterans began invading white-owned farms in early 2000 (Chitsike, 2003). FTLRP was launched in 2000 and marked the beginning of state-led land reforms in Zimbabwe. The main objective of FTLRP was to redistribute land under the banner of *third chimurenga*.[4]

FTLRP dismantled a dualistic agrarian structure inherited at independence, into a "tri-modal" structure comprising small, medium and large farms, dominated by mainly black smallholder households predominantly from communal areas (Moyo, 2011; Moyo & Chambati, 2013). The Fast Track Land Reform Programme had two models, namely the A1 and A2 models.

The A2 model was designed as a commercial farming land-use model meant to empower the black indigenous farmers (GoZ 2001; Masiiwa & Chipungu 2004:14–15). The model comprises small, medium and large scale commercial farms meant to empower the black indigenous farmers and designed to continue with commercial farming. Farms under model A2 were acquired either through invasion or applications (Gonese et al., 2000). Beneficiaries of this model are offered a 99-year lease contract by the state.

Belonging: Conceptual Issues

Belonging concerns a sense of connection to a person, place, community, thing, group and even to oneself. Many studies on "belonging" focus on migration in an urban and rural context. The prominent works on belonging written by scholars in Africa are Fontein (2011), Geschiere (2009), Geschiere and Nyamnjoh (2000) and Nyamnjoh (2006). These scholars have noted that belonging is a contested terrain in Africa. Many of the debates on belonging are positioned within the "autochthons and strangers" dynamics (Geschiere & Nyamnjoh, 2000). Belonging entails people that share values, identities, relations and practices (Anthias 2006: 21). The challenge with belonging as a concept is its vague nature. Belonging more often is discussed within the frameworks of the politics of belonging. Yuval-Davis (2011:4) argues belonging and politics of belonging need to be separated. He notes that "It is important to differentiate between belonging and the politics of belonging. Belonging is about emotional attachment, about feeling 'at home'... the politics of belonging comprise of specific political projects aimed at constructing belonging to particular collectivises". With regards to this study I will adopt a definition as noted by Mujere (2011:1126) "entails rootedness or being attached to a place. This involves an attachment to place, being an indigene or having roots in a certain place as opposed to being a stranger".

One of the recurring criticisms of belonging is its assumption that people construct new belonging. Malkki (1992), working amongst Rwandan refugees, has criticised scholars for assuming people in a singular sense of attachment and rootedness to a place, and thus failing to take account of people's ability to de-territorialised and construct new attachments to places and peoples. In Zimbabwe, studies by Dekker (2004), Barr (2004) and Kinsey et al. (1998) have indicated how belonging is fluid as new social relations, kinship ties and institutions transcending ethnic backgrounds gradually emerged in the aftermath of the land reform (Mkodzongi, 2016). While there are also studies that have indicated that "newcomers seek to construct a place they can again call home through 'negotiations with neighbours' (Castles & Davidson, 2000:130), these studies have shown that belonging is dynamic as people can define their identities when they relocate. Studies by Scoones et al. (2010), Murisa (2013), Mutopo, (2014), Mujere (2011) and Moyo (2009) have shown that households maintain connections, and in areas where links are maintained as this case study highlights, there is need to fill in a gap on the implications of maintaining belonging.

Graves are an important component of belonging. Shipton (2009:20) notes that graves are symbolic places of human attachment. Although belonging is asserted in multiple notions (Geschiere, 2005, 2009, Shipton, 2009, Cohen & Odhiambo, 1992, Chabal, 2013), Fontein (2011: 713) argues that "despite the prominence given to funerals in this literature, and the well-recognized fact that 'autochthony' implies a claim to a 'special link to the soil', there is a need to look at belonging beyond graves, to include social and economic links".

Rutherford (2003, 2008) argues that households residing in resettlement areas reconfigured and redefined the definition of "modes of belonging" which did not always fit into the definitions of belonging and not belonging. As Peters (2004:302) notes, belonging acknowledges the differentiated nature of society particularly where "Social conflict over land takes the form of stricter definitions of those who have legitimate claims to resources, or, in other words, group boundaries are more exclusively defined". Cousins and Claassens (2006:22) remark that "social identities are often multiple, overlapping and therefore 'nested' or layered in character". In this study belonging is analysed with multiple social identities overlapping into both communal areas and A1 villagised settlements.

As the literature showed belonging entails rootedness and attachment. In this study, while cognizant of the importance of land (soil), I will use linkages to explore how social, cultural and economic variables reflect belonging. Belonging is often embedded in multiple identities. As people straddle between two areas they enforce their bonds with their place of origin (communal areas) while residing in A1 settlements. While belonging as noted is often debated within the "insiders" and "outsiders" context, the relations among "insiders" show the importance of maintaining belonging. Thus, the concept of belonging is used to analyse the maintenance of links by beneficiaries of the FTLRP and households in communal areas. Therefore, belonging will be understood as relationships between households, community and land.

The Land Question in Zimbabwe

As shown in the background, the land question in Zimbabwe is better understood when located in its historical context – the colonisation of present-day Zimbabwe in 1890 marked the beginning of the land question. Zimbabwe's 100 years of colonialism, which was designed along racial lines, led to massive land "dispossession and social engineering" (Moyo, 1995:59). Colonialism distorted belonging as households were evicted from their places of origin to make way for white settlers. This notion of communal areas was carried over after independence with the rural "homes" located in communal reserves controlled by a minority European settlers (Scott 1976:56). Thus, much of the land during colonisation was transferred to a minority of settlers and after attainment of independence, land continued to be in the hands of white farmers. At independence, most African countries (Zimbabwe included) retained or modified colonial policies to give the state control over for purposes of modernization and nation-building. But they overlooked land issues (Okoth-Ogendo, 1993).

Communal areas are broadly understood as a colonial construct within the context of customary land tenure. Matondi describes communal areas as land used for communal grazing and owned under usufruct arrangements by families mostly in arid areas (Matondi, 2012). Thus, land reform in Zimbabwe after independence was premised on the need to modify communal areas towards some form of transactable freehold and/or leasehold (Moyo, 1995).

Land Reform in Zimbabwe started in 1980 and can be aptly described as an act of transferring land from white commercial farmers to blacks based on their presumed historical and social entitlement to land (Dekker & Kinsey, 2011; Moyo, 1995; Moyo & Chambati, 2013). Land reform in Zimbabwe is divided into three phases: the first phase is from 1980 to 1990, the second phase is from 1990 to 1998 and the third is from 1999 to 2002. The first phase was redistribution using a market-based approach, which was guided by the Lancaster House Agreement[5] of 1979 and employed the "willing-seller-willing-buyer" approach (Palmer, 1990: 163–181).

The period between 1980 and 1997, over 70 000 households were resettled on land that had previously belonged to white farmers (Barr, 2004). Studies by Dekker (2004) indicate that in the 1980s resettlement did not disrupt social relations between beneficiaries and family and friends in communal areas. By 1984, as much as 40% of households that had been relocated in 1980 still cultivated their communal areas (Kinsey, 1999). Like other resettlement programmes in the sub-Saharan Africa region during this period, except for Tanzania's villagisation programme, the first phase of land reform in

Zimbabwe failed to achieve its targets (Kinsey, 1999). The slow pace at which the land was redistributed during this phase was the catalyst to the Fast Track Land Reform led by war veterans. At the end of the second phase in 1998, the set targets of 1980 were not achieved. With pressure from war veterans, land reform in Zimbabwe turned radical (Sachikonye, 2003, Murisa & Chikweche, 2015).

FTLRP began in 2000 and households acquired land through various means – in some cases it was through violence and some through formalised structures. Resettlement during the FTLRP was facilitated by local chiefs, war veterans, with(out) political backing and in some cases (not) coordinated (Scoones et al., 2010, Chaumba et al., 2003). In the case of A1 settlements, most households resettled in adjacent communal areas (Chaumba et al., 2003). In some cases, as noted by Matondi, land occupations were facilitated by the Zimbabwe Republic Police (ZRP) and the District Administrator's Office and the District Land Committee (DLC), who coordinated the invasion of white commercial farm land (Matondi, 2012). In some cases, chiefs played a key role in identifying land and forwarding the names of the farms to district land committees (Murisa, 2009, Chiweshe, 2011). These committees comprised the District Administrator, the district chairperson of the war veterans, ZANU (PF) officials, national intelligence and the chief. The involvement of chiefs in the FTLRP accounts for the large number of beneficiaries from communal areas (Murisa, 2009). The fact that a number of beneficiaries originated from communal areas warrants critical analysis to understand the nature of the linkages between residents of the two settlements.

Land Occupations under Fast Track Land Reform Programme

Connections and disconnections after FTLRP

There are various studies that have been conducted on the FTLRP. Some of the issues raised in the studies include productivity, gender, labour relations, livelihoods and tenure (Scoones et al., 2010, Hammar et al., 2003, Manjengwa et al., 2013, Murisa, 2009, Mandizadza, 2010). Linkages are an important facet which few studies have provided in-depth analysis. However, the extent to which the A1 villagised model led to disconnection or connection with households in communal areas is widely debated. Without dwelling much on the process of the FTLRP itself, which a number of studies have exhaustively covered (Sachikonye, 2005; Moyo, 2000, 2011; Matondi, 2012; Hanlon et al., 2012; Chiweshe, 2011; Scoones et al., 2010), this discussion focuses on relationships between communal areas and A1 villagised settlements after the FTLRP.

Most of the debates on land reform have focused on the process and consequences of the land reform programme. In Zimbabwe, while post-Fast Track Land Reform literature has acknowledged the connections between communal areas and A1 villagised settlements, limited attention has been provided on how maintenance of these enforces belonging and social relations. Debates post-FTLRP focused on agricultural production, livelihoods and social outcomes, with few studies discussing the links between residents of communal areas and A1 villagised models. Debates on FTLPP have illustrated that beneficiaries maintain links with communal areas. Nyambara (2001:773) notes that movement of people to resettlement areas and maintenance of old communal areas has been common since the opening up of formerly wildlife areas in the 1970s and 1980s.

A survey conducted in 2007 across six districts in Zimbabwe indicated that 16.6 per cent of the households in resettlement areas were maintaining homes in communal area (Murisa, 2013). Likewise, Kinsey (1982), Barr (2004) and Dekker (2004) have noted that after independence land reform beneficiaries maintained connections with communal areas. These pre-FTLRP studies focus on the importance of kin networks for most rural families to strengthen their social capital and resource-pooling strategies. While these studies confirm the maintenance of homes in communal areas and A1 villagised settlements, the nature of the connections needs to be probed further to understand the new dynamics triggered by FTLRP.

Most of the documented reason for the A1 beneficiaries' practice of maintaining land in communal areas has to do with the uncertainty of tenure in A1 farms in the sense that they are not given lease contracts (Matondi, 2012; Mkodzongi, 2013; Moyo, 2009). However, further analysis of these linkages is required to understand the other aspects of the linkages.

On linkanges between communal areas and resettled areas, Scoones et al. (2010:53) noted in Masvingo that "59.9 per cent of households that came from rural areas were almost exclusively from nearby communal areas". Scoones further notes that most of these land reform beneficiaries are maintaining links with communal areas. This was also noted by Moyo et al., (2009:21) who observed that 65.9 per cent of A1 beneficiaries came from communal areas. They note that beneficiaries that originated in adjacent communal areas continue to straddle between the two places to aid their social reproduction and maintenance of familial links. Other studies (Mutopo, 2014; Murisa, 2013; Mkodzongi, 2013) indicated that beneficiaries maintained relations by receiving inputs from their networks in communal areas. Murisa (2013) notes there are links between communal areas and land beneficiaries who used to live in communal areas. Murisa further notes that "most (57.5%) commonly cited reasons for the maintenance of a customary area homestead is because it is still home to other members of the extended family" (2013:270). His findings affirm that most of the beneficiaries nonetheless maintain connections with their places of origin.

However, Nyawo (2015) argues that rituals and traditions which keep people together are not analysed in most studies. Nyawo (2014) further argues that the FTLRP destabilised the family unit. She further argues that men went to the resettlement areas while women remained in communal areas and doubled as fathers of households as well as doing chores traditionally associated with men (Nyawo; 2014). While Mabhena (2010) captures the conflict between A1 settlement and communal areas, his study does not capture the connections between these areas and how they might typically promote linkages. This chapter, on the contrary, argues that familial ties go beyond physical boundaries to provide social and material needs.

Fontein (2011) and Mujere (2011) have correctly argued that during the FTLRP, graves performed a prominent role in linkages and claiming land in either A1 or A2 settlements. The empirical basis of Fontein's argument of belonging derives from the shared nature of material landscapes. More specifically, he argues that ancestral graves before colonisation were used as symbols for communal households to claim land in former commercial areas. Mujere (2011), on the other hand, shows that traditional leaders play a key role in determining how belonging is negotiated. Engaging with power of political authorities, he notes, conflicts have emerged between autochthons and migrants over the control of the new resettlement areas and over the authority of village heads and chiefs. While these studies have provided insights into the social dynamics generated by land reform, what remains is to examine why beneficiaries of land reform maintain their homes in communal areas of origin.

A1 villagised model

The A1 model is a resettlement model that was designed to cater for landless people in communal and urban areas. The A1 model had two types: the self-contained and villagised models. The main objective of the A1 model was to decongest the communal areas by resettling landless people on the villagised and self-contained plots (GoZ, 2001). In the self-contained model, households were allocated one plot which comprised both arable and grazing land (Murisa, 2009, GoZ, 2001). The self-contained model was designed on composite allocations of between 25 to 50 hectares of land per household. The villagised model on the other hand comprised six hectares of arable land allocated to households and fifteen hectares of grazing lands as part of shared lands and woodlots. The A1 villagised plots were allocated arable which comprised a subdivided section of the plot, while residential plots were allocated in a way that enabled households to build homesteads near each other. Focus in this chapter is on the A1 villagised model. A large number of beneficiaries in the A1 villagised settlements originated from communal land, hence the need to explore this relationship.

The A1 villagised model is made up of smallholder farms in resettlement areas. Selection of beneficiaries was done through local government structures (District Administrators, Village Heads/Chiefs, District Development Fund and Rural District Councils), and the main criteria for land allocation was willingness to relocate, landlessness and age (Gonese et al., 2000). In Zvimba a household has an average of six arable hectares. Njaya (2015:9): notes that "under A1 villagised model, homesteads are in villages with a common grazing area akin to communal areas". Households were allocated residential and individual plots with shared woodlots, a water point and common grazing. Land was provided through Rural District Councils and local village heads and later the Ministry of Lands. The next section will explore the land question in Zimbabwe.

Linkages between A1 and Communal Areas in Zvimba

An Overview

To examine the linkages between residents of A1 and communal areas in Zvimba District, I draw from the case study conducted on Machiroli Farm (A1 villagised settlement) and adjacent Zvimba Communal Areas (Ward 3). This area was chosen because of the proximity between communal areas and resettlement areas. The insights reported here were gathered in a study conducted in Zvimba District between August 2017 and May 2018. Collection of narratives relied on in-depth interviews, life histories, observations as well as a review of Government of Zimbabwe reports and policies as secondary sources of data. Pseudonyms were used to maintain anonymity.

In Zvimba communal areas' access to land and rights is through membership to a clan or lineage group. On Machiroli Farm (A1 Villagised) land is administered and provided through state structures. Machiroli Farm has 28 A1 villagised beneficiaries. Out of the 28 beneficiaries that are on Machiroli Farm 25 are from adjacent Zvimba Communal Areas. These beneficiaries are from the wards surrounding the farm; the other three beneficiaries are from urban areas. The majority of respondents on Machiroli Farm indicated that elderly people remained in communal areas, while the younger population resettled on Machiroli Farm. Most of the primary owners of land in communal areas did not leave their homesteads. Most of the beneficiaries on Machiroli noted that they were parents, in-laws and guardians before translocating. Households in both communal areas and Machiroli Farm are differentiated. Respondents indicated four categories of households in the area, namely poor, middle, middle to rich and the rich households which determined households access or use of labour, productivity, livelihoods as well as income

(Scoones et al, 2010; Cousins et al., 1992). The next section provides details of the nature of linkages between communal areas and A1 settlements in the case study area.

Types of linkages

In Zvimba District, there are various reasons why households maintain links between communal areas and A1 settlements. Proximity of both communal areas to Machiroli Farm was one factor. Factors that support connections and belonging are varied as shown below.

Burial sites

Burial sites and funerals rituals are some of the ways households ascertain belonging. The paramount reason that beneficiaries on Machiroli Farm are maintaining links between A1 settlements and communal areas is to ensure that once they die they are still recognised as being part of the clan. While it is critical to observe that only a small proportion of the population wanted to be buried in the A1 settlements, most of the respondents indicated that being buried in their communal areas was critical for them. Some of the respondents had this to say;

> When a person dies, it is a matter of personal preference, and some believe that family graves should be in one place. However, here in Machiroli over time, I realised that generally many people want to be buried back home in the communal areas of origin. (Interview with Mrs Z, November 2017).

Another respondent observed that,

> I am not comfortable to bury my family member there in that common gravesite, grave sites are a sacred place burying my relative there might make it difficult to find rest. Besides former farm workers have different customs which might anger our ancestors. (Interview with Mr ZK, January 2017)

Another respondent concluded by saying that,

When a person dies they should be reconnected with their ancestors, here in the resettlements its farming area, if I die I will be buried in the communal area

These highlighted the importance that the respondents placed on the place where a person is buried. Geschiere and Nyamnjoh also noted that in Cameroon even people in the urban areas place emphasis on where they are buried, with most preferring to be buried in the villages in Cameroon (Geschiere & Nyamnjoh, 2000; Geschiere 2009). Therefore, although households were allocated land in A1 settlements, links through burial in communal areas portray an important role in belonging.

Funerals are some of the reasons households maintain links. Insights from the study indicate that beneficiaries on Machiroli Farm attend funerals in adjacent communal areas and some of the A1 beneficiaries are buried in communal areas. This highlights that although people relocated to resettlement areas, through attending funerals they remain connected with kin. Geschiere (2009) argues that funerals in most cases are conducted in places where a person was born rather than where he lived. Through the maintenance of these linkages, through burial in communal areas and attending funerals it indicates that households in resettlement areas have a need to belong as insights above showed.

Familial links
Familial links are an important form of illustrating belonging. Familial relations can be found at various levels and include extended and totemic family ties. Narratives from my case study suggest that households still maintain familial ties even if they have physically separated residence. In most of the cases, these relations are reciprocal between familial network members. Familial links are maintained through various ways such as weddings (paying of bride price), ceremonies, rituals and social visits. Through these links households indicated that they are taking advantage of their relatives in resettlement areas to avert some of the challenges found in communal areas such as shortages of firewood. Totemic and familiar relations have enabled households to share livestock across both

communal areas and Machiroli Farm. Most respondents in the communal areas highlighted that there are limited grazing areas for the livestock. They had hoped that the FTLRP would have addressed this overcrowding and opened more grazing land. Through these familial and totemic links access to grazing land has been made possible. This concurs with findings by Cliffe (1986) who notes that kinship networks provided important support in times of need and agricultural activities. Thus, by maintaining links with the family it enforced belonging by beneficiaries of the FTLRP.

In both communal areas and Machiroli farm households own cattle, goats, chickens and sheep. All these animals are kept for different reasons and benefit the household. Households in both areas place great emphasis on cattle production. In the communal areas there are limited grazing areas that are available, and in most cases cattle stray into other people's fields resulting in conflicts. The connection that exists between households that are in the communal areas and A1 settlements enable these households close to the resettlement area to send their livestock across for better grazing. This concurs with Mkodzongi (2013) who states how, in Mhondoro Ngezi, some households were straddling the two areas (RAs and CAs), as a way of diversifying their livelihoods. These arrangements are mostly based on kinship ties. Before the FTLRP, cattle which strayed into the commercial farms were captured or the cattle owners would pay a fine. This was explained by one respondent who stated that:

> Since we are close to the A1 settlements, our cattle now move into the Machiroli Farm. We normally ask for permission from our relatives, after harvesting to allow our cattle to graze. It is different from the times when Sean used to own the farm when our cattle strayed into his farm we would pay a fine. Now this has ceased to happen. (Interview with Mr. BN, November 2017)

The reason for straddling between these households are varied. Insights from my fieldwork revealed that households straddle for social, political and cultural purposes. Observations of A1 residents indicated that A1 villagised areas tend to be socially isolated and, as a result, they feel the need to belong and remain connected and relevant in the broader social fabric with families and friends in communal areas. Thus, households participate and maintain friendship networks also known as '*sahwiras*'. Within these *sahwira* networks, households help each other during weddings, funerals and social and cultural events in either communal areas or A1 settlements. The case study showed that through these *sahwiras* networks there are savings groups and burial societies which are still being maintained by A1 households that have left communal areas. Participating in these networks maintains links between households in communal areas and resettlement areas. These networks are an affirmation of the need to maintain belonging by the beneficiaries of the FTLRP.

Religious and cultural practices

Religion plays a significant role in maintaining interconnections between A1 and the communal area households. Religion is one of the contributing factors for households to straddle between communal areas and resettlement areas. People in Zvimba practice mostly Christianity and traditional African religion with former farm workers mainly practising Muslim. The Roman Catholic Church is the most prominent church in the area; this is due to the long history of the church in Zvimba. The Roman Catholic Church (RCC) managed to build schools, hospitals and churches in the communal areas in Zvimba. Many beneficiaries came from the communal areas that had strong ties to the RCC. The majority of the respondents on Machiroli Farm and communal areas belong to the Roman Catholic Church (RCC) due to the role of the institution in education and health. Although other respondents belonged to other churches (white garments, Methodist, and Pentecostal churches), RCC was the common church. While others which constituted a small population, most farm workers were Muslim. Links with their churches was a source of maintaining belonging among the beneficiaries of the FTLRP.

The Roman Catholic Church remains a source of connection in the case study area. Most churches are located in the communal areas and households in A1 settlements travel on most Sundays to attend church. A respondent noted that "We grew up in the Roman Catholic

Church. Even though we moved to the A1 farms, every Sunday we make sure that we go" (Interview with Mr Tamai, January 2018). While the church is the source of spiritual "upliftment", I observed that the church provides materials such as farm inputs and food wherever necessary for its members across both communal areas and A1 settlements.

In addition, the church is a social network in itself as it surpasses the geographical boundaries. Church members are from A1 settlements and communal areas. Church members provide each other with assistance, and they give each other knowledge in social, economic and political issues. Some of the A1 farmers belonging to the same church networks lend each other money and farm inputs such as seed – this is done to uphold the Christian ethos of love and unity. One of the respondents in the A1 settlements said that:

> When we moved to the resettlement one of the things that pained me was leaving my family. What provided me comfort was that the church was close so we could meet often. The church is another family which gives me advice and love. I do get seed and borrow money from my people in the church. (Interview with Mrs Tizai, May 2018)

Despite the fact that some members of households moved to Machiroli farm families remain connected through churches such as the Roman Catholic Church. There are also new Pentecostal churches also known as "white garments" or "*mapostori*". The white garments church accommodates households in both the communal and A1 settlements. The majority of white garment churches are located in communal areas. These denominations in Machiroli have created and maintained a sense of unity amongst the members of the study area. Through religion households maintain links as well as show their belonging by attending church.

Traditional practices is another factor that enables residents of both Machiroli Farm and Zvimba communal areas to maintain connection. Belonging has been enhanced through traditional practices such as *Chisi* (traditional rest day). This is a practice regarded as sacred in Zvimba District. Respondents in both Machiroli Farm from communal areas acknowledged that they observed these traditions. The concept of *Chisi* is a spiritual connection to the land and belonging, and respondents stated that it signified being at one with the soil. Hence it was the role of the people to take care of the land. In essence, a person is connected to the land from the day of birth and when a person rests so should the land. Thus, as indicated here, belonging as a process is dynamic and, in most cases, it is multi-layered as Zvimba District has shown (Antonisch, 2010). This chapter indicates implications for policy on land reforms, and lessons from the FTLRP indicate that it is difficult to separate people from their places of origin since people maintain links with their places of origin.

However, it is important to acknowledge that not all FRLRP beneficiaries value maintaining relationships with their places of origin; some have established relations within Machiroli Farm. The FTLRP has evolved the nature of social networks such as burial societies and new burial societies have emerged in A1 settlements as a way to deal with the limited access to a family as well as direct costs of death and risk when away from close family members. Mrs Taruza had this to say:

> Our families are not always here; in the event of death my neighbours will be the first people to come and provide assistance. We decided to start our own burial society. We have few former farm workers but mostly it is us, the A1 farmers in Machiroli, who assist and contribute money which we give to our members or their family in the event of death. (Interview with Mrs Taruza, December 2017)

While there are households that have established other social networks in resettlement areas, is evident from the view of most respondents that belonging in the case study area is much more fluid. Maintaining links with communal areas allows households to articulate their belonging despite participating in social networks in resettlement areas. It becomes evident that belonging include people's physical relationship with the land and other physical materials. Although belonging is socially constructed, households, particularly, when it comes to the importance of land, construct their meaning through linkages.

Labour exchanges

Labour also provides a connection between households in communal areas and Machiroli Farm. Labour is provided through family (extended) networks, friends, non-family members in communal areas and former farm workers on Machiroli Farm. On Machiroli Farm there are former farm workers that reside on the farm. These former farm workers provide their labour mostly to A1 villagised settlers. Labour from the extended family network, though provided on a limited scale, serves as a connection. This connection made it possible to mobilise labour should it become necessary to request labour from communal areas. This was confirmed by one respondent who stated that:

> Despite the fact that some have moved to the other side of Hunyani, we remain attached as we are family and share the same blood. We do assist those in Machiroli should they want assistance on their farms. (Interview with Mr Zimunya, May 2018).

Labour exchanges within the extended family are premised on reciprocity. Reciprocity through labour is one of the elements that has supported linkages. This was explained by one of the respondents who observed that:

> When it is off season communal area households do come to help us with vegetable gardens and when we do harvest we pay them in kind or from the crops that we would have harvested. (Interview with Mr Mutandwa, 13 October 2017)

Whilst there are limited financial payments that are provided to family members, payment in kind is the most popular form; households are given a share in agricultural produce. The shortage of money in Zimbabwean banks has resulted in barter trade as the major source of trade, particularly in rural areas. More often extended family members exchange labour for maize, sugar beans and seed (maize, groundnuts, round nuts). Some of the respondents that indicated that they engage their extended family who provide them "tokens" of appreciation for the services rendered; tokens were either

333

maize or groceries. In an interview in Machiroli Farm, one respondent stated that

> My young brother, a good turn deserves another turn. Our country has no money at the moment. When your relative asks for your help and pays you back with maize or vegetables it is better because access to money is a challenge. (Interview with Mr Tauya, December 2017)

Extended family members from communal areas assist A1 settlers with planting and weeding of the vegetable gardens. While there are few households that engage in this kind of arrangement between Machiroli Farm and communal areas, it enhanced the agricultural productivity of A1 settlers at the same time providing resources to households in communal areas that participated in these initiatives.

Family members in communal areas and the A1 settlements are interdependent. Households that do not have adequate finances to pay former farm workers upfront engage labour from communal areas to supplement their labour reserve. A respondent explained that "When we are pressed we ask our family members back home to send nephews to come and assist us. If we have excess we give them something after harvest" (Interview with Mr Mutandwa, 18 January 2018). Households that provide labour from the communal areas to either A1 households or communal areas are not treated the same as former farm workers. This is because, despite that these households in communal areas and A1 settlements are better off financially than poor households, in the long run, they need or require assistance from poor households. Even though labour is a means which connects communal areas and A1 settlements, labour is not a means to exploit kin. This was explained by one respondent who stated that

> In Machiroli, I realised that I cannot be giving money to the farm workers while my kin in the communal areas is struggling. In most cases, these members of the extended family assisted in planting in exchange for fertilisers and seed. In that way, I know they have a portion they manage to plant in their fields. (Interview with Mrs Zana, November 2017)

The existence of a family in the communal areas provides households in A1 settlements with assistance in times when there is a need for labour. Some respondents indicated that they received support from their families in the early days of moving into A1 settlements. This support was either in the form of agricultural equipment or labour to clear farms as most A1 farmers were allocated farms that had not been cultivated before. Labour provided to A1s was to assist with building housing as well as transporting farming equipment such as ox-drawn ploughs. After eighteen years, evidence from Zvimba District indicates that in the resettlement areas, movement of labour from communal areas still takes place, although reduced. This is due to communal households' need to focus on their agricultural production during the farming season as well as limited labour availability in communal areas. However, communal households still provide labour to resettlement areas at various levels; however, this varies from household to household.

Members of the extended family and non-family members from communal areas are employed to assist with tasks such as herding cattle, cultivation of crops, weeding and harvesting. Compared to former farm workers extended family members are believed to be loyal and a part of the family. A respondent explained that

> I suffered huge losses as some stole from me and I lost some of my livestock. I had to go and ask for my sister's son in the communal areas that had finished his Ordinary Level two years ago to help me on my farm. I pay him here and there, whenever I can. (Interview with Mr Chomu, January 2018)

Extended family members are often paid in money or food by their employers. During conversation with "employees" in this category, I observed that more often kinship ties are used to manipulate these workers by being paid little or no salaries. A respondent gave an insight into this:

> I work for my uncle and he is a good man, however, the challenge has been that I have not been paid for a long time. The initial agreement was that I would be given an allowance but ever since I got here it has

not been the case. When we harvest I do get about five bags of maize which I send to my mother in the communal areas. (Interview with Taurai, May 2018)

This strategy implied that, in some instances, social networks are used to obtain additional labour through kinships ties at the expense of those providing it. The maintenance of these links is based on the premise that since A1 settlers originate (belong) from communal areas employing family, friends or non-family members would assist reduce high costs of labour as well as provide a sense of trust as former farm workers are perceived as untrustworthy. As households interact in agrarian spaces, belonging emerges at different levels such as cultural, emotional, physical, political and social levels. These labour linkages highlight the fluid boundaries between communal areas and A1 settlements and investment in social relationships which strengthen belonging.

Discussion

While belonging is attached to land (soil), it is also highlighted in other ways such as labour relations and social relations. In Africa, as Chitonge (2018) notes, conceptualisation of land is intricately connected to the past, present and the future. Land has different implications on belonging under different circumstances. Access to land often implies obligations to family networks, kith and kin in facilitating linkages. Chabal (2013) notes that there are kinship relations which, in most cases, are closely related, family and clan members linked through marriage bound by a connection to the land. In the case area study, through belonging, households have access to resources.

Connection to the land plays a key role in maintaining the kinship relations as the insights from this case study have shown. Chabal (2013: 47) notes "… Kinship, therefore, is not the (negative) burdens or (positive) opportunities it implies, which are real enough, but the ways in which it contributes to a sense of socially meaningful belonging". These are emphasised through funerals and burial sites as this case study has shown. Funerals and burial sites are an important contribution to belonging in Africa. Geschiere (2005) notes that where one is buried is a crucial test of someone's belonging. Furthermore, this use is seen to be a powerful way to determine who is the real owner of contested land, particularly for customary tenure. Chabal (2009) notes that the very essence of social relations is through obligations. Berry (1993) states that, despite African governments' attempts to regulate land, land access is through social relations. Therefore, land, while it is the ultimate sign of belonging, is maintained through social relations as this case study has shown.

Belonging is not confined to physical boundaries or territories. Antonsich (2010) notes that belonging is often visible beyond territorial or boundary limits. Narratives from Zimbabwe indicate that despite the two settlement models, belonging transcends the space between people. Mkodzongi (2016), however, argues that autochthony and a new sense of belonging that has been created in resettlement areas redefines the notion of belonging. Insights from this case study indicate that to beneficiaries of land reform, belonging is plural and not limited to a single area in which they reside, as households straddle across different areas. Scholars such as Ehrkamp (2005) note there are multiple forms of belonging between places of origin and places of relocation. Scholars, in fact, agree that belonging cannot be treated like "a zero-sum game" (Pollini, 2005, Jayaweera and Choudhury, 2008). Thus, belonging specifically for beneficiaries of land reform is a catalyst to spill over benefits to places of origin.

Land reform has created dual belonging for beneficiaries of the land reform. This case study has highlighted how households are maintaining links in both places of origin and new places of residence. Mujere (2011:1140) notes that despite contestations over boundaries and reclamation of lost ancestral lands, land reform has also brought dual belonging as some beneficiaries' straddle between communal and resettlement areas. The maintenance of these interconnections that are in different forms, follow customary social patterns and relationships (Matondi, 2012). This case study highlights that the benefits that A1 households have spill over to households in communal areas such as access to natural resources and food as households' straddle between two areas. In this case study, I argue

337

that land reforms provide multiple benefits to non-beneficiaries through land-based livelihoods and address the colonial imbalance of land distribution. This chapter depicted that land reform is attached to belonging – narratives from Zvimba indicate that most household's beneficiaries of the FTLRP were keen to maintain linkages.

Conclusion

The fundamental notion of belonging as shown in Zvimba District sufficiently indicates that although beneficiaries willingly left communal areas they are still connected to places of origin. This chapter acknowledged that various groups benefited from the FTLRP and acknowledged that despite the fact that beneficiaries have established themselves in A1 settlements, communal areas provide significant attachments for A1 beneficiaries. Valuable insights indicated precisely that most beneficiaries desired to be continually connected to their places of origin. These were evident through graves, religion and familial connections. Insights from Moyo (2009) provided a key point of departure and with this case study I provided another distinct layer of belonging, carefully noting that land beneficiaries cannot be easily uprooted from their places of origin. For policy, narratives generated from this study highlight that future programmes which voluntarily relocate people should note that households desire to maintain links (social relations) with their places of origin. These key insights indicate that belonging is much more nuanced and can be understood differently.

Acknowledgements

This chapter was presented at a Colloquium held in November 2016 at the University of Cape Town in honour of the work of the late Professor Sam Moyo. This research was made possible by the generous funding of the University of Cape Town National Research Foundation (NRF) Research Chair: Land Reform and Democracy in South Africa, The Archie Mafeje Scholarship and University of Cape

Town International Students Scholarship. Malvern Kudakwashe Marewo PhD student (University of Cape Town).

Notes

(1) A1 villagised model of the FTLRP is known as the decongestion model for communal areas.

(2) A communal area is land held in terms of customary law. Access to and use of grazing land is communal in the strict meaning of the word; the rest of the land is owned under usufruct arrangements by families. (Matondi 2012).

(3) Agro-ecological zone is a land unit, carved out of a climatic zone, correlated with landforms, climate and the length of growing period (Pal et al., 2009).

(4) Chimurenga is a vernacular name for the armed liberation struggle against the settler colonial state. It was also used as an ideological thread capturing the undying spirit of African resistance to colonialism. (MUGABE, R. 2001).

(5) Lancaster House Agreement was an agreement between the Rhodesians (white settlers) and Guerrillas (black Zimbabweans) which brokered negotiations for independence and a constitution (Sibanda, 1990).

References

Adams, M., Sibanda, S. & Turner, S.D. 1999. Land tenure reform and rural livelihoods in Southern Africa, Overseas Development Institute London.

Antonsich, M. 2010. "Searching for belonging – an analytical framework". *Geography Compass*, 4, 644–659.

Anthias, F. 2006. Belongings in a Globalising and Unequal World, in Yuval-Davis, Nira, Kannabiran, Kalpana & Vieten, Ulrike (eds): The situated politics of belonging. London: Sage, 17-31.

Barr, A. 2004. "Forging effective new communities: The evolution of civil society in Zimbabwean resettlement villages". *World Development*, 32, 1753–1766.

Beach, D.N. 1986. *War and politics in Zimbabwe, 1840-1900*, Mambo Press.

Berry, S. (1993). No condition is permanent: The social dynamics of agrarian change in sub-Saharan Africa, University of Wisconsin Pres.

Castles, S. and A. Davidson (2000). Citizenship and migration: Globalization and the politics of belonging, Psychology Press.

Chabal, P. (2009). "Africa: The politics of smiling and suffering." University of KwaZulu-Natal Press

Chabal, P. 2013. *Africa: the politics of suffering and smiling*, Zed Books Ltd.

Chaumba, J., Scoones, I. & Wolmer, W. 2003. "From jambanja to planning: the reassertion of technocracy in land reform in south-eastern Zimbabwe?". *The Journal of Modern African Studies*, 41, 533-554.

Chitonge, H. 2018. "Trails of Incomplete Decolonisation in Africa: The Land Question and Economic Structural Transformation", The Centre for African Area Studies, Kyoto University

Chitsike, F. 2003. A critical analysis of the land reform programme in Zimbabwe. 2nd FIG Regional Conference, 2003. 2–5.

Chiweshe, M.K. 2011. *Farm level institutions in emergent communities in post fast track Zimbabwe: case of Mazowe district.* Rhodes University SA.

Cliffe, L. 1986. Policy options for agrarian reform in Zimbabwe: a technical appraisal. FAO, Harare

Cohen, D.W. & Odhiambo, E.S.A. 1992. *Burying SM (Cloth): The Politics of Knowledge and the Sociology of Power in Africa*, Heinemann Educational Books.

Cousins, B. & Claassens, A. More than simply "socially embedded": recognizing the distinctiveness of African land rights. Keynote address at the international symposium on "At the Frontier of Land Issues: Social embeddedness of rights and public policy", Montpelier, May, 2006. 17–19.

Cousins, B., Weiner, D. & Amin, N. 1992. "Social differentiation in the communal lands of Zimbabwe". *Review of African Political Economy*, 19, 5–24.

Dekker, M. & Kinsey, B. 2011. "Coping with Zimbabwe's economic crisis: small-scale farmers and livelihoods under stress". *ASC working paper.*

Dekker, M. 2004. "Sustainability and resourcefulness: Support networks during periods of stress". *World Development*, 32, 1735–1751.

Ehrkamp, P. (2005). "Placing identities: Transnational practices and local attachments of Turkish immigrants in Germany." *Journal of Ethnic and Migration Studies* 31(2): 345-364.

Fink, E. 1981. *"Ethnic scale and intensity: The Zimbabwean Experience".* Journal of

Social Forces, Vol. 59, 1981.

Fontein, J. 2011. "Graves, ruins, and belonging: towards an anthropology of proximity". *Journal of the Royal Anthropological Institute*, 17, 706–727.

Geschiere, P. & Nyamnjoh, F.B. 2000. "Capitalism and autochthony: the seesaw of mobility and belonging". *Public culture*, 12, 423–452.

Geschiere, P. 2009. *The perils of belonging: Autochthony, citizenship, and exclusion in Africa and Europe*, University of Chicago Press.

Geschiere, P. "Autochthony and citizenship: new modes in the struggle over belonging and exclusion in Africa". *Forum for Development Studies*, 2005. Taylor & Francis, 371–384.

Gonese, F., et al. (2000). Land Reform and Resettlement Implementation in Zimbabwe: An Overview of the Programme against Selected International Experiences, SN.

GoZ. 2001. "Land reform and resettlement programme: revised phase 2". In: *Ministry of Lands Agriculture and Rural Resettlement.* Harare: Zimbabwe: Government Printers

Hammar, A.J., Raftopoulos, B. & Jensen, S.E.B. 2003. *Zimbabwe's unfinished business: rethinking land, state and nation in the context of crisis.* Weaver Press

Hanlon, J., Manjengwa, J. & Smart, T. 2012. *Zimbabwe takes back its land*, Kumarian Press.

Home, R. 2012. The colonial legacy in land rights in southern Africa. In (B. Chigara, ed.)

Southern African Development Community Land Issues: Towards a New Sustainable

Land Relations Policy, pp. 8–26. Routledge, London.

Jayaweera, H. & Choudhury, T. 2008. *Immigration, faith and cohesion: evidence from local areas with significant Muslim populations.* York: Joseph Rowntree Foundation

Kanyenze, G. 2011. *Beyond the enclave: Towards a pro-poor and inclusive development strategy for Zimbabwe*, African Books Collective.

Kinsey, B.H. 1982. "Forever Gained: 1 Resettlement and Land Policy in the Context of National Development in Zimbabwe". *Africa*, 52, 92–113.

Kinsey, B., et al. (1998). *"Coping with drought in Zimbabwe: Survey evidence on responses of rural households to risk."* World Development 26(1): 89-110.

Kinsey, B.H. 1999. "Land reform, growth and equity: emerging evidence from Zimbabwe's resettlement programme". *Journal of Southern African Studies*, 25, 173–196.

Mabhena, C. 2010. Visible Hectares, Vanishing Livelihoods: A Case for the Fast Track Land Reform Programme in Southern Matabeleland, Zimbabwe. PhD Thesis, University of Fort Hare.

Makura-Paradza, G. G. 2010. *Single women, land and livelihood vulnerability in a communal area in Zimbabwe*, Wageningen Academic Pub

Malkki, L. 1992. "National geographic: The rooting of peoples and the territorialization of national identity among scholars and refugees". *Cultural anthropology*, 7, 24–44.

Mandizadza, S. 2010. The fast track land reform programme and livelihoods in Zimbabwe: a case study of households at Athlone Farm in Murehwa District. University of Witwatersrand.

Manjengwa, J., Hanlon, J. & Smart, T. 2013. "Zimbabwe takes back its land: Is this the best use of the land? Land Divided: Land and South African Society in 2013", in *Comparative Perspective*, 1–15.

Masiiwa, M. & Chipungu, L. 2004. "Land reform programme in Zimbabwe: disparity between policy design and implementation". In: M. Maiiwa (ed.), *Post-independence Land Reform in Zimbabwe: Controversies and Impact on the Economy*, 1–24. Journal of Sustainable Development in Africa.

Matondi, P.B. 2012. *Zimbabwe's fast track land reform*, Zed Books Ltd.

Mkodzongi, G. (2013). "Fast tracking land reform and rural livelihoods in mashonaland west province of Zimbabwe: opportunities and constraints, 2000-2013." The University of Edinburgh

Mkodzongi, G. 2016 "Utilising 'African Potentials' to Resolve Conflicts in a Changing Agrarian Situation in Central Zimbabwe". In: Sam Y.M. Moyo (ed.), *What Colonialism Ignored: African Potentials for Resolving Conflicts in Southern Africa.* Oxford.

Moyana, H., Sibanda, M. & Gumbo, S. 1984. "The African Heritage". *History for Junior Secondary School Book,* 2.

Moyo, S. & Chambati, W. 2013. *Land and Agrarian Reform in Zimbabwe,* African Books Collective.

Moyo, S. & Yeros, P. 2005. *Reclaiming the land: The resurgence of rural movements in Africa, Asia and Latin America,* Zed Books.

Moyo, S. 1995. *The land question in Zimbabwe,* Sapes Books Harare.

Moyo, S. 2000. *Land reform under structural adjustment in Zimbabwe: land use change in the Mashonaland provinces,* Nordic Africa Institute.

Moyo, S. 2009. *Fast track land reform baseline survey in Zimbabwe,* African Institute for Agrarian Studies.

Moyo, S. 2011. "Three decades of agrarian reform in Zimbabwe". *The Journal of Peasant Studies,* 38, 493–531.

Mugabe, R. 2001. Inside the third Chimurenga. Harare: Department of Information and Publicity.

Mujere, J. 2011. "Land, graves and belonging: land reform and the politics of belonging in newly resettled farms in Gutu, 2000–2009". *Journal of Peasant Studies,* 38, 1123–1144.

Murisa, T. & Chikweche, T. 2015. *Beyond the crises: Zimbabwe's prospects for transformation,* Weaver Press.

Murisa, T. 2009. *An Analysis of Emerging Forms of Social Organisation and Agency in the Aftermath of 'fast Track' Land Reform in Zimbabwe.* Rhodes University.

Murisa, T. 2013. "Social Organisation in the Aftermath of Fast Track: An Analysis of Emerging Forms of Local Authority, Platforms of Mobilisation and Local Cooperation". *Land and Agrarian Reform: Beyond White Settler Capitalism.* Dakar: African Institute for Agrarian Studies, Harare, and CODESRIA.

Mutopo, P. 2014. *Women, mobility and rural livelihoods in Zimbabwe: experiences of fast track land reform*, Brill.

Njaya, T. 2015. Transforming People's Livelihoods through Land Reform in A1 Resettlement Areas in Goromonzi District in Zimbabwe. Journal of Humanities and Social Sciences, 20(2), pp. 91-99.

Nyambara, P. S. (2001). "Immigrants, 'Traditional' Leaders and the Rhodesian State: The Power of 'Communal' Land Tenure and the Politics of Land Acquisition in Gokwe, Zimbabwe, 1963–1979." Journal of Southern African Studies **27**(4): 771-791.

Nyamnjoh, F.B. 2006. *Insiders and outsiders: citizenship and xenophobia in contemporary Southern Africa*, Zed Books.

Nyawo Vongai, Z. Families Divided: The Place of the Family and Women in Zimbabwe's Fast Track Land Reform Programme. 4th Global Academic Meeting, GAM 2015 10-11 October, Dubai, UAE, 2015. 18.

Nyawo, V. Z. 2014. Zimbabwe post-fast track land reform programme: the different experiences coming through. *International Journal of African Renaissance Studies-Multi-, Inter-and Transdisciplinarity*, 9, 36-49.

Okoth-Ogendo, H.W.O. 1989. Some issues of theory in the study of tenure relations in African agriculture. *Journal of International African Institute*, 59(1): 6–17.

Okoth-Ogendo, H. 1993. Agrarian reform in sub-Saharan Africa, in *Land in African agrarian systems*, edited by T Bassetand D Crummey. Madison: University of Wisconsin.

Pal, D., et al. (2009). "Revisiting the agro-ecological zones for crop evaluation." *The Indian Journal of Genetics and Plant Breeding*, *69*(4), pp.305-314. Genetics 69: 315-318.

Palmer, R. 1990. "Land reform in Zimbabwe, 1980-1990". *African affairs,* 89, 163–181.

Paradza, G. G. 2010. Single Women's experiences of livelihood conditions, HIV and AIDs in the rural areas of Zimbabwe. *AIDS and Rural Livelihoods: Dynamics and Diversity in Sub-Saharan Africa,* 77-95.

Peters, P.E. 2004. "Inequality and social conflict over land in Africa". *Journal of agrarian change*, 4, 269–314.

Pollini, G. 2005. "Elements of a theory of place attachment and socio-territorial belonging. International Review of Sociology". *Revue Internationale de Sociologies*, 15, 497–515

Rutherford, Blair (2003) 'Belonging to the Farm(er): Farm Workers, Farmers, and the Shifting

Politics of Citizenship', in A. Hammar, B. Raftopoulos and S. Jensen (eds) *Zimbabwe's Unfinished Business: Rethinking Land, State and Nation in the Context of Crisis*, pp. 191–216. Harare: Weaver Press.

Rutherford, B. 2008. "Conditional belonging: farm workers and the cultural politics of recognition in Zimbabwe". *Development and Change*, 39, 73–99.

Sachikonye, L. 2003. "The Situation of Farm Workers after the Land Reform in Zimbabwe". A Report Presented for Farmers Community Trust of Zimbabwe.

Sachikonye, L. 2005. "The land is the economy: Revisiting the land question". *African Security Studies*, 14, 31–44.

Scoones, I., Mahenehene, J., Marongwe, N., Mavedzenge, B., Murimbarimba, F. & Sukume, C. 2010. *Zimbabwe's land reform: myths & realities*, Currey.

Scott James, C. J. N. H. Y. U. (1976). "The moral economy of the peasant: rebellion and subsistence in Southeast Asia." New Haven: Yale University

Shipton, P.M. 2009. *Mortgaging the Ancestors: ideologies of attachment in Africa*, Yale University Press.

Sibanda, A.E. 1990. *The Lancaster House Agreement and the post-independence state in Zimbabwe*, Zimbabwe Institute of Development Studies, Harare

Sithole, B., Campbell, B., Doré, D. & Kozanayi, W. 2003. "Narratives on land: state-peasant relations over fast track land reform in Zimbabwe". *African Studies Quarterly*, 7.

Yuval-Davis, N. 2011. *The politics of belonging: Intersectional contestations*, Sage.

Author's email: Email: marewokm@gmail.com

Chapter 12

Land Contestations after Fast Track Land Reform Programme: Emerging Land Tenure Challenges in Zimbabwe

Moses Moyo

Introduction

This chapter looks at emerging land tenure challenges after the Fast Track Land Reform Programme (FTLRP) in Zimbabwe. Contestations are emerging in land use and ownership with some violent incidents recently reported in the national press. Evidence from a case study of Mazowe tobacco farmers shows that lack of fair and transparent land transfer mechanisms are threatening the success and sustainability of FTLRP. Conflicts are emerging as smallholder farmers compete for land to participate in commercial agricultural activities. Evidence from the review of existing literature, newspapers and a case study of Mazowe are used to demonstrate emerging contestations and intergenerational land transfer problems which are attributed to the spontaneous nature of the land reform programme in Zimbabwe which has failed to develop sound tenure systems that allow for efficient transfer of land. Research on FTLRP focused on processes and outcomes of the programme, describing how the land was taken and the effects on production and livelihoods. These studies have exhibited a high degree of polarisation both from an ideological and policy perspectives (Moyo, 2011a). In all this, Sam Moyo has been the pacesetter in land reform scholarship in Zimbabwe. Further work on land tenure systems has been done by Matondi and Dekker (2011); however the focus remained on resettled farmers. The tenure relations between resettled farmers and the communal areas often receive very little attention. This is an important aspect of land tenure, given that some of these farmers share boundaries and the resettled farmers could be occupying historical ancestral land which might be claimed by adjacent communal peasants. Further, land reform was expected to decongest and improve "… agricultural performance and incomes in place of origin (communal areas) and place of settlement (new Fast Track Farms)" (Matondi & Dekker, 2011: 18), however this has not happened and there is potential of causing land tenure insecurity for resettled farmers.

The rest of the chapter is organised as follows: the next section describes land contestations, the history and development of land tenure in Zimbabwe. This is followed by a description of post-FTLRP tenure systems and the emerging issues. The chapter then presents evidence of tenure problems observed in Mazowe and concludes that these need sound land transfer systems to avoid black on black conflicts. The last section concludes the chapter.

Sam Moyo's Contribution to Scholarship on Land in Zimbabwe

Post-independence, Sam Moyo arguably set the tone for land reform research and debates in Zimbabwe, widely contributing to academic and policy discourse. In the introduction to his book *The Land Question in Zimbabwe* Moyo (1995) he aptly identifies key issues that have shaped land discourse for the past two decades. In his words the issues are:

> … the adequacy of the quantity and quality of land redistributed, the method and costs of land acquisition and redistribution, the efficiency of land use in both the large farm and resettlement areas, the suitability of those benefiting from land redistribution, the fairness and equitability of procedures for dealing with land demands, and the economic impact of land reform (Moyo, 1995).

Moyo addressed these issues "meticulously" (Mamdani, 2009:6) with methodological rigour (Scoones 2016) that brought to the fore empirical clarity for policy makers at the same time contributing to academic debate on "… the greatest transfer of property in southern Africa since colonisation and it has all happened extremely rapidly" (Mamdani, 2009:8). Moyo advocated for expropriation of land without compensation and believed that peasants should take land,

348

and institutional and administrative issues would follow latter. This attracted debates from critics (Laurie & Chan, 2016; Cliffe et al., 2011) and the many scholars who responded to Mamdani's "Lessons of Zimbabwe". All this typified the importance of Moyo's work as shown by the robust debate that followed Mamdani's article and hence he noted; "For anyone wanting to understand the historical trajectory of land reform, the work of Sam Moyo, who directs the African Institute for Agrarian Studies in Harare, is indispensable".

Moyo's various works have stood the test of time. For instance smallholder farmers are increasing production (Scoones et al., 2011), though problems still exist particularly in areas of equitable distribution of land, poverty and congestion in communal areas. Issues of multiple farm ownership, illegal land leases and joint venture arrangements were recently reported by Muronzi and Mambo (2017) in the state media indicating problems of land transfer mechanisms. This has been exacerbated by the increased uptake of cash crop production and hence the rise in demand for land by smallholder farmers (Sachikonye, 2016; Moyo, 2011a).

Land Tenure from a Historical Perspective

In 1890 the British South African Company (BSAC), invaded Zimbabwe changing land holdings and agriculture production of indigenous people. The indigenous black population was dispossessed of their land (Palmer & Parsons, 1977; Riddell, 1980; Moyana, 1978, 2002) and their agricultural practices affected through a chain of land tenure reforms starting in the early 1900s to independence in 1980 (Moyo, 1995). These included forced resettlement, crop production and marketing restrictions through legislation, like the Maize Act of 1930 and the Husbandry Act of 1951 among others. This resulted in congested communal areas, competition for resources and passive resistance by the peasants. All this affected land tenure systems among Zimbabwean farmers with the notable creation of a dual agricultural system comprising large-scale commercial farmers on 15.5 million hectares of prime land, operating along an indigenous subsistence farming community congested on 16.4 million hectares of low potential communal areas.

In between were small-scale farmers on 1.4 million hectares, who acted as buffers between the extreme farming communities. It is during this era that communal tenure systems were crafted as explained by Cheater (1990), of which some of these systems were adopted by the post-independence government. This was despite the fact that some of these systems were deemed problematic during the colonial times. One such institution that survived is the traditional authority under chiefs who are empowered with communal land administration under the Traditional Authorities Act. However, though the chief's authority is clearly spelt out for communal areas, this has remained a grey area for settlements under the FTLRP, though recent trends point to chiefs' extending their authority onto FTLRP areas (Murisa, 2018; Chipenda, 2018).

Traditional authorities generate mixed feelings in their land administration role, with some authors viewing them as colonial puppets who served under the colonial tribal trust land (Cheater, 1990). O'Flaherty (1998) documents land administration hierarchies in Gudyanga, a district in Manicaland, showing the various roles played by the headman, the chief and the district officers among other institutions, while Cheater (1982) study in the Msengezi purchase area shows intergenerational land and transfer complications that arise from the indecisive land tenure system. This affects production relations within the farming community and hence the need for clear provisions for land tenure administration systems that are clear on use and transfer among those that demand land and those holding land rights. The starting point would be clarity on rights of current holders. This according to Hall (2009) would facilitate effective use of land after land reform. As a result Hall (2009:23) observed that:

Where land is redistributed through land reform, agriculture is the dominant, but not the only, land use. However, land reform policy has not, until now, envisaged what kinds of production are to be promoted through the process of reform, and, therefore, what kind of structural change in production, markets and settlement patterns is being pursued, alongside the de-racialisation of ownership. This is the product of a longstanding failure to locate land reform within a wider framework of agrarian reform.

A successful land reform therefore could be measured by its impact on agricultural performance post-reforms, an outcome that emanates from good tenure systems. It is this gap Sam Moyo's inspired land debates did not emphasise. According to Moyo (2011a: 939), this could be because:

> Much of the literature on both sides of a polarised debate on agrarian change in Zimbabwe has focused narrowly on the Fast Track Land Redistribution process and its immediate consequences for agricultural production.

Post-independence land tenure administrative systems that were in place favoured the large-scale commercial areas, while for "native reserves" government reacted to potential catastrophes resulting from overcrowding in communal areas. For instance, the Husbandry Act of 1951 and Alvord's extension services were a response to massive land degradation in communal areas if compared to the Intensive Conservation Area that governed land use systems in white commercial lands. These systems had differential outcomes in terms of farming practices impacts on the environment and how they were regulated. After FTLRP, such systems became necessary given that newly resettled farmers were neither under the jurisdiction of the Intensive Conservation Area nor traditional authorities. As Gonese and Mukora (2003) noted FTLRP-beneficiaries were settled with little infrastructural support and administration system to run whatever envisaged land tenure system. As illustrated by the latter, weak tenure and administrative system had devastating effects on FTLRP farms due among other things to high uptake of cash crops without proper tenure systems defining land use patterns.

All the above said, Moyo (2004) recognised that the FTLRP had excluded other sectors of society particularly youth, women, farmworkers and perceived opposition, given their limited political capital. He recognised that most of the debates on tenure were skewed towards A2 leaseholds with little attention on A1 and customary tenure. The communal areas remained congested. Transfer of use rights or access by these groups of people remained a problem and hence the need for innovative access mechanisms.

Such access mechanisms remained work in progress from Moyo's work, setting a research agenda for post-radical land reform tenure systems. This is of paramount importance as the demand for land increases due to the increasing uptake of industrial crops with better returns for emerging agricultural capitalists. The question is whether land tenure reforms proposed elsewhere would fit the "unique" radical land reform that unfolded in Zimbabwe. How would this fit in with international capital which is dominating industrial crop production? All this would require a context-specific land tenure system which ties in with the unique land reform in Zimbabwe. Below, I discuss land tenure reform as described in literature, highlighting challenges a scenario that unfolded in Zimbabwe would have in adopting such land administration systems. The next section describes land tenure.

Land Tenure Systems in Zimbabwe

Maxwell and Wiebe (1998: 4) define land tenure as "… social relations and institutions governing access to and ownership of land and natural resources", which are enshrined in the country's statutory and customary laws. Land tenure prescribes use, transfer and exclusion rights to holders of the land, which is broadly referred to as property rights within the neoliberal school of thought (Feder & Feeny, 1991). In a broader sense, social scientists (Ribot & Peluso, 2003; Berry 1993) refer to land access among members of a community, thus they focus on "the right to benefit" from the land. In a land tenure system based on access, we have property rights that are provided for in laws governing access as well as social or power relations that allow people to negotiate use of land even though they do not own it (Cotula, Dyer, & Vermeulen, 2008). Access is a more suitable option to a "unique" land reform process that unfolded in Zimbabwe. In Zimbabwe all agricultural land is owned by the state and farmers use land on the basis of "poorly" defined permits, offer letters or lease agreements of which some have no such documentation. For instance, A2 farmers are expected to operate on the basis of 99-year leases, yet most farmers have not received these. The legal status of the leases is also contested. The same applies to

A1 permits. Therefore, under the circumstances access to land use is negotiated, and rights loosely defined.

This is in contrast to title deeds held by former large-scale commercial farmers which Agrawal (1996:3) says provides "… the right and the capacity to use, dispose, exclude or another action seen fit by the holder. The enforceable claims give rise to access as a bundle of rights". Consequently, these farmers could use their land as collateral. The 99-year lease provides for use rights and does not bequeath disposal or ownership rights to the holder of the lease. As a result banks have not accepted the leases as collateral, thus affecting access to credit and crop choices of the farmers. In essence, legal experts classify a 99-year lease like any property lease, with the advantage that it has long-term benefits, while Maguranyanga and Moyo (2006) identified problems with the leases and permits offered under FTLRP and made recommendations on tenure rights that were not followed by vigorous research to address this pressing issue. Work by Rukuni (2012) on tenure reforms also seems to have received very little attention from the government. These lone voices in secure tenure research need to be complemented for a successful agrarian transition.

Zimbabwe has two tenure systems in operation namely: customary tenure which entitles peasants traditional usufruct on State Land for Communal Areas, permits for Model A Old Resettlement and for A1 farmers; statutory tenure which includes freehold title for a few farmers; short-term leases; 99 -year leases (for A2 farmers); and offer letters for most A2-farmers awaiting processing of leases (Rukuni, 2012). Rukuni (2012) believes that these tenure systems can all be secure if issues of transferability and enforceability are addressed. This will address issues of transfer of use of land to those who want to farm the land. As De Soto (2000) noted, an asset that cannot be transferred is dead capital, hence, building on such work by Rukuni, Manguranyanga and Moyo scholars from various disciplines could debate appropriate land tenure systems suitable for the Zimbabwean situation.

This needs to take into account socioeconomic structures and contexts of the various jurisdictions in Zimbabwe. Maguranyanga and Moyo (2006) explain the need for:

> ... developing appropriate land tenure systems is a complex process, with crosscutting social, political, economic and environmental implications. Consequently, land tenure development is intimately linked to the broader political economic issues of democracy, governance, social justice, empowerment, equity and development.

This can be achieved through multidisciplinary research. Moyo (2011a) noted the potential of contestations and competition among elites and the poor which could escalate into violence in the absence of secure land tenure systems. Mkodzongi (2016, 2018) describes self-provisioning and vernacular land sales due in part to weak land tenure systems. Murisa (2018) and Chipenda (2018) describe the extension of traditional authorities in A1 settlements where a permit-based tenure system is in use. All this could potentially result in conflicts or tenure insecurity which all affects productivity on farms. Already Moyo (2011c:509) reports on conflict arising from "... disputes over boundaries and land rights, the extraction of natural resources and 'inherited' access to infrastructures (2.7 per cent), to conflicts arising from the interventions related to the GoZ's land reform re-planning programme". Some of the conflicts related to the place of origin of the FTLRP beneficiaries which points to possible clashes between resettled farmers and people from the surrounding communities particularly in communities like the A1 and communal areas. Land conflicts result in those with power and resources winning the conflicts thus marginalising the poor.

In debating, developing and proposing tenure systems researchers and policy advisers should be cognisant of research elsewhere on the matter. Some of the research has shown problems in Eurocentric approaches to land reform (Mafeje, 2003). For example the market-assisted reform in South Africa was deemed a failure while reversal and remergence of traditional tenure systems were reported on by Nuesiri (2014). Further customary land tenure has been dynamic and changing with demand for agricultural land (Chitonge, 2015; Chitonge Mfune, Kafwamba & Kajoba, 2017; Migot-Adholla Hazell, Blarel & Place, 1991). For instance customary land tenure conversions in Zambia (Chitonge, 2015) and vernacular sales in Zimbabwe (Chimhowu & Woodhouse, 2006) have all facilitated access to land either for agricultural or residential purposes. Some of these transactions arise because homesteads and agricultural plots are privately owned though not titled. Consequently neoliberal economists like De Soto (2000) would argue that such land could form a basis of formal land markets in developing countries. What is important are land administration systems that facilitate efficient land use and access to productive resources, more so given policy shifts where African governments are pushing for partnerships with agribusinesses (NEPAD., 2013).

Emerging Pressures on Land after FTLRP

Post-FTLRP pertinent questions have now emerged, some of which were at the core of Sam Moyo's work especially about justice and egalitarian distribution of land among poor peasants in congested communal areas. Moyo was concerned about land concentration (Moyo, 2011b) and the emerging competition between the elites and the poor peasants in a question of land imbalances (Moyo, 2011a), issues that could potentially be solved through sound land tenure systems. Laurie and Chan (2016) document deficiencies in processes in place during FTLRP that resulted in multiple farm ownership and extortions, all perpetuated by the elites and shrewd farm invaders who negotiated wealth and cash pay-outs in the name of protection fees. The fact that all this continued beyond FTLRP era speaks to insecure land tenure systems, yet both critics and proponents focused their debates on "narrow" FTLRP processes and outcomes. All this speaks to land use rights, about who controls land and who uses land.

Recent work on FTLRP reveals emerging land administration problems among beneficiaries and peasants who did not benefit. These problems have taken various forms like:

- Extension of traditional authority to A1 resettlement areas (Murisa, 2018; Chipenda, 2018; Mkodzongi, 2016).
- Conflicts between resettled farmers and bordering communities, some who claim that the land belonged to their ancestors. For example, the Chemagora case discussed below. This is fuelled by chiefs' desire to extend authority to resettled areas.

- Emergence of vernacular land markets (Mkodzongi, 2018).
- Land self-provisioning and expansion of plots by resettled farmers onto grazing areas (Mkodzongi, 2016).
- And in Mazowe the increased demand for land to produce commercial crops has resulted in various forms of lease arrangements among FTLRP beneficiaries, communal farmers and urbanites (Author, interviews).
- Environmental Management challenges (Author, own data).

Further, population growth remains a challenge. Without sound land-use transfer mechanisms this could change the nature of land conflicts. Current work on land reform in Zimbabwe has focused on correcting colonial injustices, that is, it has been a black and white issue the latter being the perpetrator of injustice while the former is the victim. However, work by Riddell (1980) shows that in 1977 communal areas were overpopulated by two and half times, carrying 675,000 households and these households almost doubled to 1,100,000 after FTLRP (Moyo, 2013). Herbst (1991) shows that around the time of his study forty thousand households were added to the congested communal lands, showing that congestion and justice needed more than settling 127,000 families under FTLRP. There is need for a strong intergenerational land transfer system to avoid land conflicts among blacks. In Mazowe and other communal areas (Chipenda, 2018; Murisa, 2018; Mkodzongi, 2016) land administration and claims are emerging issues. In Mazowe environmental issues are concerns as well. These issues are discussed below.

Land Contestations after FTLRP

Land contestations have a history stretching from the 1890 to the present day. Land appropriations by the British South Africa Company (BSAC) resulted in the first Chimurenga, and subsequent struggles that resulted in Zimbabwe gaining its independence in 1980. During this colonial period contestations pitted white colonial settlers and blacks whose land was annexed. Contestations revolved around statutory land use provisions such as the Land Appropriation

Act, land management provisions and the inadequacy of land allocated to blacks. Post-independence, the government through land reform tried to correct some of these injustices though with very little success. For instance, the FTLRP was aimed at decongesting communal areas and provide for adequate access to land for farmers to meet their production and livelihood needs. This did not happen, as shown by the prominence land tenure issues received in the 2008 Global Political Agreement (GPA) signed by ZANU PF and the two MDC formations. Though the parties agreed that FTLRP was irreversible, they all acknowledged that work was needed to bring the land question to its logical end in Zimbabwe.

Scholars, like Murisa (2016) while celebrating Moyo's work, identify land tenure reform as a gap still to be resolved to avoid land contestations, competition for resources and elite capture of the FTLRP. Media reports in Zimbabwe also report of land contestation pitting resettled farmers and adjacent communal areas, and political leadership has consistently referred to the need to finalise land issues. All this reflects Moyo's (2007:12) observation that "An effective land administration system which supports and enforces the new rights is also critical to ensure equity". This chapter adds to calls for research on land tenure systems, to facilitate smooth transfer of land use among users in rural areas. There is a further need to reduce emerging contestations and environmental catastrophic land use patterns from increased cash crop production by the new farmers. While the problem affects both commercial and smallholder farmers, the focus of this chapter is on rural smallholder farmers in A1 and communal settlements. This is because most A1 resettlements share boundaries with communal areas and have unique land tenure concerns. Post-independence land reforms need to refocus land tenure systems to new challenges facing farmers.

FTLRP debates focused on results of the FTLRP outcomes without analysing how land would be accessed or transferred after land reform. Hence the land question is alive and still a topical issue in Zimbabwe. The former president often raised the issue of land expropriation at every opportune time when addressing his supporters at rallies. While acknowledging that "farmers are farmers" President Mnangagwa has indicated that the FTLRP is irreversible though the issue of compensation of former white farmers has taken centre stage in the new dispensation's international re-engagement policy. Remedying the shortfalls of the land reform has proved to be a painful process and a long-drawn effort. A recent book by Laurie and Chan (2016), has opened old debates about Mugabe's motives of the FTLRP emphasising perceptions that "… coercion; corruption and incompetence; cronyism in the redistribution of land; lack of funds and an absence of agricultural activity – have come to stand for the whole process" (Mamdani 2009: 7); issues underplayed by proponents of FTLRP. These issues have resurfaced. The new government has moved with speed to implement the land audit to correct multiple farm ownership and deficiencies of the fast tract land reform, issues Moyo raised in his later work when evaluating the outcomes of FTLRP.

From Moyo's work and the debate that ensued it is evident that most issues received considerable attention with the exception of "… the fairness and equitability of procedures for dealing with land demands, and the economic impact of land reform" (Moyo, 1995:1). By this, it is understood that Moyo, referred to land tenure and administration issues. Land tenure problems became evident with the rapid growth of agricultural commercialisation, particularly the high uptake of tobacco and cotton production reported by Sachikonye (2016). Increased uptake of cash crop production is often associated with increased demand for land (Cotula, Dyer & Vermeulen, 2008). This can create tensions and conflicts which normally deprive the poor of their land and threaten their food security. For example, where tenure security is weak, the poor might be coerced to rent out their land for commercial crop production. In certain instances, they might be enticed into producing for contractors at uncompetitive prices.

In his latter writings (Moyo, 2011a) was weary of the competition for resources among the elites and the ordinary peasantry, and reports of struggles for land ownership and resource access. More telling is the social differentiation in terms of assets and land among farming communities. Of the 70% of land owned by 1,300 million families among communal farmers and FTLRP beneficiaries in Zimbabwe (Moyo, 2011b) by 2003 only 127,000 A1 and 7,260 A2 farmers got land on 6,429,894 hectares of FTLRP-land (Utete, 2003), a sign of widening land ownership differentiation. These figures might have changed over time as new beneficiaries were added, changing land use in A1 settlements (Ncube, 2018). However, land transfer processes, tenure security and administration have been questioned by property rights proponents (Richardson, 2005). While inheritance of FTLRP has been clarified, transfer among farmers either through subletting or leasing has remained a grey area. For instance, joint ventures require the Minister of Agriculture's authority. These processes are deemed cumbersome to potential investors. More importantly, this limits land transfers among users, with the possibility of excluding those who did not benefit from FTLRP from commercial agriculture. This creates struggles and conflicts explained by (Moyo, 2009, 2011b) which raise a new dimension to the land question.

Critics of the FTLRP (Richardson, 2005) point to this tenure problem as the source of poor agricultural performance. This though is more applicable to A2 farmers entitled to leasehold tenure. Moyo (2009: 6) countered by alleging that critics fail to understand the "... emergence of a new land tenure regime in terms of the forms of access to land, the right to inclusion or exclusion, and the protecting mechanisms of such access and use tends to be disregarded". However, contestations and competition for land and resources mirror deep security of tenure problems. In addition, the fact that most studies neglect the plight of over 1,100 million communal peasant households still congested in rural areas, leaves a gap in research on access and tenue security problems in Zimbabwe's agrarian structure. This could result in blood conflicts, like the recent small-scale farmer who was hacked to death by illegal settlers from Chemagora communal lands in Gower (Mhlanga, February 2019). The local chief was implicated for inciting the invasion which resulted in the farmer's death.

In the FTLRP areas of Ngezi, Mkodzongi (2016, 2018) reports of tenure concerns have emerged as farmers expand their official allocations beyond the set cadastral boundaries prompted by local "vernacular land sales" by traditional authorities. In Mazowe, farmers rent land through various mechanisms while Moyo (2011b) reports of FTLRP beneficiaries hiring former white farmers against the spirit of land reform. Recent plans to create a "new city" in Mount Hampden which borders Zvimba has seen government issue warnings to land barons (some FTLRP beneficiaries) converting agricultural land to lucrative urban settlements. All this points to emerging issues of tenure security, particularly in the disposal and bequeathing of use rights by farmers. This is not surprising as tenure security has historically been a poorly defined issue in Zimbabwe (Cheater, 1990). This is the core of contestations within the land reform discourse in Zimbabwe and threatens to perpetuate the culture of "violent land access" in Zimbabwe (Sachikonye, 2011a; 2011b). The problem is further clouded by analysing land tenure issues under the property rights paradigm, yet A1 and A2 have different land tenure systems. As Moyo (2007) observed, the A1 permit system is more like a customary tenure system.

Land Tenure Challenges after FTLRP: Evidence from Mazowe

Evidence from a Mazowe case study reveals land contestations and underlying problems of land tenure insecurity among A1 farmers as land demand increases and farmers participate in contract farming for cash crops like tobacco, soya beans and maize under the lucrative command agriculture (a programme sponsored by the government). These farming interventions resulted in farmers increasing area under crop production. In a case study of tobacco farmers in Mazowe the researcher observed that farmers that participated in contract farming increased plots under tobacco from a low average of 0.84 hectares before joining contract farming to 1.3 hectares. This was a 54 per cent increase. Non-contract farmers increased their plots by 8 per cent and these were mainly in communal lands. Elite farmers also participated in soya bean and maize command agriculture production. As a result, the five-hectare plots were not enough for such farmers, which was the same with communal farmers all who responded by renting in more land as described below. All this created tenure problems, competition for resources and social tensions within the Mazowe community.

Gender inequalities in the control and use of land

In Mazowe women and youth were discriminated against in terms of land ownership under fast track. From a sample of 150 respondents, only thirteen women (only 9%) accessed land under the FTLRP, and youth complained that they could not access contract farming because they had no land of their own. Of the thirteen women only three were in tobacco production and felt there were excluded from contract farming because of gender bias in the allocation of contracts. Two women used their husbands to produce under contract and the contracts were in their husbands' names. While some women had access to land, access to farming resources affected their land-use options. Youth who had no land rented land in some form of share cropping to produce cash crops. This meant they were also not registered as tobacco producers which affected their economic activities and direct participation in agricultural markets. A 20-year old youth said:

> I work for an A1 farmer in return for a half-hectare plot where I produce my tobacco. I also sell my tobacco through this farmer. Government needs to provide me with my own plot so that am not exploited by a fellow black farmer (Personal Communication, 29 August 2017).

A headman in Chiweshe explained that he had a long list of people under the age of 30 years who were awaiting land as promised by the local political leadership. The headman said,

> Our leaders asked us to register people for land, which they said would be availed from the surrounding farms. People were asked to pay US$5 per month. Now it turns out that the land is small residential stands measuring 200 square metres. People feel cheated, they need agriculture land. And besides the stands are still a dream and even if we got them how do we build houses with no money? (Personal Communication, 29 August 2018).

All this points to simmering land access problems which are waiting to explode and hence a need for lasting land transfer mechanisms that allow for intergenerational transfer of land. For example, the farmer who worked for an A1 farmer believed that he was entitled to land in the area, before "foreigners" could be allocated land. He added, "I was born here, and this is my ancestral land and yet it's being taken away again, this is not right". Through desperation youth were participating in land rental and share-cropping arrangements which they felt were exploitative and unfair. The local chief felt that locals should have first preference to surrounding farms available for resettlements and was against the settlements of *vabvakure* (people from other districts) on their ancestral land. He felt people from Mazowe were being deprived of their land for the second time. An A2-farmer on the boundaries of Chiweshe communal lands was being threatened with *Jambanja* because he came from another district and was "giving back land" to the white farmer. The farmer partnered with a former white commercial farmer which was unacceptable to the locals. The former president publicly chastised such practices and the locals were quick to threaten *Jambabnja* in support of the president.

Growing demand for land

A land rental and share cropping market was observed in Mazowe. This was driven by increased demand for land to meet subsistence and cash crop production under contract production. Some farmers who accessed land under FTLRP were renting out because they lacked resources to work their plots and did not qualify to join contract farming because they lacked initial assets. Yet, they were farmers who had access to contracts and demanded more land. These came from the rural and urban areas; some were A1 farmers whose land was not enough for their cropping mix. The demand–supply situation observed in Mazowe can be explained by Akram-Lodhi (2005) reasoning on why farmers rent in and rent out land, which is driven by profit motive on one hand, and unexpected expenses or resources access challenges for those renting out and increased income for surplus farmers.

The development of the rental market is characterised by individualised informal agreements, paid for both in kind or cash, and involves the poor and rich. All interviewees who said they paid fixed rentals for land were contract farmers and wanted to expand plots under tobacco, and the poor were involved in some form of sharecropping based on labour exchange or sharing output. A member of the Committee of Seven at Thorncreek farm, indicated that they were aware of the practice; however, it was necessary, because "… they all want enough for survival" (Personal communication, 25 August 2017). However, he indicated that land rental was illegal but only became "commercialised" out of greed after people realised that farmers were making money from contract farming. The communal and A1 land tenure system does not allow for land rentals. Further discussions revealed that A1 farmers rented out land to keep the farm productive for fear of repossession.

Three categories of people renting land were observed:

- Landless urbanites, generally to embark on cash crop production. These had access to resources, such as cash and contract farming, which they accessed through illicit means, and rented land from A1 farmers. One farmer indicated he was brought into the scheme by a friend, who is the extension officer in the scheme, and they decided to start this partnership. The partnership worked well because of insider trading which normally meant their tobacco attracted a better price (Personal communication, 30 July 2017).

- Communal people expanding into cash crops and who were short of land. These rented lands from communal areas and A1 farmers to allow for crop rotation and increased plots under tobacco production after concluding contracts. In addition, there were communal farmers involved in some form of share cropping, where they worked plots of rich peasants in exchange for a small plot to produce staple crops. A communal farmer in Ndire, who was producing under contract, rented all the plots where he produced his tobacco. A letter of introduction to TIMB that allowed him to get a grower number was based on his communal plot, as he noted, "nobody makes a follow-up" and hence, anybody could get a letter of introduction from the headman even if they didn't have land (Personal communication, 16 July 2017).

- A1 farmers expanding operations rented land from fellow A1 farmers. These produced multiple cash crops, such as beans and soya beans, and were involved in command agriculture as well as tobacco contract farming. These were also among the accumulators observed in Mazowe. Through patronage, they had good access to resources; some were said to be active in politics as sponsors, though they themselves never occupied political office. Some of the favours included transporting people to political rallies.

An A1 farmer, who rented out his plot, indicated that he had no resources or knowledge of farming, had no job and hence he was reaping the fruits of his participation in *Jambanja* through renting out his plot (Personal communication, 16 July 2017). Access to resources and asset endowment were key drivers of the developing land rental market and the sharecropping arrangement (De Janvry, Sadoulet, & Zhu, 2005) and, hence, those able to access resource-providing institutions or draw from personal resources were able to participate in rental markets.

The local leadership complained that land rentals were benefiting people from other regions as the A1 farmers preferred to deal with urbanites who had better resources and were not a threat to their ownership of the land. An officer at the chief's court supported this view observing, "It is illegal to rent out land and very soon we will weed out such A1 farmers from our land. Our people have no land, yet some hold it for speculative purposes". This shows the animosity that was developing between those holding the rights to land and the adjacent communal households living on congested land. This animosity was worsened by the preferential treatment resettled farmers got in contract farming arrangements.

Challenges in accessing contract farming arrangements

Communal farmers in Mazowe faced problems in accessing contract farming arrangements, and it was observed that there was competition for these contracts. This was bitterly received by the communal farmers who felt excluded because of their small landholdings. A communal farmer had this to say, "We were servants of the white commercial farmers who took our land and now the government gave land to people from other districts and we are now servants of our brothers" (Personal communication, 16 July 2017). He went on to say he believed surrounding farms should have been first allocated to locals. This he believes could have improved their economic fortunes.

Environmental challenges: deforestation, land degradation and climate change
"The land has lost its cover", lamented a Ndire resident. Thus, what meets the eye as one drives through the Mazowe farmlands. This epitomises land use problems in FTLRP areas. Trees are cut for curing tobacco in an unsustainable manner, in that no recovery time or replacement is done (Farmer, ward 21, October 2017). The Environmental Management Agency (2014) cites tobacco curing as the number one cause of deforestation in Zimbabwe. Most tobacco farmers surveyed indicated that they plant gum trees for use in tobacco curing, however there were no plantations in the wards visited. In wards 10 and 9 local leadership indicated there were plans to establish a plantation but the problem was delayed deliveries of seedlings. LANGA (2017, December) reports on eight million dollars of tobacco funds deposited in the TIMB account that were not being used for the intended purpose which confirms the dilemma faced by leadership in wards 10 and 9. Langa quotes the Minister of Agriculture telling parliament that:

> No progress has been made in establishing woodlots towards the fund because the constitution of the Afforestation Fund is yet to be presented to and registered with Parliament as per the requirements of the Public Finance Management Act, [Chapter 22 (19)] by the Minister of Finance and Economic Planning.

As the bureaucratic wheel turns farmers continue to harvest the few natural woodlots that remain. For instance, (Siddiqui, 1998) has argued that people's search for economic opportunities and inept policies and policy implementation are the key contributors to deforestation. Lambin et al. (2001:265) put the blame on globalisation and note:

> Markets trigger commercial intensification of agriculture in a commodification pathway changing economic conditions, mediated by

institutional factors created by markets and policies, increasingly influenced by global factors.

For instance, in Zimbabwe tobacco as the key foreign exchange earner finds a government hesitant to enforce regulations or antagonise contractors who supply capital. This is despite of the existence of regulation like the Forest Act (Chapter 19:05) and the Communal Land Forest Produce Act (Chapter 19:04). Most of the tree cutting is now concentrated in A1 farms and then sold or exchanged for services with communal or other A1 farmers and land tenants, A1 farmers claim they are clearing land for cultivation. However, a farmer in ward 32 queried this explanation and observed: "There is no planning here, people just cut trees everywhere and nobody holds them to account, it's not for cultivation it has become big businesses." Some people actually hold stacks of firewood for sale to tobacco farmers in exchange for goods or farming land. Communal areas are land deficient and there is need for alternative energy sources and yet:

> TIMB has avoided using the afforestation fund collected since 2015 as it awaits administrative processes so that it can scale up its activities to the establishment of 20 000 hectares of woodlots per year for the next 5 years. (Chikwati and Mutasa, 2018 January)

Given land shortages in communal areas, 20,000 of the proposed woodlots might not reach the communal lands as one farmer queried, "Where will they plant the trees, when we don't even have land for our staples" (Interview with non-tobacco farmer, ward 15, 25 July 2017). An extension officer in ward 10 expressed concern about the proposed woodlots in the area as he thought they would disturb the ecosystem, particularly the wetlands. This view is strongly shared by environmentalist and World Health Organisation scholars fighting tobacco production, who argue it disturbs biodiversity (WHO, 2017).

Farmers in Mazowe were provided with coal to supplement firewood, which was observed lying beside the tobacco barns and farmers said they couldn't use it because it didn't burn well if not fired by electricity. An electricity project stalled and benefited few as explained earlier. However, the use of coal is also being blamed for heavy carbon emissions and hence the multinationals resolved they would not buy coal-cured tobacco starting 2020. Farmers within the survey sample were not aware of this proviso and indicated it would not affect them because they never used coal in the first place.

Contractors in Mazowe were not involved in plantation programmes, ostensibly because of the one-year contract offered to farmers. The short-term contract meant that contractors could not tie their investment to individual farmers. The legislation cited above forbids harvest of wood for commercial purposes like tobacco-curing energy, however enforcement is lacking. On its website EMA observes, "Traditional leaders also use the Traditional Leaders' Act (Cap 29:17) and their traditional norms and values to control deforestation issues". While chiefs in Mazowe knew of the provision of this act, there were no coordinated efforts between EMA, the Forestry Commission and local leadership in managing natural resources, presumably turning a blind eye for the production of the white gold to flourish.

In the absence of this, the contractor was more likely to treat the soil and environment badly. BAT a tobacco contractor in Kuria, Kenya, required tobacco farmers to have 5-acre plots with provision for fuel wood and plant 1,000 plants for three years for tobacco curing (Heald, 1991). Such an arrangement, enforceable by the regulator upon registration of tobacco contractors, could have a positive effect on the environment and sustainability of tobacco-farming operations in the long run.

Heavy reliance on indigenous trees for fuel wood in curing tobacco will eventually deprive the community of alternative livelihoods like the wild fruit sugarplum (mazhanje), hunting space and cooking energy. It could be in the interest of contractors to work with local leadership to enforce the prohibition against harvesting indigenous trees, and planting exotic trees for sustainable sources of curing energy. This is an urgent issue given that the tobacco oligopsony will be banning the use of coal, an alternative curing energy source for Mazowe tobacco farmers. The local leadership in Mazowe were moving towards the control of the A1 resettled farmers, which the latter resisted. Access to fuelwood, water sources and earth was a contested issue as chiefs sought to impose their authority on the A1 farmers. Lack of clarity on the permit system aided to the confusion that ensured in Mazowe.

Land degradation

Tobacco production involves the use of heavy chemicals which are blamed for soil fertility problems. The problem is acute in communal areas where land shortage is high and crop rotation is minimal. This means land has no time to recover, however most farmers rented land to mitigate this. Survey data show that farmers deal with tobacco diseases through two main processes: applying chemicals (34.3%) and crop rotation (61.4%), leaving chemicals applied during production as the main environmental concern. Environmentalists would argue that these chemicals damage biodiversity, though this argument is countered by the fact that intensive agriculture is damaging to the soil as farmers are forced to use a disproportionate number of fertilisers to maximise yields. However, while crop rotation was said to be good for soil management, the researcher observed that most fields still had tobacco stalks in October that was said to be a ready source of diseases to the adjacent fields.

The Zimbabwe Broadcasting Corporation confirmed this observation in Hwedza (ZBC 2018, June) reports of farmers who have not destroyed tobacco stalks two weeks after the expiry of the legalised deadline. Farmer organisations and government extension officers blame this on lax controls by contracting firms who are the main sponsors of the tobacco crop. An agribusiness extension officer who blamed the situation on the structure of the contract said,

It's a one-year contract, which ends with the harvesting and sale of the crop, during the marketing season, my focus is on tobacco deliveries to the firm, am not in the field and what happens there is out of my control.'

During the marketing season agribusiness is concerned with recruiting and offering contracts for the coming season and delivery of inputs at the expense of field management activities because the contract ends when the crop is delivered and a new one starts.

Towards A Secure Land Tenure System

Matondi and Dekker (2011:3), citing Rukuni (1998:2) observed that land tenure security consists of:

- **Use rights**: are rights to grow crops, trees, make permanent improvement, harvest trees and fruits, and so on;
- **Transfer rights**: are rights to transfer land or use rights, i.e., rights to sell, give, mortgage, lease, rent or bequeath land;
- **Exclusion rights**: are rights by an individual, group or community to excluded others from the rights discussed above; and
- **Enforcement rights**: refer to the legal, institutional and administrative provisions to guarantee rights.

These four rights are often associated with the property rights school of thought (Richardson, 2005), however these could fall short for communal tenure described above. For example, transfer of rights is limited for both communal and A1 areas. The right to transfer is important under customary tenure which was exercised by traditional authorities. As discussed above, this is now an area of contestation as chiefs are now encroaching into A1 settlements. The Chemagora example points to new claims which could destabilise land tenure in resettlement areas. As observed in Mazowe this is exacerbated by demand for land to produce cash crops as well as to access credit from contracting firms.

The challenge is now for the government to formalise land transfer mechanisms in rural areas to allow those who need land for farming to benefit, either through a rental market or share-cropping system. For instance, farmers who lack resources could be allowed to rent-out part of their land for agricultural purposes just like in the A2 system but with authority at the local level. Further the role of traditional authorities needs to be recrafted or explicitly extended to the new resettlement areas. This would allow for dispute resolution among A1 and communal farmers as they arise as well as natural resource management.

As observed by Matondi and Dekker (2011), the government also needs to balance the allocation of developmental resources. This would reduce competition between neighbouring A1 and communal areas.

Conclusion

Land reform is a just cause and there is cause to celebrate Sam Moyo's work for advancing the same. However, there is a need to build on such work to facilitate Zimbabwe's development to a highly productive nation. Insecure land tenure systems constrain agricultural productivity, and this is beginning to manifest through conflicts among resettled farmers and adjacent communal areas. Traditional authorities are also extending their jurisdiction to A1 settlements though this is contested. The need for capital is also creating smouldering tensions as people compete for resources. Land and environmental degradation is on the increase due to vacuums in land management systems. This calls for consolidated tenure systems which would help preserve the environment. These emerging issues threaten land tenure security and livelihoods in resettled areas and the adjacent communal areas. This requires land transfer and sustainable use mechanisms that facilitate transfer of land to users with minimal conflict. Sam Moyo recognised the need for this and his work reveals these potential conflicts. He even opened debate on this need (Maguranyanga & Moyo, 2006). While this chapter offers no remedies, it is important for scholars to build on work by the Rukuni Commission and Matondi and Dekker (2011) who are among a few who have looked at this issue. However, emphasis needs to be put on the new commercial agriculture trajectory the government has taken and the realisation that land tenure has broader effects that go beyond rural people. Urbanites have shown their hunger for land for economic reasons. This will increase competition for land and informal tenure systems will sprout out with damaging agricultural production relations in rural areas. It is with this view that institutions of land governance need to be strengthened through due legal processes.

References

Agrawal, Arun. 1996. "Not Having One's Cake, Nor Eating It: Intellectual Property and "Indigenous" Knowledges". Paper Prepared for the Colloquium Series of the Program in Agrarian Studies, Yale University, New Haven, CT, April 19, 1996.

Akram-Lodhi, A Haroon. 2005. "Vietnam's agriculture: processes of rich peasant accumulation and mechanisms of social differentiation", *Journal of Agrarian Change*, 5: 73-16.

Berry, Sara. 1993. "No condition is permanent: The social dynamics of agrarian change in sub-Saharan Africa." In.: Madison: University of Wisconsin Press.

Cheater, Angela. 1990. "The ideology of 'communal'land tenure in Zimbabwe: Mythogenesis enacted?", *Africa*, 60: 188-206.

Cheater, Angela P. 1982. "Formal and Informal Rights to Land in Zimbabwe's Black Freehold Areas: A Case-Study from Msengezi", *Africa*, 52: 77-91.

Chikwati, Elita, and Mellisa Mutasa. 2018 January. 'Farmers still to benefit from $19m tobacco levy", *The Herald Zimbabwe*. Retrivied https://www.herald.co.zw/farmers-still-to-benefit-from-19m-tobacco-levy/

Chimhowu, Admos, and Phil Woodhouse. 2006. "Customary vs private property rights? Dynamics and trajectories of vernacular land markets in Sub-Saharan Africa", *Journal of Agrarian Change*, 6: 346-71.

Chipenda, Clement. 2018. "After Land Reform in Zimbabwe: What about the Youth? Conference Paper No. 73", *Emancipatory Rural Politics Initiatives (ERPI) 2018 International Conference - Authoritarian Populism and the Rural World*.

Chitonge, Horman. 2015. "Customary land at crossroads: contest for the control of customary land in Zambia", *SADC Law Journal*, 4: 45-67.

Chitonge, Horman, Orleans Mfune, David Kafwamba, and Gear Kajoba. 2017. "Hybrid land markets: monetarised customary land transactions in Zambia", *Canadian Journal of African Studies/Revue canadienne des études africaines*, 51: 123-43.

Cliffe, Lionel, Alexander, Jocelyn, Cousins, Ben and Gaidzanwa, Rudo. 2011. "An overview of fast track land reform in Zimbabwe: editorial introduction", *Journal of Peasant Studies*, 38: 907-38.

Cotula, Lorenzo, Dyer, Nat and Vermeulen, Sonja. 2008. *Fuelling Exclusion?: The Biofuels Boom and Poor People's Access to Land* (Iied).

De Janvry, Alain, Sadoulet, Elisabeth and Zhu, Nong. 2005. "The role of non-farm incomes in reducing rural poverty and inequality in China". CUDARE: Working Paper, Department of Agricultural and Resource Economics, University of California, Berkeley

De Soto, Hernando. 2000. *The mystery of capital: Why capitalism triumphs in the West and fails everywhere else* (Basic Civitas Books).

Feder, Gershon, and Feeny, David. 1991. "Land tenure and property rights: Theory and implications for development policy", *The World Bank Economic Review*, 5: 135-53.

Gonese, Francis, and Mukora Charles M.. 2003. "Beneficiary selection, infrastructure provision and beneficiary support", *Delivering land and securing rural livelihoods: post-independence land reform and resettlement in Zimbabwe. Harare and Madison, Centre for Applied Social Sciences, University of Zimbabwe, and Land Tenure Center, University of Wisconsin-Madison.*

Hall, Ruth. 2009. "Land reform for what?", *Another.* 22.

Herbst, Jeffrey. 1991. "The dilemmas of land policy in Zimbabwe", *Africa Insight*, 21: 269-76.

Lambin, Eric F, Turner, Billie L, Geist, Helmut J., Agbola, Samuel B, Angelsen, Arild, Bruce, John W , Coomes, Oliver T., Dirzo, Rodolfo, Fischer, Günther and Folke Carl. 2001. 'The causes of land-use and land-cover change: moving beyond the myths', *Global environmental change*, 11: 261-69.

Langa, Veneranda. 2017, December. '$8m afforestation funds lie idle", *Newsday*. Retrivied https://www.newsday.co.zw/2017/12/8m-afforestation-funds-lie-idle/

Laurie, Alexander Charles, and Chan, Stephen. 2016. *The land reform deception: Political opportunism in Zimbabwe's land seizure era* (Oxford University Press).

Mafeje, Archie. 2003. *The agrarian question, access to land, and peasant responses in sub-Saharan Africa* (United Nations Research Institute for Social Development Geneva).

Maguranyanga, Brian, and Moyo, Sam. 2006. *Land Tenure in Post FTLRP Zimbabwe: Key Strategic Policy Development Issues* (African Institute for Agrarian Studies Harare).

Mamdani, Mahmood. 2009. 'Lessons of Zimbabwe: Mugabe in context', *Concerned African Scholars Bulletin*, 82.

Matondi, Prosper B, and Dekker, Marleen. 2011. 'Land Rights and Tenure Security in Zimbabwe's Post Fast Track Land Reform Programme', *A Synthesis report for LandAc. Project ID WS*, 320005.

Maxwell, Daniel, and Wiebe, Keith Daniel 1998. *Land tenure and food security: A review of concepts, evidence, and methods* (Land Tenure Center, University of Wisconsin-Madison Madison, WI).

Mhlanga, Blessed. 2019 February. 'Farmers bay for Chief Njelele's blood ', *Newsday Zimbabwe*. Retrivied https://www.newsday.co.zw/2019/02/farmers-bay-for-chief-njeleles-blood/

Migot-Adholla, Shem, Hazell, Peter, Blarel, Benoit and Place, Frank. 1991. 'Indigenous land rights systems in sub-Saharan Africa: a constraint on productivity?', *The World Bank Economic Review*, 5: 155-75.

Mkodzongi, Grasian. 2016. "I am a paramount chief, this land belongs to my ancestors': the reconfiguration of rural authority after Zimbabwe's land reforms', *Review of African Political Economy*, 43: 99-114.

———. 2018. "Peasant Agency in a Changing Agrarian Situation in Central Zimbabwe: The Case of Mhondoro Ngezi", *Agrarian South: Journal of Political Economy*, 7: 188-210.

Moyana, Henry. 1978. *Land apportionment in Rhodesia 1920-1960* (University Microfilms.).

———. 2002. *The political economy of land in Zimbabwe* (Mambo Press: Gweru, Zimbabwe).

Moyo, Sam. 1995. "The land question in Zimbabwe", *SAPES Books, Harare*.

————. 2004. "The land and agrarian question in Zimbabwe." In *first annual colloquium (30 September 2004) at the University of Fort Hare.*

————. 2007. "Emerging land tenure issues in Zimbabwe. African Institute for Agrarian Studies

————. 2009. *Fast track land reform baseline survey in Zimbabwe* (African Institute for Agrarian Studies).

————. 2011a. "Changing agrarian relations after redistributive land reform in Zimbabwe", *Journal of Peasant Studies*, 38: 939-66.

————. 2011b. "Land concentration and accumulation after redistributive reform in post-settler Zimbabwe", *Review of African Political Economy*, 38: 257-76.

————. 2011c. 'Three decades of agrarian reform in Zimbabwe', *Journal of Peasant Studies*, 38: 493-531.

————. 2013. "Land reform and redistribution in Zimbabwe since 1980", *Land and agrarian reform in Zimbabwe: Beyond white settler capitalism*: 29-78.

Murisa, Tendai. 2016. 'Prospects for Equitable Land Reform in Zimbabwe: Revisiting Sam Moyo's Work on the Land Question', *Agrarian South: Journal of Political Economy*, 5: 240-64.

————. 2018. "Land, Populism and Rural Politics in Zimbabwe". ERPI 2018 International Conference - Authoritarian Populism and the Rural World Conference Paper No. 51(17-18 March 2018 International Institute of Social Studies (ISS) in The Hague, Netherlands). '.

Muronzi, Chris, and Mambo, Elias. December 2017. "Mugabe leases Interfresh land", *The Independent Zimbabwe*. Retrivied https://www.theindependent.co.zw/2017/12/08/mugabe-leases-interfresh-land/

Ncube, Senzeni. 2018. "The role of social capital in the Fast Track Land Reform Programme (FTLRP) of Zimbabwe: a case of Rouxdale (R/E) Farm, Bubi District, Matabeleland North Province", University of Cape Town.

NEPAD., New Partnership for Africa's Development. 2013. "African agriculture, transformation and outlook". Johannesburg: The New Partnership for Africa's Development.'.

Nuesiri, Emmanuel O. 2014. "The re-emergence of customary authority and its relation with local democratic governmen Authority and its Relation to Local Democratic Government." RFGI Working Paper No. 6. Dakar: CODESRIA.

O'Flaherty, Michael. 1998. "Communal tenure in Zimbabwe: divergent models of collective land holding in the communal areas", *Africa*, 68: 537-57.

Palmer, Robin H, and Parsons, Neil. 1977. *The roots of rural poverty in Central and Southern Africa* (Univ of California Press).

Ribot, Jesse C, and Peluso, Nancy Lee . 2003. 'A theory of access", *Rural sociology*, 68: 153-81.

Richardson, Craig J. 2005. "The loss of property rights and the collapse of Zimbabwe", *Cato J.*, 25: 541.

Riddell, Roger. 1980. "Zimbabwe's land problem: the central issue", *Journal of Commonwealth & Comparative Politics*, 18: 1-13.

Rukuni, Mandivamba. 1998. "Where Should Land Tenure Policy be in Southern Africa?", *Paper prepared for the Scandinavian Seminar College "Sustainable Africa Initiative" keynote paper presented at a workshop in Harare in September 1998.*

———. 2012. "Why Zimbabwe needs to maintain a multi-form land tenure system", *Sokwanele Land Series*.

Sachikonye, Lloyd. 2011a. *When a state turns on its citizens: 60 years of institutionalised violence in Zimbabwe* (African Books Collective).

Sachikonye, Lloyd Mambo. 2011b. *Zimbabwe's Lost Decade: Politics, Development & Society* (African Books Collective).

———. 2016. "Old wine in new bottles? Revisiting contract farming after agrarian reform in Zimbabwe", *Review of African Political Economy*, 43: 86-98.

Scoones, Ian. 2016. "Livelihoods, Land and Political Economy: Reflections on Sam Moyo's Research Methodology", *Agrarian South: Journal of Political Economy*, 5: 221-39.

Scoones, Ian, Marongwe, Nelson, Mavedzenge, Blasio, Murimbarimba, Felix, Mahenehene, Jacob and Sukume, Chrispen. 2011. "Zimbabwe's land reform: challenging the myths", *Journal of Peasant Studies*, 38: 967-93.

Siddiqui, Kalim. 1998. "Agricultural Exports, Poverty and Ecological Crisis: Case Study of Central American Countries", *Economic and Political Weekly*: A128-A36.

Utete. 2003. "Report on the presidential land review committee, under the chairmanship of Dr. Charles M.B Utete. Main report to His Excellency, the President of the Republic of Zimbabwe", *Harare: Presidential Land Review Committe (PLRC)*.

World Health Organisation (WHO). 2017. Tobacco and its environmental impact: an overview. Retrieved http://apps.who.int/iris/bitstream/handle/10665/255574/9789241512497-eng.pdf

ZBC. 2018, June."Destroying tobacco stalks critical", *Zimbabwe Broadcasting Corporation*. Retrieved http://www.zbc.co.zw/destroying-tobacco-stalks-critical/

Author's email: moyobrendon@gmail.com

Chapter 13

The Legacy of Steve Biko and the Japanese Social Movements

Yoichi Mine

Setting the Scenes

Reflecting renewed interest in 1968, a number of books and articles that review the political events that took place about a half century ago and thereafter are currently being published in Japan. Most of them are written by young scholar-activists who belong to the post-1968 generation.

The Japanese radical student movement that started with the occupation of university campuses enjoyed a broad popular support, possibly broader than its Western counterparts for the initial period, due to the rapid expansion of tertiary education in the post-war period. The number of new students was swelling. The 18-year-old population increased from 1.6 million in 1953 to a record high of 2.5 million in 1968, while the university enrolment almost tripled from 0.13 million in 1955 to 0.33 million in 1968. In consideration of strict class categories, university students are part of the petty bourgeoisie. The old and new petty bourgeoisie combined may become a distinctive social force through fascist parties as discussed by Nicos Poulantzas (1970), or otherwise may transform into a social force committed to the liberatory cause if they succeed in "class suicide" as argued by Amilcar Cabral (1969).

As vividly depicted in the novels of Hiroshi Noma, Haruo Umezaki, Kazumi Takahashi and others, a queer feeling of having incidentally survived World War II captured the mind of the war generation. Then, the core generation of Japan's 1968 grew up in the aftermath of Japan's defeat in the war. As the post-war baby boomers entered the universities, some of the masses started to form a broad support base of militant activists, largely affiliated to the New Left. The occupation of university campuses in 1968 was ignited by the discontent of students over an increase in tuition fees and other campus-specific issues. After a series of showdown battles with riot police, the campuses became "normalized", but the frustrated activists wanted to continue mobilizing students around broader social and political issues.

From 1955 to 1973, the Japanese economy maintained an annual growth rate of more than 10 per cent on average, although the distribution of wealth was far from equitable. Some students who retained the memory of post-war poverty and destitution felt that they would betray their home communities and possibly their parents with lower education by stepping up the ladder of social hierarchy. They may have been aware that they could be trapped into uneasy elite positions if they pursued their own personal interests and careers. Then, after campuses were forcibly normalized by the police authority in 1968, people formerly deprived of their voices started to raise critical voices, inspired by the direct action of students. They were women, foreigners, people with disabilities, underclass workers, and other socially marginalized groups of people. Their messages were crushing and far-reaching, making the heart of young activists waver between embarrassment, guilt and defiance.

In many respects, the impact of voices raised by the socially marginalized in Japan was parallel to the impact brought by the Black Consciousness movement in South Africa. The collection of political writings of Steve Biko (1946-77), *I Write What I Like,* which was translated into Japanese in 1988, was welcomed by the Japanese audience and is still in print. While Japanese and South African political activists at the time did not exert visible, large-scale mutual influence, activists from both countries communicated face-to-face since the early 1960s (Makino 2018). They were basically separate but synchronized like quantum entanglement.

Biko enrolled in the University of Natal in 1966, organized South African Students' Organization (SASO) in 1968, and was banned in 1973. He and the Japanese 1968 activists were true contemporaries. In this essay, the narratives of activists in Japan are juxtaposed to the narratives of Biko, in order to shed light upon the resonance of political voices in Southern Africa and East Asia.

Negation and Self-Negation

Biko once delivered fierce criticism to the shallow, hypocritical attitude of so-called "white liberals" in his article entitled "Black Souls in White Skins?", an apparent spoof of *Black Skin, White Masks* by Frantz Fanon (1967). Biko was a medical student at the time, but student organizations were dominated by white students from racially segregated whites-only universities. He describes hypocrisy as follows:

> If you ask him to do something like stopping to use segregated facilities or dropping out of varsity to work at menial jobs like all blacks or defying and denouncing all provisions that make him privileged, you always get the answer – "but that's unrealistic!" It only serves to illustrate the fact that no matter what a white man does, the colour of his skin – his passport to privilege – will always put him miles ahead of the black man. Thus in the ultimate analysis no white person can escape being part of the oppressor camp (Biko 1978 [originally 1970], pp. 22-3).

Biko gave pungent expression to the awkwardness of persons who were not oppressed but spoke eloquently on behalf of the oppressed. The same logic of rejecting complacent "friends of natives" was presented by the Chinese Youth Struggle Committee (Kaseito), a group of young Chinese activists in Japan imbued with Maoist thinking and the ethos of the Cultural Revolution of the time. After student radicalism was violently suppressed in 1968, Japanese New Left factions with all sorts of Marxist creeds started to compete with each other, purge comrades, and seek out a fresh issue for political mobilization. They eventually tried to seize control of a new wave of the movement against xenophobia as a means of political manoeuvring. At one of the rallies in 1970, Kaseito decisively broke away from the New Left parties in protest of their predator behaviour, and the New Left leaders were forced to make bitter self-criticism in front of their supporters. Kaseito disbanded at the same time. In a document, Kaseito referred to the Great Kanto Earthquake in 1923, when thousands of Koreans and anarchists were brutally killed by Japanese vigilante groups instigated by security police and the army:

> Now that the authorities conspire to restage the abhorrent massacre of Koreans that occurred at the time of Great Kanto Earthquake, we cannot help but feel great fear. Japanese can secure an escape route, as long as they are Japanese, by taking a self-satisfied position of non-commitment. We, however, cannot even take refuge. As long as we are treated as potential criminals, being forced to carry alien registration cards, even passive Japanese bystanders are criminals in our eyes, not to mention those Japanese who identify with imperialists [Kaseito 1970].

Biko challenged privileged student activists to drop out from universities. In the meantime, some participants in student movement in Japan, especially from elite national universities such as Tokyo and Kyoto Universities, cherished the discourse of "self-negation" and cried out slogans such as "Down with Imperial Universities!" Although class suicide could not be a main theme of popular movement, the self-reflective mind set was shared by the elite student community and made their leaders receptive to unreserved criticisms such as those raised by Kaseito.

A student of Hiroshima University, Shuji Funamoto (1945-75), quit the university and lurked in *yoseba* (urban communities of homeless people; literally, this term means places to be gathered) as a maverick revolutionary. Typically, day labourers were people who emigrated from the agrarian countryside, lost touch with their families and engaged in heavy labour on daily contract in city construction sites. The largest *yoseba* called "Kamagasaki" was located in the south of Osaka City. Funamoto eloquently articulates "self-negation" in his own way as follows:

> "Self-negation" means to deny the present real state of self. For labourers, self-negation is not to be elevated from the status of labourers to that of recruiters, but to negate their own way of living in surrender and despair, being obedient under the thumb of the white pigs – being fussed over when young and healthy, then exploited, and

once their bodies are worn to rags with age, thrown out on the streets, dying like dogs, and eventually used as specimens for dissection in medical universities..... The basis of our organizing principle is not to organize indebtedness on the part of the "strong" but to organize humiliation and grudges on the part of the "weak"..... If you are the guardian of a weapon (i.e. knowledge), you should either direct this weapon against the state, or hand it over quietly to the "weak" who know the best usage of the weapon (Funamoto 1973).

Funamoto was born in Manchuria, the northeastern part of China that Japan colonized. Even if it were uncommon, there were always a number of students like Funamoto who "disappeared" from the campus and got immersed in under-class communities. After engaging in the radicalization of the movement of day labourers for the liberation of *yoseba*, he immolated himself in Okinawa in political protest.

Contradictions among the People

The strategy of Black Consciousness was to withdraw from the would-be inclusive student organization dominated by a group of glib, privileged people and to organize their own group that will grow at their own pace and on their own responsibility. As the unity of the oppressed is prioritized, those who flirted with people on the opponent's side were considered dangerous elements, as described by Biko:

> They have been made to feel inferior for so long that for them it is comforting to drink tea, wine or beer with whites who seem to treat them as equals. This serves to boost up their own ego to the extent of making them feel slightly superior to those blacks who do not get similar treatment from whites. These are the sort of blacks who are a danger to the community (Biko 1978 [originally 1970], p. 23).

In the indictment by Kaseito, they warned against Chinese "selfish upstarts" or "clever men" who plead for better treatment from Japanese, crying "Please help me, at the least", in the delusive information technology age (Kaseito, 1970). However, even if they are "dangerous", are such persons really the enemy of people?

The same question of betrayal was asked by Mitsu Tanaka (1943), the most influential leader of Japanese urban radical feminism at its inception. Radicalized by the student movement around 1968, Tanaka questioned why female student-activists always prepared meals for their male counterparts who passionately talked about the revolutionary army and the emancipation of the human race amongst themselves and stepped out to clash with police. The term "women's lib (liberation)" spread rapidly in the 1970s, as the writing of Tanaka was read widely and their movement gained momentum. Some vigorously campaigned for legal reforms for women's rights, while others set up women's collectives. Her *For Women of Life* still enjoys a wide audience as the manifesto of "women's lib" and contemporary Japanese feminism. She currently runs an acupuncture clinic in Tokyo. Here she describes the dynamics of solidarity in women's liberation.

> "The enemy of 'Lib' is also women, isn't it?", some men say. Sure, those women who should not feel humiliation about "being women" are the enemy. Those women who do not express sympathy with women who were forced to commit infanticide are the enemy. Those women who assume their *neutrality* and say frivolously, "You are in the camp of women's liberation", are the enemy. However, I never condone men calling those women out as our enemy, because those who have changed sides are still *the enemy within the boundary of friendship.* We never sell them out, even if they sell us out (Tanaka 2010 [originally 1972], p. 185).

Tanaka underlined that "women's lib" should be firmly anchored in one's own suffering. She asked, "Why do the voices raised by Koreans and Chinese in Japan bear such an essential importance? This is because those people are the agents of the struggle based on their own pains" (Tanaka 2010 [originally 1972], p. 253). For Tanaka, the division between women was basically a contradiction among the people (Mao 2007 ["On the Correct Handling of Contradictions among the People" written in 1957]), while the divide between men and women could be an antagonistic contradiction.

If the enemy is concentrated in the oppressor's camp, it is easy to stay out of touch with them. It is also possible to avoid direct contact with a person of the other sex. However, it is not an easy task to cut ties with one's own mother, from whose womb one was born. But what if she attempted to kill you because of the very fact that you are alive? Koichi Yokozuka (1935-78) was born with cerebral palsy (CP) and eventually became a leading figure in an organization of persons with disability, called the Society of Green Lawn. Notably, this organization campaigned against a popular petition that called for a reduction in sentence for a mother who killed her child with severe disability. If this kind of homicide was justified, the right to life of people with disabilities would be denied categorically, as noted by Yokozuka:

> When a mother rises from her slumber after delivery and sees her baby for the first time, she tries to confirm if all of its limbs and fingers are fine. But I think this has grave implications to we people who live with CP. How is it if the baby has physical defects? How is it if it is born with CP? After birth, we are treated as those who appear to deviate from normalcy, or more precisely, as beings that should not have existed. This is when the struggle between parents and their children with CP starts..... Because the cause of our movement is to bring into the open the real state of people with CP, it boils down to calling for our liberation from our parents. Even with running tears, even with apologies for our unfilial attitudes, we are destined to kick over parental love (Yokozuka, 2007 [originally 1970], pp. 24, 27).

Return to the Source

Biko wrote that the "most potent weapon in the hands of the oppressor is the mind of the oppressed" (Biko 1978 [originally 1973], p. 92). With the objective of escaping from this control, one needs to keep a certain unmoving point of reference in the mind, which cannot be the same as conventional social norms. Yokozuka asked,

"In this world, is there any person who leads a life wishing to be understood day and night in the first place?" (Yokozuka 2007 [originally 1970], p. 65), while Tanaka wrote, "Persons who are suffering at the moment do not have the luxury to explain lucidly about their pains. Because the expression of true feelings based on one's own pains emanates from one's very existence, it is no use replying to those who want to demand words from us" (Tanaka 2010 [originally 1972], pp. 88-9).

In these circumstances, where is the unshakable point of reference, the source to which one eventually should return? For Cabral, it was the African countryside where imperialist penetration was still partial and the authentic African way of life was preserved (Cabral 1973). In apartheid South Africa, Biko considered a sort of "Africanness" the source of emancipatory inspiration. While he envisioned "a colourless and non-exploitative egalitarian society" in which the Black Consciousness approach would be irrelevant, he believed that this synthesis would be achieved only after waging a frontal battle between the industrial and military values of the West and the spiritual and humanistic values of Africa. For Biko, the power of Africa lay in the modalities of contextual and intimate communication:

> One of the most fundamental aspects of our culture is the importance we attach to Man. Ours has always been a Man-centred society. Westerners have on many occasions been surprised at the capacity we have for talking to each other – not for the sake of arriving at a particular conclusion but merely to enjoy the communication for its own sake. Intimacy is a term not exclusive for particular friends but applying to a whole group of people who find themselves together…..
> (Biko 1978 [originally 1971], p. 41).

While many of the first-generation Koreans and Chinese in Japan were forcibly uprooted from their home nations before and during World War II, the subsequent generations have taken pains to make a living in Japanese environments. For the latter, the question was not to go back physically to their original home nations, although there was a large-scale campaign for Koreans to "Return to North Korea" from the 1950s with unpleasant outcomes for the returnees. Kaseito noted some of the challenges the Korean and Chinese diasporas faced:

More than a half of 600,000 Koreans and 50,000 Chinese [at that time] grew up as the post-war generation. While our parents think in their mother languages, speak them, and live in an inconvenient language environment, we of the second and the third generations forget these languages. Here we face enormous contradictions. The first generation feels loneliness and bleakness with which they have to bury their agony and joy into the land of the alien country. If we end up being uprooted, we may not be able to draw on the nourishment of our national soul forever from the land on which our parents treaded. To restore national culture is not to repossess what has been lost, but to build something anew and create what has not been there (Kaseito, 1970).

For the Kaseito activists, paying respect to the historical experience of their ancestors was indispensable, but this does not contradict their attempt to create a new identity in this alien land where they were born. The Kaseito document signified that wandering in liminal spaces and taking resolute action would not be incompatible.

Funamoto found that *yoseba* was the urban shore of drifters. Like his contemporary activists, Funamoto was affected by the influence of the abstract Hegelian dialectic. However, he must have marvelled at the diversity of workers on the ground in the *yoseba* when he chose to live there in his twenties. "Buraku" are the communities of Japanese outcast minorities entrenched during the feudal era. Funamoto argues:

For the *Anko* (day labourers), Kamagasaki is the node of a circuit of migrants from agricultural villages, fishing villages, unliberated Buraku, Korean communities and Okinawa, as well as from abandoned mines. After very hard work, villages are scrapped, and people are fired on the pretext of industrial restructuring, "forcibly recruited" from Okinawa, or driven out of Buraku. Kamagasaki is a relay point of their wandering. As long as their struggles remain in an individual, pre-reflective state, these are destined to be mutually segregated and buried

385

forever. Our principle is to make these discrete struggles of the *Anko* develop into the struggle of all people, and to develop the partial reason to the universal reason (Funamoto, 1973).

As discussed by Cabral and Biko, cultural dignity matters, and this has something to do with the modalities of communication. Tanaka's remarks about men's language of enlightenment and women's language of existence seem to correspond to the distinction between low-context and high-context cultures recently "discovered" by anthropologists. In her manifesto of Japanese feminism, Tanaka reinstated the value of irrationality in a logical way:

> Around us, so many people espouse the value of words. One who relies on words in communication tries to varnish one's blunt body with words. The language flying out of men's neatly sorted drawers is a lifeless language, of enlightenment, which leans toward the dominant side. Modern rationalism separates words from bodies, expelling insanity from bodies. As such, women's confusion, or words spoken with confusion, has something to do with regenerating our bodies, to reinstate insanity. While men speak about insanity with their words, women speak about insanity through their existence. Confusion is the most beautiful weapon of women, the soul of women itself (Tanaka 2010 [originally 1972], p. 167).

Yokozuka thinks that the people with serious disabilities embody the universality of human beings precisely because of the fact that disabled people have been a target for elimination by their fellow humans. If people who consider themselves to be normal continue to murder those who are perceived as different, the planet will become empty sooner or later. By implication, Yokozuka's discussion attests to the absurdity of racism:

> Power always excludes certain minorities from society, thereby implanting a superiority complex and discriminatory consciousness in the mind of the majority. From the viewpoint of those who are in power, discarding deficient descendants is "a procedure deemed to be necessary for the progress of the humankind". Many people may be

convinced by such words, or become quiet if not convinced, because they assume that they are not on the side of being eliminated. However, if the one in last place is eliminated, the next appear one after another, and the process will continue until a time when only one remains in the world. I don't care about whatever "wonderful society" emerges after I am eliminated as a "defect", because I will be non-existent by then (Yokozuka 2007 [originally 1972], p. 132).

Concluding Remarks

Let me conclude this essay by commenting on the divergence and convergence of post-1968 experience in South Africa and Japan.

In the age of anti-apartheid struggle in South Africa, social issues faced by individual persons were subordinated to the cause of national liberation, and the Black Consciousness language galvanized the liberatory mass movement by the end of the 1960s. Given the collusive relationship between apartheid and racial capitalism, it was assumed that all serious discrimination would be buried forever when the apartheid regime collapsed. The millenarian rhetoric prevailed, even though the mainstream leadership espoused the two-step theory of National Democratic Revolution.

Now, it is very clear that the abolition of institutional apartheid only marked the first step in overcoming various forms of oppression including ethno-centrism. The BPC (Black People's Convention)/SASO Trial was based on the criminalization of solidarity with the Mozambique Liberation Front (FRELIMO) that was expressed by the Black Consciousness movement, which aspired to pan-African internationalism. When Mozambique achieved independence in 1975, nobody could have anticipated the spate of xenophobic violence that would occur in South Africa after the collapse of apartheid in 1994.

In the period following 1968, as described in this essay, multiple issues came to light in Japanese society; those issues persisted for the long term – may have been so since the birth of the humankind – but were invisible in Japan in the era of rapid economic growth and urbanization until the activists of the 1968 generation raised voices.

After a half century, the social energy of 1968 is conserved in numerous small groups that take up their own issues and scatter throughout the country. However, Japanese progressive forces did not succeed in consolidating a single liberatory agency both in and out of parliamentary politics. Brutal infighting among New Left factions devastatingly alienated their sympathizers in the 1970s and 1980s.

Now that inequality has worsened and absolute poverty has intensified in every nation of the world, the demand for group entitlements on the winning side of people never engenders emancipatory politics. The privileged should be able to nurture respect for the intrinsic value of other human beings, rather than protecting their own dignity. On the other hand, a person may face not single but multiple layers of oppression, or belong to both camps of the oppressed and of the oppressors simultaneously; the law of non-contradiction may not necessarily be true. In the visionary classic, *Pedagogy of the Oppressed* by Paulo Freire (1970), the line separating the two camps was described as relatively rigid despite the emphasis on mutual learning and transformation. We need a fresh association of resilient individuals who are determined to return to their own source collectively, recognizing the simple fact that class and race are still significant but neither is the single factor in determining the position of a person in society.

References

Biko, Steve, 1978. *I Write What I like: A Selection of His Writings*. London: Heinemann.

Cabral, Amilcar. 1969. *Revolution in Guinea: Selected Texts*. New York: Monthly Review Press.

----------. 1973. *Return to the Source: Selected Speeches*. New York: Monthly Review Press.

Fanon, Frantz. 1967. *Black Skin, White Masks*. New York: Grove Press.

Freire, Paulo. 1970. *Pedagogy of the Oppressed*. New York: Continuum.

Funamoto, Shuji. 1973. "'Jakusha' no tatakai kata ni manabi, 'jakusha' no seikatsu shiso wo taitoku shi, 'jakusha' no kakumei shiso wo kochiku suru tameni (To Learn from the Way of Struggle of the 'Weak', to Capture the Living Thought of the 'Weak', and to Forge a Revolutionary Thought of the 'Weak')". Mimeo.

Kaseito: Kakyo Seinen Toso Iinkai (Overseas Chinese Youth Struggle Committee). 1970. "Nyukan toso wo tatakau nakakara minzoku no tamashii no fukken wo (Restore the National Soul through the Struggle against the Immigration Control)". Mimeo.

Makino, Kumiko. 2018. "Travelling for Solidarity: Japanese Activists in the Transnational Anti-apartheid Movement." In *Migration and Agency: Afro-Asian Encounters.* edited by Scarlett Cornelissen and Yoichi Mine. London: Palgrave, pp. 247-70.

Mao, Tse-Tung. 2007. *On Practice and Contradiction.* London: Verso.

Poulantzas, Nicos. 1970. *Fascisme et dictature: La IIIe internationale face au fascisme.* Paris: Maspero.

Tanaka, Mitsu. 2010. *Inochi no onna tachi he: Torimidashi uman ribu ron (For the Women of Life: Confusion and Women's Liberation).* New Edition. Tokyo: Gendai Shokan.

Yokozuka, Koichi. 2007. *Haha yo korosuna! (Mother, Don't Kill!).* New Edition. Tokyo: Seikatsu Shoin.

*Translation of the Japanese texts is only tentative.

Author's email: ymine@mail.doshisha.ac.jp

www.ingramcontent.com/pod-product-compliance
Lightning Source LLC
Chambersburg PA
CBHW060020030426
42334CB00019B/2116